# LINES DRAWN UPON THE WATER

# LINES DRAWN UPON THE WATER
*First Nations and the Great Lakes*
*Borders and Borderlands*

KARL S. HELE, editor

ABORIGINAL STUDIES SERIES

Wilfrid Laurier University Press

We acknowledge the financial support of the Government of Canada through the Book Publishing Industry Development Program for our publishing activities.

## Library and Archives Canada Cataloguing in Publication

Lines drawn upon the water : First Nations and the Great Lakes borders and
    borderlands / Karl S. Hele, editor.

(Aboriginal studies series)
Proceedings of a conference held at University of Western Ontario,
    London, Ont., Feb. 11–12, 2005.
Includes bibliographical references and index.
ISBN 978-1-55458-004-0

1. Indians of North America—Great Lakes Region (North America)—History.
2. Métis—Great Lakes Region (North America)—History.  3. Canada—Boundaries—
United States.  4. United States—Boundaries—Canada.  5. Water boundaries—Ontario.
6. Water boundaries—United States.  7. Great Lakes Region (North America)—History.
I. Hele, Karl S. (Karl Scott), 1970–   II. Series: Aboriginal studies series (Waterloo, Ont.)

E78.G7L46 2008               971.3004'97               C2007-906611-9

Cover image: "Dividing the Land" (2006), pen-and-ink drawing on paper by Lorraine
Trecroce. Cover design by P.J. Woodland. Text design by Catharine Bonas-Taylor.

© 2008 Wilfrid Laurier University Press
Waterloo, Ontario, Canada
www.wlupress.wlu.ca

This book is printed on Ancient Forest Friendly paper (100% post-consumer recycled).

Printed in Canada

This volume is dedicated to all those who
live in the Great Lakes borderlands.

# CONTENTS

# LIST OF ILLUSTRATIONS
# AND MAPS

# ACKNOWLEDGEMENTS

This book and the workshop it came from originated from my experiences growing up along the Canadian–American border. The very existence of the border was so ingrained in my psyche and taken for granted as an inconvenience rather than an actual barrier that it took my dissertation supervisor, Professor Catherine Desbarats, to remind me that I was discussing a border region. I thank her for this kind and humorous reminder. I would also like to express gratitude to David McNab and Ute Lischke, series editors at Wilfrid Laurier University Press and dear friends, for encouraging me to proceed with this volume when the task appeared overwhelming. Additional thanks are extended specifically to Dr. Tanya Gogan and Ken Hogue for their judicious advice and kind lessons on style, to my student assistant Sadie Donovan, who graciously ran down odd or incomplete references, and to Lorraine Trecroce for her wonderful art. Speaking on behalf of the contributing authors, both those who were and those who were not part of the original workshop, it is necessary to thank all those unnamed individuals who offered advice both individually and collectively to the various authors. Lastly, I would like to thank all the contributors, the Wilfrid Laurier University Press's editors, the anonymous reviewers, the University of Western Ontario (specifically the departments of History and Anthropology), and above all the Social Sciences and Humanities Research Council, Aid to Research Workshops and Conferences in Canada, and the First Nations Studies Program at the University of Western Ontario, which provided the funding for the workshop and the publication of this volume.

"Drawing/Erasing the Border" (2006), by Lorraine Trecroce.

# INTRODUCTION

Prompted by my own interest in the Anishinabeg and Métis living in the Sault Ste. Marie borderlands, discussions with colleagues interested in similar regions, and several recent studies on the Canadian–American border, I organized the workshop that became the basis of this volume. Over the course of three days in February 2005, participants discussed, within the context of their own work, how the impositions of colonial and national boundaries have influenced First Nations populations within the Great Lakes region. As the workshop proceeded, participants came to appreciate the artificiality of confining the discussion of Aboriginal people to settler-created states and boundaries. While the past, present, and future of individual First Nations and the collective experience of all Aboriginal people in the region is not easily approached without reference to the international border, much can be learned by exploring those relationships that have existed and continue to exist despite the political and physical boundaries in the borderlands.

The Great Lakes region consists not only of lakes Superior, Huron, Michigan, Erie, and Ontario but also of the lands drained by them (see map 1). Contemporary political boundaries include Canada and the United States (US), as well as the contiguous province of Ontario and the states of Ohio, Indiana, Illinois, Michigan, Wisconsin, Minnesota, New York, and Pennsylvania. Yet these political entities are relatively recent creations and their existence fashions the borderlands. In terms of populations, the Great Lakes region prior to contact (ca. 1534) was home to hundreds of thousands of Aboriginal Nations living both in direct proximity to the lakes and their watershed or regularly making

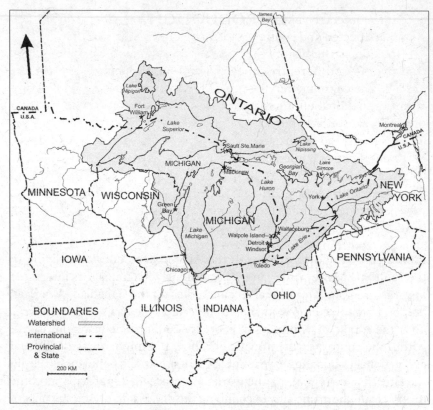

**Map 1:** Great Lakes Watershed and Political Boundaries, by Louise Ridely Buck.

seasonal use of the region. Generally speaking, the populations can be broken down into at least three language groups: Algonquian, Iroquoian, and Siouxian. The Iroquoian nations include, but are by no means limited to, the Five Nations (consisting of the Mohawk, Seneca, Cayuga, Onondaga, and Oneida) or Iroquois (Haudenasaunee), and the Huron, Neutral, and Petuns. The Algonquian nations include the Ojibwa (Chippewa, Anishinabeg, Anishinabek, Anishnaabeg), Ottawa (Odawa), Potawatomie, Sauk, Fox, Miami, and Illinois. The Siouxian-speaking nations include the Winnebago (HoChunk) and Dakota (Sioux).[1] Individually and collectively, the lands of these unique and independent Aboriginal nations have been claimed and then divided amongst various colonial powers since the 1600s. While this volume does not address all the various experiences of each First Nation, it does examine aspects of the borderland existence for the Anishinabeg and Haudenasaunee nations. It is hoped that this foray into the Great Lakes borderlands will encourage others to view the region as a whole despite the artificial division that affected and continues to affect all who live within it.

To address the history of the Great Lakes region beyond national frameworks, a differently conceived and more dynamic approach is needed. The contemporary impact of the international border on communities, national efforts to enforce the boundary, and the determination of local groups to pursue their interests and to define themselves is better understood by analyzing the region as a borderland and, indeed, as a multiplicity of borderlands. Significant differences obviously exist in terms of the nature and extent of the border as a concrete reality from the seventeenth century through to the present. Even so, local residents have persistently regarded the border as an artificial construct. The inability of colonial and state authorities to police the border effectively has certainly contributed to this view. Beyond this, from the perspective of the residents, the border represents a contested zone of interaction between Native residents, non-Native authorities, and national interests.[2] From this vantage point, dynamic interactions in the region can be seen to flow from First Nations, Métis, and non-Natives pursuing their own distinct interests. It is also conditioned by the degree to which outside authorities have been able to intervene in local affairs and by the ability of local groups to play off the interests of these same outside colonial and, subsequently, national authorities.

Borders are lived experiences. While non-Natives and Natives regularly cross to and from the United States and Canada for pleasure or work, real differences in culture and experience can significantly set apart the lives of people living along one side of a border from those living a mere drive across it. The simple experience of transiting the border will not be the same for all. For instance, those living in the Sault Ste. Marie or Windsor–Detroit borderlands regularly engage in what is officially deemed to be the smuggling of goods and services across the border. This is such a lived experience that from youth we are trained not to volunteer unsolicited information and to understate the reasons for a brief foray across the international line. If the border guard fails to ask about alcohol or other goods in the trunk, few are apt to declare its presence. Likewise, we learn that wearing newly acquired clothing even for a few minutes creates a fiction to relieve the burden of paying duties because the clothes are now used. Such calculations and actions, while commonplace among borderland residents, can shock and occasionally appall those who did not grow up near the border. Their experiences are far less likely to have equipped them with the repertoire of half and hidden truths that often underlie the responses of borderland residents to the routine questions of grim-faced border guards. Borders, however, are relevant far beyond the simple daily movement of goods and individuals; these demarcations—particularly those in the Great Lakes—divide families, communities, and cultures. The multiplicity of borders include not only the line separating Canada and the United States but also the lines drawn between sovereign First Nations' territories and settler societies, as well as those frontiers that we draw between ourselves based on perceived differences.

This volume, building on the 2005 workshop entitled "Lines Drawn upon the Water: The First Nations Experience with the Great Lakes' Borderlands and Borders," emphasizes the idea that some boundaries are mere lines drawn upon the water, often disrupted or even erased altogether by the lived experiences of First Nations people. By bringing together essays that make use of a borderlands perspective to provide insight into the history of the Great Lakes region, the editor hopes this collection encourages scholars in Canada and the US to look beyond their national borders and simplistic comparative studies between regions or cities on either side of the border. After all, borderlands are regions within themselves. The borderlands concept was initially posited by Herbert Eugene Bolton in his 1921 volume, *The Spanish Borderlands*. Bolton's work, while conceived as a complement to Frederick Jackson Turner's frontier thesis, has inspired subsequent generations of scholars to examine the evolving complexity of social, economic, spiritual, and political interactions in regions where two or more groups, usually interpreted as colonial powers, cannot effectively exert their authority.[3] In the context of the Spanish/Mexican and American border region, this line of inquiry has produced numerous historical and contemporary studies.[4]

While comparative studies of Canadian and American issues abound, relatively few works address issues specifically associated with Canadian–American borderlands. In the last decade, the number of published works examining the Canadian–American borderlands have gradually increased. The majority of these studies, however, examine the borderlands west of Great Lakes and are situated within the nineteenth century—the most recent being *The Borderlands of the American and Canadian Wests* (2006) and *Living with Strangers* (2006).[5] Both of these studies provide examples of how to approach First Nations living within a borderlands. This volume draws attention to the need to understand an earlier and often more complex border region. By expanding the discussion to the broader Great Lakes region, this volume shows that borderland processes are not static and have not been defined and fixed in relation to the creation of the Canada–US border. Although the Canadian and US governments regard the border as being clearly defined politically and geographically, local communities continue to contest the artificial divisions imposed by this international boundary. In many ways, these communities define spatial and human relationships within the borderlands in their own terms and in a manner that pays little heed to the international boundary.

Vital to understanding the borderlands discussed in this volume is Jeremy Adelman and Stephen Aron's article, "From Borderlands to Borders."[6] They present a theory of borderlands that emphasizes how local history is shaped by imperial rivalries and Aboriginal attempts to exploit these differences "partly to resist submission but mainly to negotiate intercultural relations on terms more to their liking."[7] Borderlands, according to these authors, consist of the "contested boundaries between colonial domains." These contested boundaries arose and persisted beyond the initial period of colonization where neither side possessed the ability to exert power effectively. By examining three contemporaneous borderlands—the Great Lakes, the Lower Missouri Valley, and the Greater Rio Grande Basin—Adelman and Aron effectively sketch out the wiggle room that people experience when living in border zones; and yet, according to the authors, the borderlands they examine ceased to exist in the early nineteenth century, when imperial rivalries receded and ethnic and social relations became solidified as "empires were succeeded by incipient nation-states" and the present enforceable borders emerged. Particularly relevant to the present volume is Adelman and Aron's claim that the Great Lakes borderlands ceased to have meaning after the War of 1812 with the confirmation of the border between British North America (BNA) and the United States.[8]

As the essays in this volume demonstrate, First Nations living within the Great Lakes borderlands did not disappear, nor did they assume British Canadian or American identities with the demarcation of the border under the Treaty of Paris in 1783 or its reaffirmation by the 1814 Treaty of Ghent. Both the British–Canadian and American authorities were, in subsequent years, unable to control their respective borders effectively. The initiatives undertaken in the years since the events of 11 September 2001 clearly demonstrate the ongoing difficulties experienced by the Canadian and American governments in this regard, particularly in the Great Lakes region. Recent American proposals to patrol the waters using military helicopters and more and better armed Coast

Guard vessels echo, in effect, earlier efforts in centuries past to build forts along the border to establish regulated crossings. Even US citizens, calling themselves "minutemen," more appropriately referred to as vigilantes or potential terrorists, have been patrolling the northern and southern US borders in an effort to prevent illegal immigration and terrorist infiltration.[9]

While such efforts along the border may further divide communities, their ultimate impact remains unknown. Certainly, First Nations people in the region will continue to assert their rights and shape their identity through public and private actions. By exploring borders and borderlands through cross-disciplinary and national perspectives, we hope to overcome the limitations in perspective imposed by the border and to explore the living traditions of Great Lakes Aboriginal communities as they strive to maintain existing relationships and to establish new connections despite the imposition of what is, in reality, a nebulous line drawn upon the water.

The essays collected in this volume explore how the presence of two or more cultures and/or colonial states have influenced First Nations living throughout the Great Lakes watershed. The creation of the border in 1783 and subsequent efforts to control this national/colonial boundary based on local, regional, international, and strategic concerns have indisputably affected the First Nations of the region. Those who participated in the workshop that inspired this volume emphasized in their individual contributions how the First Nations have attempted to mediate the affects of this artificially imposed border on their communities. Many First Nations individuals, in the context of their economic pursuits, kinship links, religious and political affiliations, Indian policy, and many other intangibles, made decisions to reside on one side of the border or the other while maintaining community ties across it. Their efforts have tended to render meaningless such designations as American Indian and Canadian Native.

In most instances, and this is reflected in the nature of the contributions to this volume, the lived experience of the borderlands is discussed in terms of political, social, and economic relationships. This is the case, for example, when discussing the ongoing struggle of the Great Lakes First Nations to exercise their rights under the 1794 Jay Treaty. This debate is often cast in terms of Canada's failure to recognize the treaty's confirmation of Native rights to transport goods—whether they be cigarettes, alcohol, or other American products—into Canada, but it is more than this. The issue ultimately concerns the struggle of First Nations to force Canada to recognize the right of Great Lakes peoples to move freely across the border in search of economic and social independence.

As several contributions to this volume demonstrate, the issue of the borderlands can also be configured within a metaphysical and epistemological framework. Conversations between spiritualities and forms of knowledge and power can also be viewed as a contest between the colonizers and the colonized. The resulting conversation is more than a simple dialectic of non-Native versus Native. Attempts to colonize the mind and spirit, and efforts to recast power relationships can evoke a myriad of responses that create not only solid lines of difference but also blurred distinctions between individuals, communities, and nations.[10]

This volume aspires to foster a new way of thinking about First Nations' experience in the Great Lakes by making scholars and the public on both sides of the border aware that one cannot truly speak of, for instance, Iroquois or Ojibwa pasts, presents, and futures without exploring the nature of their relationship to the international border and those relationships that transcend it. Workshop participants stressed the importance of looking beyond national and comparative perspectives to employ increasingly fluid models to expand our understanding of Native–White relations in the Great Lakes borderlands.

The first two chapters of this volume examine the larger Great Lakes watershed. In chapter one, Edmund J. Danziger Jr. explains that, while Aboriginal peoples responded to US and Canadian policies in the nineteenth century in various ways, they were inspired by a desire to defend cultural, political, and economic independence by building on long-standing patterns of mutual respect and cooperation with the Euro-America newcomers. Chapter two builds on this in more specific detail and offers a discussion of cross-border treaty signers among the Anishinabeg (Ojibwa/Chippewa). Philip Bellfy shows that the most capable among the Anishinabeg, regardless of the side of the border on which they lived, led the treaty negotiations with the rapidly expanding settler states. In effect, the reality of the experience saw "American" Anishinabeg participate in negotiating British–Canadian treaties, and vice versa. Beyond ensuring that the expansion of the Euro-American nations proceeded in a relatively peaceful way, treaties were seen by the Anishinabeg as a way of ensuring their independence. Thus, treaty negotiations helped forge a greater sense of Anishinabeg nationhood that transcended the US–Canada border. Finally, by signing treaties on both sides of the border, the Anishinabeg people ensured their right to live throughout their Great Lakes homeland.

Chapters three to six draw attention to specific communities within the Great Lakes region and expand upon the analyses initiated by Danziger Jr. and Bellfy. In chapter three, Mark Meuwese focusses on how the Flemish Bastard, a Mohawk war chief, international messenger, and "Christian Indian," experienced the colonial borderlands of New York and New France in the mid-seventeenth century. Meuwese thus illustrates how Aboriginal peoples living in the space between empires were affected by European rivalries. Individuals such as the Flemish Bastard and nations like the Mohawk found the borderlands experience to be conditioned by ambiguity, danger, and opportunity that could and would affect sovereignty and identity. Similarly, Karl Hele's examination of the nineteenth-century Sault Ste. Marie borderlands, in chapter four, further illustrates the ambiguities of living between competing empires—British–Canadian and American—by exploring how the locals, in an effort to maintain political and economic independence, interacted with the border that artificially divided their community and territory. In the end, the effort to control the border proved impossible for the emergent states, and its presence remains an inconvenience that has negative, positive, and indeterminate effects on the Anishinabeg and Métis communities. Chapter five presents a detailed study of the Métis in the Sault Ste. Marie region to show how they are truly a "people in-between." Alan Knight and Janet E. Chute's study shows not only how the Métis people used their dual heritage to participate in both worlds but also how their family connections cut across the borders between racialized groups, ethnicities, and polities. From the Upper Lakes region as represented by Sault Ste. Marie, David T. McNab changes focus, in chapter six, to the Lower Lakes region in his study of the Bkejwanong (Walpole Island First Nation) territory. McNab lays out a series of stories that illustrate how the people of Walpole Island First Nation resisted imperialism in the larger context of the mutability and invisibility of artificially imposed borders and how local populations were affected by the political exertions of larger, outside power centres. McNab argues that Walpole Islanders continued to cross the border as their right but that, at the same time, they remained subject to the terrorism of the nation/colonial state and individuals claiming the nation/colonial state's protection. Euro-American squatters, poachers, and Indian agents all engaged in terrorizing the Native population of Walpole Island in an effort to destroy the community and to usurp its land base and resources. Thus, for McNab and the islanders, homeland security is as much about protecting territory as it is about culture, politics, and sovereignty.

Chapters seven and eight both deal specifically with the Baldoon community, which is located near Walpole Island and the community of Wallaceburg, the home of an Anglo-Canadian settler population consisting largely of Scots. In chapter seven, Lisa Philips and Allan K. McDougall explore the legend known as the Baldoon Mystery. As it mutated over time, whether it was framed around ghosts, avenging spirits, witches, or protesting Natives, this tale is at its heart about fears associated with cross-cultural communication, land appropriation, and resistance. Each retelling of the Baldoon Mystery, the authors argue, reflects the character of the people in the era in which it was advanced. They contend that the Baldoon Mystery evolved from an expression of First Nations connections to the land to reflect Euro-Canadian frontier tales and western assumptions concerning ghosts, land, and myth. For Philips and McDougall, the Baldoon Mystery is decidedly about both physical and metaphysical boundaries. Rick Fehr continues the examination of the Baldoon settlement in chapter eight. Instead of exploring the legend, Fehr focusses on how the environment has been affected through the imposition of economic and political process from outside the region. Rather than examining physical boundaries between people or nations, Fehr discusses the boundaries between concepts of the development, settlement, and sustainable use of the local environment as held by the local Scottish and Anishinabeg communities. In the end, Fehr suggests that the local populations, Native and non-Native, need to cooperate to develop a hybrid framework of land ethics that respects the natural environment and ceases to impose boundaries upon the waters of Bkejwanong.

The remaining four chapters continue the exploration of metaphysical and epistemological borderlands. Catherine Murton Stoehr, in chapter nine, connects the land, military history, and religion in her exploration of Anishinabeg Nativism and the role of Methodist Christianity in the community. She argues that a hybrid movement evolved among the Anishinabeg in Southern Ontario that combined the Nativist message that Indians were one people and that new ceremonies could restore lost spiritual power with, in particular, Methodist Christian ideas of salvation and apocalyptic teachings. The emergent guiding principle in this movement held that both spiritual and material improvements could only occur through the ethical actions of First Nations people in the region. Significantly, Stoehr maintains that the Methodist–Nativist hybrid was truly an indigenous invention that made use of the language of Christianity to critique the settlers, colonial governments, and even the missionaries.

Its development and growth was directly influenced by events and experiences in the United States and British North America. Within the borderlands of spirituality, Anishinabeg people developed a Nativist ethos that successfully incorporated aspects of Methodism and offered an explanation for the contemporary situation and hope for the future.

Michelle A. Hamilton, in her study of First Nations and anthropology, extends the idea of borderlands as a geographical reality to encompass an intellectual space. This allows her to examine, in chapter ten, the conversations within the discipline of anthropology and how First Nations people, specifically individual Haudenosaunee from the Grand River in Ontario, became involved in studying themselves either independently or in association with a professional anthropologist. In a metaphysical landscape, individual Haudenosaunee people found that their motives and activities were deeply affected by cultural identities, family, religion, the influence of mentors, and mainstream society. Hamilton maintains that Aboriginal people were more than mere informants; instead they were full participants in defining anthropological investigations. The borderlands of cultural study is, in effect, shown to be as ambiguous, dangerous, and replete with opportunity as living between competing states.

In chapter eleven, Norman Shields's study of the Grand General Indian Council of Ontario's response to Indian status legislation builds further on the concept of the borderlands as a non-geographical space. Shields demonstrates that the borderlands of law, politics, gender, and "race" intersected in the late nineteenth century to generate a split between the Six Nations and the Anishinabek, as well as within the ranks of the Anishinabek. The Six Nations consistently argued that the legalities of the legislation violated their culture of matrilineality, whereas the Anishinabek became divided over the loss of women to their bands through marriage to non-status and non-Canadian Native people. While marriage to non-Natives was a concern, Anishinabek/Ojibwa women who married Anishinabek/Potawatomi men lost their status even though they had married other "Indians," albeit ones who were not legally recognized as such. This cut to the heart of the Three Fires Confederacy, an ancient alliance between the Ojibwa, Odawa, and Potawatomi that spanned the whole of the Great Lakes region. The effect of the legislation and British and Canadian refusal to live up to their responsibilities helped create artificial borderlands within Native communities and literally broke hearts.

Chapter twelve stands apart from the other essays in this volume by examining literary interpretations of the border. By focussing on Louise

Erdrich's stories about borders, Ute Lischke draws our attention to the importance not only of Native literary conventions and the meanings of borders but also to the acts of resistance contained with the stories themselves. Erdrich's stories, like the histories examined in this volume, reveal the uneasy relationship that First Nations peoples maintain with the international border. Lischke's work ultimately examines the transcendence of borders and how First Nations people have maintained their sense of identity, cultural continuity, and even political sovereignty.

Taken together, the twelve chapters constitute a unique exploration of the effects of the borderlands on the Great Lakes First Nations. While the majority of the essays examine the Anishinabeg, perhaps reflecting their dominance in the region politically and militarily, the implications and conclusions are applicable to all Aboriginal nations contending with imperial, national, and intellectual boundaries. It is clear that physical, metaphysical, and epistemological borderlands are a lived experience that conditions the past and present and will continue to condition the future of nations, communities, families, and individuals.

Much is made of Canada and the United States sharing the world's longest undefended border. Less examined is how that border has artificially divided hundreds of Aboriginal territories and First Nations peoples for over 300 years. Beyond simply comparing Canadian and American experiences, much can be discovered by examining the ebbs and flows of experiences within borderland regions. This is true regardless of whether the focus is on borderlands in the Maritimes, the St. Lawrence River, the Great Lakes region, or along the forty-ninth parallel in the Prairies or British Columbia. As such, this volume is by no means the final word on the borderlands centred on the Great Lakes, but it does represent a starting point from which further discussions can evolve. It is also part of a new and growing field of study as Canadian and American scholars turn to examining the border not as a barrier but as a crucible where conflicting currents of identity, history, and culture shape local and national communities.

# "WE HAVE NO SPIRIT TO CELEBRATE WITH YOU THE GREAT [1893] COLUMBIAN FAIR"
## *Aboriginal Peoples of the Great Lakes Respond to Canadian and United States Policies During the Nineteenth Century*

━━ ⊯◊⊱ ━━

EDMUND J. DANZINGER JR.

## Introduction

In 1893, Chief Simon Pokagon, a sixty-three-year-old Michigan Potawatomi, spoke at the Chicago World's Columbian Exposition. His words carried the authority and the pain of one who endured both Indian removal and the ordeal of reservation life:

> We have no spirit to celebrate with you the great Columbia Fair....
>
> Where these great Columbian show-buildings stretch skyward, and where stands this "Queen City of the West" *once* stood the red man's wigwams; .... All [the resources of the region] were provided by the Great Spirit for our use; we destroyed none except for food and dress; had plenty and were contented and happy.
>
> But alas! The pale faces came by chance to our shores, many times very needy and hungry. We nursed and fed them, fed the ravens that were soon to pluck out our eyes and the eyes of our children....
>
> The cyclone of civilization rolled westward; the forests of untold centuries were swept away; streams dried up; lakes fell back from their ancient bounds; and all our fathers once loved to gaze upon was destroyed, defaced, or marred, except the sun, moon, and starry skies above, which the Great Spirit in his wisdom hung beyond reach....
>
> As the hunted deer close chased all day long, when night comes on, weary and tired, lies down to rest, mourning for companions of the morning herd, all scattered, dead, and gone, so we through weary years have tried to find some place to safely rest. But all in vain! Our

throbbing hearts unceasing say, "The hounds are howling on our
tracks." Our sad history has been told by weeping parents to their
children from generation to generation....

   We never shall be happy here any more; ... We only stand with
folded arms and watch and wait to see the future deal with us no better than the past.[1]

The nineteenth century was indeed hellish for Great Lakes Aboriginal peoples. They were no longer needed as military allies and fur-trading partners by Great Britain and the United States, whose rapidly expanding
populations in the region coveted Aboriginal resources. One by one, Iroquoian and Algonquian nations ceded most of their homeland and either
relocated west of the Mississippi River or, by the 1850s, accepted small
reservations scattered throughout the Great Lakes basin. Ontario lands
included fifty-one such parcels, and in the United States there were
twenty-three. By 1870, officials estimated the Native population at
41,500.[2]

   During the reservation years of the later nineteenth century, it made
little difference whether Aboriginal people lived north or south of the
international border drawn upon the water. All were buffeted by the
"cyclone of civilization" driving westward and northward: White farmers and labourers, aggressive entrepreneurs, a transportation revolution,
federal policy-makers and their coercive field agents, and evangelistic
school teachers and missionaries.

   Prior to the 1814 Treaty of Ghent, the British–American border also
helped shape the region's history. Both countries jockeyed for control
of the Old Northwest's fabulous resources—from farmland and furs to
fish and timber. The lakes provided as well a gateway to northern and
western frontiers. Britain occupied military and trading posts on American soil until the Jay Treaty of 1794. London also encouraged Indian
nations to remain faithful allies while resisting Yankee expansion. The
United States meanwhile established a factory system of trading posts
to hold Indian trade and loyalty, enacted two land ordinances to stimulate White settlement south and west of the lakes, and adopted a schizophrenic Indian policy that sought simultaneously to "civilize" Aboriginal
peoples and encourage their cession of most homelands east of the Mississippi River. America's policies triggered powerful responses from the
Shawnee Prophet and his brother Tecumseh, whose accomplishments
on both sides of the border are well chronicled. In 1812 their resistance
campaign merged with an Anglo–American war.[3]

The consequences of these hostilities and the Treaty of Ghent were momentous for Native residents of the region. Their world flattened. Whether villagers dwelt north or south of the international border made much less difference. Britain and the United States began demilitarization of the Great Lakes and jointly surveyed their border, whose lines upon the water had been murky since the 1783 Treaty of Paris. Henceforth, though boundary lines theoretically divided the region, waves of change battered both sides of the border. American and British (later Canadian) Indian policies likewise became almost indistinguishable, as were Native responses to them in Ontario, Minnesota, Wisconsin, Michigan, or New York.[4]

Be they Canadian or American, Native community leaders and individual families valiantly and creatively defended their cultural traditions, as well as their economic and political independence. Reservation leaders, drawing upon long-standing traditions of mutual respect and cooperation with non-Natives, sought a workable balance between the new and the old, between accommodation to changing circumstances and protection of their peoples' resources and traditions. There was no monolithic Native response to the exercise of power wielded by government agents and missionaries; rather, groups and individuals responded in various ways—from accommodation to resistance—and made use of the resources available to them.

The Aboriginal story is worth telling because reservations were important battlegrounds where Native people fought to protect their self-sufficiency, identity, and sovereignty. Here, too, Canadian and United States frontiersmen sought control of remaining Native resources. Other newcomers, in hopes of saving the Indian from extinction, worked diligently to "civilize" and ready reservation families for absorption into the mainstream. The outcome of these Great Lakes struggles would shape the future of both sides of the watery international border.

## Winds of Change

The four decades following the War of 1812 redirected the course of Great Lakes Native history. The rush of settlers and developers out to the lakes via the Erie Canal and other new transportation arteries forced dozens of Indian land cession treaties. Many nations, like the Wyandot, gathered on reservation islands amid a rising White sea. Troubles beset even these sanctuaries. Canadian and United States Indian agents and missionaries tried to regulate Native–White relations and to convert their Wyandot charges at Ohio's Grand Reserve and elsewhere to the White way of life. Some Indians accepted part of this message and sought economic self-sufficiency through farming. Others, sometimes called the "Pagan" party or faction, clung to traditional lifestyles and searched for a means to slip the government's tightening noose. Crafty diplomacy, piecemeal accommodation, and other adaptive Indian responses could not stem the growing local and national demands to move Great Lakes Aboriginal nations, however. British policy-makers, less influenced by frontier lobbyists than their United States counterparts, permitted Aboriginal nations to keep portions of their homeland rather than push them west of the lakes.

Unlike the wholesale expulsion of tribes from the southern United States, the policy developed three variations in the American Old Northwest. Removal was applied only to Native enclaves south of a line that ran from the eastern end of Lake Erie to Milwaukee, Wisconsin. This zone embraced fertile farmland and strategic real estate needed for booming Midwestern settlements such as Buffalo, Cleveland, Detroit, Chicago, and Milwaukee. Neither resource, it was argued, could be left in Native hands. North of "the line" was an area of pine forests, marginally fertile soils, and long, tough winters. "This is the Midwestern Outback," wrote William Ashworth, "the area once referred to by Henry Clay in a famous Senate speech as 'a place beyond the remotest extent of the United States, if not in the Moon.'"[5] Once Aboriginal peoples were elbowed aside to permit the development of prime timber and mineral resources, they were allowed to stay on restricted holdings. The Great Lakes Indian relocation differed from events elsewhere in the United States because of the nearby Canadian escape hatch. Some Iroquois, Ottawa, Chippewa, and Potawatomi families, whose homes lay south of "the line" and who were targeted for removal west of the Mississippi, found refuge and then permanent homes east of Lake Huron and the St. Clair River. This process, finished by the mid-1850s, removed some groups entirely from the Great Lakes. These were the Wyandot, Shawnee, Sauk and Fox, Kickapoo, Miami, and Illinois tribes located west of the Mississippi, and the Iroquois, Ottawa, and Potawatomi families who joined them but left many fellow tribesmen behind.[6]

Those living on Great Lakes reservations in the mid-nineteenth century faced an uncertain future. Unlike their uprooted cousins to the west, they had at least retained part of their homeland. Moreover, Indian agents and missionaries had made few radical changes in Native lifestyles. On the darker side, from the Native point of view, their reservations were too small to maintain a traditional hunting-fishing-gathering economy. More than ever, they depended on White largesse. Their precarious economic position and confinement to reservations also made them vulnerable to British and American government programs of forced acculturation. Before the 1850s, the Great Lakes Aboriginal peoples had enjoyed the freedom of adopting only those features of White culture that appealed to them. The luxury of selectivity was no longer theirs; when chiefs touched their pens to cession and relocation treaties, Aboriginal peoples began a new journey down the White road.

What made this passage so challenging were the winds of change sweeping the lakes at this time. By the 1850s, government officials and entrepreneurial private citizens believed that exploitation of Great Lakes resources was essential to the future prosperity of Canada and the United States. "Let the merchants of Toronto consider," proclaimed well-known journalist George Brown in the *Globe*, "that if their city is ever to be made really great—if ever to rise above the rank of a fifth rate American town—it must be by the development of the great British territory lying to the north and west."[7] Develop they did—at a breathtaking pace. By the century's end, tidy farms and swelling cities blanketed the southern drainage basin of the Great Lakes. Meanwhile, farmers, lumbermen, miners, fishers, town builders, tourists, and federal bureaucrats transformed parts of the pristine northern hinterlands. By 1891, Ontario's population was 2.1 million, double that of forty years earlier.[8] As anxious eyewitnesses, Aboriginal peoples hunkered down north and south of the international border and struggled to hold on against these tempestuous winds of change.

Several factors spurred Great Lakes developments besides the commercial dreams of George Brown. The scarcity of good farmland south of the Canadian Shield combined with exploding Canadian and United States populations, partly due to immigration, propelled people into urban areas or north to more marginal lands. Industrialization and urbanization impulses within both nations created homes and work for those living around the southern lakes, as well as markets for raw materials such as timber and minerals shipped from the northland treasure trove.[9]

Two additional factors facilitated events. First, a transportation revolution integrated Great Lakes industries, then linked them with distant western and eastern markets. Second, during the late 1800s, the Canadian and United States governments continually opened Native lands for resource exploitation. When officials permitted White settlement on most of Manitoulin Island in 1866, for example, the Aboriginal population was only 1,250. Within four years, noted the historian James P. Barry, the island was "fairly well settled. Between 1872 and 1880 its population grew by 15,000 people, largely drawn there by lumbering."[10] George Brown's dream was realized, but with profound consequences.

## Federal Indian Policies

In 1892, Captain Richard H. Pratt, founder of the Carlisle Indian boarding school, remarked astutely, "It is a sad day for the Indians when they fall under the assaults of our troops, ... but a far sadder day is it for them when they fall under the baneful influences of a treaty agreement with the United States whereby they are to receive large annuities, and to be protected on reservations, and held apart from all association with the best of our civilization. The destruction is not so speedy, but it is far more general."[11] The reservation system was implemented during the last half of the nineteenth century by Washington and Ottawa policy-makers who set two goals for their Indian wards: continued reduction of Native land holdings and the "civilization" of "savage" reservation residents in preparation for integration into mainstream society.

Several assumptions guided Uncle Sam's thinking. Frontiersmen would applaud the opening of Aboriginal lands to White settlement as they had for over two centuries. Federal officials also hoped that "civilized" neighbours would be a good influence on fledgling Native farmers. Certainly the United States no longer had room for traditional Native cultures, whose inefficient use of the land included hunting, gathering, fishing, and, at times, bloody intertribal warfare.[12] "We are fifty millions of people, and they [Indians] are only one-fourth of one million," reported Commissioner of Indian Affairs Hiram Price in 1881. "The few must yield to the many." Later that decade, another commissioner, Thomas J. Morgan, warned that Indians must adapt to American civilization or "be crushed by it." Advocates of "civilizing" Aboriginal peoples obviously believed, furthermore, that they were capable of learning the English language and of adopting an alternative, superior mode of life. A desire to solve the long-standing "Indian problem" motivated policy-makers like Commissioner Price. To "allow them to drag along year after year ... in their old superstitions, laziness, and filth ... would be a lasting disgrace to our government," he argued. To transform them into self-sufficient and productive citizens would be "a crown of glory to any nation."[13]

Meanwhile, north of the Great Lakes, the Province of Canada assumed responsibility for Indian affairs in 1860. Canada continued

Britain's policy of Native assimilation begun in the 1830s. It was the government's duty, wrote Secretary of State Sir George Murray in 1830, gradually to reclaim Natives "from a state of barbarism" and introduce "amongst them the industrious and peaceful habits of civilized life."[14] Legislation enacted by the British and Canadian parliaments spelled out Indian policy during the last half of the century. Most notable was the suffocatingly paternalistic Indian Act of 1876, whose 100 separate sections sought to control every aspect of the lives of Aboriginal people. Their legal status became that of minors under a federal guardianship until one by one they became enfranchised. Such was the goal. Even membership in Native communities (registered or "status" Indians were eligible for government services and treaty payments) came to be determined by Indian Department officials.[15]

To attain their common goals for the Indian, the Canadian and United States governments used similar strategies. The keystone was a paternal reservation system: dozens of halfway houses that temporarily isolated Great Lakes Native communities from society and simultaneously enabled government officials to control the civilization and assimilation process. Over the years, their methods became increasingly interfering and menacing. They included (1) the promotion of Indian economic self-sufficiency through sedentary farming, allotment of reservation land in severalty, and the power to confer citizenship on Natives who had jettisoned tribal ways; (2) the formal education of their young; (3) the replacement of "pagan" beliefs and ceremonies with Christianity; and (4) attacking Aboriginal political leaders who resisted Ottawa's and Washington's acculturation program. For all persons concerned, the challenges of integrating Aboriginal peoples into a capitalistic foreign culture were momentous; yet optimism prevailed in Ottawa and Washington.

To implement these strategies, Ottawa and Washington turned to governmental agencies, particularly Indian agents stationed in the field. They laboured to turn semi-nomadic, communal Natives into self-sufficient farmers who owned individual plots of land, whose children attended schools, whose families worshipped in Christian churches, and whose leaders had been elected by the community. History would show that these elaborate Canadian and American plans—for "civilization," assimilation, and reservation resource development—clashed with Aboriginal agendas.

## Native Responses

Aboriginal peoples' responses to the winds of change blowing across their Great Lakes homelands were diverse and, over time, varied from community to community—even between individuals. Nevertheless, some generalizations are possible. Aboriginal community leaders understood what was happening economically across the Great Lakes and in the vicinity of their reserves, yet they did not surrender to these events as passive victims. Neither land loss nor assignment to reservations crushed them. Despite their relatively small numbers and very modest economic and political resources, they adjusted and resisted—in a variety of ways—as best they could. Usually, they altered traditions when they felt it was necessary or desirable. Their choices were informed and not made solely because of government policy and the chiding of field officials about the advantages of "civilization." Likewise, Aboriginal people of the Great Lakes continued to defend their rights, to negotiate in good faith, and to play a prominent role in Great Lakes history.[16] Such a high-stakes contest between worthy opponents became an exciting story, full of the surprising twists and turns of unforeseen consequences and historical accidents. It began with the Ottawa and Washington campaign to turn their Native "wards" into self-sufficient farmers.

In response to government Indian policies and other changes sweeping the Great Lakes in the late 1800s, reservation peoples adjusted in order to feed themselves and preserve community autonomy. For hundreds of Aboriginal families, especially in the south, this meant a major commitment to plow agriculture. The decision seemed reasonable: the land could support farming, and their communities had strong gardening traditions. Furthermore, Canada and the United States offered technical assistance. Nearby markets beckoned their surplus crops. Even the more northern reserves, where farming was less feasible, explored new ways to provide for their people. They, too, took advantage of federal help and the economic opportunities offered by expanding regional industries: commercial fishing, railroad construction, shipping, and lumber.

Within Native nations the currents of change and continuity ran strong. Families that focussed on plow agriculture altered gender roles, housing, day-to-day living including diet, and relationships with the local Indian agent and non-Native neighbours. Adherence to more traditional economic ways—seasonal hunting, gathering, and fishing—though evident in the south, still characterized the northern reserves in Ontario and the American Great Lakes states. Here the climate and soil were much less hospitable to farming. Nevertheless, economic changes that affected the North, such as the decline in fur markets and the influx of White commercial fisherman, challenged historic subsistence patterns. Complex patterns of change and continuity existed throughout the region.

Farming was fundamental to many Great Lakes Aboriginal families and to federal government agencies responsible for Native welfare during the last half of the nineteenth century. This was not a story of utterly mistaken government expectations for its Aboriginal wards or of outright betrayal; nor was it a tale of great differences in policy and administration between the United States and Canada. As to Great Lakes Natives, theirs is not an account of wholesale rejection of federal programs and a mulish persistence in time-honoured ways. The history of Native agriculture was far more complex and important than such one-dimensional renderings.

During the last half of the nineteenth century, many Native communities made a trial commitment to plow agriculture. Although part of their effort was ultimately undermined by a variety of factors over which they had little control, the accomplishments of energetic Iroquois and Algonquians were enormous: land cleared and cultivated, crops produced, permanent homes and outbuildings constructed, farm implements acquired and used, and livestock raised. Particularly notable were production statistics at Walpole Island, Six Nations, and upstate New York Iroquois reservations. Their residents harvested a variety of crops— grains, vegetables, fruits—and hosted agricultural fairs. At the 1871 New York Iroquois Agricultural Society fair, members displayed about a thousand entries "in all the departments." The state report also noted, "Grain and vegetables displayed at this fair can not be excelled in this country, as the remark was made by many competent to judge who were visitors from abroad." The value of Walpole Island farm products in 1898 was $15,668 and at Six Nations $63,810.[17]

Farm success derived not from a reservation's location in either the United States or Canada, but from suitable geography, gardening traditions, a solid commitment to plow agriculture, and a nutritive sprinkling of Indian department assistance in both countries. The farther north Native peoples lived within the Great Lakes basin, the less practical was plow agriculture. Zealous American and Canadian officials pushed northern Aboriginal communities to farm, and plow agriculture was attempted with government help at places like Manitoulin Island, Fort William, and Wisconsin's Menominee reservation. They cultivated thousands of acres and planted seeds. They built houses and barns. Reported yields were impressive. However, short growing seasons, the high cost of clearing land, and the availability of off-reservation food sources and wages offered by White neighbours convinced North Country men and women over the years not to rely heavily on farm crops. Pine woods and waters continued to be their farms. This pattern of seasonal rovings to supplement their garden patches persisted on both sides of the international border from Georgian Bay and Lake Huron west across Michigan and Wisconsin and as far north as Lake Nipigon and Grand Portage, Minnesota.

Mixed economies even characterized the Six Nations and Walpole Island First Nation, the heart of Native farm country. Besides their impressive and fruitful commitment to agriculture, families relied heavily on other income sources by the late 1890s. In addition to the $63,810 value of their farm products, the Grand River Iroquois earned $78,499 in wages and received $3,307.75 from land rentals. Farming provided 61.5 percent of Walpole's income; the rest came from fishing, hunting, land rentals, government assistance to the poor, and "other industries."[18]

Dependence on non-farming resources, which increased the farther north Native communities were located, remained an important part of the Great Lakes Aboriginal economy during the last half of the nineteenth century. As with agriculture, these activities demonstrated both continuity and change. Traditional hunting, gathering, and fishing persisted among Aboriginal families; they also developed new sources of income from lumbering, land sales, and off-reservation wage work. Paternalistic federal Indian agents tried to manage these pursuits whenever possible.

The limited success of reservation cash-crop farming and non-agricultural economic initiatives prompted Washington and Ottawa legislators to try new strategies. Otherwise, their hope for Indian community self-sufficiency and assimilation into the White mainstream would be unfulfilled. The twin ideals of family-owned homesteads and citizenship dominated reformers' experiments in the late 1800s. To stimulate this integration and break down communal economic ties, American and Canadian Indian treaties and legislation pressured Aboriginal families to select and improve modest-sized, private farm sites either on or off reservations. Their reward would be fee simple titles. Freedom and equality also awaited those who followed the examples of White citizens. Such was the dream—and the promise.

Great Lakes Native experiences with allotment and location tickets must have disappointed reformers and federal policy-makers. The 1887 Dawes Act of the United States Congress triggered some resistance and extensive loss of Indian lands and timber resources without producing widespread economic self-sufficiency through commercial farming. Likewise, the Canadian location ticket system met much local resistance. Actually the entire Indian Act, of which enfranchisement and these tickets were a part, became a notorious source of abusive, misguided federal Department of Indian Affairs power over Great Lakes Native communities well into the next century. On both sides of the international border, it was a disturbing and oft-repeated story: non-Indian do-gooders and frontier developers separated Aboriginal communities from even more of their homeland, and in the process weakened their cultural ties, economies, and political defenses.[19]

By the 1890s, severalty had fostered only modest agricultural success. For example, the American Lake Superior Ojibwa, whose allotted lands totaled 212,034.52 acres, farmed only 2,865 acres. Agents optimistically pointed out that increasing percentages of reservation men who laboured in "civilized pursuits." American Indian Bureau officials also hoped that allotees would use wages and timber-sale profits to improve their homesteads and purchase farm machinery. However, large numbers of self-sufficient, commercial farmers remained but a hope. Of the ninety-nine allotments at Fond du Lac in Minnesota, only two families even lived on their lands.[20]

On the American side of the lakes, perhaps the most negative consequence of Washington's severalty program was lost reservation land. Helen Hornbeck Tanner writes that at every stage of the process—from allotment selection and receipt of trust certificates to presidential land patents—"interference came from land speculators, loan sharks, lumbering interests, and aggressive settlers, at times working in collusion with Indian agents and the federal land offices." The Indian Bureau had implemented severalty among the Ottawa and Ojibwa of the Upper Great Lakes since the mid-1800s, with the result that "close to 90 percent of allotted reservation land passed rapidly into non-Indian possession, usually before patents were received."[21]

Not content with restructuring Native economies, Canadian and American policy-makers bent on bringing Native wards into the mainstream proposed to change the inner character: "The time for fighting the Indian tribes is passed," remarked President Merrill Gates of the Lake Mohonk Conference in 1891. "We are going to conquer the Indians by a standing army of school-teachers, armed with ideas, winning victories by industrial training, and by the gospel of love and the gospel of work." Once again, Aboriginal peoples became an object for alteration. This time children had to modify their behaviour, whether in a day or boarding school.[22] Boys and girls, along with their families, were required to bend like saplings before the powerful and superior ways of White culture. This new form of warfare, which turned classrooms into battlegrounds, created momentous change within reservations and drew into the fray Native leaders, parents, pupils, school teachers, missionaries, Indian agents, and other federal officials. The struggle was fierce and extended into the next century.

Scholarly focus on the harmfulness of boarding schools and absenteeism in day schools has obscured much of the positive Aboriginal response to both types of schools.[23] Many families and community leaders, north and south of the international border, believed in the importance of some formal education for their youngsters, though their agenda was not always the same as that of the White newcomers. Aboriginal peoples pressured or at least allowed the federal governments to establish schools in their midst—twenty-five among the New York Iroquois alone in the mid-1880s. Natives often helped finance construction and then maintained the structures. A school board at Six Nations on the Grand River set educational policy. Some schools had Aboriginal teachers. Aboriginal parents sent thousands of their children over the years to day schools and boarding schools. As in any community, not everyone supported the local schools, and ideas changed over time, as well. Families became disenchanted with schools or came to the realization that formal education was necessary. Many parents, especially up north, regularly took children out of class so they could help with off-reservation hunting, trapping, fishing, and gathering. Whether fathers and mothers supported or resisted the day and boarding schools, they exercised far more control over the influential educational process than heretofore given credit. The same may be said of the children, whose resistance to boarding-school procedures at times bedeviled administrators and even terminated operations by burning buildings. True, boarding schools crippled some children emotionally, leaving them unable to function well in either the Native or White world, but the continuing support of boarding schools like Saint Joseph's on the Menominee Reservation and the desire of so many Wisconsin Aboriginal parents to enrol their children at Tomah, for example, cast a more positive light on Native–boarding school relationships.[24]

The overall plan of policy-makers, Indian agents, missionaries, and school teachers to transform Great Lakes Natives through their children did not succeed any more than earlier programs to transform Aboriginal economies. The fault lay once again in unrealistic and ethnocentric goals, the unwillingness of federal governments—despite their sense of urgency—to commit enough funds for a long enough period, and the unwillingness of Native families and community leaders to be pushed around like pawns on a chessboard. Instead, Natives supported those schools and school activities that they believed benefitted students and the reserves. Those that did not were ignored, as were requests from the Canadian Department of Indian Affairs and the US Office of Indian Affairs that all reservation residents become commercial farmers. Some families tried formal education and some did not. Nearly all kept their options open and refused to totally accept any culturally transforming program coming out of Washington or Ottawa. Though hard pressed and in need of new skills and new approaches as they faced a challenging future, Great Lakes Native people continued to direct as best they could the course of their lives.

Educational and economic programs were not the only ones to "blow across the bow," disturbing and challenging Native communities. The exhortations of Christian evangelists stirred up menacing waves, as they had been doing for over 200 years on the Great Lakes. Their hope was to save Indian souls and ready them for assimilation and citizenship within Canadian and American societies. Although many Native families dismissed the missionaries and their message, it would be mistaken to assume their role was inconsequential.

Missionaries made a difference for a variety of reasons and in diverse ways. First, their strong motivation to spread the Gospel message was supported by powerful church organizations and by both federal governments, which saw church workers as junior partners in the program to "civilize" Indians. Second, the seeds sown by evangelists yielded an impressive harvest of churches that sprang up and thrived on many reservations. Some had more than one house of worship. Third, because missionaries tried to change nearly all aspects of Native cultures, their influence reached beyond the churchyard. They urged and assisted Native people in dividing reservations into family plots, fencing land, and taking up horse-and-plow agriculture. Missionaries also advocated that Aboriginal families live in permanent homes, wear "citizens'" clothes, lead healthy lives, and abstain from alcohol use. Churches often sponsored reservation day schools and residential schools, and supplied teachers for both. Missionaries were also involved in local politics, often at the request of Native leaders who recruited local ministers and priests to be supporters and cultural brokers. During President U. S. Grant's administration, the churches helped determine civil appointments to Indian agencies. Finally, C. L. Higham's study of United States and Canadian Protestant missionaries documented how they helped fashion public perceptions of Native peoples as well as national Indian policy. She concludes, "As the nineteenth century came to a close and their work ended, missionaries left behind their most important contribution to Canadian and American societies—their ideas, opinions, and evaluations of native groups and the frontier. Their observations became part of the scholarly literature and were discussed often throughout the twentieth century."[25]

What shaped Native responses to evangelists were the troublesome winds of change sweeping their homelands. Aboriginal interests demanded that they adapt to Canadian and American newcomers in order to preserve their communities, obtain desirable merchandise—from tools to household goods—and get the skills necessary to compete in the workplace and safeguard the land of their birth. Native decisions about Christian conversion must be seen against this environmental background. Their reactions to Christian churches proved remarkably discriminating, as they had been with Indian agents, school teachers, and others who urged them to make top-to-bottom cultural changes. There was no pell-mell rush to accept the Gospel or reject it; rather, Aboriginal responses were noticeably mixed—from enthusiastic acceptance of Christianity at one extreme to outright denial on the other—and subject to fluctuation over time. It was the Native way to decide individually how to keep a spiritual balance.

The same was true for politics. Aboriginal families and their communities exercised as much independence in governance as they did in making a living, educating their children, and relating to the spirit world. They were autonomous communities that reacted to a changing world in ways that seemed to serve them best. "How could it be otherwise?" writes Joel W. Martin.[26] Such was the way of their forefathers, who dealt with French fur traders and British Redcoats who encroached upon the Great Lakes country. Aboriginal people canoed through history with hands on the paddles, guiding their own destiny.

A number of factors provoked the attack on traditional politics between Natives and non-Natives in the late nineteenth century. American reformers, disappointed with President Grant's Peace Policy, regarded reservations as a barrier to cultural change rather than a refuge for beleaguered Native families. The consensus-style Aboriginal government systems and the inability of chiefs to command obedience contributed to the painfully long process of reaching binding agreements and the sluggish rate of "progress" in economic development, education, and the abandonment of "paganism." Canadian and American officials likewise grumbled about the cost of subsidizing reservations and protecting their borders from encroaching Whites. An attack on Aboriginal political independence got additional support from aggressive land developers; they liked any policy change that promised to open Native lands for settlement by a rapidly expanding frontier population. Decidedly different from these entrepreneurial motives were those of American and Canadian social engineers. Although they, too, pushed for abandonment of reservations and traditionalist tribal governments, they did so with the goal of elevating and assimilating Aboriginal peoples and thereby creating a homogeneous citizenry.[27]

Between 1857 and 1890, a series of Canadian and American laws confined Indians to the legal status of minors and made the federal government their guardians with the power to oversee every aspect of reservation life. This legislation weakened the position of reservation leaders and generally curtailed Native sovereignty. The Canadian government, for example, would henceforth supervise the selection of chiefs and councillors. Parliament would decide the powers that local officials could exercise, impose a municipal model of government, and oversee all Native actions. Gone would be the practice of nation-to-nation negotiations, and in its place a client people would be guided by the Crown's gatekeepers: resident Indian agents.[28] Such blatant interference in the political affairs of reservation communities, all the in name of civilization and protection, similarly characterized the United States government during this period.

Each Great Lakes Aboriginal community responded in a unique way to the powerful internal and external pressures it faced during the second half of the nineteenth century. A few generalizations can be made, however. Local chiefs and councils realized that they must at times accommodate the demands of aggressive, resourceful Washington and Ottawa policy-makers and their functionaries. The result was a governing partnership between Indian headmen and federal officials, in the field and in the national capitals. Together, they staged elections for reservation officials, set and approved their salaries, and grappled with critical, everyday resource issues such as allotments, leases, fishing rights, and tribal membership. Political cooperation enabled chiefs and councils to preserve much of their homeland and their identity as Aboriginal peoples while they sailed into the twentieth century. To portray Aboriginal leaders largely as victims of oppressive colonial powers is to disregard the fruits of these hard-won, productive partnerships with federal departments. Cooperation was a dominant political theme, but it could not mask the underlying, natural tensions between Native councils and federal officers at all levels. Native communities regularly challenged and refused to do the bidding of assimilationist bureaucrats. Great Lakes Native people were just as assertive politically as they were in matters of religion, education, or making a living.

Another corrective to the notion of uniform, suffocating federal political dominance was suggested by Canadian Agent William Van Abbott in 1894. He visited the Michipicoten and Big Heads on Lake Superior only once a year.[29] Otherwise, these isolated and independent bands directed the activities of their own families and villages, free from Ottawa's interference. How different their situation was compared to that of southern Indian communities, who regularly contended with aggressive White neighbours, missionaries, school teachers, and resident agents.

Another indicator of the importance of Great Lakes Aboriginal politics was intertribal cooperation. It took various forms. One was the ongoing Grand General Indian Council of Ontario. It met on a different reserve every two years during the last half of the 1800s and included nearly all Canadian Great Lakes Ojibwa bands.[30] The Grand Council had counterparts elsewhere. The Iroquois Confederacy continued to function on both sides of the international border, although its former sphere of influence—intertribal and international affairs—was greatly restricted. Claims against the United States government prompted the Ojibwa of Lake Superior to work more closely together. Reservations sent delegates to meet at Bad River, Wisconsin, late in 1895. Here they agreed to hire attorneys to help get the monies Washington owed them because of 1854 treaty commitments. Cooperating reservations later signed contracts with local lawyers, as well as a Washington, DC, law firm.[31]

For Aboriginal political leaders determined to protect and advance their communities' interests, hiring attorneys and working intertribally were but two strategies employed. Another was outright resistance. Individuals, as noted above, simply refused to cooperate with federal officials. Some kept their children out of school, stayed away from churches, and would not "take up the plow." Resistance was also corporate when reserves refused to accept an electoral system for choosing their leadership or other types of outside interference in their political affairs.

Rather than choose outright resistance to Ottawa and Washington, a more common approach was to consult with local agents and try to influence the thinking of distant policy-makers. Numerous petitions, memorials, and letters preserved in Ottawa and Washington archives show the intensity and shrewdness of Aboriginal political leveraging. Petitions reveal that their writers understood how to influence the government bureaucracy as well as high-level policy-makers. These documents also show what issues troubled Native leaders at a particular place and time. Menominee, for example, clearly understood Washington's treaty obligations, were aware of bills brought before Congress that touched Native interests, and were prepared to take their case to lawmakers and central administrative offices—even if forbidden to do so by their agent and the Indian commissioner. Though remarkable, the Menominee campaigns were similar to those of other regional Native communities.[32]

Lobbying trips now and then proved successful. In the late 1800s, the Shawano, Wisconsin, Businessmen's Association sent a representative to promote passage of a bill giving them access to reservation timber. A Menominee group followed him to Capitol Hill to protest such legislation. Washington responded by sending its own special agent to Wisconsin. He spent twenty days looking into the possible consequences of the bill; then he filed a devastating report about the economic harm that would be done to the Menominee if Congress enacted such a law.[33]

What distinguished these dealings with federal governments was the political savvy of Great Lakes Native people. They clearly understood their own interests. They championed them vigorously and creatively, while skilfully working within the White governmental system. Chiefs repeatedly bypassed local agents if they did not trust them or wanted to sway policy-makers. Aboriginal councils made their voices heard in several ways: writing petitions, memorials, and letters; lobbying among White friends; hiring attorneys; and sending delegations to national capitals. Aboriginal people, as non-citizens, obviously lacked political clout; but they were a population to be taken seriously. Native people had treaty rights and valuable land. Their history had been intertwined with that of Euro-Canadians and Euro-Americans for over 400 years.

By 1900, the well-laid plans of Washington and Ottawa to transform Aboriginal governments into handmaidens of acculturation and assimilation had to a significant degree failed. Federal legislation in both countries weakened the powers of chiefs and councils, and intrusive Indian agents demanded and obtained a powerful voice in reservation affairs; yet, despite marginality, factionalism, and a colonial status, Aboriginal leaders remained keen interpreters of reservation interests and, with some success, championed the self-determination and sovereignty of their people. In politics, as in other spheres of Great Lakes reservation life, Aboriginal people showed remarkable resilience, adaptability, and diversity. Though no longer masters of their fate, chiefs and councils played a much stronger role than heretofore portrayed, during their own day and as heroes for later generations.

## Conclusion

By 1900, Native peoples of the Great Lakes had forged a new set of relationships with Whites on and off the reservations, north and south of the international boundary. No longer the freewheeling, semi-nomadic owners of vast Great Lakes resources of which Chief Pokagon spoke to persons assembled at the Chicago World's Columbian Exposition, Aboriginal lives centred on island communities that were expected to enter the Canadian and American mainstream before long. As the century drew to a close, Native people on reservations had stepped partway into the current. Most families lived in permanent frame or log houses, and earned at least part of their living by farming or from wage work close to home. Gone were the distant expeditions to trapping grounds, isolated trading posts, and enemy encampments. Other features of their traditional cultures were being replaced. Day schools and residential schools enrolled a significant number of Native boys and girls. Many reservation Natives regularly attended local Christian churches. All facets of tribal life were supervised by government agents, from farming and timber harvests to education and community government. In the coming years, a powerful mainstream tugged forcefully at Great Lakes Native people with offerings of the good life, if only they would let go of the past. On both sides of the border, the year 1900 saw these moderately acculturated Natives poised between two worlds and two centuries. A more consequential dividing line was the one discerned by environmental historian William Ashworth and discussed above: between the Great Lakes outback to the north and the more southern areas of fertile farmland and large population concentrations.

Sixty years later, when the Red Power Movement of the 1960s exploded onto the Canadian and American stages, it drew guidance and strength from Native leaders of the past. Some were battlefield commanders: Joseph Brant, Tecumseh, Sitting Bull, Geronimo. Others were Great Lakes chiefs and councillors and clan mothers: protectors of their homelands and champions of their people by peaceful means during the reservation years of the 1800s. These leaders kept alive the dream of economic self-sufficiency, of self-determination, of Native sovereignty. In today's parlance, they had agency.

That they remain influential survivors "is a remarkable tribute to the strength and endurance of Aboriginal people," remarked Canadian Minister of Indian Affairs and Northern Development Jane Stewart in January 1998. Moreover, she went on to say,

> The Government of Canada recognizes that policies that sought to assimilate Aboriginal people, women and men, were not the way to build a strong country. We must instead continue to find ways in which Aboriginal people can participate fully in the economic, political, cultural and social life of Canada in a manner which preserves and enhances the collective identities of Aboriginal communities, and allows them to evolve and flourish in the future. Working together to achieve our shared goals will benefit all Canadians, Aboriginal and non-Aboriginal alike.[34]

A similar apology by the United States government[35] promised the beginning of a new Great Lakes era—north and south of lines drawn upon the water—for Aboriginal people and their non-Aboriginal neighbours.

# CROSS-BORDER TREATY SIGNERS
## *The Anishnaabeg of the*
## *Lake Huron Borderlands*

—⊷ ✲◇✲ ⊶—

PHIL BELLFY

## Introduction

From the swirling waters of the St. Mary's rapids at the Twin Saults, to the St. Clair River delta that gives rise to Walpole Island, the Lake Huron Borderlands comprise a true Indigenous nation. Native people have lived in this area since the glacial waters subsided and the Great Lakes took on their present configuration—about 2,500 years ago. The rich fishery and abundant wildlife induced them to stay in the region, having migrated west from their ancient homeland on the Great Salt Sea in the land of the rising sun far to the east.

We, the Anishnaabeg, thrived for millennia in this rich area, and our lives changed little; but when the Europeans arrived in the early seventeenth century, we were forced to adapt to a radically different way of life in a relatively short span of time, and our culture was changed forever. Change that may have taken untold generations in the past to unfold now took place within a generation or less. Regional disputes that we might now call "low-intensity conflict" became more intense, often fuelled by Continental European conflicts and the cruel methods of war introduced by European "fathers." Conflict over the fur trade and access to trapping territories exacerbated ancient rivalries, and warriors often found themselves hundreds of miles from home, fighting enemies they barely knew for reasons they may have never fully understood.

Yet, throughout these European proxy wars, the Native people of the area fought mainly for their own interest, which simply was to maintain control and occupancy of their homelands. For example, the dominant society has portrayed the actions of Pontiac and his allies as "Pontiac's *Rebellion*." Native people are more inclined to view Pontiac as one leader—among many—who vigorously defended the homeland against the European settler invasion (in this case, the "Americans").

After the Europeans and their settler brethren more or less settled their differences in North America with the Treaty of Ghent in 1814, the Native people of the area—once seen as a military threat—were now relegated to the role of abandoned allies, left to fend pretty much for themselves in their new dealings with either the new "American" government or the British North American authorities. Instead of being "courted" by one side or the other (or, as often happened, by both sides) to tip the "balance of power," they now found themselves divided by a new line drawn through the heart of their homeland—the lines drawn upon the water. Of course, the Anishnaabeg were not completely ignored, in fact, they were still "courted" in one sense by both sides, and that new courtship was intended to foster good relations that, it was hoped, would lead to peace among all groups. A result of this new tranquility, the settler states sought agreement from the Anishnaabeg that their colonial expansion could proceed without impediment through land-cession treaties.

The new threats the Anishnaabeg faced were no longer military ones—the days of Tecumseh and Pontiac were over. Instead, the new threat was legal and diplomatic, with guns and arrows giving way to pen and paper; but throughout this treaty-making period, one thing remained steadfast—the quiet determination of the area's Native people to continue living in their home territory, enjoying the fruits of the land where the Creator had put them and where the bones of their ancestors were buried.

The overwhelming importance of this goal meant that when the time came to negotiate a treaty with the British, the Anishnaabeg did not feel compelled to send only "Canadians" to the council but rather to send their most capable people, just as any threatened group would do. When they sat down with the Americans, they again sent their best and most capable people without regard to their residence on one side of the border or the other. The result of this treaty-making process, with both the British and the Americans, is an astonishing number of "cross-border" treaty-signers—individuals who signed treaties on behalf of the area's Native people with both British and American governments.

This chapter tells their story—the story of the People of the Upper Great Lakes, and the individuals who ably represented them at various treaty councils—making what, for their nation, were the best deals possible under very difficult circumstances. After detailing some of the important treaties and their signers, the paper will conclude with a brief look at the contemporary state of Indigenous life in the Lake Huron Borderlands and the People's enduring sense of nationhood—a nationhood forged in the salt air of an ancient sea, tempered in the cool waters of the Upper Great Lakes, and matured in the political fires of North American nation-building.

## The Barbarians and the Borderlands

The area was a significant part of an empire that embraced most of the known world, transformed from a land of warring, primitive and almost entirely illiterate tribes into a united realm under an administration based on the rule of law.

The early policy of employing friendly chieftains as client "kings" was never intended to be more than a temporary expedient. The process of absorbing the tribes into the normal framework of the provincial administration greatly encouraged the adoption of "civilized" ways.

Based on considerations of manpower and expense, it was decided to hold only that part which was reasonably easy to control and which was profitable.

Considerable trouble occurred in the region before, but it paled into insignificance before the tremendous destruction wrought by a *barbaric conspiratio* when, in unnatural alliance, the tribes attacked simultaneously. The garrison fell, but it was not in fair fight.[1]

To anyone the least bit familiar with European imperialism since 1492, this passage might refer to virtually any part of the planet, save Europe itself. In fact, these quotations are adapted from a 1965 book by Peter Salway called *The Frontier People of Roman Britain*, which discusses the ancient Roman experience in Britain from AD 43 to the early 5th century when the Romans withdrew, leaving the island to fall into—in Salway's words—the "province of the Dark Age historian."[2] Specifically, Salway refers to the "borderlands" between ancient British and Scottish peoples. However, the same sentiments might just as well be from a book called *The Frontier People of the Great Lakes*. In such a book, these quotations might illuminate some of the "Dark Age" quality that characterizes much of the written history of the Indigenous people of the Lake Huron borderlands of the Upper Great Lakes region of North American. As you read what follows, I hope you see how the "histories" of the

Anishnaabeg were, and are, often distorted by European contact and the imposition of imperial hegemony over their territories, especially the imposition of the US–Canada border through the centre of their homelands.

## The Significance of the 1794 Jay Treaty

While the passage of time since the American Revolution and the obvious difficulties engendered by serving two masters (the US and Canadian governments) has eroded the day-to-day interaction of the various Anishnaabeg communities along the border, a common language, a common history, and a common culture still serve to identify us as one People. Perhaps the most notable of these unifying forces is the 1794 Jay Treaty. The passage of over two centuries has not diminished the relevance of this document to the Anishnaabeg of the Lake Huron borderlands.

Article 3 of the Jay Treaty between the United States and Great Britain mentions by name three distinct segments of the North American population: British subjects, citizens of the United States, and "Indians dwelling on either side of the said boundary line." It has been argued since at least 1795 that this statement is tacit recognition of the sovereignty of Native peoples.[3] Despite this tacit recognition, the Canadian and the US governments now refuse to recognize the provisions of the Jay Treaty that mention "Indians," the most important of which is the right of Native people to "freely pass and repass" the border between the two countries exempt from custom duties.

Despite the US and Canadian governments' refusal to recognize any Jay Treaty rights, one of the most visible and political manifestations of Anishnaabeg sovereignty in the Great Lakes is the fact that Native people of the area continue to exercise their Jay Treaty rights by "passing and re-passing" the border and refusing to pay duty on the goods they "import." The obvious consequence of the assertion by Native people of assumed Jay Treaty rights is a plethora of court cases in both the US and in Canada, court cases that have never been decided in favour of Native people; yet the people persist in asserting those rights, and defending those rights in the courts. The most recent of these court cases is the 2001 Canadian Supreme Court decision in *Mitchell v. M.N.R.*, whereby the court, while recognizing an "Aboriginal right" under Canada's Constitution, nevertheless denied Chief Mitchell, and by extension the Mohawks of Akwesasne, the right to "import" goods duty-free from one side of their reserve to the other. The reserve (called St. Regis on the US side) is split by the US–Canada border where New York, Ontario, and Quebec come together in the St. Lawrence.[4]

## The Significance of "Cross-border" Treaty-signers

While a border implies "division," the border, and its association with the land and its people, may also be viewed as a strong link that has served to maintain unity among the Anishnaabeg during the period of European control over the lives of these People. A common language and culture are also obvious links, but the unity achieved through common political struggle—struggling *against* the border—is a significant factor in their sense of nationhood. In the pages that follow, I argue that this unity is exemplified by what I call "cross-border treaty-signers." I maintain that the mere fact that cross-border treaty-signers exist in significant numbers demonstrates that the sovereignty of the Anishnaabeg has not only been maintained but also recognized and strengthened by the British and the American acceptance of these treaty-signers. Everyone knew what they were doing at the time—the Anishnaabeg were in no way trying to deceive British and American authorities by hoping that the settler states would not notice that the same individuals were involved in all sorts of treaty negotiations on both sides of the border. Other cross-border treaty-signers, while not signing treaties with *both* governments, nonetheless signed treaties with one government while maintaining very strong ties to communities on the other side of the border. Again, this practice reinforces the Anishnaabeg sense of "nationhood" and sovereignty.

## Significant Treaties of the Great Lakes Borderlands

Before I get into a discussion of various treaty-signers, I need to address a few questions that may be raised concerning my inclusion of certain individuals who, some may argue, are not the same due to spelling vagaries, etc. First, it must be noted that nineteenth-century spelling conventions were essentially non-existent. The case of the Potawatomi chief Topinabee is instructive in this matter. While Topinabee is not a treaty-signer of any of the treaties discussed in this paper, he did sign several treaties for the Potawatomi, and, in fourteen references to him in these treaties, we find his name spelled twelve different ways. In fact, in one treaty (signed in 1833), we find three variations: Topenebe, Topenebee, and Jo-pen-e-bee.[5] In an interesting twist, the spelling variation that I chose to introduce this issue—Topinabee—is the postal designation of a small community in Cheboygan County in Northern Michigan, and this spelling variation does not appear in any of the treaty documents (it is very unlikely that the historic Potawatomi chief has any connection to this Northern Michigan community; his tribal homeland was the area surrounding the lower and western reaches of Lake Michigan).

In addition to these caveats concerning spelling, it should be added that in several cases I chose to not include some duplicate names in the appendices due to a perceived geographic or chronological distance that might render their inclusion suspect. Rather than include sets of names with dubious integrity, I decided that it was more prudent to include only those names that would withstand close scrutiny. With these concerns in mind, let us now take a look at a few of the significant treaties signed during this era.

## 1820 Treaty at Sault Ste. Marie, with the Americans

Long after the Revolutionary War, and even after the War of 1812, the Anishnaabeg of the Upper Great Lakes were still in control of their homelands and neither side (British or American) were much inclined to assert their purported "authority" until 1820, when the US attempted to finally assert sovereignty over its claimed portion of the Sault Ste. Marie area, at the foot of Lake Superior, when the territorial governor, Lewis Cass, travelled to Sault Ste. Marie to establish a fort and raise the US flag over it. The Indigenous people of the region were none too pleased with this affront to their supremacy in the area; but the threat of escalating hostilities, and the realization that their British "fathers" would not come to their defence persuaded the Native people to sign a treaty ceding land for the American fort.[6] Among the treaty-signers was Shingwauk, the influential area leader who was living at Garden River (on the "British" side of the border) at this time.

Shingwauk signed the 1820 treaty as "Augustin Bart," his French name, and, after the treaty-signing, returned to his residence on the "British" side of the St. Mary's River.[7] After securing land at the Sault, the US government installed Henry Rowe Schoolcraft as Indian agent in 1822. He was instructed to foster good relations with all of the area's important Native leaders without regard to their residence, that is, without regard to whether they lived on the American or the Canadian side of the border.[8] In Schoolcraft's words, Shingwauk was "a person of some consequence among the Indians.... His residence is ... for the most part, on the British side of the river, but he traces his lineage from the old Crane Band here" ("here" means the entire Sault area, without consideration of the border).[9]

It is also significant that during this period the US and Canadian governments were engaged in the giving of presents as an inducement to the Native people to maintain their alliance with one side or another. This policy proved to be wholly ineffective for the simple reason that both US and Canadian agents were instructed to treat all Native people equally, again, without regard to their residency, so Native people collected presents from both sides. In fact, the Canadian government recognized Native people who were coming to British territory from the US for their presents as simply "visiting Indians," acknowledging that their residency was not the determining factor in the British recognition of their obligation to the Anishnaabeg for previous support they received from Native people.[10] On the US side of the border, Schoolcraft was instructed to ignore residency when engaged in his own US presents distribution.

## The 1836 Treaties

The 1836 British treaty was essentially designed to turn Manitoulin Island into a kind of "Canadian Oklahoma" for Upper Great Lakes Indigenous people. Consequently, a treaty was needed to show that the Indigenous residents of the island would allow other Native people to live on "their" territory. Among the treaty-signers for this British–Anishnaabeg treaty was Assekinack (Blackbird), who was a Northern Michigan chief from the Petoskey area. Kitchemokman, a chief from the US Straits of Mackinaw area, was another 1836 Manitoulin treaty-signer. Other "US" chiefs that signed the 1836 Manitoulin Island treaty are Kimewen, Mosuneko, Paimausegai, and Chigenaus.[11] It should be noted that by the inclusion of such a large number of "US" Anishnaabeg treaty-signers, the British authorities recognized that such an important decision had to be made by as large a representation of area Native leaders as could be assembled if the decision were to have any legitimacy.

The same considerations of legitimacy could be attributed to American authorities as they negotiated a treaty in 1836 with the Ottawa and Chippewa people as they ceded about one-third of what is now Michigan: essentially, the northwest quarter of the Lower Peninsula and the eastern one-third of the Upper Peninsula. Given its scope and significance, the treaty-making process attracted a large number of Anishnaabeg leaders from throughout the area. Among them was Gitchy Mocoman (Kitchemokman),[12] who also signed the 1836 Manitoulin Island Treaty, as did Kimmewun, Mosaniko, Pamossegay, and Saganosh (all 1836 Manitoulin signers, as shown above). Others who signed the 1836 Michigan land cession treaty with "Canadian" connections are Akosa, Chingassamo, Kawgayosh, Keezhigo Benais, Maidosagee, Magisanikway, Muckadaywacquot, Oshawano, Shaniwaygwunabi, and Shawunepanasee (names can be found in Appendix 1; cross-border connections can be found in Appendix 2).

## The 1850 Canadian Robinson-Huron Treaty, Signed at Garden River

The 1850 Robinson-Huron Treaty was a land-cession treaty, equivalent in significance to the 1836 Michigan land-cession treaty. Through this treaty, the Anishnaabeg ceded a vast area to the British, essentially all the land from Lake Huron's shore to the height of land, north to what was then Rupert's Land (Land of the Hudson's Bay Company). Among the treaty-signers of this 1850 Canadian Robinson-Huron treaty was Assikinock, the "Michigander" who also signed the 1836 Manitoulin treaty; and Shinguakouce, who signed the 1820 Sault treaty as Augustin Bart. Other "US" Native people who were associated with the 1850 Robinson-Huron Treaty are Aquasa, Aneuwaybe, Kagegabe, Matawaash, Nebenaigoching, Shawunegonabe, and Tagawinini (see Appendix 2 for these connections).

These few examples recount only a small portion of the dozens of treaty-signers my research has uncovered among only a few treaties (and only from a thirty-year period) from the upper reaches of the larger "borderlands" area. To see the breadth and strength of these cross-border treaty-signing connections, I refer the reader to the appendices at the end of this chapter.

## Conclusion: Jay Treaty and Beyond

After the mid-1800 land-cession treaties mentioned above, the Anishnaabeg's main struggle was simply to survive as a People—and survive they did. They continually and steadfastly refused to recognize the US–Canada border as a line of division; rather, they continued to "use" the border as a symbol of their sovereignty and unity. Quite often, these symbolic acts involve an assertion of Jay Treaty rights to "duty-free importation" of goods; these actions take place in spite of the US and Canadian governments' refusal to recognize these rights.

Anishnaabeg assertion of Jay Treaty rights are not, however, restricted to duty-free passage. In 1928, a Native of Walpole Island, claiming a right to pass freely across the border to seek employment in Algonac, Michigan, was denied entry on the grounds that he could neither read nor write. After a spirited protest to Washington, the US government allowed his free passage.[13] In 1974, a federal district judge in Maine ruled that the Jay Treaty and a 1928 immigration statute gave Native people born in Canada the right to live and work in the United States so as to "preserve the aboriginal right of American Indians to move freely throughout the territory originally occupied by them on either side of the U.S. and Canadian border."[14] John Price, in *Native Studies: American and Canadian Indians*, argues that forceful assertion of a Native right to unimpeded border-crossing "violates the values of both laws and nationalism of Americans and Canadians": but, he adds, "their claim of a right to do this is one of the few things which sets Native people apart from all others. To Natives it is a symbolic act which validates their identity [and creates] a new proud ideology and social cohesiveness."[15]

One might add that Great Lakes Native people appear to realize that the boundary of a country is only as viable as the people being separated allow it to be, though they are keenly aware that the central government's job is to attempt to maintain that division, unnatural as it may at times appear. Furthermore, it seems—at least in the case of the Anishnaabeg—that the boundary "is far removed from the changing desires and aspirations of the inhabitants of the Borderlands" and, where culture and autonomy are involved, the border is very often ignored.[16]

For example, the thrust towards greater Anishnaabeg cultural unity can be seen in the return of traditional societies throughout the borderlands area. The Three Fires Society, active among the Anishnaabeg of Ontario, Manitoba, Michigan, Wisconsin, and Minnesota, is but one representation of this movement. Members of this re-formed society follow the teachings of the Midewiwin. Among their prophetic beliefs is the prediction that "In the time of the Seventh Fire a new people will emerge, to retrace their steps and history, to find what was left by the trail.... Their task is not easy. It will take time, hard work, perseverance and faith. The new people must remain strong in their quest, but in time there will be a rebirth, and a rekindling of the sacred fire, which will light the Eighth, and Final Fire of eternal peace, understanding and acceptance over the entire world."[17] According to this tradition, now is the time of the Seventh Fire, and a return to the more traditional ways is the essence of what it means to be Anishnaabe.

The drive for unification is political as well as spiritual. Political unions are fast becoming an Anishnaabeg hallmark. By 1986, forty-six Ojibway and Cree bands (including bands along the US–Canada border) had formed the Nishnawbe-Aski Nation; nine Ojibway, Potawatomi, and Missisauga bands in Ontario's northern cottage country formed an alliance in 1989; seven Ojibway bands along the Georgian Bay North Channel formed the North Shore Tribal Council in 1991; and Ojibway bands on the Bruce Peninsula presented a united front in fishing-rights confrontations in 1992.[18] On the US side, the Inter-Tribal Council, head-quartered in Sault Ste. Marie, Michigan, represents all twelve of Michigan's federally-recognized tribes, all representing Anishnaabeg people. Cooperation among these organizations is high, and if, as in the past, the Native people of Canada under the authority of the North Shore Council organize a Jay Treaty border-crossing action, they can be assured of support from their fellow Anishnaabeg from the United States.[19]

A recent example of this "cross-border" collaboration between tribes and federal officials can be seen in the US Environmental Protection Agency's Great Lakes Declaration of 2004. This international declaration on the protection and restoration of the Great Lakes was concluded by representatives from both the US and Canadian authorities, as well as representatives from tribes from across the entire Great Lakes watershed, tribal officials from all of the Anishnaabeg organizations mentioned above.[20] A partial list of the participants in this Great Lakes initiative include "Federal agencies, Great Lakes Governors, [and] Great Lakes Tribes"; thus, we see the language of the declaration echoing the Jay Treaty language, which recognized "His Majesty's subjects, ... the citizens of the United States, and ... the Indians dwelling on either side of the said boundary line," reinforcing the *international* recognition of tribal sovereignty implicit in the Jay Treaty of over 200 years ago. When we look historically at the provisions of the Jay Treaty, the presence of dozens of cross-border treaty-signers for a period of close to 100 years, and the most recent (December 2004) international declaration on Great Lakes water quality, we see not only an assertion of sovereignty by the Anishnaabeg of the Lake Huron Borderlands, but also a recognition of that sovereignty by both the US and Canada.

As we look back through this history and into today's world, we see that the Anishnaabeg have persisted as a strong, identifiable, sovereign Lake Huron Borderlands Nation. They may seem to be "divided" by a "line drawn upon the water," and they may be living in relatively isolated small communities throughout what was once a vast homeland belonging to no one but themselves, but they were never vanquished, they are not divided by a "border," and for the most part, they were not "removed," nor are they dispersed. They are simply Three Fires People, living with a profound sense of unity and a persistent cultural sense of being Anishnaabe, despite these many centuries of assault.

## Appendices

In Appendices 1 and 2 the spellings are given as they appear in the cited source. Spelling variations in Native names were the norm during the entire treaty-signing period; further complicating the spelling issue is that the Anishnaabeg "b" and "p," "d" and "t," and "k" and "g" have the same pronunciation values. In these tables, the name of the individual is followed by a number that designates the year of the treaty or other source, and is labelled either "A" for the United States or "C" for Canada. The "S" designation refers to the source of the information: 1839-S refers to the Ottawa and Chippewa Payroll of 1839 from the Schoolcraft Papers; 1985-S and 1991-S are referenced in the appendix. The Robinson Treaty Voucher #2 from Sault Ste Marie, Canada, designated as 1850-V, represents individuals who were paid by the Canadian government for cessions in the Robinson-Huron Treaty of 1850. An explanation of these references, treaty descriptions, and other sources are in Appendix 3.

### Appendix 1: Anishnaabe Canada–US Treaty-signers

| Signer Name | Treaty | Treaty-signing Location and/or Comments |
|---|---|---|
| Sheganack | 1817-A | N. Ohio |
| Sigonak | 1819-A | Saginaw |
| Assekinack | 1836-C | Manitoulin Island |
| Assikinock | 1850-C | Sault Ste. Marie |
| Assiginack | 1862-C | Manitoulin Island |
| Chemokcomon | 1817-A | N. Ohio |
| Kitchmookman | 1819-A | Saginaw |
| Chemogueman | 1820-A1 | L'Arbre Croche & Mackinac |
| Kitchemokman | 1836-C | Manitoulin Island |
| Gitchy Mocoman | 1836-A | Wash., DC (N. MI-EUP cession) |
| Keezhigo Benais | 1836-A | Wash., DC (N. MI-EUP cession) |
| Keghikgodoness | 1862-C | Manitoulin Island |
| Keywaytenan | 1790-C | Detroit |
| Kewaytinam | 1819-A | Saginaw |

## Appendix 1 (*continued*)

| Signer Name | Treaty | Treaty-signing Location and/or Comments |
|---|---|---|
| Kimewen | 1836-C | Manitoulin Island |
| Kimmewun | 1836-A | Wash., DC (N. MI-EUP cession) |
| Kemewan | 1839-S | Ottawa/Chippewa list. |
| | | |
| Macounce | 1796-C | Thames River |
| Macquettequet | 1807-A | Detroit |
| Eshtonoquot | 1836-A1 | Wash., DC (St. Clair region) |
| "Little Bear"[21] | 1985-S | |
| Ishtonaquette[22] | 1991-S | |
| | | |
| Meatoosawkee | 1798-C | St. Joseph Island |
| Maidosagee | 1836-A | Wash., DC (N. MI-EUP cession) |
| | | |
| Magisanikway | 1836-A | Wash., DC (N. MI-EUP cession) |
| Mahgezahnekwa | 1859-C | Garden River. |
| Megissanequa | | Moved to Garden River by 1840.[23] |
| | | |
| Mosaniko | 1836-A | Wash. DC (N. MI-EUP cession) |
| Mosuneko | 1836-C | Manitoulin Island |
| | | |
| Nanguey | 1795-A | Greenville |
| Nangee | 1796-C | Thames River |
| Nangy | 1800-C | Windsor |
| | | |
| Nawogezhick | 1855-A | Detroit |
| Nawwegezhick | 1855A1 | Sault Ste. Marie |
| Nawwegezhick | 1855-A2 | Detroit (Sault cession) |
| Nahwegezhig | 1859-C | Garden River |
| Naway Kesick | 1867-C | Garden River |
| | | |
| Negig | 1796-C | Thames River |
| Nekiek | 1805-A | Fort Industry (N. Ohio) |
| Negig | 1807-A | Detroit |
| Negig | 1827-C | Amherstburg |
| | | |
| Nemekass | 1795-A | Greenville |
| Annamakance | 1796-C | Thames River |
| Nemekass | 1807-A | Detroit |
| Animikince | 1827-C | Amherstburg |
| Nimekance | 1991-S | "Chief of Sarnia Band"[24] |
| | | |
| Paanassee | 1815-A | Spring Wells |
| Panaissy | 1850-C | Sault Ste. Marie |
| | | |
| Paimausegai | 1836-C | Manitoulin Island |
| Pamossegay | 1836-A | Wash., DC (N. MI-EUP cession) |
| | | |
| Shawanoe | 1820-A1 | L'Arbre Croche/Mackinac |
| Kewayzi Shawano | 1836-A | Wash., DC (N. MI-EUP cession) |
| Oshawano | 1850-C | Sault Ste. Marie |
| Shawano | 1855-A | Detroit |
| Oshawano | 1855-A | Detroit |
| Oshawawno | 1855-A2 | Detroit (Sault cession) |

**Appendix 1** (*continued*)

| Signer Name | Treaty | Treaty-signing Location and/or Comments |
| --- | --- | --- |
| Ouitanissa | 1790-C | Detroit |
| Wetanasa | 1789-A | Fort Harmar |
| | | |
| Penash | 1790-C | Detroit |
| Penosh | 1814-AA | Greenville |
| | | |
| Penashee | 1832-A | Tippecanoe |
| Penashi | 1842-A | LaPointe |
| Penashe | 1859-C | Garden River |
| | | |
| Peyshiky | 1796-C | Thames River |
| Peeshickee | 1826-A | Fond du Lac |
| | | |
| Sagunosh | 1819-A | Saginaw |
| Shaganash | 1820-A1 | L'Arbre Croche/Mackinac |
| Saganash | 1827-C | Amherstburg |
| Chigenaus | 1836-C | Manitoulin Island |
| Saganosh | 1836-A | Wash., DC (N. MI-EUP cession) |
| | | |
| Saugassauway | 1819-A | Saginaw |
| Sagawsouai | 1822-C | Thames River |
| | | |
| Shawanapenisse | 1798-C | St. Joseph Island |
| Shawunepanasee | 1836-A | Wash., DC (N. MI-EUP cession) |
| | | |
| Sawanabenase | 1807-A | Detroit |
| Shawanipinissie | 1827-C | Amherstburg |
| | | |
| Shawshauwenaubais | 1819-A | Saginaw |
| Shashawinibisie | 1827-C | Amherstburg |
| Shashawaynaybeece | 1855-A2 | Detroit (Sault cession) |
| | | |
| Shebense | 1790-C | Detroit |
| Chebaas | 1818-A1 | St. Mary's, Ohio |
| Chebause | 1832-A | Tippecanoe |
| Ghebause | 1832-A | Tippecanoe (variant spelling?) |
| | | |
| Shinguax | 1817-A | Miami River, Ohio |
| Shingwalk | 1819-A | Saginaw |
| "Augustin Bart" | 1820-A | Sault Ste. Marie |
| Shinguakouce | 1850-C | Garden River |
| Shingwahcooce | 1859-C | Garden River |
| | | |
| "Shingwalk Jr." | 1819-A | Saginaw |
| Ogista | 1859-C | Garden River |
| Augustin | 1867-C | Garden River |
| Augustin | 1873-C | Garden River |
| | | |
| Tegose | 1855-A1 | Detroit |
| Tagoush | 1867-C | Garden River |
| Tegouche | 1873-C | Garden River |
| | | |
| Waubogee | 1826-A | Fond du Lac |
| Waub Ogeeg | 1836-A | Wash., DC (N. MI-EUP cession) |

**Appendix 1** (*continued*)

| Signer Name | Treaty | Treaty-signing Location and/or Comments |
|---|---|---|
| Waubooge | 1859-C1 | Garden River |
| Wawbowjieg | 1854-A | LaPointe |
| Waubojick | 1855-A | Detroit |
| Wawbojieg | 1855-A1 | Sault Ste. Marie |
| Wawbojieg | 1855-A2 | Detroit (Sault cession) |
| Wauweeyatam | 1819A | Saginaw |
| Wawiattin | 1822-C | Thames River |
| Wacheness | 1795-A | Greenville |
| Wittaness | 1796-C | Thames River |
| Wetanis | 1800-C | Windsor |

## Appendix 2: Other Anishnaabeg–Canada–US Treaty Connections

| Signer Name | Treaty | Comments (with treaty and tribal affiliation, when given) |
|---|---|---|
| Akosa | 1836-A | Washington (Ottawa & Chippewa) |
| Aquasa | 1850-V | On 1850 Robinson Treaty Voucher |
| Anewaba | 1819-A | Saginaw (Chippewa) |
| Aneuwaybe | 1850-V | On 1850 Robinson Treaty Voucher |
| Chingassamo | 1836-A | Washington (Ottawa & Chippewa); moved from Cheboygan area to Canada; left power vacuum that Schoolcraft had to mediate[25] |
| Kagegabe | 1850-V | On 1850 Robinson Treaty Voucher |
| Kawgagawbwa | 1855-A | Detroit (Ottawa & Chippewa) |
| Kawgayosh | 1836-A | Washington (Ottawa & Chippewa); referred to by Schoolcraft as Gitshee Kawgaosh, a British Chief[26] |
| Kaybaynodin | 1855-A | Detroit (Ottawa & Chippewa) |
| Kebaynodin | | Signed Sault area petition to Canadian government[27] |
| Keneshteno | 1847-A | Fond du Lac (Chippewa) |
| Kenishteno | 1854-A | Moved to Canada[28] |
| Makitewaquit | 1800-C | Signed Canadian Deed of Sale |
| Mukutay Oquot | 1836-A | From Grand River, Western MI |
| Muckadaywacquot | 1836-A | Washington (Ottawa & Chippewa); from SSM (see text) |
| Matwaash | 1817-A | Miami River (Chippewa) |
| Matawaash | 1850-V | On 1850 Robinson Treaty Voucher |
| Muckuday peenaas | 1826-A | Fond du Lac (Chippewa) |
| Mawcawdaypenayse | 1854-A | La Pointe (Chippewa); moved to Canada[29] |

**Appendix 2** (*continued*)

| Signer Name | Treaty | Comments (with treaty and tribal affiliation, when given) |
|---|---|---|
| Mizi | 1842-A | La Pointe (Chippewa) |
| Mezye | 1847-A | Fond du Lac (Chippewa); moved to Canada[30] |
| Nebenaigoching | 1850-C | With Shingwauk, moved to Canada and became chief of "Western" Sault area and other major 1850 Robinson treaty signer |
| Ogemawpenasee | 1839-S | On Ottawa and Chippewa Payroll of 1839 (US) |
| Ogemahbenaissee | 1859-C | Garden River (Ojibway) |
| Paybaumogeezhig | 1826-A | Fond du Lac (Chippewa) |
| Pawpomekezick | | Petitioned to move to Canada in 1850s[31] |
| Pasheskiskaquashcum | 1815-A | Spring Wells (Chippewa) |
| Pazhekezkqueshcum | | Moved to Walpole Island in 1820s[32] |
| Bauzhigiezhigwaeshikum | | On Walpole Island ca. 1845[33] |
| Pensweguesic | 1817-A | Miami River (Chippewa) |
| Penaysewaykesek | 1819-A | Saginaw (Chippewa) |
| Penasewegeeshig | 1845 | "Deserving Chippewa Warrior" at Port Sarnia in 1845[34] |
| Piawbedawsung | 1855-A | Detroit (Ottawa & Chippewa) |
| Piawbedawsung | 1855-A1 | Sault Ste. Marie (Chippewa); Shingwauk's son-in-law; lived on Sugar Island; was also a signer of petition to Canadian government asking that Garden River be made a pan-Ojibway settlement;[35] referred to as the chief of the Garden River band[36] |
| Sabo | 1819-A | Saginaw (Chippewa) |
| Saboo | | Signed Sault area petition to Canadian government[37] |
| Shawanoe | 1814-A | Greenville (either Miami or Odawa); Moved to Walpole Island[38] |
| Shaniwaygwunabi | 1836-A | Washington (Ottawa & Chippewa) |
| Shawunegonabe | 1850-V | On 1850 Robinson Treaty Voucher |
| Tagawinini | 1850-C | Sault Ste. Marie (Ojibway); lived at Saginaw; moved to Canada[39] |
| Toposh | 1832-A | Tippecanoe River (Potawatomi) |
| Toposh | 1845 | "Common Potawatomi Chief" on Walpole Island in 1845[40] |
| Waanoos | 1785-A | Fort MacIntosh (Chippewa) |
| Wawanosh | | Early 1800s chief of the Canadian Saugeen Chippewa (St. Clair region);[41] "Deserving Chippewa Chief" on Walpole Island in 1845[42] |

## Appendix 3: Treaties Referenced in Appendix 1

In the data that follow, the treaty or reference cited in the tables is given first, followed by its signing date; information is organized chronologically. The location of the signing and the names of the tribes are given next; this is followed by a brief description of the treaty. Finally, the names of the treaty-signers are given.

If explicitly denominated within the treaty or reference, the names of signers are preceded by a [C] for Chippewa or Ojibway, [O] for Odawa, and [P] for Potawatomi. If no reference to the tribe is made in the following summaries, and only one tribe is listed, it can be assumed that all signers are members of the listed tribe. In some cases tribal affiliation is not given in the treaty itself but must be determined by other sources.

Unless otherwise referenced, all US treaty data are taken from Charles J. Kappler, ed., *Indian Treaties: 1778–1883* (New York: Interland, 1972); all Canadian treaty data are from Indian *Treaties and Surrenders*, 3 vols. (Ottawa: C. H. Parmelee, 1973).

| Date and Location | Tribes | Description | Signers |
|---|---|---|---|
| 1785-A<br>21 January<br>Fort MacIntosh | Wyandot<br>Delaware<br>Ottawa<br>Chippewa | Attempt to fix line separating Indigenous nation from US, with cession of some Native land | Waanoos |
| 1789-A<br>9 January<br>Fort Harmar | Wyandot<br>Delaware<br>Ottawa<br>Chippewa<br>Potawatomi<br>Sauk | Confirmation of 1785 Fort MacIntosh treaty with further cession of lands retained by Natives in that treaty | [C]<br>Wetanasa |
| 1790-C<br>19 May<br>Detroit | Ottawa<br>Chippewa<br>Potawatomi<br>Huron | Cession of Essex County except Anderdon Twp. and part of West Sandwich; Kent County except Zone Twp. and Gores of Chatham and Camden; Elgin County except Bayham Twp. and parts of South Dorchesterand Malahide; in Middlesex County, Delaware and Westminster twps. and part of North Dorchester | [C]<br>Ouitanissa<br>Wasson<br><br>[P]<br>Penash<br>Keywaytenan<br>Shebense |
| 1795-A<br>3 August<br>Greenville | Wyandot<br>Delaware<br>Shawnee<br>Ottawa<br>Chippewa | Establish peace between the government and the Native peoples of the western regions; establish an "Indian Territory" | [P]<br>Wacheness<br><br>[C]<br>Nanguey |

**Appendix 3** (*continued*)

| Date and Location | Tribes | Description | Signers |
|---|---|---|---|
| | Potawatomi Miami Eel River Wea Kickapoo Piankashaw Kaskaskia | | Nemekass |
| 1796-C 7 September River Thames | Chippewa | Cession of London Twp. and part of North Dorchester, Middlesex County; part of North Oxford Twp., Oxford County | Nangee Peyshiky Negig Macounce Annamakance Wittaness Wasson |
| 1798-C 30 June St. Joseph Island | Chippewa | Cession of St. Joseph, Cariboux, or Payentanassin Island, between lakes Huron and Superior | Meatoosawkee Shawanapenisse |
| 1800-C 11 September Windsor, ON | Ottawa Chippewa Potawatomi Wyandot | Deed of sale; Huron Church Reserve[43] | Makitewaquit Nangy Wetanis see Deed of Sale 1800 in Bibliography |
| 1805-A 4 July Fort Industry | Wyandot Ottawa Munsee Delaware Shawnee Chippewa Potawatomi | Cession to US for a Connecticut land company in Northern Ohio | [O] Nekeik  [C] Macquettoquet Little Bear |
| 1807-A 17 November Detroit | Ottawa Chippewa Wyandot Potawatomi | Treaty adjusts Greenville treaty line separating "Indian territory" for the lands of the US | [C] Sawanabenase Negig Macquettequet Nemekas |
| 1814-A 22 July Greenville | Wyandot Delaware Shawnee Seneca Miami Potawatomi Ottawa Kickapoo Eel River Wea | Post–War of 1812 peace treaty | [P] Penosh Shawanoe [listed as Miami but Bauman claims he was Odawa][44] |

**Appendix 3** (*continued*)

| Date and Location | Tribes | Description | Signers |
|---|---|---|---|
| 1815-A<br>8 September<br>Spring Wells | Wyandot<br>Delaware<br>Seneca<br>Shawnee<br>Miami<br>Chippewa<br>Ottawa<br>Potawatomi | Following War of 1812, treaty establishes peace and affirms the 1795 Greenville Treaty | [C]<br>Pasheskiska-<br>   quashcum<br>Paanassee |
| 1817-A<br>29 September<br>On the Miami<br>River, Ohio | Wyandot<br>Seneca<br>Delaware<br>Shawnee<br>Potawatomi<br>Ottawa<br>Chippewa | Cession of land in Northern Ohio | [C]<br>Shinguax<br>Pensweguesic<br>Chemokcomon<br>Sheganack<br>Matwaash |
| 1818-A<br>2 October<br>St. Mary's<br>(N. Ohio) | Potawatomi | Northern Ohio land cession | Cheebaas |
| 1819-A<br>24 September<br>Saginaw | Chippewa | Cession of remaining portion of Southeast Michigan | Wauweeyatam<br>Sagunosh<br>Sigonak<br>Saugassauway<br>Kewaytinam<br>Penaysewayke-<br>   sek<br>Kitchmookman<br>Shingwalk<br>"Shingwalk, jr."<br>   (Augustin)<br>Shawshauwen-<br>   aubais<br>Aneuwaybe |
| 1820-A<br>16 June<br>Sault Ste. Marie,<br>MI | Chippewa | Cession of 16 square miles at Sault Ste. Marie to Governor Cass for military fort | The Ojibway chief Shingwauk signed under his French pseudonym "Augustin Bart" |
| 1820-A1<br>6 July<br>L'Arbre Croche and<br>Michilimackinac | Ottawa<br>Chippewa | Cession of St. Martin Islands in the Straits of Mackinac area | Shawanoe<br>Shaganash<br>Chemogueman |
| 1822-C | Chippewa | Cession of 580,000 acres lying | Sagawsouai |

**Appendix 3** (*continued*)

| Date and Location | Tribes | Description | Signers |
|---|---|---|---|
| 8 July River Thames | | on the north side of the River Thames in the London and Western districts of Ontario | Wawiattin |
| 1826-A 5 August Fond du Lac | Chippewa | The Chippewa recognize the authority and the jurisdiction of the US government and agree to allow the US to explore and mine any minerals in their country | Peeshickee Waubogee Muckuday Peenaas |
| 1827-C 10 July Amherstburg | Chippewa | Cession of 10,280 acres, adjoining Lake Huron and the St. Clair River in the Gore and Home districts of Ontario | Shashawinibisie Negig Shawanipinissie Saganash Animikince |
| 1832-A 27 October Tippecanoe River | Potawatomi | Cession of Potawatomi lands in Indiana, Illinois, and Michigan south of the Grand River | Toposh Penashee Chebause Ghebause |
| 1836-C 9 August Manitoulin Island | Ottawa Chippewa | Agree to set aside Manitoulin Island chain for use of all Native people who wish to reside there | Chigenaus Kitchemokman Assekinack Paimausegai Kimewen Mosuneko |
| 1836-A 28 March Washington | Ottawa Chippewa | Cession of the northwest portion of Michigan's Lower Peninsula and the eastern half of the Upper Peninsula | Keezhigo Benais Waub Ogeeg Saganosh Chingassamo Kewayzi Shawano Mosaniko Pamossegay Gitchy Mocoman Maidosagee Kimmewun Shawunepanasee Kawgayosh Mukutay Oquot (from Grand River) Mukudaywac- quot (from Sault Ste. Marie) Akosa Shaniwaygwun- abi |

**Appendix 3** (*continued*)

| Date and Location | Tribes | Description | Signers |
|---|---|---|---|
| 1839-S | | Ottawa and Chippewa Payroll 1839; from the Henry Rowe Schoolcraft Papers | Kemewan Ogemawpenasee |
| 1842-A 4 October LaPointe | Chippewa | Cession of the western half of Michigan's Upper Peninsula and areas of northern Wisconsin | Mizi Penashi |
| 1845 Walpole Island and Sarnia, ON | Chippewa Potawatomi | Mentioned in account of presents distribution on Walpole Island and at Sarnia, ON. In 1844 all distribution of presents by Canadian government to "visiting Indians" ceased. This 1845 list thus implies that listed individuals are residents of Canada. | [C] Penasewegeeshig [P] Toposh |
| 1847-A 2 August Fond du Lac | Chippewa | Cession of land in central Minnesota | Mezye Keneshteno |
| 1850-C 7, 9 September Sault Ste. Marie, ON | Ojibway | The Robinson Treaties: two treaties that ceded the north shore of Lake Superior from the US–Canada border at Minnesota to Lake Huron and the Georgian Bay to Penetanguishene to the height of land that separates Ontario from the lands of the Hudson's Bay Company. The names listed are all from the Lake Huron portion of the treaty. | Panaissy Oshawano Tagawinini Nebenaigoching Shinguakouce Assikinock [listed as interpreter] |
| 1850-V 7 September Sault Ste. Marie, ON | Ojibway | As part of the Robinson Treaty negotiations, payments were made to the affected Native people, whose names and amounts paid were entered on vouchers. Voucher #2 lists Native people from Sault Ste. Marie affected by the 1850 Robinson-Huron Treaty. | Anewaba Kagegabe Aquasa Shawunegonabe Matawaash |
| 1854-A 30 September La Pointe | Chippewa | Cession of land in the far northeast of Minnesota | Mawcawdaypenayse Wawbowjieg Kenishteno |
| 1855-A 31 July Detroit | Ottawa Chippewa | This treaty eliminated the threat of removal from the remaining Ottawa and Chippewa people of Michigan and granted them | Oshawano Tegose Piawbedawsung Nawogezhick |

**Appendix 3** (*continued*)

| Date and Location | Tribes | Description | Signers |
|---|---|---|---|
| | | allotments of land within those areas they already held by virtue of the 1836 treaty. The treaty also contained a clause that expressly included the members of the Garden River band, i.e., Canadian residents who may have been signatories to the 1836 treaty. | Kawgagawbwa Waubojieg [also listed as Waubojick] |
| 1855-A1 27 June 1856 Sault Ste. Marie | Chippewa | Local ratification of the 1855 Treaty of Detroit | Wawbojick Nawwegezhick Piawbedawsung Tegose |
| 1855-A2 2 August Detroit | Chippewa | Although in dispute, this treaty cedes to the US the right of fishing and the encampment granted the Chippewa in the 1820 treaty. | Shashawaynay-beece Nawwegezhick Oshawwawno Wawbojieg |
| 1859-C 10 June Garden River | Ojibway | Cession of Laird, Macdonald, and Meredith twps. and land on Echo Lake and Garden River; also Squirrel Island in Lake George | Shingwahcooce Nahwegezhig Ogemahbenais-see Ogista |
| 1859-C1 29 July Gros Cap near the Sault | Batchewana and Goulais bands of Ojibway | Cession of reserves set aside in 1850 Robinson Treaty with the exception of Whitefish Island in the rapids, which is used as a fishing station | Waubooge |
| 1859-C2 11 June Bruce Mines | Ojibway | Cession of land at Thessalon and agreement to move to Garden River | Penashe Nahwegezhig Ogemahbenais-see |
| 1862-C 6 October Manitoulin Island | Ottawa Chippewa ("and other occupants") | Cession of Manitoulin Island except for certain reserves; also Barrie and Cockburn islands | Assiginack (not as interpreter) Keghikgodoness |
| 1867-C 9 July Garden River | Ojibway | Cession of a block of land on Peltier River, near Garden River, for gristmill | Augustin Naway Kesick Tagoush |
| 1873-C 20 May Garden River | Ojibway | Cession of land for erection of church | Augustin Tegouche |

# FROM INTERCOLONIAL MESSENGER TO "CHRISTIAN INDIAN"

## The Flemish Bastard and the Mohawk Struggle for Independence from New France and Colonial New York in the Eastern Great Lakes Borderland, 1647–1687

MARK MEUWESE

The seventeenth-century Mohawk war chief, negotiator, intercolonial messenger, and "Christian Indian" of Dutch-Mohawk descent who is best known as the Flemish Bastard has remained an obscure individual in the historiography of Native–European relations in colonial North America. It is true that the Flemish Bastard has been recognized by some scholars. Historians of the Iroquois League of Five Nations, comprising the Mohawk, Oneida, Onondaga, Cayuga, and Seneca nations during the seventeenth century, have noted that the Flemish Bastard gave an important speech to French colonial officials in 1654 regarding the political structure of the Iroquois Confederacy. Several scholars have also correctly identified him as a prominent Mohawk war chief and negotiator during the First French–Iroquois War (ca. 1650–1667). Nevertheless, so far no comprehensive biographic study has been attempted about the Flemish Bastard. This is surprising, since the Mohawk leader functioned as a valuable and trusted messenger between French officials in Quebec, Mohawk chiefs in Iroquoia, and Anglo-Dutch authorities in Albany, New York, during the 1650s and 1660s. It is especially remarkable that the Flemish Bastard did not become a subject of the recent historical studies that analyzed the activities and roles of individuals who functioned as interpreters, brokers, or negotiators between indigenous peoples and European colonists.[1]

One possible reason why the Flemish Bastard has been neglected so far by contemporary historians is the lack of primary sources. There are a handful of references to him in the Jesuit *Relations*, the annual reports written by Jesuit missionaries and published in France to support the Jesuit missionary program in North America. There are also several references in other French documents, as well as Dutch and English colonial sources. However, many aspects about his life remain unclear. For example, between 1667 and 1687 there are no references to be found about the Flemish Bastard in the existing French, Dutch, or English colonial records.[2]

Another explanation for the Flemish Bastard's relative obscurity in the historiography is that he was known under different names by the Iroquois and the various imperial European powers. The French Jesuits labelled the Mohawk chief the "Bâtard Flamand" (Flemish or Dutch bastard) because they viewed him as "an execrable issue of sin, the monstrous offspring of a Dutch Heretic father and a pagan woman."[3] Contemporary French colonial officials and later historians of New France followed the Jesuits in using this name to denote the Mohawk chief and negotiator. Interestingly, Dutch colonial records do not refer to the mixed descent of the individual known to the French as the Flemish Bastard. Instead, Dutch colonists and officials at Fort Orange and Beverwijck (later Albany) always used "Smits Jan," a Dutch name. It is not known whether Smits Jan was his baptismal name or a later name given to him by Dutch colonists and officials. When English colonial authorities made use of his services after the English conquest of New Netherland in 1664, they anglicized his Dutch name to "Smits John." Finally, according to one Dutch colonial record, the Flemish Bastard also had an indigenous name. In a letter from Johannes Dijckman, West India Company commander at Fort Orange, to Jean de Lauson, governor of French Canada, dated 25 December 1653, a person who is almost certainly the Flemish Bastard is referred to as Canaqueese. Since this individual was carrying messages to de Lauson on behalf of the Mohawks and was described by Dijckman as "a savage who is much beloved by the Maquas [Mohawks]," it is likely that Canaqueese was a name given to the Flemish Bastard by the Mohawks.[4]

The confusion among historians about the various Dutch, French, and Iroquois names for the Mohawk war chief and negotiator has been amplified by the ongoing tendency of historians to impose anachronistic international boundaries on colonial North America. This inclination has especially been strong among scholars of New France and colonial New York. Recent studies have persuasively shown that colonial northeastern America was an interconnected region in which Aboriginal peoples and the various English, Dutch, French, and Swedish colonies were often dependent on one another for trade, communication, protection, and information. Despite this new scholarship, the influence of nationalistic approaches in history remains strong in the United States and Canada. The neighbouring colonies of New France and colonial New York continue to be treated as self-contained political entities belonging respectively to the national histories of Canada and the United States.[5]

Because of this nationalistic historiographical approach, individuals such as the Flemish Bastard, who interacted with officials in both Quebec and Albany, are inadequately discussed by historians. For example, scholars of French–Iroquois relations in Canada have usually focussed solely on the individual known by the name Flemish Bastard. Thomas Grassman's well-documented entry on the Flemish Bastard in the authoritative *Dictionary of Canadian Biography* omits a discussion of the Flemish Bastard's role as a mediator under the Dutch name of Smits Jan between Dutch colonists and Algonquian-speaking peoples of the Upper Hudson Valley in 1663. Likewise, scholars of intercultural interactions in colonial New York have often not connected the activities of Smits Jan with those of the Flemish Bastard.[6]

In the light of these sometimes inaccurate and limited observations, the Flemish Bastard deserves a closer look. As some of the previously mentioned historians have shown, he performed various roles in his documented life. To explain these multi-faceted aspects of his life, it is best to understand his actions and motives in the context of an emerging borderland between New France and colonial New York during the mid-seventeenth century.

Recent historians such as Jeremy Alderman, Stephen Aron, and Evan Haefeli have redefined the early twentieth century historiographic concept of borderland in order to obtain a better understanding of intercultural relations in North America. While the influential concept of the frontier has continued to be useful for historians describing relations between European colonizers and Aboriginal peoples in certain North American regions, frontier studies frequently ignored the complicated repercussions that intercolonial and transatlantic rivalries had on Aboriginal peoples. According to Haefeli, a borderland can best be defined as a geographic zone of interaction "where autonomous peoples of different cultures are bound together by a greater multi-imperial context." In order to incorporate this intercolonial and imperial context into studies of Aboriginal–European interactions, recent scholars have proposed using the concept of borderlands when discussing intercultural relations in North America.[7]

The Iroquois League of Five Nations of central and western New York State were the creators of and the participants in a heavily contested borderland that arose out of a complex series of intertribal wars and intercolonial rivalries in the New France–colonial New York borderland during the second half of the seventeenth century. This borderland originated when Dutch and French colonizers realized the economic and strategic potential of the Five Nations. Whereas the French primarily viewed the Iroquois nations as obstacles to economic, diplomatic, and religious relations with the Iroquoian-speaking Hurons and Northern Algonquian peoples of the Great Lakes, Dutch colonists in the Upper Hudson Valley developed close economic ties with the neighbouring Mohawks. In return for supplying the Dutch with beaver pelts and other animal hides, the Mohawks received material goods ranging from metal utensils to muskets. Accompanying this growing system of intercultural economic exchange were intimate liaisons between Mohawk women and Dutch men. While Mohawk women received valuable trade goods from their Dutch partners, colonial fur traders gained access to Iroquois hunters who were relatives of their Mohawk partners. It was out of these informal unions that children of mixed descent such as the Flemish Bastard were born.[8]

Tragically, relations with Europeans also exposed the Five Nations to deadly old-world pathogens to which the Iroquois had no biological or medical defences. Although the Iroquois population of about 21,000 people was cut in half by a major smallpox epidemic during the 1630s, the Five Nations recovered demographically by waging a series of "Mourning Wars" against Aboriginal neighbours to replace deceased relatives. Most of these wars were waged against the Iroquoian-speaking Huron, Erie, Petun, and Neutral neighbours of the Five Nations during the 1640s and 1650s. Strength in numbers, together with access to Dutch muskets and gunpowder, gave the Five Nations definite military advantages and resulted in the effective destruction of the Hurons, Eries, Petuns, and Neutrals as independent polities. After a decade of intensive fighting, the Five Nations had stabilized their population at approximately 10,000 by incorporating thousands of Huron, Erie, Petun, and Neutral captives into their villages. According to some scholarly estimates, war captives made up about half of the total Five Nations population by 1660.[9]

After having secured their physical survival by incorporating Aboriginal neighbours, the Iroquois Confederacy was faced with increasing Dutch, English, and French pressures from the mid-seventeenth century onwards. Although New Netherland lacked the resources to threaten

Iroquois independence, the Mohawks' growing material dependency on Dutch trade goods resulted in the first land transactions between the Five Nations and Europeans during the early 1660s. Following the English conquest of New Netherland in 1664, Fort Orange/Beverwijck was renamed Albany and became a strategic English imperial outpost on the eastern border of the Iroquois Confederacy. From this Anglo-Dutch town, colonial officials tried to recruit the Five Nations as allies in the struggle with New France over the valuable fur trade in the Great Lakes region. Meanwhile, on the northern border of the Five Nations, the authorities of New France attempted to neutralize the Iroquois Confederacy by using a combination of military force and Jesuit missionaries.[10]

Despite these growing European pressures, the Five Nations maintained considerable autonomy in the New France–colonial New York borderland from the 1650s until the era of the American Revolution through a combination of factors. Because of the Iroquois' military successes in the Mourning Wars and due to the confederated nature of the Five Nations, the English and the French were unable to force their will on the Iroquois peoples. Through a delicate diplomatic strategy, the Five Nations also succeeded in preserving independence by negotiating treaties of friendship or neutrality with both colonial New York and New France. The diplomatic success of the Five Nations was especially remarkable in the face of the intensifying imperial rivalries between England and France in North America after 1680.[11]

As some recent historians have emphasized, however, living in a borderland had disadvantages as well as advantages. Although the Five Nations were able to maintain sovereignty through a skilful system of diplomatic treaties with New France and colonial New York, the borderland conditions often also brought the English and French imperial powers right into Iroquois territory. The Five Nations could only maintain security and independence if they could keep the peace with both the French and the English; but often the only way to do that was by granting the English and French economic, missionary, or military access to the villages of the Five Nations.[12]

The intertwined opportunities and dangers of living in a borderland also exemplified the career of the Flemish Bastard. On one hand, his bicultural background allowed him to function as a negotiator and a trusted messenger between Quebec and Albany officials. At the same time, increasing French imperial pressures on the Mohawks forced him to seek a closer association with New France. Although the Flemish Bastard did never fully give up his autonomy as a prominent Mohawk, borderland conditions forced him to make compromises with European colonial powers.

According to the standard biography by historian Thomas Grassman, the Flemish Bastard first enters the documentary record in the summer of 1650. A recently discovered letter written by a Dutch merchant operating in New Netherland in December 1647, however, suggests an earlier reference to the individual of Mohawk-Dutch descent. In the letter, written by the prominent merchant Govert Loockermans to a business associate in the Dutch Republic and dated 21 December 1647, Loockermans discussed an incident that had recently occurred at Fort Orange on the Upper Hudson Valley. According to Loockermans, the local West India Company merchant Harmen Meijndertsz van den Bogaert had been suspected of having had sexual relations with his "black boy," a euphemism for his African slave. In an attempt to escape likely harsh judicial punishment by Dutch colonial authorities who viewed homosexuality as a considerable crime, van den Bogaert and his African slave escaped from Fort Orange and made their way to nearby Mohawk territory. It was not surprising that van den Bogaert sought refuge among the Mohawks because he had made an important diplomatic visit to them more than ten years earlier, in the winter of 1634–1635. He probably expected that the Mohawks, with whom he had established valuable commercial relations, would shelter him and his slave from Dutch prosecution.[13]

The relevance of this incident to our understanding of the Flemish Bastard is Loockermans's reference in his letter to a certain Swist Jan who accompanied van den Bogaert and his slave to the Mohawks. It is possible that Swist Jan was an entirely different person than the Flemish Bastard, who was, as previously noted, known among the Dutch as Smits Jan. However, circumstantial evidence strongly suggests that Swist Jan could very well have been the Flemish Bastard. Names were not always consistently spelled in early modern Dutch documents. As a result, "Swist Jan" could easily have been a misspelling of "Smits Jan." Second, it is not very likely that there was another person in New Netherland with a name similar to that of Smits Jan who had a close connection to the Mohawks. Finally, while Dutch officials eventually tracked down van den Bogaert without Mohawk interference, it appears that Swist Jan continued to live among the Mohawks. Throughout the history of New Netherland, there are no other recorded instances of colonists moving from colonial society to Aboriginal communities. Swist Jan's willingness to reside among the Mohawks therefore suggests that he had a familial relationship with this Iroquois nation. Since the matrilineal Mohawks viewed children born out of liaisons between Mohawk women and European fathers as fully Mohawk, it is very probable that Swist Jan, like the Flemish Bastard, was a person of Mohawk-Dutch descent.[14]

If the Flemish Bastard was indeed the same individual as Swist Jan, his motive for running away from Fort Orange to the Mohawks in 1647 could be that he felt more comfortable among the Mohawks than among the Dutch. This was not surprising since the Flemish Bastard was almost certainly raised by his Mohawk mother and her male relatives in a Mohawk village. In his childhood and teenage years, he probably frequently accompanied his Mohawk relatives to visit the neighbouring Dutch communities on the Upper Hudson Valley. Throughout the period of Dutch colonial rule in New York, Mohawk men, women, and children regularly travelled to Rensselaerswijck, Fort Orange, and Beverwijck during the summer months to exchange beaver pelts for European goods. During these visits, the Flemish Bastard may have learned some Dutch, received the name Smits Jan, and met his Dutch father.[15]

Despite these likely interactions with Dutch colonists, all the available European documents indicate that the Flemish Bastard primarily identified himself as a Mohawk. Whenever he visited the small face-to-face communities of Rensselaerswijck, Fort Orange, and Beverwijck after 1647, local Dutch officials, who presumably knew him personally and were likely familiar with his Dutch background, always labelled him as a Mohawk. The Flemish Bastard therefore must have resembled the Mohawks in physical appearance, clothing, and everyday customs. Mohawk irritation at the Dutch failure to prevent the frequent mistreatment of Mohawk visitors to Fort Orange and Beverwijck by aggressive fur traders may also not have encouraged the Mohawk-raised Flemish Bastard to cultivate close ties with the Dutch. A final indication of the Flemish Bastard's identity as a Mohawk is that he reportedly had a Mohawk wife and children at the time of a major French military expedition against the Mohawks in the fall of 1666.[16]

Because the Flemish Bastard grew up as a Mohawk, he actively participated in the brutal Mourning Wars that the Iroquois waged during the 1640s and early 1650s. There are no records documenting the participation of the Flemish Bastard in the combined Seneca–Mohawk attacks that destroyed the Huron confederacy of southern Ontario in 1649. One year later, however, the Jesuit *Relations* described him as a leader of a Mohawk war party who attacked the strategic French community of

Trois-Rivières, located midway between Quebec and Montreal. Since Iroquois war leaders were usually selected on the basis of merit on the battlefield, the reference to the Flemish Bastard as a war chief in the Jesuit *Relation* of 1650 strongly suggests that he had successfully participated as a young warrior in the Iroquois campaigns against the Hurons in the late 1640s.[17]

The Flemish Bastard's participation in a Mohawk assault against Trois-Rivières in the summer of 1650 was part of the First French–Iroquois War, which lasted until 1667. This intercultural war originated out of the Mourning Wars between the Iroquois and the Hurons. The French rightly concluded that the Iroquois campaigns greatly hindered the fur trade with their Huron and Northern Algonquian allies, upon which New France was economically dependent. For their part, the Iroquois felt that the French alliance with the Hurons and Northern Algonquians posed a great military threat to the Iroquois confederacy. During the First French–Iroquois War, the Flemish Bastard proved a skilled commander in organizing ambushes, which were traditionally favoured by the Iroquois to minimize their own casualties and to inflict maximum damage on their opponents. According to the Jesuit *Relations*, the Mohawk warriors and the Flemish Bastard repeatedly lured eager French pursuers into traps that cost the French "some of our best Soldiers."[18]

Although the Five Nations had the upper hand in the wars against the French and their Huron and Northern Algonquian allies during the early 1650s, the Iroquois confederacy also needed warriors for Mourning War expeditions against the Iroquoian-speaking Eries and Susquehannocks on the western and southern borders, respectively, of Iroquoia. For this reason, the Senecas, Cayugas, Onondagas, and Oneidas started independent negotiations with French officials in the fall of 1653. The Mohawks, who felt militarily confident because of direct access to Dutch firearms and powder at Fort Orange, were initially skeptical of the negotiations but eventually sent their own envoys to New France in order to avoid being diplomatically isolated. Since the French in Canada were badly equipped and not organized to fight a prolonged war against the Iroquois Confederacy during this period, Quebec officials were very eager to conclude a ceasefire with the Iroquois Nations. Throughout the winter of 1653 and 1654, the French made several separate peace treaties with the Five Nations.[19]

Due to his bicultural background and his status as a prominent war chief, the Flemish Bastard played a valuable role in the negotiations between the Mohawks and the French. To make his embassy to French colonial officials more effective and persuasive, he skilfully used the Dutch at Fort Orange and Beverwijck as diplomatic middlemen. Before embarking on an arduous winter journey to Quebec, the Flemish Bastard visited Fort Orange in late December 1653. During his visit, he persuaded the court of Fort Orange and Beverwijck to write a letter of recommendation that he could give to French officials. It is very likely that he took this course of action because he personally knew the Dutch from earlier visits to Fort Orange and Beverwijck. The Dutch magistrates wrote a sympathetic letter to French governor Jean de Lauson in which they urged the Frenchman to treat the Flemish Bastard well. The Dutch officials also informed de Lauson that the Mohawks were willing to conclude a peace with the French as long as the French kept out of the Iroquois wars against the Hurons and the Northern Algonquian-speaking peoples.[20]

By shrewdly utilizing his Dutch connections in the New France–colonial New York borderland, the Flemish Bastard was able to persuade the French that the Mohawks were sincerely committed to peace. Although several Mohawk missions and delegations from other Five Nations visited New France to discuss the details of the treaties, it was not until the arrival of the Flemish Bastard that French officials became convinced that the Mohawks were truly concerned with ending the fighting. According to the Jesuits, who had considerable influence in New France at this time, the French remained suspicious of Mohawk peace offers during the first months of 1654. Their skepticism was finally abandoned when "an Anniehronnon [Mohawk] Captain, the son of an Iroquois mother and a Dutch father, brought us letters from the Captain of Fort Orange in New Holland and from some Dutch tradesmen, who all assured us that now they really saw a disposition for Peace on the part of the savages allied to them." After having personally negotiated with the French governor, the Flemish Bastard promised to return to Quebec in the summer months to deliver two French captives as a sign of good intentions on part of the Mohawks.[21]

When he returned to Quebec in July 1654, the Flemish Bastard gave a speech chastising the French for sending a recent diplomatic mission to the Onondaga nation rather than to the Mohawks. This speech is significant because it is the earliest surviving written document discussing the political structure of the Iroquois League. The Jesuits, who had viewed the Flemish Bastard as "an execrable issue of sin" during the Mohawk attack on Trois-Rivières in 1650, now considered him a skilled orator who spoke "with cleverness and intelligence." Several days before he arrived in Quebec, French officials had dispatched the Jesuit Simon

Le Moyne on an official diplomatic mission to the Onondaga nation. The French sent Le Moyne to the Onondagas because they had been the first Iroquois nation to contact the French regarding a possible truce. The French had probably also deliberately passed over the Mohawks because, of all the Five Nations, they had done the most damage to the French colony. French authorities may also have been informed by Iroquois captives or Huron allies that the ceremonial seat of the Iroquois confederacy was at the Onondaga nation. By sending Le Moyne to the Onondagas, the French may have wanted to secure a ceasefire that would be honoured by all the Five Nations.[22]

When the Flemish Bastard heard about Le Moyne's mission, he used typical metaphorical Iroquois political language to criticize the French. Comparing the Iroquois League to an Iroquoian longhouse, the traditional residence of the Iroquois peoples, the Flemish Bastard pointed out that the Mohawks were the keepers of the eastern door of the longhouse because of their easternmost geographic position within the league. According to the Flemish Bastard, by sending Le Moyne to the Onondagas, who lived at the geographic and political centre of the Iroquois Five Nations, the French had contacted the Iroquois League through the central chimney of the longhouse. In the opinion of the Flemish Bastard, it was a considerable breach of diplomatic protocol "to enter by the roof and through the chimney" rather than by the door. Following the speech, the French governor presented some gifts to the Flemish Bastard. The governor also instructed him to pursue Le Moyne and to tell the Jesuit to pay a diplomatic visit to the Mohawks as well. Although the Flemish Bastard failed to catch up with Le Moyne, the French governor's instructions reveal that the highest officials in New France took the Flemish Bastard's speech and warnings seriously.[23]

The Mohawks were greatly angered after Le Moyne's diplomatic visit to the Onondagas resulted in the construction of a large Jesuit mission post in Onondaga territory in 1656. The Onondagas planned to use the Catholic mission to maintain the loyalty of hundreds of Christian Hurons who had been captured and incorporated in Iroquois villages since 1649. The Onondagas also wanted to attract to Onondaga the remaining Huron refugees, who were now living in the vicinity of Quebec. Since most of the Huron captives and refugees had been baptized by Jesuits and practised Christian rituals, the Onondagas hoped to secure stability in their villages by inviting the missionaries. The Onondagas also welcomed the Jesuits in the expectation that the missionary outpost would give them direct access to European trade goods.[24]

After learning of the Onondaga–French rapprochement, the Mohawks began a campaign of harassment against both the Onondagas and the French to prevent losing their privileged status as the only Iroquois nation with direct access to European trade goods. At the same time, they wanted to avoid open warfare with the Onondagas because a civil war could destroy the Iroquois Confederacy. The Mohawks were also careful not to destroy the recent French–Mohawk truce because it forced the French to stay out of the ongoing Mohawk wars against the Aboriginal allies of New France. Mohawk raids against French colonists and Jesuits were therefore complimented by frequent Mohawk peace envoys to New France.[25]

The Flemish Bastard actively participated in the complex Mohawk strategies. In the late summer of 1656, he took part in a sophisticated Mohawk ambush of a large canoe flotilla consisting of Hurons, Northern Algonquian-speaking Ottawas, and two French Jesuits on the Ottawa River near Montreal. The numerically inferior Mohawk warriors fired a devastating volley into the ranks of the first six canoes by using well-positioned snipers. Leonard Garreau, one of the two French missionaries, was among the injured. When the Huron and Ottawa survivors pursued the Mohawks, the latter retreated to a well-fortified stronghold that they had build in preparation of the ambush. Unwilling to take more losses by storming the Mohawk fortress, the Hurons and Ottawas gave up the siege and abandoned the gravely wounded Garreau to the Mohawks. To preserve the carefully negotiated peace with the French, the Flemish Bastard did not kill Garreau but delivered him to Montreal officials as a sign of goodwill. Although Garreau died of his wounds shortly after arrival in Montreal, the French appreciated the compassionate gesture. After having convinced French officials that a French deserter among the Mohawks had shot Garreau, the Flemish Bastard was allowed to leave Montreal unharmed.[26]

The contradictory Mohawk policies towards New France, alternating between violent raids and peaceful negotiations, did not have the desired effect but only intensified French suspicions of Mohawk intentions. Moreover, although the Mohawks successfully forced the Jesuits to abandon their mission post at Onondaga in March 1658, the Mohawk campaign of intimidation quickly backfired as angry Onondaga warriors retaliated. Even more problematic for the Mohawks was renewed warfare with the Susquehannocks on their southern borders and with New England Algonquian peoples on their eastern borders in the late 1650s and early 1660s.[27]

To avoid encirclement by their French and Aboriginal enemies, the Mohawks turned to their Dutch trading partners as possible allies and diplomatic middlemen. In September 1659, they succeeded in renewing their valuable diplomatic and economic alliance with the Dutch during a special council held at Caughnawaga, the Mohawk village closest to Fort Orange. Despite this successful meeting, the Dutch were reluctant to become actively involved in the Mohawk struggles against the French and neighbouring Aboriginal peoples. From a Dutch perspective, the alliance with the Mohawks and other Iroquois nations was primarily valuable for commercial reasons. Even when the Dutch requested the assistance of the Mohawks in negotiating an end to a frontier conflict between Dutch colonists and the Algonquian-speaking Lenape people at Esopus Creek, midway in the Hudson Valley, in 1659, New Netherland officials refused Mohawk requests for military aid.[28]

The Flemish Bastard and other Mohawk envoys eventually intervened in the Dutch-Algonquian war at Esopus in order to preserve their valuable relationship with the Dutch. Since the Esopus region was strategically located along the main communication line between Fort Orange and Manhattan, the intercultural war threatened the flow of firearms, gunpowder, and other important Dutch trade goods to the Mohawks. Moreover, by intervening in the Esopus–Dutch war, the Mohawks could reassert their influence over the Algonquian peoples that lived along the Hudson Valley. In June 1663, the court magistrates of Fort Orange were visited by "the savage, called Smith's Jan [Smits Jan], who presented himself and offered his services, saying that he felt himself driven to it by his conscience" to ransom Dutch captives of the Lenapes at Esopus. That the Dutch officials failed to recognize Smits Jan as a child of a Dutch father reveals that the man was a Mohawk in behaviour and dress. The reference to his conscience may have also indicated that the Flemish Bastard felt obliged by his part-Dutch background to help the colonists.[29]

On 27 June 1663, the Flemish Bastard, together with three other Mohawks, the Dutch interpreter Jan Dareth, and the Mahican chief Skiwias, left Fort Orange in a Dutch yacht to travel to the Esopus region. Although the Flemish Bastard worked hard to obtain the release of Dutch hostages, his mission had only limited success. Some of the Lenape chiefs were unwilling to release their hostages because the Flemish Bastard did not provide enough gifts and wampum. The Mohawk war chief was eventually able to secure the release of one captive by giving "his own strings of wampum" to a Lenape sachem. When the Flemish Bastard returned to Fort Orange in early July, he tried to put a positive spin on his failed rescue mission by boasting that he could go down to the Esopus region and attack with "44 Maquaes [Mohawks], there being 44 prisoners still in their [Lenape] hands."[30]

Although Petrus Stuyvesant, the director general of New Netherland, was initially excited about the proposal of the Flemish Bastard, Dutch authorities at Fort Orange rejected it as "too dangerous." They clearly did not entirely trust the Mohawk. According to Fort Orange magistrates, the Flemish Bastard "was tipsy at the time" he made the offer. Moreover, the officials claimed that he had "made the offer without knowledge of the older fellow-chiefs of the Maquaes." This assertion confirms the earlier suggestion that the Flemish Bastard was a war chief who traditionally lacked influence in Mohawk politics. Because he had less influence than he claimed, Dutch officials decided not to make further use of his services during the Esopus Wars.[31]

After his failed negotiation effort at Esopus in 1663, there is no information available about the Flemish Bastard for three years. By the time he reappears in European written documents in 1666, the diplomatic, economic, and military circumstances in the New France–colonial New York borderland had dramatically changed for the Mohawks and the other four Iroquois nations. In late summer 1664, an English naval force conquered New Netherland and the Dutch colony was renamed New York. The English conquest initially did not appear to have much of an impact on the Five Nations. Realizing the strategic and economic significance of the Iroquois peoples, English officials quickly negotiated a treaty of friendship with representatives of the Five Nations at Albany in September 1664. Likewise, most Dutch colonists continued to live in New York and import European goods to exchange for beaver pelts with the Five Nations on the Upper Hudson Valley. The Second and Third Anglo–Dutch Wars (1664–1667 and 1672–1674), which were fought especially hard on the Atlantic and North Sea trade routes, did have a negative impact on the Five Nations, however, as the flow of trade goods from Europe to colonial New York was occasionally interrupted.[32]

The Flemish Bastard successfully adjusted to the European regime change on the Hudson Valley by serving as a messenger for the new English colonial authorities. He was probably hired by English officials because of his experience and familiarity in dealing with Dutch colonists and the New Netherland and New France officials during the 1650s and early 1660s. In one of his letters to Albany officials, Colonel Richard Nicholls, the first governor of colonial New York, based at Manhattan, explained that he favoured the Flemish Bastard as a messenger "because he is reported to love both English and Dutch." The bicultural Mohawk chief was employed not only to carry letters and messages between Albany and Manhattan but to bring letters back and forth between Albany and Quebec. The use of Aboriginal postmen was not a new policy. Colonial authorities of New Netherland had already successfully used Native messengers during periods when the Hudson River was not navigable.[33]

By serving as a messenger on behalf of colonial officials, the Flemish Bastard not only received some material compensation but was also able to maintain close personal ties with authorities in New France and colonial New York. These face-to-face relations with Dutch, French, and English officials were useful in securing his status as an influential chief among the Mohawks. Even more valuable, his personal contacts with colonial officials provided him with intelligence detailing the intentions and policies of New France and colonial New York toward the Five Nations. His status as a trusted carrier between Albany and Quebec enabled him to supply the Mohawks with precious information that they could use in their struggle to maintain security and independence.

The Flemish Bastard was only able to benefit from his strategic position as an intercolonial messenger as long as either colonial New York or New France did not directly threaten the status quo in the New France–colonial New York borderland. When more than a thousand well-armed regular French soldiers and an aggressive imperialistic new government arrived in New France in the summer of 1665 with direct orders from the new French King Louis XIV to destroy the Five Nations, however, the Flemish Bastard quickly lost the ability to benefit from his status as a neutral postman.[34]

When the Five Nations learned of the intentions of the newly arrived regiment and colonial government in Quebec, the Senecas, Cayugas, Onondagas, and Oneidas were quick to dispatch peace envoys to New France in order to avoid a potentially devastating French invasion of their communities. The western four Iroquois nations became especially alarmed after the French troops constructed a series of forts along Lake Champlain. Unwilling to take high casualties against the French troops and faced with ongoing battles against the Susquehannocks along the Susquehanna Valley, the Senecas, Cayugas, Onondagas, and Oneidas held a series of negotiations with the new French colonial government at Quebec in December 1665. In 1666, these four Iroquois nations formalized a peace treaty with New France and promised not to fight the Aboriginal allies of the French any longer.[35]

Unlike the other Iroquois nations, a majority of Mohawks wanted to continue their low-intensity guerilla war, which effectively pinned down the French in the St. Lawrence Valley. Despite a looming invasion by French troops, the Mohawks felt secure through their trade relations with Dutch colonists on the Upper Hudson Valley. Perhaps the Mohawks also expected their Dutch trading partners and the recently arrived English officials at Albany, with whom they had made a treaty in September 1664, to aid them against any French attacks. The Mohawks were sorely mistaken, however, when a force of several hundred French soldiers and colonial militia penetrated deep into the lands of the Mohawks in January 1666. Although the French expedition failed because the soldiers and militiamen got lost in a snowstorm and were forced to seek shelter at the Dutch hamlet of Schenectady (located between Albany and the Mohawk town of Caughnawaga), the Mohawks must have been greatly alarmed by the presence of heavily armed Frenchmen on their borders.[36]

What was even more disheartening for the Mohawks, however, was the friendly reception the French troops received at Schenectady and from Albany officials. Instead of coming to the aid of their trading partners, the Dutch colonists actively sheltered the Mohawks' French enemies. Although the Dutch colonists viewed the Mohawks as valuable trading partners, they clearly did not want to enter into a conflict with a large invading French army. Likewise, while English officials from Albany viewed the French expedition in colonial New York as an infringement on their territorial claim, they did not protest the French attempt to attack the Mohawks.[37]

The benign attitudes of the Dutch and English toward the French must have been an especially sobering experience for the Flemish Bastard. When the destitute French soldiers arrived at Schenectady, he was staying near the Dutch community together with his Mohawk kinsmen and other followers. The hungry and exhausted French troops immediately attacked and looted the two structures in which the small Mohawk band was living in order to look for food. Although the Flemish Bastard and the other Mohawks were able to seek safety by fleeing into the walled community of Schenectady, the bicultural Mohawk chief was likely dismayed when the Dutch colonists supplied food and other aid to the same French troops who had only shortly before attacked him. In this borderland situation, where Dutch and English allies of the Mohawks were more concerned with maintaining friendly relations with the French than with their Aboriginal trading partners, the Flemish Bastard concluded that the Mohawks should not rely on colonial New York for help.[38]

Realizing the increasingly isolated position of the Mohawks, the Flemish Bastard and several other Mohawk leaders started negotiations with the French on their northern border. The Mohawks were also willing to start peace talks with the French after renewed warfare with the Susquehannocks on their southern border and increasing clashes with the Mahicans and Algonquian peoples from the Connecticut Valley on their eastern border forced them to fight a desperate three-front war. When a large military force of some three hundred French soldiers, militia, and Northern Algonquian allies, led by captain Pierre de Saurel, neared the Mohawk villages in August 1666 in retaliation for the Mohawk capture of several French officers at Lake Champlain, a Mohawk delegation led by the Flemish Bastard met the French expedition with an offer to hold negotiations. The embassy of the Flemish Bastard persuaded de Saurel of the sincerity of Mohawk intentions by releasing the recently captured French officers.[39]

Although de Saurel took the Flemish Bastard to Quebec for further peace talks, the viceroy of New France, Alexander Prouville, Seigneur de Tracy, refused to hold negotiations with the Mohawk mediator. Instead of discussing a peaceful end to the ongoing Mohawk–French conflict with the Flemish Bastard, Tracy, after some deliberation with senior French colonial officials, organized a third major military expedition. During the preparations for this campaign, Tracy treated the Flemish Bastard and his Mohawk companions as hostages and forced them to make snowshoes for the French troops.[40]

At the same time, the Flemish Bastard was treated with considerable respect by Tracy. According to the Quebec-based Ursuline nun Marie Guyart, the Flemish Bastard was treated "like a great lord; to honour him, Monsieur de Tracy gave him a fine suit of clothing for his use and promised him his life before he set out with the army." Unlike the other Mohawk envoys, the Flemish Bastard was also not kept in chains but was allowed to move about freely in the French town in the company of armed guards. Guyart believed that the Flemish Bastard received this favourable treatment from Tracy because the Mohawk chief had released the captured French officers, one of whom was a relative of Tracy. It is also possible that Tracy treated the Flemish Bastard with consideration because the viceroy viewed the bicultural Mohawk leader as a valuable mediator who could be persuaded to work for the security of New France in the future.[41]

For all the respect he received from French officials at Quebec, the Flemish Bastard was powerless to stop the invasion. When Tracy and

Daniel Remy de Courcelle, the new governor of New France, departed from Quebec with fourteen hundred soldiers, militia, and Aboriginal allies in mid-September 1666, the Flemish Bastard was forced to witness the large military force as it marched out of the French town. The Flemish Bastard reportedly cried when he saw the large number of French troops and Aboriginal warriors leave for an attack on his people, but he also warned Tracy "'that many of your fine young men will remain behind, for ours [the Mohawks] will fight till the end.'" It is unknown how Tracy responded to this threat, but the French viceroy promised the Flemish Bastard to spare the life of the Mohawk chief's wife and children and bring them to Quebec if possible.[42]

After the French and Aboriginal forces returned victorious to Quebec on 5 November 1666, the Flemish Bastard and other Iroquois hostages were ordered by Tracy to return to their people "with the mandate to tell them that if they stirred again he [Tracy] would go back to see them and this time they would not get off so lightly." The Flemish Bastard was also instructed to return to Quebec "within the space of four moons" with several Northern Algonquian and Huron captives as a sign of goodwill. Upon learning of the devastating success of the French–Aboriginal expedition, the Flemish Bastard had no choice but to accept Tracy's demand. Although Tracy and Courcelle had not engaged any Mohawk warriors, the French and Aboriginal forces had destroyed all four Mohawk villages, had burned food supplies, and had taken back to Quebec many Mohawk possessions.[43]

Faced with serious French threats to Mohawk independence and realizing that aid from colonial New York was not forthcoming, the Flemish Bastard began to associate more closely with the French. Although he returned to Quebec in April 1667 without bringing any Huron or Northern Algonquian captives, he informed French officials "that he would remain as a hostage; and that he himself would come to live, with his family, in the colony, in order to prove the sincerity which led him to come to ask for peace." The Flemish Bastard was not the only Mohawk who concluded that aligning with the French was the best hope for survival. Throughout the spring of 1667, several other Mohawk families joined the Flemish Bastard and his relatives in relocating to the St. Lawrence Valley. Furthermore, those Mohawks who remained skeptical of the French concluded that making peace with New France was the only way to prevent military destruction. In the summer of 1667, representatives of all Mohawk factions accepted the peace treaty that the French had earlier made with the other four Iroquois nations.[44]

Soon after having moved to New France, the Flemish Bastard was asked to carry several letters to the Upper Hudson Valley. Tracy wanted to inform Albany officials, some of whom had persuaded the Mohawks to make peace with the French, of the impending treaty negotiations between the French and the Five Nations. In order to convey this message to Albany in writing, Tracy instructed the Flemish Bastard to travel to the Upper Hudson Valley in May 1667. In a letter to Arent van Curler, a Dutch colonist who played a prominent role as negotiator between the Iroquois and colonial New York, Tracy wrote, "I shall always treat him [the Flemish Bastard] favorably out of consideration for you [Van Curler]." Tracy also wrote to Van Curler that he "entertained friendship" for the Flemish Bastard and that he had granted the Mohawk leader special permission to travel between New France and Albany throughout the month of June.[45]

Unfortunately, there is no documentary evidence that the Flemish Bastard actually arrived at Albany. He may have feared that Albany officials would probably not welcome him anymore because of his recent decision to move to New France. In this context, it is significant that some Dutch colonists living at Manhattan had heard rumours already in the fall of 1666 that "Smits Jan hath received so much kindness from the French that hee is turned French man." At the same time, Albany officials would not have harmed the Flemish Bastard because they were as dependent on the services of the experienced Mohawk messenger as Tracy was. The physical dangers of travelling from Albany to Quebec remained very real for European colonists; for example, Arent van Curler drowned under mysterious circumstances on Lake George while travelling to Quebec in the summer of 1667. Moreover, senior English authorities did not believe that the Flemish Bastard would seek close ties with the French. Responding to the rumours among Dutch residents at Manhattan, Colonel Nicholls concluded that "hee hath drawne so much blood from the French that he cannot be so foolish as to thinke that they have good intentions for him onely to serve their present Ends." It was precisely the French threat to the Mohawks, however, that had forced the Flemish Bastard to relocate to New France.[46]

The Flemish Bastard does not appear to have functioned as an intercolonial messenger after Tracy's reference to him as a courier to Albany in the spring of 1667. His sudden absence from Dutch, English, and French records after May 1667 suggests that his disillusionment after colonial New York failed to come to the aid of the Mohawks in 1666 may have led him to refuse to travel to Albany. Following the conclusion of the Iroquois–French peace treaty of 1667, with conditions favourable to New France, and the release of the Mohawks' French, Huron, and Northern Algonquian prisoners, the French also no longer needed the Flemish Bastard to maintain frequent contacts with Albany.[47]

Having ended his career as an intercolonial courier, the Flemish Bastard's identity after 1667 was closely linked with that of the so-called "Canadian Iroquois," "Settled Indians," and "Christian Indians" who emerged as autonomous Aboriginal communities in the vicinity of Montreal and Quebec during the late 1660s and early 1670s. Like the Flemish Bastard, most of the Aboriginal peoples who resettled along the St. Lawrence Valley in this period were Iroquois refugees who sought protection and a new life within the orbit of New France following the French military invasions of the Five Nations in 1666. Since many of the Iroquois refugees were former Huron captives who had been baptized by Jesuit missionaries, most Iroquois families resettled in towns that were administered by the French black robes. Despite the presence of Jesuits and their close association with New France, the newly established Aboriginal villages were self-governing and often followed their own foreign policies in the era of French–English imperial rivalries from the 1680s to the 1760s.[48]

During his first years as a Mohawk refugee in the St. Lawrence Valley, the Flemish Bastard and his relatives and followers established an independent community near Montreal, from which they hunted for food and animal pelts. At one time, the Flemish Bastard and his hunters supplied Montreal merchants with so many furs that the price of imported Canadian furs in France dropped by half. After several years, he and his hunting band may have relocated to one of the mission towns in order to cultivate crops that, together with hunting, were the main sources of subsistence among the Iroquois peoples. It is not known whether he was baptized or considered himself a Catholic. In this respect, the bicultural Mohawk leader was not unusual, since many of the Canadian Iroquois created their own brand of Christianity, which often blended Catholic rituals with traditional Iroquois beliefs.[49]

The Flemish Bastard appears for the last time in European documents in 1687. Twenty years after resettling in the St. Lawrence mission towns, he participated in a Christian Indian war party that accompanied a major French expedition against the Senecas in western New York. This expedition was part of a campaign by French Governor Jacques-Rene de Brisay de Denonville to punish the Senecas for obstructing the French diplomatic and mercantile alliance with Aboriginal peoples in the Great Lakes region. With a force of some two thousand French troops and militia, as well as one thousand Aboriginal allies, Denonville marched into Seneca country in the summer of 1687.[50]

If the testimony of one captured Christian Indian, given to colonial New York officials, is to be believed, the Flemish Bastard rallied the Aboriginal allies of the French during a critical point in the campaign when the Christian Indians, many of whom were Mohawks, opposed Denonville's ruthless tactics of destroying Seneca villages and food supplies. By persuading Christian Indians to support Denonville, the Flemish Bastard implied that he was willing to support the same severe tactics of burning and looting against the Senecas that the French had used against the Mohawks in 1666. His call upon his fellow Mohawk and other St. Lawrence Iroquois to attack the Senecas was not necessarily an indication of his abandonment of an Iroquois identity. Political and diplomatic solidarity among the Five Nations was never strong during the seventeenth century. As we have seen, the Mohawks had openly clashed with the Onondagas during the 1650s in order to prevent the Onondagas from establishing a valuable diplomatic and commercial alliance with the French. Since the Iroquois refugee communities on the St. Lawrence Valley were politically independent from the Five Nations, the Flemish Bastard may have sincerely viewed the Senecas as an obstacle to the interests of the Christian Indians.[51]

At the same time, by actively calling upon the Christian Indians to follow Denonville against the Senecas, the Flemish Bastard indicated that he associated more closely with the French than the rest of the Iroquois allies of New France. While the Canadian Iroquois were unwilling and hesitant to openly confront the Senecas on the battlefield, the Flemish Bastard was more concerned with preserving the alliance with the French. As a negotiator who had interacted with the French for several decades, he probably remained an influential liaison between New France and the Iroquois refugee towns of the St. Lawrence Valley. Since he had always been well-treated by the French, he viewed a close relationship with New France as more valuable than maintaining Iroquois unity. Although there is no indication that he became a political pawn of the French, his active support for Denonville in 1687 suggests that the bicultural Mohawk chief who had once strongly opposed the French had now become a loyal ally of New France's imperial ambitions.

The career of the Flemish Bastard demonstrates that, as long as diplomatic conditions in the New France–colonial New York borderland remained stable, the Mohawks were able to maintain security and autonomy. By using his bicultural background, the Flemish Bastard was able to function as a valuable negotiator and intercolonial messenger between Fort Orange/Albany and Quebec. However, the arrival of an aggressive and heavily armed colonial government in New France in 1665 quickly altered borderland circumstances for the Flemish Bastard and his Mohawk kin. Faced with French military invasions and unable to receive support from their Anglo-Dutch allies in Albany, the Flemish Bastard and many other Mohawks sought security by closely aligning themselves with their former French enemies. Although the Flemish Bastard's relocation to the St. Lawrence Valley in 1667 secured physical and political survival for himself and his Mohawk followers, the move simultaneously pressured him to collaborate more closely with his French hosts.

Viewed from a larger, theoretical perspective, the life of the Flemish Bastard shows that Aboriginal peoples who lived in the geographic space between competing European powers were impacted by intercolonial rivalries in complex ways. On the one hand, Aboriginal peoples such as the Five Nations in the New France–colonial New York borderland were able to maintain effective political independence by using one European power to neutralize the threat of another. During the 1650s and 1660s, the Flemish Bastard and the Mohawks used their alliance with Dutch traders at Fort Orange/Albany to keep New France in check. On the other hand, when Aboriginal peoples were no longer able to exploit the rivalries between the competing European colonial powers, Indigenous nations were forced to relinquish some autonomy to the aggressive European colonial powers in order to survive. As the experiences of the Flemish Bastard make clear, life in a borderland was marked by both opportunity and danger for Aboriginal peoples.

# THE ANISHINABEG AND MÉTIS IN THE SAULT STE. MARIE BORDERLANDS

*Confronting a Line Drawn upon the Water*

━━ ⩔⩕ ━━

KARL S. HELE

## Introduction

The creation and survey of an international boundary by drawing a line through the water irrevocably and artificially divided the Sault Ste. Marie Anishinabeg and Métis communities. This was certainly the view of the Baptist Reverend Abel Bingham, who observed in 1844 that a new era had definitively begun for the Indians when the British and American governments agreed upon a boundary line.[1] In contrast, Lord Selkirk, upon learning of the boundary's placement, more effectively summed up the contemporary impact of the newly established border under the 1783 Treaty of Paris. A philanthropist and colonizer best known for establishing colonies at Red River and Baldoon, Lord Selkirk was intimately familiar with the difficulties of imposing authority and establishing European presence in the North American wilderness, and it was his considered opinion that the "boundary was established by fools."[2] The context of his remarks indicates that he saw authority as being too far removed from the reality of the newly established border regions to appreciate the difficulties of imposing what could only amount to an artificial and arbitrary line on a map.

The geographic reality of the region as a borderland is abetted by the will of individuals to conduct their affairs despite the existence of the border. Considerably more room, no doubt, existed for the local residents to evince their "Sault-ite" determination to subvert authority and to directly assert their own interests prior to 1870. By examining the pre-1870 era, it is possible to see that the Anishinabeg community actively strove to assert itself in its interactions with the adjacent communities and with the two expanding settler states. The scale of the borderland itself and the Anishinabeg community's place within it can best be appreciated by recognizing that borderlands are as much human context as they are geographic space—the borderlands' true scale tracks the interests and imperatives of individuals and groups within the Native, Métis, and White, British North American, Canadian, and American communities.

Looking back from the present, it is hard to disagree with this statement; but what did the border actually mean for the First Nations inhabiting the region? This question, of course, has no easy answer. Through a thematic examination of the border, it is possible to discern how, in the absence of effective control, individual agents, whether as state officeholders, clergy or lay missionaries, tribal chiefs, kinsmen, or economic actors, negotiated, as adversaries and allies, the terrain of relationships that established the Sault Ste. Marie region along St. Mary's River as a distinctive borderland in North America. With no outside powers able to exercise absolute, uncontested sovereignty in the early years of colonization and settler-nation-building, the activities of individuals such as Crown Lands Agent Joseph Wilson, US Indian Agent Henry Rowe Schoolcraft, Chief Shingwaukonse, and Chief Piabetassung played crucial roles in shaping reality on the ground. Over time, the dynamics of their interactions, along with the activities of countless others, fundamentally altered local relationships in terms of rights, land and resource use, and structures of authority. State initiatives to solidify control over and advance a governing agenda on each side of the border sought to divide the community, but local residents maintained opportunities to negotiate and pursue their own interests, producing a skein of relationships that existed independent of and even despite the presence of border. For the Sault Region Ojibwa and Métis, these areas of contested authority have shaped local history as people—Indian, Métis, and Europeans—sought cultural, social, and economic outcomes more to their own liking.[3]

This chapter explores the difficulties of imposing and enforcing a border in the Sault Ste. Marie region. This thematic approach highlights the various implications of the boundary's presence in the Sault region for local Aboriginal peoples and state policies. "Drawing the Line" briefly examines the creation of the border. "Defining the Indian and Métis" discusses government policies for defining spheres of control. "Rum along the Border" highlights not only local will to subvert the border's presence but the manipulation of state-created identities. Both "Establishing Control" and "Tensions along the Border" discuss efforts to control the boundary and the tensions created. Finally the "Effects on the Native Economy" draws attention to how government attempts to police the border affected the Aboriginal economy. By its very nature, a thematic approach chronologically overlaps themes as the reader moves between them. However, taken together, the themes ably illustrate the central point of this paper and collection, that the lines drawn upon the water by colonial states affected First Nations, Métis, and governmental policies in a variety of ways.

## Drawing the Line

By 1820, the Sault Ste. Marie area was theoretically divided between the United States (US) and British North America (BNA). Boundary definitions were finalized by the 1840s, but the American and British authorities remained unable to exert effective control over the entire region's population until after the 1870s. The gradual pace of intrusion was such that Euro-American commentators took scant note of the region's character. Few in Upper Canada and the eastern United States gave much thought at all to the area. Early tourists travelling in the region prior to the 1850s remarked upon a picturesque but wild and primitive landscape dominated by Indians and the fur trade. This resulted in conflicting images of empty spaces that were nonetheless occupied by Indian bands existing upon the edge of starvation, reliant on the largesse of traders, and trading in furs.[4]

Hudson's Bay Company (HBC) personnel in the region regarded themselves as existing beyond the pale of Upper Canada.[5] The Whites who resided at the Sault congregated along the north and south shores of the St. Mary's River prior to 1820, but they were almost completely isolated from, though loyal to, Britain. Despite increasing attempts by the US and BNA to exert control, as late as the 1860s the region remained remote and was seen as inhospitable for settler populations.[6] The nature of the local economy meant that most residents had closer ties to the fur-trade elites of Montreal and Mackinaw. This meant that, despite establishing their homes in British North America or the United States, residents maintained business and social connections on both sides of the border.

The Native people living along the St. Mary's River, which flows from Lake Superior into Lake Huron, occupied a region that extended well beyond the north and south shores of the river. Based on oral and written records maintained by the Anishinabeg and various US and Canadian archives, it is clear that the northern and southern boundaries were thought of, and can best be discussed, in terms of territories defined in terms of alliances, kinship, and ties of ethnicity, as well as in terms of borders set out in the provisions of treaties with outside colonial and early national authorities.[7] In the broadest geographical terms, the southern boundary runs from Whitefish Point on Lake Superior in the west, to Neebish Island and Munuscong Lake at the mouth of Lake Huron in the east, and to the height of land on the southern interior. The northern boundary runs from Coppermine Point and Batchawana Bay on Lake Superior in the west, to Lake George and Pumpkin Point at the mouth of Lake Huron in the east, and to the height of land on the Northern interior (see map 1). Within this region, the Sault was "a place marked out by nature as a centre."[8] It was further defined by the presence and patterns of life of the Ojibwa occupying the territory on both sides of the river that came to define the border between BNA and the US. Early on, outsiders recognized the pivotal importance of the Sault; in particular, missionaries established bases for themselves in either village from which they could organize their travels and activities throughout the region.[9]

The end of the American Revolution and the signing of the 1783 Treaty of Paris divided the region with a border demarcating areas of US and British jurisdiction. The Treaty of Paris stated that the international border ran through the middle of the Great Lakes, but it neglected to define how the St. Mary's River and its islands should be divided. The British refusal to abandon its posts in the American Northwest, which were south of the Upper Great Lakes, made a mockery of these early efforts to define a border. Later, in 1794 with the Jay Treaty, Britain agreed to cede control of its interior posts south of the 1783 boundary line, although the treaty again failed to specify how the waters and islands in the St. Mary's River itself were to be divided. Despite the absence of clarity on such finer points, the treaty did confirm that the South Shore was to be American while the North Shore was to be British. Steps towards defining the border more precisely were taken under the 1818 Anglo–American Treaty. In this pact, the US and Britain agreed to appoint a commission to investigate and decide various outstanding border issues, including the disposition of the boundary line through the St. Mary's River.

After investigating matters, the commissioners by 1828 settled upon a boundary running through the St. Mary's River that largely followed the main fur-trade canoe route. Their decision, while merely confirming agreements contained within earlier treaties, permanently and irrevoca-

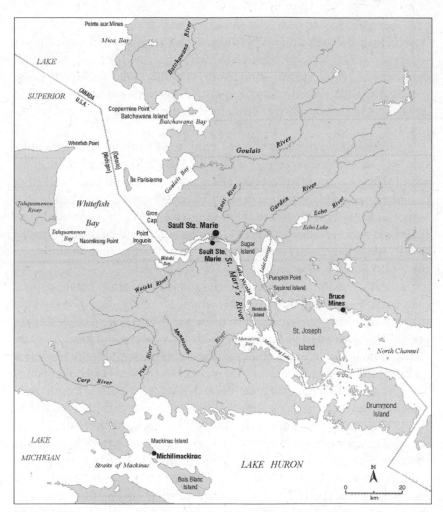

**Map 1:** Sault Ste. Marie Borderlands

bly divided control over the local Ojibwa and Métis communities between
two outside settler societies in the form of a colonial state in the north
and an emerging nation-state in the south. While these outside authorities largely agreed on the boundary drawn upon the water, they nonetheless contested the ownership of several islands.

In one notable case, both the British and the Americans claimed
Sugar Island. Two years before the announcement of the 1828 boundary
commission's conclusions, the Sault Ojibwa acknowledged the American claim to the island when they negotiated and signed a treaty with the
United States in 1826. The Treaty of Fond du Lac recognized the rights

of Oshawguscodywayquay and her descendents to a portion of Sugar Island based on their Ojibwa heritage. This treaty technically acknowledged the US claim, and from 1826, with the assent of the local residents, the US gained jurisdiction over the island in law.[10] Nevertheless, it took eight additional years of negotiations between the Americans and British before the US was confirmed as the island's governing power in 1842.[11]

Determining the ownership of Drummond Island proved less difficult but had a far greater impact on the St. Mary's River borderland community. By awarding Drummond Island in 1828 to the US, the British military abandoned the area in favour of a naval base at Penetanguishene, Upper Canada. The Métis and the non-Native merchant community on the island simply relocated with the troops.[12] This effectively decimated British settlement in the area and severely limited Britain's authority on the North Shore of the Sault region for many years.

Initially, the imposition of a border did little to affect local peoples' lives at the Sault. The Ojibwa, Métis, and local settlers ignored the border, crossing and recrossing the river in search of game, fish, and trade goods. The river was a barrier that could easily be crossed in summer by canoe or boat and in winter by snowshoes or sled, and it only became a real obstacle during the spring thaw and fall freeze. For the Anishinabeg, hunting, fishing, and sugaring activities, as well as seasonal variations in the food supply, determined the side of the river on which they would live during the year. For the Métis, hunting, fishing, trading, farming, and temporary employment with one of the many trading outfits at the twin Saults, as well as family connections, determined where they built their houses. For non-Natives, the limited availability of suitable soil for farming and the relative distance from their competitors and confederates in trade determined their residence and social schedule. For instance, as dispersed as White society in the region may have been, its own social schedule helped knit it together. Many troops and officers from Fort Brady on the US side regularly ventured across the river to attend events hosted by prominent traders such as Charles Oakes Ermatinger or HBC officers. Similarly, those living in BNA crossed the river to enjoy the hospitality of the American traders and military troops.[13]

## Defining the Indian and Métis

In the years following 1840, concerted British and American efforts to define the status of Native populations increasingly affected the character of the borderland.[14] While British policies were framed within the context of maintaining good relations with the US, they were in fact shaped by fiscal constraints and the interests of diplomacy. By 1840, British desires to appease American fears of interference with its Indians led to a restriction of gifts or presents to those living in BNA; the practice ceased altogether by 1858.[15] Initially, to determine eligible recipients, the British government developed three separate categories of "Indians"—visiting, resident, and wandering. Native people classed as visiting or American Indians were discouraged from remaining in Canada West and encouraged to return to the US.[16] Resident or Canadian Indians were those living or originating within BNA's boundaries who had a fixed or identifiable residence. The people at Garden River in 1848, for instance, qualified as residents because they had an identifiable village, even though they continued to exploit the seasonal availability of resources throughout the borderland. Finally, those who belonged to BNA but who did not have a permanent or readily identifiable place of residence were classified as "wandering Indians" and so also fell under the general rubric of Canadian Indians.[17] The US authorities, at least in the Sault area, developed similar classifications based upon precedents set by treaties and observable residency patterns.

Beginning in the 1850s, the Canadian and American governments created new regulations that affected group membership. The United Canadas passed a series of legislative acts that further defined the term "Indian," including the Act for the Protection of the Indians of Upper Canada from Imposition, and the Property Occupied and Enjoyed by Them from Trespass and Injury (1850), the Act for the Better Protection of the Land and Property of the Indians of Lower Canada (1851), and An Act of the Gradual Enfranchisement of Indians (1869). Collectively these legislative acts created the concept of "status" (registered) and "non-status" (unregistered) Indians. The 1851 and 1869 acts stated that patrilineal descent determined whether or not an individual could be considered a status or registered Indian. While initially sporadically enforced, the law became an effective tool for government control of Native groups. Canadian governments continued to tinker with the definition of "Indian," with the last significant adjustments being undertaken in 1985.[18] This legislation was and remains a direct attack on First Nations' sovereign ability to determine their own group membership. The 1859 and 1869 acts proved to be effective weapons against the Ojibwa living in the borderlands.

On the South Shore, the American Treaty of 1855 included a clause that dissolved the Sault Ojibwa's tribal government. In effect, after the payment of compensation and the selection of individual allotment lands, the Chippewa–Ottawa tribal structure south of the border ceased to exist. The policy arose as an effort on the part of the Bureau of Indian Affairs to end the fiction that the Ottawa and Chippewa formed one tribal government. This fiction had been created by Henry Rowe Schoolcraft, amateur anthropologist and the Indian superintendent for Michigan, and by former governor of Michigan and federal secretary of war Lewis Cass in 1836. In the process, all the artificially created tribal governments were dissolved. Consequently, in the view of the US federal government, the St. Mary's River area Ojibwa were no longer a tribe since their tribal or national structure had been terminated. In short, the 1855 treaty defined Natives individually as citizens of Michigan and thereby the US. Legally and administratively, this terminated the special collective relationship that the population had enjoyed with the US federal government, placing individual US Ojibwa on a nominally equal footing with their White neighbours. Beyond this, internally, their American Indian identities were defined by individuals and groups within the Aboriginal community and, externally, through the prism of the largely racist views held by Euro-Americans.

The Métis, for their part, were never truly recognized as an Indigenous community at the Sault. While the US treaties of 1836 and 1855, for instance, included pay-outs to half-breeds and quarter-breeds, the Canadian treaties of 1850 and 1859 recognized no distinctive Métis rights. It took a Supreme Court of Canada decision in 2003 to recognize the historic and continued existence of the Sault Métis as an Aboriginal community.[19] Interestingly, the half- and quarter-breed distinctions made in the US treaties did not fall neatly along the commonly understood Indian–European divide. The term Métis legally referred to anyone who was part Chippewa/Ojibwa and something else, whether it be Indian, Black, or White.[20] Moreover, the US officially limited its treaty payments to those resident on the US side of the river despite knowledge on the part of the lead negotiator, Henry Rowe Schoolcraft, that the Indian and Métis communities maintained ties across the artificial boundary.

Métis residents of both Saults complained about the allocation of cash disbursements by the US government. A "Parole" or petition addressed to President Andrew Jackson, dated 13 November 1836, and carried by Pierre Cadotte, a Métis from Sault Ste. Marie, Michigan, alleged that Schoolcraft had paid several people inappropriately while denying others their due and just compensation.[21] The "Parole" noted that Charlotte Johnston McMurray, Schoolcraft's sister-in-law and the wife of Anglican missionary William McMurray, and her son received payment as a first-class Métis despite the fact that her father had been Irish and her mother had been half-Chippewa and half-Dakota. This heritage made their offspring second-class Métis under the 1836 treaty. Moreover, Charlotte Johnston McMurray should not have been paid since she and her child resided in Sault Ste. Marie, Upper Canada. Treaty payments to individuals residing outside the territories of the US were contrary to official policy and almost certainly illegal.[22]

Another incident developed in October 1836, when Schoolcraft wrote directly to the commissioner of Indian Affairs contesting the validity of complaints about the treaty payments made to John Bell, a mixed-blood resident of Upper Canada and [?] Cadotte, a mixed-blood resident of Michigan. While specific correspondence could not be located, the nature of the complaints can be hypothesized based on the 1836 treaty's articles. Bell and Cadotte, both Métis and traders, were likely displeased with their share of the half-breed money, did not like the prevalent favouritism, or believed that they failed to receive monies due to them based on the clauses under which debts owed to traders were paid.[23] Since both Upper Canada and the US officially denied treaty annuity payments to non-subjects and Métis, the fact that "American" and "British" Ojibwa signed and believed themselves to be part of each treaty negotiated in the region proved problematic. Indian agents on both sides of the river regularly attempted to prevent "foreign" Indians from receiving treaty payments.

Additionally, acceptance of a treaty payment could lead to a denial of status or denial of residence in the respective country of residence. The long-term result was that, under government pressure, centuries-old residency patterns of group membership in the borderlands could not be easily maintained. Chief Piabetassung and his followers' residency in both Upper Canada and the US resulted in the band's demise in the late 1850s and early 1860s. This band resided on Sugar Island, Michigan, and on the east side of the mouth of Garden River, Canada West.[24] After signing both the 1850 BNA and 1855 US treaties, Piabetassung and his followers accepted annuity payments and government largesse from both countries. British Canadian officials declared Piabetassung's band to be American after learning that the group had accepted US treaty payments. The US in turn used the band's acceptance of Canadian annuities as well as the termination clause of the 1855 US treaty to deny them recognition and residency in Michigan. This convergence of US and Canadian colonial definitions that did not include dual national residency tore the group apart, forcing former band members to blend into the recognized groups on both shores or to leave the area entirely.[25] The issue of annuity payments to Canadian and American Indians created with the signing of the various treaties in the region remain largely unresolved.

## Rum along the Border

Rum-running along the St. Mary's River, an enduring tradition thanks to the river's many islands, certainly attests to the border's reality. The practice dates back to at least the 1830s when American and then-British authorities, in conjunction with local missionaries, attempted to prohibit the sale of intoxicating drinks to the Indians. This effort eventually collapsed once it became apparent that little could be done to arrest the flow of alcohol across the border. Traders and tavern keepers during the period seized upon a legal loophole to facilitate their trade. From their vantage point on either side of the river, they were inclined to argue that American laws applied only to American Indians or that Canadian laws similarly governed only Canadian Indians. Conveniently, when selling alcohol to an Indian, the trader simply informed any inquiring officials that the customer did not "belong" to that particular country, thus using the border to the advantage of both customer and trader. This illicit trade continued unabated, attaining an altogether broader scale a century later in the 1920s and 1930s with Prohibition. Interdiction efforts were also notoriously unsuccessful, although much was made in the media outlets of the time of the government struggle against rum-runners.[26]

## Establishing Control over the Ojibwa from the 1820s to 1830s

To pry Ojibwa living on the South Shore away from British influence, the US established an Indian agency at Sault Ste. Marie in 1822 under the direction of Henry Rowe Schoolcraft. Schoolcraft immediately informed the Ojibwa that they must cease visiting the British military and Indian department establishment on Drummond Island, as well as those located elsewhere.[27] Throughout the 1820s and 1830s, Schoolcraft also kept the War Department apprised of Native travels to and from British territory while he attempted to win their allegiance for the US.[28] According to Schoolcraft, "the establishment of a military post, and Indian

Agency, at this place, enables the president to carry into effect, in this remote part of the union, the benevolent views of the American government with respect to the condition and the wants of the Indian tribes; … to open a proper intercourse with the most distant bands residing within the northwestern limits of the United States."[29] With the withdrawal of British forces from Drummond Island in 1828, the US became the dominant non-Native force in the region. The closest British post, at Penetanguishene on Lake Huron, was at least a two days' journey away by sail, and in winter the trip took at least a week. Essentially, the British Sault's non-Native population stagnated and even regressed after the loss of the troops at Drummond.[30]

In response to American assertions of sovereignty on the South Shore, the Anglican William McMurray was appointed lay preacher or missionary and Indian agent to the North Shore in 1832.[31] McMurray's appointment, like that of Schoolcraft, represented an imperialist government's attempt to control and influence the lives of the Anishinabeg at the Sault. By placing McMurray in charge of the spiritual and temporal welfare of the Ojibwa, the Upper Canadian government under Lieutenant-Governor Sir John Colborne aspired to implement a policy of gradual assimilation, while hoping that a civilized village of loyal Ojibwa on the border would help defend the British colony from US aggression.

The inherent fluidity of the borderland played a fundamental role in shaping the course of McMurray's tenure at the Sault. First, McMurray and Schoolcraft married sisters from a prominent fur-trade family, the Johnstons, creating a transnational familial bond between government representatives—this despite the fact that John Johnston, the family's patriarch, fought for Britain in the War of 1812, without ever thereafter becoming an American citizen regardless of his continued residence on the South Shore. While working to promote His Majesty's interests, McMurray also regularly resided on the American shore for extended periods in either the Johnston or Schoolcraft homes. Schoolcraft and McMurray, judging from the surviving correspondence found in the Henry Rowe Schoolcraft Papers, had a cordial relationship and cooperated in their efforts to promote Christianity and civilization among the Indians.[32]

Even so, Schoolcraft regularly wrote to the American War Department concerning the negative effects and continued influence of Britain on the Indians. Ironically, he was assisted in this by McMurray: McMurray, during the civil disturbances in Upper Canada beginning in 1837, continued his regular correspondence with Schoolcraft, passing on information about British troop movements as well as other events of note in the colony.[33] Although McMurray and Schoolcraft served as state representatives for BNA and the US, respectively, they shared ties of residence and kinship that blurred the boundaries of government policies and authority. As such, their activities at Bawating are a case study in and of themselves, illustrating the complex interactions and relationships possible within a borderland.

## Tensions along the Border

The transborder interchanges between officials stemmed in large measure from their inability to exert effective control of their respective territories in the borderland. This was notably apparent when news of the rebellions affecting Lower and Upper Canada reached the Sault. In early 1838, Hudson's Bay Company Factor William Nourse feared that the Métis planned to capture the post in an act of support for their rebellious French brethren in Lower Canada. To forestall the attack, he asked the US garrison to either arrest, or assist in crushing, the dissidents should the need arise on either side of the border.

For their part, the Ojibwa misconstrued the problems elsewhere in Canada to mean that Britain and the US would soon be at war. In preparation, the chiefs allegedly made plans to surprise the poorly manned Fort Brady as a precursor to driving the Americans from Ojibwa territory. George Johnston, the mixed-blood son of Susan and John Johnston and a US Indian interpreter, claimed that he prevented war by forewarning the fort's commander. The situation was such that the HBC took action to dispel rumours and to encourage the Ojibwa to remain at peace with the United States.[34]

Tensions in the region subsided until September 1838 when American Fort Brady unexpectedly opened fire on the British Sault. Colonel Croghan, embittered since his War of 1812 defeat at Mackinac Island and rumoured to be intoxicated, ordered his troops to fire. Since the shot passed harmlessly into the hillside, local British officials on the North Shore downplayed the incident and took their time in notifying British authorities at York and Quebec.[35] Once Croghan left Fort Brady, the officers of the garrison apologized for their commandant's actions, as did General Brady when he heard of the incident.[36] After this, tensions in the Sault region dissipated as the peaceful cross-border nature of the community reasserted itself.[37]

Despite the low-key nature of the incident, a series of letters from the Sub-agent James Ord at Sault Ste. Marie to Henry Schoolcraft, the

Michigan Superintendent of Indian Affairs from March to May 1838—at the height of tensions in the region—show that real concerns existed over the apparent power of the Ojibwa in the borderlands.[38] Ord wrote to Schoolcraft, "there is much discontent among the Indians in this sub-agency." He recommended non-confrontational "efforts to remove it," specifically by sending presents to the Sault for distribution, including oxen, chain, and a cart.[39] Apparently unimpressed by these US gifts, the Indians solicited and received assurances about the munificent nature of the Queen's bounty from British agents. While this correspondence does not reveal how such gifts affected Ojibwa behaviour, a letter written in September 1838 indicates that the practice resulted in the Ojibwa collecting numerous gifts from both countries.[40]

Knowledge among non-Natives of the resource value of the region from the 1840s helped move the direction of policy away from appeasing the Ojibwa with gifts. In 1841, the South Shore was preoccupied with a boom in mineral speculation. This speculation eventually spread to the Canadian settlement on the North Shore. As the Upper Canadian government issued mining leases in violation of the 1763 Royal Proclamation, the British Sault Ojibwa under the leadership of Shingwaukonse and Nebenagouching protested these illegal actions. In July 1849, a petition signed by the two leaders calling for justice appeared in the *Montreal Gazette*. This petition elicited a response from one of the mineral lessees, a self-proclaimed expert on Indians, former Indian agent and speculator William Keating. In a 15 August 1849 letter to the editor of the *Chatham Chronicle*, Keating stated that the Sault region Ojibwa did not have any legitimate claim to the land or its resources since they were American Indians.[41] The accusation was loosely tied to reality since Shingwaukonse and Nebenagouching, along with many of their followers, were born in the US and maintained residency rights on the South Shore. In his letter, Keating knowingly made the most of this while ignoring the historic patterns of life in the region. Nonetheless, the Ojibwa objections, as well as the contradictory claims presented in Keating's letter and in D. B. Papineau's 1847 report on Ojibwa claims (which claimed the Ojibwa had originated on Mississippi before violently wresting control of the region from its true inhabitants), both of which denied Native rights, led the Crown to establish a commission to investigate mining claims along lakes Huron and Superior.[42] This ultimately resulted in the negotiation and signing of the Upper Canadian 1850 Robinson-Huron Treaty, which, among other things, sought to confine Natives to reserves and allowed non-Natives to access mineral lands without fear of Ojibwa retaliation.

## Effects on the Native Economy

The various revenue sources maintained by the Ojibwa revolved around their normal seasonal subsistence activities—logging, trapping, and hunting in the winter on family hunting territories; planting and fishing while producing maple sugar in the spring; fishing, tourism, and guiding during the summer along the St. Mary's River; and fishing during the autumn, followed by a return to the bush in late fall to begin logging once again.[43] This multi-faceted economy allowed the Native community to support itself despite the high price of provisions. The Ojibwa participated in the emerging market economy, relied upon trade in kind, and built reserve stores of food that helped guarantee their survival and independence.[44]

Pre-treaty or traditional fishing rights in the rapids appear to have depended on the degree of connection to the Sault band that maintained a permanent presence on the South Shore. Everyone who lived within the larger Sault region had fishing rights in the rapids. Their traditional locations determined the points at which they could camp and/or from which they could fish. For instance, the Sault band held rights to access the rapids from the South Shore, as well as to launch boats to access the rapids. Those from Tahquamemnon / Bay Mills appear to have had the right to fish from some of the islands in the middle of the rapids. Others held fishing rights to the North Shore and islands just downstream from the main rapids.

In 1820, the Anishinabeg leadership made a concerted effort to protect their fishing grounds when the US proposed a treaty to erect a military post alongside the rapids. Unable to refuse the treaty, the Sault band negotiated a clause within the 1820 treaty that "secure[d] to the Indians a perpetual right of fishing at the falls of the St. Mary's, and also a place of encampment upon the tract hereby ceded, convenient to the fishing ground."[45] The subsequent 1836 US treaty, which saw the surrender of further lands, continued to protect Native access to fishing sites. Chippewa representatives managed to obtain guarantees in respect of lands at

> Sugar Island, with its islets ... Six hundred and forty acres, at the mission of Little Rapids. A tract commencing at the mouth of the Pississowining river, south of Point Iroquois, thence running up said stream to its forks, thence westward in a direct line to the Red water lakes, thence across the portage to the Tacquimenon river, and down the same to its mouth, including the small islands and fishing grounds, in front of this reservation.[46]

Native fishing rights at the site along the shoreline in front of the Euro-American Sault village finally ended with the construction of the shipping canal in the 1850s. In 1853, Charles T. Harvey, who was in charge of the canal construction, paid the Ojibwa US$10 to US$15 for each "cabin" (Native homes) and then ordered all Indians off their fishing site within twenty-four hours.[47] The land was dredged for a canal, which destroyed the fishery at that location.

Prior to the signing of the 1850 Robinson-Huron Treaty, Chief Shingwaukonse hired a lawyer to represent his people's interests before the Upper Canada government against non-Native mineral speculators in 1848–1849. In payment for his services, Chief Shingwaukonse granted his lawyer, mineral speculator and ally Allan Macdonell, several leases, including some islands in the St. Mary's River. The Reverend James Cameron, a mixed-blood Baptist minister who was a member of the Tahquememnon community through marriage, pronounced the action illegal. Specifically, he claimed that the islands in the St. Mary's River, despite their location in Canadian waters, were not Shingwaukonse's to lease. In his correspondence, Cameron made use of indirect evidence derived from the Baptist Reverend Abel Bingham's diaries and oral accounts to allege that the Tahquamenon and Naomikong bands of Michigan owned the islands. Not incidentally, these were Cameron's supporters and kin. These islands served as a camping ground where members of these two bands stayed while visiting the Sault or during the biannual whitefish runs. Shingwaukonse, as leader of the Garden River Band, needed to consult not only the Tahquamenon and Naomikong bands, but also the Crane chiefs of the Sault region who resided in Michigan, before negotiating a lease with Macdonell or a treaty with British Canadian authorities. He did not have the authority to negotiate the surrender of another community's land or rights. Cameron's protests about the leases and treaty were centred around customs, rights, and traditions of the Bawating Anishinabeg.[48] Obviously, within the borderlands, traditional Ojibwa rights and privileges could not be contained neatly by a line drawn upon the water by Euro-Americans. This resulted in a dizzying array of assertions and counter-assertions that the colonial states ignored in their efforts to assert their views about who held what rights and who belonged on which side of the border.

On the North Shore, the Ojibwa similarly continued their efforts to protect their fishing rights under the terms of the 1850 Robinson-Huron Treaty. Specifically, the Batchawana Indian band, under the leadership of Nebenagouching, reserved "a tract of land [extending from

Wanabekinegunning west of Gros Cap to the boundary of the lands ceded
by the chiefs of Lake Superior and inland ten miles throughout the whole
distance, including Batchewanaug Bay], and also the small island at Sault
Ste. Marie used by them as a fishing station."[49] The waters and shore-
lines included within this area represented some of the band's best fishing sites.

In the end, with the signing of the various treaties in the region and
government efforts to regulate the cross-border movements of the Métis
and Ojibwa, many of the regional communities found their traditional
fishing stations in another country to which they were denied access.
With the completion of the Sault canal, the US Sault Ojibwa lost their
best access points to fishing in the rapids. Continued exploitation proved
difficult since they now had to compete with non-Natives for the rights
they once enjoyed. On the Canadian side, Native people were gradually
restricted from selling their whitefish catches, although subsistence fishing appears to have persisted well into the early twentieth century. The
whitefish fishery in the rapids finally collapsed after 1901 with the advent
of industrialization and the increasing pollution of the St. Mary's River
as a result of the erection of two hydroelectric plants and a steel mill.

Logging in the region proceeded in a similar cross-border fashion
among the Ojibwa and Métis. They had always sold their logs to passing steamships and to storekeepers, whether the boats or businesses
were Canadian or American. If this meant British Canadian harvests
were sold to US store owners or vice versa, the Native people did not
much care. The British Canadian and US governments, however, viewed
matters differently. Both government and church representatives tried to
capitalize on the issue of access to timber resources and points of sale
to control the Ojibwa. In 1835, the Roman Catholics of Sault Ste. Marie
sent a petition to Lieutenant-Governor Sir John Colbourne requesting government intervention to prevent Anglican deacon and British Indian
agent William McMurray from interfering with the cutting and sale of timber into the US for the construction of a Catholic church. The petitioners noted that McMurray's actions violated Chief Shingwaukonse's
authority to regulate community access to resources.[50] The petitioners
failed to realize that McMurray was acting not only on sectarian motives
but on behalf of Upper Canadian government interests in his attempts
to stop timber shipments.

With the passage of legislation by the United Canadas, the government formulated a policy that envisioned placing Native people in stable, settled agricultural communities. Operating within this framework,

the Indian Department deemed logging an improper form of labour because it encouraged wasteful resource use and was a seasonal activity. Nevertheless, logging remained an important source of funds for the Native community. The sale of cordword to passing British or American steamers, as well as for construction purposes on both sides of the river, increased as more and more ships and people ventured to the Sault region beginning in the 1840s. Throughout the 1850s and 1860s, various government agents arrested and jailed Ojibwa loggers for cutting timber on their own lands, meddled in contracts, or simply confiscated all harvested trees.

Despite their religious differences, Roman Catholic, Methodist, and Anglican missionaries protested these actions, but not necessarily in unity, citing the inability of the soil to sustain large-scale agriculture common in southern Upper Canada and the lack of markets for produce. Moreover, according to the missionaries, logging gave the Ojibwa a ready source of cash and encouraged industry or steady work habits, both of which the missionaries keenly tried to instill.[51] Indeed, Anglican, Catholic, and Methodist missionaries actively encouraged the Ojibwa to integrate into the emerging White cash economy through continued logging, albeit under licences issued by the Canadian government. This strategy recognized the long-standing practice of selling wood to steamers on the St. Mary's River. The passing steamers would stop alongside wharfs erected by the Ojibwa to purchase cordword for their boilers, or knees and other wood products useful in ship construction and repair.[52] Moreover, the Ojibwa, who generally subscribed to Methodism, regularly sold berries, maple sugar, and crafts, as well as logs, to P. Church, a fellow Methodist and storekeeper on Sugar Island, Michigan.[53] The cash earned by these endeavours went toward subsistence, farm improvements, and supplies for the next season's logging activities.

In the face of a growing lumbering business on the Garden River reserve and evidence of Ojibwa success, Upper Canada stuck fast to its belief in the benefits of farming. The government sent seed to the Reverend James Chance of the Church of England for distribution to those willing to farm, while at the same time imposing timber regulations designed to frustrate Ojibwa participation in the growing lumber industry on the Great Lakes. For instance, in 1862, William Spragge, Deputy Superintendent General of Indian Affairs, informed his agents that an order-in-council granted the Department of Indian Affairs the authority to administer Native logging. The government, considering reports from an investigator sent by the New England Company, concluded that the

Indians were misusing and thus wasting a valuable resource. The New England Company's investigator, Hector Lister, stated that the Indians "had not allotted the land among the different families," which meant that "any man could cut timber where he liked, and sell it for a mere nothing to the first speculator."[54] Thus he argued that government regulation of lumbering would place the Indian "on the same footing as the white men" and protect the valuable timber resource from being squandered by those who lacked rights to the reserve.[55] Ironically, it was the Department of Indian Affairs that was squandering the Garden River band's timber resources by irresponsibly leasing lands to non-Native lumbering interests at lower rates than those set for non-reserve Crown lands.

To ensure that the department's plans for the Indians and their resources were successful, Lands Agent Joseph Wilson was ordered to ensure that the Natives did not cut more trees than they needed for fuel, fencing, or construction. If the Ojibwa desired to sell the cut logs, a licence would have to be issued by Wilson. The stated object of the regulations was to "impress forcibly upon the Indians ... the right to sell which (for their own benefit) was neither their Grandfathers, nor theirs, nor their children, but whenever sold, must be made the means, as their land when it is sold, of yielding a permanent Fund for the support, education, and advancement of their and their people for all time to come."[56] In 1864, the Canadian legislature clarified the regulations by "empower[ing] the Governor-General in Council to deal with Indian lands and timber as with the Crown lands and timber. Indians at Garden River are now ... required to pay all the dues and taxes imposed upon lumber men on the Crown lands; and a license is insisted upon before the Indians can cut timber on their own reserve."[57] All contracts between the Ojibwa and non-Natives were now subject to ministerial approval. Failure to obtain a licence could result in the confiscation of timber, a jail sentence, and/or the cessation of annuity payments.[58] Moreover the minister of Indian Affairs had the right to set the price that Ojibwa loggers would be paid for the timber—often at a lower rate than that being paid to Euro-Canadian loggers. Meanwhile, the Ojibwa living on the American side of the St. Mary's River earned approximately US$8,000 in one year making and moving boat knees, telegraph poles, and cedar posts.[59]

In response to government policies, missionaries in the region and their churches protested the unfair treatment, arguing that government restrictions would unduly impoverish the Ojibwa. Jesuit Father Auguste Kohler supported François Biron, a Métis who maintained residency on both sides of the river, when he was arrested for illegally cutting timber. Reverend George McDougall helped Garden River members sell timber to S. E. Harvey, US canal engineer, that would be used in the construction of the American shipping canal.[60] Similarly, Reverend Chance threatened to inform the Christian public of the government's activities at Garden River after three residents were sent to the penitentiary for inciting Native unrest—essentially, they were logging and encouraging others to do the same.[61] The missionaries also attempted to obtain timber leases where their Indians could log legally. The New England Company even forwarded £5 to assist three individuals of good character in obtaining licences from the Canadian government.[62]

From 1864 to 1869, Crown Lands Agent Joseph Wilson and Indian Agent Charles Dupont sought to intervene in the sale of Garden River reserve timber to US citizen and shopkeeper Mr. Church. The sale of timber across the border also put into issue the question of the chief's authority and access to resources. Chief Ogista of Garden River complained of unfair treatment when he noted that Mr. Maitland, a friend of Crown Lands Agent Wilson, had sold timber to Mr. Church on Sugar Island.[63] This practice of selling timber to US residents had been pioneered by the Ojibwa long before Whites asserted their interest in the trade. Even so, Wilson regularly confiscated Ojibwa logs destined for sale to the American merchant.[64] In 1864, one year after Wilson's interdiction of Chief Nebenagoching and his followers' US timber trade, the government chose to focus on the money being generated by the sale of ships' knees, shingle-timber, and other products by Ogista to Mr. Church. Little note was taken of White activities. Despite government efforts to halt the sales, the band(s) continued to sell timber to the US side with or without licences.[65]

## Conclusions

The Sault region emerged as a borderland as British Canadians and Americans sought to extend their control to the north and west in North America. However, throughout much of the nineteenth century, British Canadian and American authorities were unable to control their respective territories around the Sault. Where incoming settlers, resident settlers, traders, Métis, and Anishinabeg attempted to negotiate their place in the emerging order on the ground, outside authorities increasingly intervened to pursue their own agendas. While I did not deal with how the non-Native settlers attempted to circumvent the border, it is apparent that they too were affected by its creation and adopted strategies to circumvent its impact. Indeed, without making distinctions as to race, when the initial boundary survey was being made in the 1820s, government commissioners warned that it would be difficult to establish an effective border control over the region's population. This control even to this day remains limited—residents on both sides of the border regularly engage in smuggling goods and services across the boundary. Current controls, while curtailing some of the more blatant aspects of local efforts to "save a buck," are still proving largely ineffective in controlling smuggling and cross-border traffic in the region. It is this eighteenth-century line in the water that continues to artificially divide the people of the Sault. While the European settlers have assumed different identities, the Métis and Ojibwa of the region continue to struggle with the insistence that they become either American or Canadian. Likewise, recent US efforts to police the border in an effort to halt the drug and human trade, as well as counter potential terrorist threats, will continue to falter when faced with human ingenuity, local determination, and the artificiality of the boundary drawn upon ever-moving water.

Thus the border through the St. Mary's River, while serving to define whether one has entered Canadian or American claimed space, is as fluid and as subject to cross-currents as the waters on which it is drawn. The border's presence, now as in the nineteenth century, proffers benefits and poses obstacles to the people that it purports to separate. For the Ojibwa, it remains an outside imposition that divides their homeland, their community, and their kin.

# IN THE SHADOW OF THE THUMPING DRUM
## The Sault Métis—The People In-Between

＊＋＝ ≍◊≋ ＋＊

ALAN KNIGHT
JANET E. CHUTE

I went to rest last night with the heavy murmuring sound of the falls in my ears, broken at short intervals by the busy thump-thump-thump of the Indian drum ...
—Henry Rowe Schoolcraft, Sault Ste. Marie, 8 July 1822

## The Origins of the Sault Métis to 1828

A prevailing perspective has been that Sault Ste. Marie was little more than a retirement village for petty merchants and former voyageurs (known commonly as the "comers and goers"), a sheltered haven away from the vicissitudes of the trading world. From as far away as the Red River, the Sault was viewed as a minor player in the métis community of the Great Lakes, an area that itself constituted an inchoate entity "snuffed out" after 1814, when it lost its utility as an intermediary between encroaching metropolitan powers and hinterland indigenous populations.[1] Our work reviews this thesis and argues that, owing to an unusual sequence of events, the Sault Ste. Marie métis community, instead of dying out or subsisting as a politically and culturally sterile backwater, actually revitalized itself after the War of 1812. In its energized state, it contributed substantially to the vitality and resilience of the broader Native milieu.

Before examining this contention closely, it is necessary to explain this study's specialized use of the two terms, "métis" and "Métis." Our use of the uncapitalized métis denotes the population of mixed Native and European ancestry residing in the Upper Great Lakes area, as distinct from the capitalized Métis, which refers to the *New Métis Nation* that burst upon the Red River scene in 1816.[2]

George Woodcock has contended that Victorians regarded the Red River Métis as a rootless and improvident race, so divorced from their French antecedents that they literally became devoid of culture: a "transitional and traditionless people."[3] The métis community dwelling near the St. Mary's River rapids (Sault Ste. Marie) was not born out of cultural chaos but rather in relationships fostered and nurtured over two hundred years of prior occupation. During the French era, *métissage* left a lasting stamp on Native society. Individual métis, raised within or otherwise still attached to the Native community, were unusually cognizant of their mixed ancestry. Ojibwe annals kept tabs on the activities of all group members. A German visitor to Lake Superior, Johann Georg Kohl, wrote about Ojibwe chroniclers who knew exactly if a girl had married outside the band, to whom, the reasons for her so doing, and whether a child had been born. By providing a basis for the regularized inclusion of métis into Ojibwe society, these mechanisms endowed individuals of mixed ancestry with a sense of identity even during the tumultuous transition accompanying the fall of the French regime and the rise of the British presence in the Upper Great Lakes arena. Influential métis individuals aided the British in understanding and complying with Native demands for continuance of the cultural "middle ground" of formalized Native–White interrelations developed prior to 1763.[4] By the time Britain and the United States had come to offer annuity payments in return for land cessions, J. G. Kohl noted, bands could determine to what degree a métis person was "related to the tribe, and how far he/she [had] a claim to share in the [government] tribute."[5]

Middle ground tenets also influenced Britain's drafting of the terms of the Royal Proclamation of 10 October 1763, gauged to regulate land transactions between Native and non-Native on the frontier. Despite its prohibitions on individuals bargaining for Aboriginal territory, such compacts were made with considerable regularity at the Sault.[6] One of the earliest was a land agreement contracted between Jean Baptiste Cadotte Sr. (b. 1723 in Batiscan, Trois-Rivières, Quebec) and a head chief named Kitche Okanejeed (Gitcheojeedebun), or "Great Crane."[7] Great Crane's grant entitled Cadotte to unmolested residence on a French seigneury held from 1750 to 1759 by Louis Legardeur de Repentigny (1721–1786) and Louis de Bonne, Sieur de Missegle (ca. 1717–1760). His tenure to his trading establishment secure,[8] Cadotte occupied de Repentigny's fort until his own death, which occurred sometime between 1803 and 1812. Among the Ojibwe, Cadotte was known as "a great village orator," and "Fort Cadotte" remained the sole European feature on the landscape for many years.

At Michilimackinac, on 28 October 1756, Cadotte married Marie (Catherine) Athanasie, a Nipissing woman (an Equaysayway or "Travelling woman"), who bore him at least two daughters, including Marie-Renee (1756–1786) and Marie-Charlotte (1758–1769), and two sons, Jean Baptiste and Michael.[9] Recognizing that the richest trapping grounds at this time extended westward from the headwaters of the Mississippi, Cadotte travelled annually to this region. Between 1762 and 1765, he and Alexander Henry (1739–1824) established both eastern and western extensions to their business concerns: to the east, on the south side of St. Joseph's Island at the entrance to the St. Mary's River; and to the west, at La Pointe, Wisconsin, and Red Lake in what was later the state of Minnesota. In 1770, they spent the winter at Grand Portage and trapped the region west of Lake Superior.[10] Cadotte eventually joined with the North West Company (NWC) in 1796 as their agent at Fond du Lac.

His son, Jean Baptiste Cadotte Jr. (1761–1818) was educated in Montreal at the Sulpician College of Saint-Raphael (1773–1780) (where he was an honour student from 1776 to 1780) and married the métis daughter of Sault fur trader Joseph Piquette,[11] Marie Janette Piquette (1780–1859), also called Sangemanqua,[12] by whom he had three children. Early in life, Jean Baptiste Jr. gained a reputation as a fiddle player and was much in demand at local dances. Involved in trading southwest of Lake Superior and west into the Dakotas, from the fort he had constructed in 1798 at the junction of the Red and Clearwater rivers in Minnesota, he rarely spent long periods at the Sault.[13] He did attain a degree of status when he was accepted into a partnership in the NWC in 1801 (1/46 share) but was dismissed two years later due to habitual drunkenness and placed on a NWC pension of one hundred pounds a year. From 1808 to 1817, Cadotte was employed as an interpreter at the British military post on St. Joseph Island and played a prominent part in the attack on Fort Mackinac.

Younger brother Michael (1764–1837),[14] popularly known as Kechelmeshane or "Le Grande Michel," married Ossinahjeeunoqua (Equaysaway, or Marie Madeline) of La Pointe, the daughter of Waubojeeg[15] (The White Fisher), in 1787, set up trade near his father-in-law's encampment and later rebuilt the Old French Fort on the Madeleine Islands in Wisconsin. He also had posts at Courte Oreille, and on the

Wisconsin, Chippeway, and St. Croix rivers. In 1798, it was estimated that Michael Cadotte was doing $40,000 in annual business at Grand Portage. That year he joined forces with the NWC and was placed in charge of their post on the Tortue River in the Fond du Lac District. He transferred his business concerns at La Pointe to his sons-in-law, Truman and Lyman Warren of Massachusetts, in 1823. For the next fifteen years, Lyman Warren worked for the American Fur Company (AFC)[16] as chief factor at La Pointe, which soon replaced Sault Ste. Marie as the AFC's centre of operations on Lake Superior. Truman Warren, known as "the Prince," died in 1825 of pneumonia.

By the late 1780s, the Cadottes' picketed fort at Sault Ste. Marie was flanked by seven traders' houses.[17] Most of the inhabitants were French (and some were only seasonal):the Cadottes, Jean Baptiste Nolin; Jean Baptiste LaChausse; Pierre Parrent; Joseph DuChene; Jean Baptiste, Laurent and Lavoine Barthe; Francois Cameraire; Joseph Piquette and his son Francois; Jean Baptiste Perrault, and one merchant of Irish extraction, John Sayers. In return for their merchandise, they traded not only fur but fish, vegetables, corn, maple products, preserves, and game.[18] Under the provisions of the Quebec Act of 1774, which extended French civil law to the Upper Great Lakes region, French fathers and their métis offspring operated within a milieu that sustained their French identity despite British dominance of the upper fur-trade echelons. Knowledge that certain French Canadian bourgeois could amass sizable fortunes[19] further sustained a subtle French nationalism among French residents and their métis offspring, geographically separated but not entirely divorced from their Lower Canadian heritage.

Another noticeable trend was the ability of several Sault traders to form long-term relationships with Native women of high status, a few of whom played important intermediary roles during times of major historical transition in the region.[20] Jean Baptiste Cadotte Sr.'s first wife Athanasie saved Alexander Henry's life following the Native capture of Michilimackinac in 1763 by interceding with her kinsman Madjeckewiss (1735–1805), who had instigated the attack.[21] Jean Baptiste Nolin's (ca. 1742–1826) métis wife, Marie-Angelique Couvret, helped her husband in 1794 obtain land at the rapids through her kinship ties to the Sault band.[22] British traders who emulated the French in this respect reaped similar benefits. Dr. David Mitchell's (1750–1832) wife Elizabeth Bertrand, a woman of French and Odawa ancestry, recruited Odawa military assistance from l'Arbre Croche during the War of 1812, and afterwards ran a retail business in her own right on Mackinac Island while her husband acted as chief medical practitioner at the British post on nearby Drummond Island.[23]

Even more striking were the actions of Oshasuguscodaywayqua, or Woman of the Green Prairie (1772–1843), who in 1793 became Susan, the wife of John Johnston (1762–1828), a member of the Irish gentry.[24] Mrs. Johnston not only carried on a commercial sugar-making and fur-trading operation in her own right but, when her husband was absent in Ireland in 1820, demonstrated exceptional negotiating acumen by quelling a volatile situation between an American military party and the Ojibwe at the rapids.[25] Her incisive commands, heeded because she was the daughter of the aforementioned Waubojeeg (The White Fisher), restored harmony after Sassaba or Ussaba, a head man (and Chief Shingabowo'ssin's younger brother), threatened to injure the Americans.[26]

Johnston was a relative latecomer to the rapids, yet, when he first arrived in 1791, the Sault presented the same lack of occupational diversity as it had when Alexander Henry first encountered it thirty years before.[27] Johnston was one of the first English-speaking residents at the Sault. As an employee of the firm of Todd and McGill, he had initiated a trading operation at La Pointe in the 1790s. For most of his career, Johnston regarded himself as an independent trader, sending his furs to the Jewish merchant David David of Montreal (beginning in 1792), where he obtained his supplies and trading goods, and visited periodically, often to attend meetings at the prestigious Beaver Club. He and Susan had seven children.[28] Like the French traders, Johnston sent his sons Lewis and George to school in Montreal and, although their attendance was irregular, George gained a reputation locally for his literacy and fluency in French, English, and Ojibwe. The youngest, John McDougall Johnston, with the aid of Ramsey Crooks of the American Fur Company, attended school in Lewis County, New York State. Unlike his French neighbours, John Johnston was a learned man and possessed an extensive library from which he instructed his children in the academic subjects while his wife taught them the Ojibwe language, culture, and household skills. Later commentators have remarked on the interesting lilt to the adult Johnstons' spoken English, which revealed the influence of their father's Irish accent. Though the Johnston establishment was an unimposing clapboard frame structure set back from the rapids, the nature and breadth of the Johnston family's Native kinship relationships endowed it with formidable political force in the Upper Great Lakes region.

In the years prior to the War of 1812, other British incomers, among them John Askin (1739–1815), who served as commissionaire at Michili-mackinac in the 1760s, relied on established French trading families like the Barthes to promote their own economic and social careers. After begetting two daughters and a son, John Jr. (1762–1820), by an Odawa woman from l'Arbre Croche, John Askin married Archange Barthe[29] in 1772 and retired to Detroit where he died.[30] Askin's extended family included Jean Baptiste Barthe (1753–1827),[31] Askin's forwarding agent at Sault Ste. Marie,[32] and Jean Baptiste's brothers, Laurent, Louis, and Levoine. Their kin network had a covert side. In the spring of 1778, Jean Baptiste Barthe noted in his account book that he was supporting an Ojibwe woman with a son by the name of Lavoine, the same name as his younger brother.[33] When his brother Lavoine[34] left for the Wisconsin Portage later the same year, the young boy remained with his mother at the Sault where they continued to receive assistance from the Barthe and Askin families. This was a common practice: total abandonment was unusual, particularly given the close monitoring of births and deaths by the Native community. As the boy grew to manhood, he became known both as Augustus Lavoine and Lavoine Barthe, though he mainly went by his Ojibwe name Shingwaukonse, or Little Pine (1773–1854).[35] Little Pine's career advanced in stages, from trading chief, orator, warrior, Native religious practitioner, and finally to a Sault head chief.

Little Pine's knowledge of his métis ancestry benefitted him in later life as it granted him latitude to choose among dual identities in the negotiating forum.[36] Such certainly was also the case for Nebenai-gooching (1808–1899),[37] also known as Joseph Sayer or Sayers, a métis grandson of Sault trader Jean Baptiste Perrault (1761–1844).[38] Perrault's daughter, Isabell, reputedly had married Wabejejauk (The White Crane), the head chief at the Sault who was killed, along with his brother Kab-mosah, at Fort George in the War of 1812. Nebenaigooching and his bereaved mother claimed the attentions of both the trader and the Native communities, who jointly took them under their wing. In 1819, British authorities on Drummond Island, knowing the boy's background, vested him with the chiefly status and the medals held by his late father, even though he was only "eight" (eleven) years old at the time.[39] Nebe-naigooching always lived a métis lifestyle. As a young man, he spent several years in the Fond du Lac region, reputedly with John Sayers's métis sons, especially John Charles Sayers (1780–1838), of La Pointe, as well as Jean Baptiste Cadotte Sr.'s son Joseph Cadotte (b. 1788), and probably Shingwaukonse.

Nebenaigooching had adopted the surname "Sayers" from the Irish trader John Sayers (1750–1818).[40] Sayers began as an agent for Joseph Howard at Mackinac and was active independently in the Fond du Lac trade at Red Lake and Leech Lake, Minnesota, as early as 1778. He later worked in association with Jean Baptiste Cadotte Sr. and Jean Baptiste Perrault. John Sayers wed Obemauunoqua (also called Marie or Bionne-quay), the daughter of Chief Mamongeseda (Mamongazida, Loon's Foot, or Big Foot) of La Pointe and sister to Waubojeeg (Little Pine's, Marie Cadotte's and Susan Johnston's aunt). From the late 1770s to the early 1780s, intricate kin networks of this nature replicated themselves over time. By his first wife, Sayers had at least two daughters and three sons, the best known being Pierre Guillaume.[41] By 1790, Sayers and his family occupied a commodious dwelling at the Sault on a large lot with an extensive garden.[42]

Sometime in 1806 or 1807, a new face, Charles Oakes Ermatinger (1776–1833),[43] entered the Sault arena, after having been stationed with the North West Company (NWC) near Winnipeg and along the North Saskatchewan River under the supervision of William McKay. In 1799, Ermatinger had been employed, in secret, by John Ogilvy[44] in connection with the newly formed New North West Company (sometimes called the XY Company), to fathom future business prospects in the Fond du Lac area. Charles Oakes was the son of the Swiss-born Montreal merchant Lawrence Ermatinger (1736–1789), who arrived in Canada in 1760 and soon became involved in the fur trade through the influence of his brother-in-law, Forrest Oakes (d. 1783).[45] Oakes, along with partners Peter Pangman, Joseph Fulton, and Charles Boyer, was active at Michilimackinac (1761), at Sault Ste. Marie, and at the Grand Portage near the head of Lake Superior between 1771 and 1781. Charles's father also provided the financial backing for Richard Dobie's initial exploration of the Fort Temiscamingue region in 1767 and other independent traders such as Charles Larche, William Shaw, James Finlay, John Gregory, and Isaac Taylor.

Appointed the NWC agent at the Sault, Charles Oakes Ermatinger leased Jean Baptiste Nolin's trading establishment, which included a very fine house and large wharf. Around 1800, he took a fifteen-year-old Ojibwe girl named Charlotte (1785–1850), daughter of Chief Katawbidai (Broken Tooth or De Brechedent) (1750–1828)[46] of Sandy Lake in the Fond du Lac district, as his country wife, by whom he eventually had thirteen children.[47] In 1807, Ermatinger left the NWC and relied upon his father-in-law's kin networks to advance his trade southwest of Lake Superior. His reliance on Sandy Lake kin connections was later emulated by Samuel Ashmun (1799–1866), the AFC's agent at l'Anse (1818–1824), and Lac de Flambeau, who, in 1824, wed Keneesequa or (Nancy), the youngest daughter of Katawabidai.[48] William Aitkin (1785–1851),[49] an AFC partner who eventually turned independent trader, also followed Ermatinger's lead after he married Charles Oakes Ermatinger's daughter Marguerite, while Charles's nephew, James Rough Ermatinger (1808–1866), married the widowed Charlotte Cadotte Warren (1805–1887), daughter of "Le Grande Michel." James Rough Ermatinger's mother was Catherine McKee, the granddaughter of John Askin and daughter of Therese Askin and Thomas McKee (1770–1814) (superintendent of Indian Affairs for the Northwest Department, 1796–1814).

Given the resilience of this trading society, it is not surprising that traders' offspring evinced considerable aptitude as interpreters, recruiters of Native military strength in time of war, and diplomats in time of peace. Jean Baptiste Cadotte Jr. rose to become one of the most accurate, and hence the most sought-after, interpreters in the Lake Superior region.[50] John Askin Jr. (1762–1820), along with his son Jean-Baptiste Askin (1788–1869) and several of the Johnstons, served the British Indian Department. At the close of the War of 1812, all métis spoke Ojibwe, the language of trade,[51] employed totemic representations derived from their mothers' clan affiliations, appropriated Native clothing traits into their own wardrobes, and occasionally participated in Native religious and medicinal practices.[52] Though this early nineteenth-century trading society still showed signs of affluence, powerful, irreversible forces undermined its economic viability. In 1817, Washington banned British trade from American soil, and the AFC was left to command the trade along the southern shores of the Great Lakes.[53] John Johnston, whose fortunes diminished when his establishment was burned to the ground during the war, nevertheless continued to trade owing to his ties to the AFC and his Native kin networks.[54] Charles Oakes Ermatinger also thrived, due to his Ojibwe father-in-law's willingness to run furs down to his establishment en route to the British present distribution on Drummond Island. In 1822, the trader still felt financially secure enough to construct a sizable stone house on the British shoreline, along with a large wharf, storehouse, windmill, and grist and saw mills. For others, however, especially many métis youths, the future looked bleaker.

Although he was appointed a militia captain, along with Johnston and Ermatinger, among others, for the attack on Fort Michlimackinac in 1812,[55] Jean Baptiste Nolin was too ill to engage in the battle; but his sons

Augustin and Louis were placed in command of a small group of Ojibwe warriors. After the war, Louis served as an interpreter at the Red River Settlement and, in 1816, Lord Selkirk sent a personal invitation to Louis' father to join the struggling community. In 1818, Augustin Nolin, along with his son Francis from the British shore, and accompanied by Native kinfolk from Fond du Lac, joined with Alexis Xavier Biron in signing a one-year agreement with the HBC to oppose the NWC near Michipicoten.[56] This arrangement could only be temporary, since dwindling fur resources made long-term compacts between large trapping parties untenable. To leave their graciously furnished household[57] must have been a difficult choice, yet the following summer Jean Baptiste and Augustin left permanently to join Louis for Red River, where, in 1820, they received grants of three choice pieces of land in the Assiniboia.[58] Jean Baptiste's eldest son, Adolphe, had married John Sayer's daughter Julie and moved to Penetanguishene where he plied his trade as a tinsmith.

Others chose to stay and seek or create new opportunities. Alexis Xavier Biron (1787–1866) had met his wife, Angelique Cadotte (1794–1885), at Rice Lake in Wisconsin, where most of his children were born.[59] Biron, Joseph Boisseneau, Joseph LeFond, and at least one of the Nolins had accompanied Colonel William McKay and Captain Thomas Anderson for the retaking of Prairie du Chein, Wisconsin, in 1814. Biron returned to the Sault and settled on a plot reserved for him in 1815 by the written permission of Major Winniet, the British commander at Drummond Island, in return for his participation in the war. Biron proved occupationally versatile, for soon he was supplementing his trading income by commercial fishing and, later, by running a small ferry service across the St. Mary's channel. Both were a major remove from the lucrative enterprise he once had carried on at Fond du Lac, yet, despite financial setbacks, his prestige as a community leader remained intact. Biron exhibited an aristocratic demeanour, which earned him the sobriquet "Lord Biron."[60] In 1823, HBC Factor John Siveright noted that he was still affluent enough to drive around in an elegant carriole even though "he has given up the Collectorship[?]" and "his means of supporting rank" were diminishing.[61] Until his death, the patriarch of the Biron family remained well respected by all sectors of the Sault.

Like Biron, Joseph Boissoneau Sr. (1786–1866)[62] also demonstrated a range of occupational proclivities. Once a skilled tradesman in the service of the HBC, he proved such an impressive carpenter that he later became a construction contractor for the first Roman Catholic church, Sacred Heart, at the British Sault.[63] Boissoneau had numerous children by two wives: the first was a Cree métis from Red River named Marguerite Guilmont and the second a Native woman, Ninon Metous (Naawe Metas).[64] His descendants intermarried with the Birons, a pattern of association that continued down through several generations. The Boissoneaus continued to cherish French historical traditions, values, and skills. They may have acquired the trader and voyageur disposition to eschew intensive farming,[65] but they proved excellent horticulturists. Joseph Boissoneau was "celebrated for his roses, the true provence roses from Provence in France"[66]—obviously emblematic of his pride in his French roots.

The lives of Alexis Xavier Biron and Joseph Boissoneau spanned momentous transitions in Upper Great Lakes history. Since the 1790s, formerly workable cultural accommodations between Native and non-Native had been deteriorating in the face of severe intercompany competition.[67] The union of the HBC and NWC in 1821 relegated the Sault to little more than a supply depot. Many former Nor'Westers and their métis offspring found themselves economically destitute in the wake of company retrenchment. The impact of this abrupt transition proved profound. Sayers's abandoned establishment with its reputedly magnificent garden burned to the ground in 1818. Symbolic of the decay of the old order, the Nolin house, once a prominent landmark on the southern shores of the rapids, by 1820 stood in a decrepit condition. Soon to be torn down to make way for Fort Brady, it temporarily accommodated American military officers and their families.

## Revitalization of the Métis Community on the British Shore, 1829 to 1849

John Johnston's military burial in 1828 signified, for many at the Sault, the end of an era.[68] The fur trade had recruited men of extraordinary resilience and internal fortitude and, after 1828, only a few belonging to the old order remained. One such man was John Dugald Cameron (1777–1851),[69] who had been a partner with the NWC, and as the HBC's chief factor at LaCloche had competed with George Johnston and David Mitchell's sons for scarce furs. Like Johnston before him, Cameron possessed an inquiring mind, furnished his frontier quarters with an excellent library,[70] supported the education of his sons to the best of his ability, yet he did not drive them to attain a status far above that of their métis counterparts, nor did he force them to function in an uncongenial milieu.[71]

Cameron's two sons, James Dugald (1806–1861) and William (b. 1808) attended Upper Canada College and were trained for the Anglican priesthood. Upon arriving in the Sault in 1832, however, James Dugald found the Baptists more appealing,[72] and for three years he worked as a lay preacher along the eastern shore of Lake Superior before his ordination as a Baptist minister by the Reverend Abel Bingham at Sault Ste. Marie on 5 June 1836. In 1835, he had married a daughter of Chief Shingabaw'ossin,[73] and he became the principal organizer of the giant revival meetings jointly sponsored by the Presbyterians, Methodists, and Baptists, held in open fields on the south shore of the St. Mary's River and at Whitefish Point. William Cameron, who owned nearly fifteen acres of land in the British Sault (1843–1845), also resided south of the border on Sugar Island, where he married Sophia, a great-granddaughter of Jean Baptiste Nolin.[74] Cameron's sister Marie, meanwhile, married John Sayers's son, Henry, and his niece, Mary, daughter of William Clouston, HBC factor at Michipicoten, and Elizabeth Cameron, married the Reverend Gustavus Anderson,[75] son of Thomas Anderson, Upper Canada's northern superintendent of Indian Affairs, and grandson of David and Elizabeth Mitchell. Under the terms of the American Fond du Lac Treaty of 1826, the Johnstons each obtained a section of land on Sugar Island from the United States government,[76] and William Cameron and Marie Sayers settled near them.[77] Sugar Island presented an enclave where the métis could examine their identity vis-à-vis others in the Upper Great Lakes area.[78] This was necessary, for the Sault was not isolated from ephemeral wildcat schemes such as "General [James] Dickson's[79] plan" in 1836 to establish a Native state in Texas.[80] This expedition attracted sons of the old Nor'Westers, including such men as John George McKenzie, John McLoughlin Jr., Martin McLeod, Alexander Roderick McLeod Jr., and Charles McBean, the son of John McBean, the HBC chief factor stationed at LaCloche, but most of the Sault Ste. Marie métis ignored inducements to join such ill-fated enterprises.[81]

By the middle of the nineteenth century, the majority of elderly traders and retired métis voyageurs who headed families at the British Sault had coalesced into a tight-knit community. They maintained a strict system of allocating land rights that reflected norms transferred from Lower Canada. Although they ubiquitously and outwardly espoused Roman Catholicism, their religion proved a syncretistic mix of interdenominational Christianity[82] and Native practices. The Roman Catholic community lacked a neighbourhood church, and although itinerant priests arrived periodically from the American side[83] and a few pious souls made the regular Sunday river crossing for mass, burial practices collectively evidenced strong Ojibwe traits. American journalist and poet William Cullen Bryant noted, "Some of the graves were covered with a low roof of cedar bark, others with a wooden box; over others was placed a little house like a dog-kennel, except that it had no door; others were covered with little log cabins." A cross usually stood in front, "some of them inscribed with the names of the dead, not always correctly spelled."[84] Clothing reflected a combination of European and Native traits. A well-dressed gentleman disported a *capot*, calico shirt, leggings, moccasins, finger-woven sash, and a silk turban around his head. During one of his visits to a métis cabin, Bryant noted that "we were received with great appearance and deference by a woman of decidedly Indian features, but light complexioned, barefoot with blue embroidered legging falling over her ankles and sweeping the floor, the only peculiarity of Indian costume about her. The house was clean as a scouring could make it, and her two little children, with French physiognomies, were fairer than many children of the European race … they speak Canadian French, more or less, but generally employ Chippewa language in their intercourse with each other."[85] There was a diversity of educational standards. Most residents were illiterate; yet educated polyglot residents, among these Alexis Xavier Biron, Jean Baptiste Perrault, and Jean Baptiste Cadotte Jr., could speak Ojibwe, French, and English, and write some Latin. The Cameron brothers were reputedly reasonably fluent in Greek and Hebrew.

Since the chief means of transportation was by water rather than road, settlement at the Sault was confined chiefly to the riverfront. Approximately thirty wooden dwellings flanked the north shore on marshy ground, in what would soon become the first concession, south of Wellington Street. These structures, constructed of vertically driven cedar pickets and occasionally covered with clapboard, were small but comfortable even in winter. Cedar bark provided roofing material, and clay and mud plaster coated the inside walls. In front of these, "clinker-built" pointers (a smaller, narrower version of the old York boat) and bark canoes were drawn up on the beach alongside wooden storehouses, which housed nets and other paraphernalia used in the fishery. Lots were arranged in a similar pattern to the *rang* settlement "strip lots" along the St. Lawrence Valley. The frontages on the St. Mary's River were narrow. Lots were bought, sold, rented, or kept for absentee residents by close kin. Territorial boundaries were strictly respected. Behind, fields trailed northward, melding into common grazing pasturage and reserved lots where every settler had the right to claim a "hay privilege" for winter silage. Unlike the usufructuary practices adopted by the Western Métis, a Sault family vacating a lot for a number of years rarely returned to find others occupying their land in the family's absence.[86]

Community leaders were expected to evince a magnanimous spirit regardless of vicissitudes, and all echelons participated equally in an arduous round of economic activities. Since critical resources were seasonal, time was of the essence. Maple sugaring began in April, after which fences had to be repaired in readiness for potato planting. Whitefish runs at the rapids in the spring and fall proved exceptionally busy times, for after the economic dislocations of the early 1800s, fishing had emerged as the financial mainstay of the community. Whitefish prices soared to five dollars a barrel and trout to four dollars in response to demand from White frontier settlements in Ohio and Illinois, which, still lacking a secure agricultural base, had to rely on fish for subsistence.[87]

During the summer, women gathered berries, which they made into preserves both for domestic use and for sale. Young men engaged in trade transactions, outfitted brigades, joined exploring expeditions, transported mail, and, when home, entertained friends and neighbours. All respected the independence of others, in keeping with prominent Ojibwe values. When not away guiding, trading, visiting, or engaging in fishing, both sexes sold maple sugar products, handicrafts, furs, timber, preserves, firewood, and produce from their vegetable gardens—potatoes, turnips, pumpkins, and some corn—to American interests and passing tourists. A number of merchants, whose offspring eventually intermarried with the métis community, resided on nearby Sugar Island, among them Philetus Swift Church,[88] John Sebastian, Michael J. Payment, Henry Leask, and Malcolm McKerchie. These men maintained connections with Michigan, New York, Ohio, and Illinois, and so provided the métis with a wide range of market options.

Haying took place in late summer on the beaver marshes and meadows east of the Sault, as few of the community lots provided enough pasturage to supply enough animal fodder and straw bedding over the winter for a family's small cattle herd, a horse or two, a few pigs, and flock of fowl.[89] The métis diet consisted of fish, pork, chicken, potatoes, onions, garlic, dried meat and fish, pemmican, a bread made from corn (or bannock if the dough was fried), and occasionally, barley, turnips, and peas. Game (ducks, pigeons, partridge, rabbits, deer, and moose) was common, and women proved resourceful in making jam and jellied preserves of various wild berries and fruits. The winter's supply of fish was taken near Thessalon,[90] at Grand Batture (near present-day Blind River) and eastward along the Lake Huron shoreline. Surpluses were sold to purchase flour, tea, clothing, and other necessities.[91] Younger men headed out on winter traplines, but, unlike the Ojibwe, did not maintain a hunting territory system. Older men stayed near home looking after the animals, collecting firewood, and fishing for herring under the ice. Older women were often left to care for the younger children.[92] At any time of the year, men engaged in blacksmithing, making sleighs, building houses, and constructing canoes and wooden fishing boats. Younger family members generally took care of their elders, and the indigent usually received some measure of community support. Residents would turn out for a barn raising or aid others in time of crisis. As one resident stated somewhat nostalgically years later, "They made their own laws, rules and regulations which each one observed as there was no white people in the Soo now so called by the Canadians in those days."[93]

Almost all of these métis could adopt an Ojibwe identity if such promoted their interests. It appears that members of the Cadotte family, regardless of their complexion or whether or not they had been educated, could assume the mantle of "Indianness" fairly readily and act under an Ojibwe name. Many of Michael Cadotte's sons and daughters had returned to the Sault and formed a distinctive core group within the métis community. Another important extended kin unit centred on Nebenaigooching (Joseph Sayers). Although regarded by the British Indian Department as strictly Ojibwe, Nebenaigooching was fluent in French and felt equally comfortable in both the métis and the Ojibwe milieu. By contrast, Little Pine was not conversant in French, although his sons, Jean Baptiste and Pierre Lavoine Tegoosh, were and for many years preferred to identify themselves exclusively as métis. Nicknamed Tegoosh (Hardwood), "Pierre l'Avoine ... Chief's son" assisted other residents in directing petitions to Sir John Colborne and the Right Reverend Alexander Macdonell, the Roman Catholic Bishop at Kingston, for a permanent priest and materials to build a Roman Catholic chapel.[94] Between 1835 and 1850, the revitalized British Sault métis community had come to view the construction of a church as an auspicious symbol of its unity and aspirations for the future. What its members did not count on was the depth of bigotry in their own clergy[95] and the opposition they would encounter from the local Anglican missionary, William McMurray (1810–1894).

McMurray had received a generous welcome from both métis and Ojibwe on his arrival in 1832. Though he seemed even more highly esteemed after his marriage in 1833 to Charlotte Johnston (1806–1878), or Ogenebugoquay (Woman of the Wild Rose), he soon angered the métis by trying to appropriate the entire British Sault as an Anglican preserve. This was in keeping with the British idea that the Church of England was the established church, a concept that later events would prove was not applicable in Upper Canada. In 1834, he went so far as to direct a letter to Lieutenant-Governor Sir John Colborne to remove the métis, whom he branded as mere whiskey smugglers. Colborne responded by contacting two HBC factors to investigate McMurray's allegations. Chief Factor Angus Bethune[96] at Michipicoten considered the missionary's suggestion a boon: to remove the métis would mean less competition from free traders.[97] The HBC's Chief Trader at the Sault, William Nourse, also welcomed the idea but for a different reason. The métis freemen, he mused, "knowing we cannot do without them are often very saucy, to keep them in humour credits are often given to them—and money often lost." It would be more feasible to dispense with the *habitants* and employ only Ojibwe.[98]

Initially the Ojibwe believed they would prosper from an Anglican mission in their midst. The government promised to build houses and supply farming implements if they accepted the Church of the Crown. When, in 1835, Thomas G. Anderson, the British Indian superintendent, appointed Little Pine as head chief in Nebenaigooching's stead, the wily power-holder took advantage of his favoured position. He presented Anderson with a map of the coast with his jurisdiction clearly marked, and pressed the agent to recognize his territorial rights.[99] In response, Anderson and McMurray urged the Ojibwe leader to put a stop to métis cutting wood for sale to the Americans and prevent any scooping of whitefish at the rapids on the Sabbath.[100]

George Johnston and Thomas Ogista soon discovered that Little Pine's resource monitoring could work to their benefit. Upon entering the Mackinac fish trade with Ogista as his assistant, George Johnston had obtained permission from Little Pine to establish an outpost at Batchawana Bay, north of the Sault. Discovering Samuel Ashmun and John Dougald Cameron's son William taking fish at nearby Goulais Bay, Johnston reported it to Little Pine. Little Pine, in turn, contacted Chief Trader Nourse, who immediately put a stop to Ashmun's illegal venture.[101] For the métis community as a whole, however, such self-interested disputes threatened the very fabric of the cohesive, distinctive identity they were trying to nurture.

By 1835, the favouring of Protestants over Catholics at annual present distributions[102] and the HBC's backing of the mission scheme not only pitched Catholic against Protestant, but also split the formerly seamless métis community into American and British factions. The impression was, in the minds of many, that Nebenaigooching had been deprived of the status conferred on him in 1819 on the grounds that he was a Roman Catholic.[103] The métis denounced the outside interference in their vital seasonal economic affairs. McMurray's actions prolonged construction on a Roman Catholic chapel at the American Sault, which burned soon after it had been built.[104] Owing to his opposition, stones and wooden timbers also lay abandoned near the Roman Catholic graveyard on the British side.[105] Anderson also objected[106] to the formation of a separate métis community, since he was wedded to the promotion of an Ojibwe farming settlement at the rapids and the idea of an independent métis community was anathema to him. Such an enclave, he felt, would prove disruptive by encouraging illicit trading practices and prolonging reliance on fur trapping. He further arranged matters so that houses promised to the Ojibwe would be built only after the métis vacated the waterfront. If métis identity had been merely inchoate before, it now crystallized under these new pressures into a distinctive community consciousness. In response, Pierre Lavoine and several others addressed a petition to the lieutenant-governor, stressing that lines of authority at the Sault had become convoluted and contradictory. McMurray, they argued, even had contravened Little Pine's authority, since they had "previously obtained the consent of the principal chief" before beginning to construct their church.[107] On being ordered by Anderson to move to Manitoulin Island, they requested £1,800 for their strip lots, a move guaranteed to discourage the government from pursuing the issue any further.[108]

The most astute analysis of the situation at the rapids in 1835 issued from John Bell (1802–1872), an interpreter, tanner, farmer, and petty merchant, who noted that the exclusivity of the Anglican faction had destroyed the mission.[109] Bell, the son of a Scottish trader named McFarlane and an Ojibwe woman from Nipigon, maintained close associations with the Cadotte family at both La Pointe and Sault Ste. Marie. Bell and his brother Peter MacFarlane[110] had received a degree of education and John, in particular, became a proficient interpreter and shrewd trader. Both men had returned to the Sault around 1836, the year in which John entered the network of Sault kinship connections by marrying Michael Cadotte Sr.'s daughter Marie (1800–1860).[111]

The disturbing state of affairs observed by Bell did not last long. In 1837, with the outbreak of rebellion in the Canadas, Anderson was directed to abandon the removal policy and distribute gifts of food, clothing, and other items to loyal métis, as well as the Ojibwe. For a brief interlude, both groups were treated once again as allies of the British Crown rather than merely burdensome dependents or wards of the state. Little Pine seized the moment. The preceding year, Washington had advised that the southwestern Ojibwe would be removed west of the Missouri River within twenty years. Aware that these Ojibwe were also suffering from scarcity of game and fur-bearing animals, the chief devised a visionary plan to relocate them on British soil, and he used the 1837 present distribution as a forum in which to announce his new scheme. Adopting his métis identity, he declared, "I went last year to the Head Waters of Lake Superior to a friend (a half-breed like myself) to inform him of how good our Great Father was,"[112] inferring that the British should encourage this proposed backwash of peoples from the frontier. Rather than depend on outsiders for favours that never materialized,[113] he continued, Native people should work together to build a large, unified community in which Ojibwe and métis would play integral roles.[114] For the next two years, Little Pine journeyed westward to the headwaters of the Mississippi, recruiting further support for his Native settlement scheme.[115]

For educated métis, the very civilization they had been expected to respect and emulate granted them little peace. With time, incoming settlers introduced a new perspective on the Upper Great Lakes social order, which drew a strict dichotomy between White and Native, and then drained the latter of positive substance and potential. The Bells, Camerons, Cadottes, and Johnstons, in an effort to challenge the derogatory barbs cast at persons of Native ancestry, readily assisted local chiefs in disputes and negotiations.[116] Educated métis like Louison Cadotte (1804–1871)[117] and James Dugald Cameron became important aides to Little Pine and Nebenaigooching since they could translate Western concepts into terms that made sense to the Ojibwe. Since they all evidenced greater attachment to Native than White society, they and their descendants came to be assimilated into Ojibwe bands.[118]

The métis living on the north side of the rapids faced a different challenge. Copper finds in Michigan had touched off speculation as to the value of the lands on which they resided and, in consequence, the United Canadas had extended jurisdiction over the British Sault in October 1845. Lieutenant Harper of the Royal Navy, dispatched northward by the Crown Lands Department, reported that the local métis appeared to be loyal subjects of the Crown and recommended their lots be surveyed; yet Harper attributed the precariousness of métis tenure to the position

Little Pine had adopted in 1834 and 1835: "[Not] one individual ... owns one foot of soil or land, " he cautioned, "their Houses are built and their little gardens are planted under fear that they may be ordered off at any moment and lose all—no title deed can be got as the Natives here claim all the land."[119] As the result of Harper's prompting, the following summer a government surveyor, Alexander Vidal (1819–1906),[120] was directed to plot the métis' properties and enumerate the occupants.[121]

Occupants' surnames read like a roster from the early trading settlement on the opposite shore. Many were HBC retirees.[122] Vidal found that eighteen of the forty-four strip lots extending along the waterfront had been taken up by former employees of the HBC (Belleau, Boissoneau Sr., Bouille, Brassard [Bourassa], LeCharite, Contien, Crochieres, Driver, LaBatte, LaRoche [La Rose], Leask, LaFond, Mastat, Miron, McKay, Perrault and Jollineau).[123] Twenty-two lots lay between the HBC post and the old Ermatinger establishment (Souliere, Guidon, Mastat, La Roche [LaRose], Belleau, Bouille, LeCharité, La Rose, Perrault, Biron, Brassard [Bourassa], Labatte, Miron, LeFond, LaRose, Biron, LaRose, Jollineau, Cadotte, Trott, the Roman Catholic Church and burial ground, and Brassard),[124] twenty-one extended eastward on the opposite side of the Old Stone House (Contien, Perrault, Mastat, Seyer, Seyer, Saurette, LeSage, Perrault, Crochières, Boissoneau, Leask, Denomée, Martin, Cameron, Driver, Trott, Church of England church and cemetery, and Seyer).[125] Joseph Wilson (1818–1904),[126] of Medonte township near Lake Simcoe, was temporally residing in Ermatinger's deteriorating mansion. "A good friend, a bitter enemy, Highland Scotch to the backbone," Wilson was appointed to the Sault as collector of customs in 1845 but soon came to fill the roles of Crown lands agent, Indian agent, postmaster, fishery overseer, captain (and later major) of the local volunteer militia, magistrate, and "general government factotum."[127]

In addition to the occupants of the waterfront or first concession, a number of métis lived on a thirty-acre piece of land on the southeast corner of the twelve hundred acres claimed as the HBC property.[128] It was west of the town plot in an area that came to be dubbed "Frenchtown." They worked as voyageurs, hunters, and fishermen and, within the confines of the fort, as coopers constructing barrels for the shipping of fish, repairing and building boats and canoes, mending tools and fishing nets, manning the warehouse, and serving as general labourers. Hyacinthe Davieaux was 41 years of age in 1846. The Davieux family gave its name to Davignon Creek (Fort Creek), which ran through that quarter. Heads of families in this section include Michael Belleau Sr., 27; Pierre Brassard

[Bourassa], 36; Michael Boyer Sr., 42; Brissett, Thomas Cadran (known as Quadrant), 39; Joseph Dubois, 41; Joseph Jourdain, 42; Pierre Colin Laliberte, 48; Jean Baptiste LeMais (known as Quebec), 36; Joseph Mousseau, 52; John McKay, 60, locally known as McCoy or McKai; his son Jean Baptiste McKay, 23; Michael Neveau, 22; François/Frank "Wattap" (Spruceroot) Nolin, 27; Benjamin Riel, ca. 22; Joseph Savard Sr., ca. 35; and John Whalen, 32.[129] Except for the longest-residing occupants—Alexis Biron, Joseph LeFond, Joseph Boissoneau, and an absentee lady named Mademoiselle St. George, who each had received military patents to their lands after the War of 1812[130]—the rest were considered squatters.[131]

Since 1836, Little Pine and his band had resided eastward at Garden River, known in Ojibwe as Kitigon Sebee and in French as both Rivière au Desert and Vieux Desert,[132] an early supply station for brigades travelling along the north channel of the St. Mary's River. His family maintained kinship ties with Michael Cadotte Sr.'s descendants, many of whom by this time were residing at the Sault or on Sugar Island. This branch of the Cadottes employed the totem of the Crane, their mother's designating mark.[133] Identity proved far more a product of ideology than biology at the Sault; for instance, the Cadottes were regarded as more Native than European, yet not as fully Ojibwe as Little Pine and Joseph Sayers.[134]

Nebenaigooching's band also grew during these years. When an elderly chief from La Pointe, named Mezai,[135] moved to the Sault region, his daughter Charlotte married Hyacinthe Davieau Sr.; another daughter, Angelique, married Alexis Biron, the son of Alexis Xavier Biron and Angelique Cadotte; and his son, Francis Mezai, also wed an Angelique Cadotte. Hyacinthe Davieu's first wife was Josette, a granddaughter of Joseph Piquette and sister to Marie LeMais and Justine Johnston. Such kin interrelations were important to métis individuals for a range of personal reasons,[136] but especially when they eventually sought admittance into bands. By the 1830s, residents of the British shore had kin networks that spread both eastward and westward, owing to intermarrying with voyageur and independent trader families from Penetanguishene, Manitoulin Island, Sugar Island, Drummond Island, Thessalon, St. Joseph's Island, l'Anse, La Pointe, the Fond du Lac, Red River, and Pembina.[137]

Despite the mining fever on the American shore, métis life at the British rapids carried on relatively unchanged until 1849.[138] For Little Pine, however, time was of the essence. The Sault métis possessed skills that impressed him: carpentry, coopering and wooden boat building.[139]

Some métis were educated enough to draft petitions for assistance on behalf of the Native constituency.[140] When the government proved reluctant to negotiate, he grew impatient and engaged a lawyer, Allan Macdonell (1808–1888), to assist him with his campaign.[141] While Macdonell's family's roots lay deep in the NWC trade, as early as the late 1840s he was already espousing an incipient expansionist attitude.[142] Little Pine's vision of a Native community participating as an integral part of a rising new dominion appealed to him, and at various times he called upon his metropolitan connections, including Chief Justice John Beverly Robinson and George Brown of the Toronto *Globe*, to aid the Native rights cause. More subtle yet pervasive was the strain of modern French nationalism echoing north of the Great Lakes. Possibly because of Little Pine's concern with issues of nationhood, an oral tradition persists at Garden River that he was the son of Napoleon Bonaparte.[143]

When the government continued to stall, thirteen Canadian métis, one French Canadian, three American Ojibwe (Chippewa), five American métis, and twelve Canadian Ojibwe set out with Allan Macdonell and two of Macdonell's associates,[144] in November 1849, in Macdonell's schooner *Falcon*, and dispossessed the Quebec and Lake Superior Mining Association of its holdings at Mica Bay, on the north shore of Lake Superior. One of the American Ojibwe was undoubtedly Oshawano, a Crane totem chief who also went by the name Cassaquadung (He Who Hallows).[145] Métis persons also bearing the Crane totem, either by descent or marriage, such as the Cadottes—and those intermarried with the Cadottes, such as Alexis Biron, Michel Belleau, William Perrault, François La Rose, Hyacinthe Davieau, and John Bell—would be expected to go.[146] The party's sudden appearance led to the evacuation of the mine site, after which the Macdonells, Shingwaukonse, Nebenaigooching, and three métis individuals surrendered themselves to the authorities.

It was not a large métis contingent that joined the expedition, although others would have been employed lighting fires on the hillsides to guide the expedition or been posted as sentinels.[147] The métis participants who turned themselves in to the authorities were young men. Pierre LeSage, the eldest, was thirty, while his brother Eustace was only sixteen.[148] Charles Boyer[149] also was only in his teens. None of this group had previous personal connections with the HBC; their predecessors had been engaged in the free fur and fish trade. Without family connections to the HBC they would have been passed over for wage work in favour of others in the community. New companies, moreover, were threatening their fishing livelihood.[150] As all were young men concerned about their future economic prospects, Little Pine's resource campaign must have appealed to them.[151] They also felt at ease working in a prominently Native milieu. Pierre LeSage later proved sufficiently acculturated into Ojibwe society to employ the totem of a reindeer in 1858 when signing a treaty document.[152] The fact that Little Pine and Nebenaigooching willingly and easily switched ethnic identities from Ojibwe to métis and back would have made support for the chief's Native rights movement appealing to young métis men eager for adventure.[153]

Many other métis individuals had sound reasons for not joining the expedition, however. Those employed with the HBC or by missionaries, government officials, and miners refused to offend potential employers. For instance, George Johnston and Thomas Ogista, who were working for mining interests near Thessalon, as well as the Camerons,[154] were stoutly opposed to the expedition. John Bell's son Peter, who had joined Anderson and Vidal on a tour around Lake Superior earlier in 1849,[155] likely was guided by similar compunctions. Individual priorities ruled. Hyacinthe Davieau, employed as one of the crew on Allan Macdonell's vessel *Falcon*, probably felt obliged to participate out of loyalty to their ship's master, Alexander Clark.[156] Meanwhile, Henry Sayers, whose nephew Pierre Guillaume Jr.'s trial for free trading at Red River in 1849 had set a precedent by being suspended despite HBC opposition, must have found himself in a quandary. As a free trader for many years and a close associate of Nebenaigooching, he may have experienced stirrings of loyalty towards the Native cause. At the time, however, he was stationed at Mississagi in the employ of the HBC. Unlike the Boyers, Cadottes, and LeSages, who not only were dedicated to the cause but also less vulnerable to negative repercussions, Henry Sayers probably opted for the safe alternative and stayed home.

Although the mine's manager, John Bonner, placed the blame for the Mica Bay incident squarely on Allan Macdonell,[157] it is evident that Little Pine had been mustering recruits for his vision of a combined Ojibwe and métis community as early as 1837. By 1849, the chief's words may have been couched in more military terms, but they elicited responses from only a few. Françoise Joachim Biron (1821–1903), in recalling the mine takeover years afterwards, claimed that "Several years before the Robinson Treaty was made [1850]—Shinquaconse of the Garden River Band called a Council—and the Half-breeds of Sault Ste. Marie were invited to attend—so we all went. The Chief told us, that if we would join his Band and be his men or soldiers—that he (the chief) would work for us, and that we would get the presents that his band

was then getting. That some day he might sell his land—and that if so—
his claim should be our claim—and that we half-breeds would have a
right to a share of what he, the Chief, might get for it." Most felt secure
enough in the métis identity to decline the offer, however, as Biron continued, "only four of us agreed to join his Band—Myself (Josham Biron),
my brother Alexis Biron, John Bell and Louison Cadotte.[158] All the other
Half-breeds said that they were already Indian enough without binding
themselves to be under an Indian chief: And they all left the council
room."[159] None of these attachments, or lack of them, seem to have
reflected the paramilitary organizational norms evidenced by the highly
corporate bison-hunting Plains Métis.[160] The fact that a few young men,
mostly related by descent or marriage to the chiefs, joined in taking over
the mine demonstrates that Great Lakes Ojibwe rather than Plains tribal
organizational principals were operating.

## The Robinson Treaties and Post-treaty Adjustments

Owing to Macdonell's family and political connections with Chief Justice John Beverly Robinson, the trial date for the Mica Bay incident was
suspended indefinitely. The affair had cut through the bureaucratic
lethargy, however, and a government negotiating party headed to the
Sault the following summer. Under the terms of the Robinson Treaties
of September 1850, the Ojibwe surrendered a vast tract lying north of
lakes Huron and Superior to the Crown. During the course of the negotiations, neither chief had forgotten their earlier promises to help secure
métis land rights.[161] The métis did not rely solely on the chiefs to advance
their interests, however; they directed two petitions of their own to
Toronto.[162] In 1850, the métis community, for a short while at least,
could retain its distinct identity. Socially and economically viable, it did
not need to adopt "Indian" status.

   To accommodate métis like the Birons and Cadottes who had chosen to join his band, Little Pine granted land at Garden River for a Roman
Catholic Church.[163] In 1850, Joachim Biron also designated part of his
property in the Sault for the purpose of erecting Sacred Heart Church,
later built by Joseph Boissoneau. Following the arrival of the métis at Garden River, Ketigon Sebee underwent an astounding transformation.
Houses, wharves, wooden boats, and even a few small stores appeared,
and an official survey and town plan was drawn up but never used.[164] The
logging industry thrived, and petitions were sent to the government

requesting that dispensation measures be taken to allow sale of wood and other articles across the border to Philetus Church's and other merchants' establishments on Sugar Island. Missionaries of three denominations, Roman Catholic, Anglican, and Methodist, whose churches were full, could hardly believe the suddenness of the transformation. All recognized that the motivation behind the movement towards change was internal; the denominational exclusivity of the 1830s had vanished.

Acting in consort with his lawyer, Allan Macdonell, Little Pine prepared for yet more Native immigration and invited long-time Native friends—the general labourers Antoine, Michael, and Naughton Missegan, and long-lived lumbermen John Columbus (1791–1896), and Jacob Thompson (1807–1911), from the Michigan Chippewa, along with the Pottawatomi Greensky and Noonday families from Wisconsin—to join him at Garden River. All were Episcopalians and quickly became members of St. John's Anglican Church at Garden River, which may have been a means by which Little Pine hoped to leverage denominational strengths within the life of the reserve.

The Chief and his supporters were to be dealt a bitter blow. Anxious to prevent the formation of large Aboriginal congregations so close to the American border, the government denied the southwestern Ojibwe access to the Sault, forbade trade with Sugar Island, and implemented legislation that prevented Natives and non-Natives from assuming strong intermediary roles on behalf of Aboriginal interests. Although the Mica Bay incident had sponsored lively press debates about Native rights to land and resources, this controversy ended abruptly in 1853 when Attorney General Robert Baldwin introduced a bill capable of impounding any person perceived as being an instigator of Native unrest.[165] If one were pressed to pinpoint a date when the time-honoured métis intermediary role north of the Great Lakes finally disappeared once and for all, it would have to be 1853, with the appearance of what became known as the Baldwin Act.[166]

Deprived of a voice as the cutting edge of frontier development passed over them, the métis and Ojibwe both faced a difficult future. Between 1853 and 1858, Joseph Wilson,[167] the local Crown lands agent, promoted White entrepreneurial interests while the Native community suffered from sanctions against the sale of wood to the American side[168] and the erosion of their fishery through competition from large fishing companies. Access to the Sault waterfront became more difficult as settlers coveted the water lots, and soon most of the offshore waters fell into the hands of others. This, combined with the decline of voyaging and trapping, brought economic hardship. Métis families began to drift slowly towards Garden River or onto the Batchawana tract north of the Sault reserved for Nebenaigooching's people in 1850. Chiefs retained discretionary rights to allocate lump sums transferred to them annually at treaty payments, and both Shingwaukonse and Nebenaigooching began to extend monies to these persons. They also attained annuitant status for many of the métis incomers by using their powers of persuasion with George Ironside (1806–1863),[169] the Indian superintendent on Manitoulin Island. By 1855, a large number of métis, after exercising prior kinship ties in their choice of which group to join, had become full legal members of the Garden River and Batchawana bands.

The chiefs' welcoming gestures provided relief in a time of crisis, but for many métis joining an Ojibwe band was not a one-way process. The Birons, although band members, retained land at the Sault.[170] Many métis resided on the reserves between 1853 and 1865 because of the prejudice they faced and pressure tactics from settlers coveting Native lands and resources. In 1858, one official, John William Keating, did not even bother to negotiate with band leaders; he dealt them a draconian ultimatum—those who did not agree to a surrender would simply be left out of the three-hundred-pound compensation package being offered by the government. Owing to Baldwin's Act, no strong voice could be raised in protest on the Canadian side; but the métis Episcopalian missionary at Sugar Island, William Cameron, vehemently denounced Keating's actions in a letter to the British superintendent of Indian Affairs.[171]

Wilson and the local Indian superintendent, George Ironside, operated in diametrical opposition to each other. Wilson cut métis petty traders from annuity lists because he viewed such persons as irresponsible plunderers of local resources.[172] Meanwhile, Ironside, urged on by the importunity of the chiefs, continually added new métis names to the rolls.[173] Nebenaigooching, whose band was composed mainly of Roman Catholics, responded to Wilson's tactics by arranging for a collection to be made among his band's members and the proceeds distributed to métis cut off the list, but still residing within his group.[174] In 1855, the Indian Department revised annuity distributions so that payments under the Robinson Treaties would henceforth be made directly to individuals, rather than lump sums being paid to chiefs to distribute as their discretion. The new system, for the first time, allowed monitoring of annuitant numbers. In 1850, the Garden River annuitant list had stood at 266, but in 1856 it had risen to 344. Numbers then experienced a sharp drop in 1860 to 211—well below the original number of band members registered in 1850. In part, this reflected the ejection from the reserves of persons registered on American band rolls, such as Chief Akewenzee (Old Man) Oshawano.[175] In 1858, the Sault Pennefather Surrender resulted in Nebenaigooching's band ceding a large reserve lying north of the Sault[176] except for a tract at Goulais Bay purchased out of treaty monies.[177] Supposedly to reduce overcrowding and depletion of local resources following the resettlement of the Batchewana band at Garden River, this was one of Wilson's strategies as he sought new ways to force the métis off the reserve. By the 1860s, he was engaged in divide-and-conquer tactics by granting reserve timber licenses only to Protestant band members.[178]

After 1856, many métis truly found themselves caught in an unenviable "betwixt and between" position. On one hand, they faced the constant threat of having their legal status as "Indians" revoked; on the other, they confronted competitive pressures and increased social prejudice within the Sault milieu that was once their home. The first concession drew land speculators who vied for prime lots in close proximity to stores and wharves, in addition to property water rights along the shoreline of the St. Mary's River. From the time the registry office for the District of Algoma opened at the Sault in 1858 until the formation of the Municipality of Sault Ste. Marie in 1871, there were 114 property transactions relating to the first concession. The métis (not including Ermatinger or Cameron) originally had occupied 60 percent of the land at the rapids, yet they were involved in only 18 of these 114 exchanges, or 16 percent of overall land transactions, and on all occasions as a seller or mortgagee.[179] Evidently, the majority of incomer–métis property transactions had occurred during the mid-1850s, before the registry office came into being.

New legislation widened the chasm dividing newcomers and métis. While no property taxes were levied prior to the formation of the municipality in 1871, according to the statute labour laws every able-bodied man was required to submit a certain number of days' work each year to his community. The lists of labourers employed on road construction and other local public works in the 1860s reveals only métis names and the names of farmers directly benefitting from such labour. Merchants and professionals had accumulated sufficient capital to pay others to do their work for them, a state of affairs that drew a sharp dichotomy between métis and White; labour and capital; town and country.[180] In 1872, the municipal council further affirmed White dominance by granting Joseph Wilson permission to release members of his militia unit, the majority of whom by this time were White citizens, from statute labour.[181] That same year, tavern licensing laws included a section prohibiting liquor sales not only to those who were known to be Native, but also to those "appearing to be 'Indian.'"[182] For these and other reasons, by the end of the nineteenth century the public identification and group classification of the métis became as transitory as the smile on Lewis Carroll's Cheshire cat and as difficult as distinguishing the forest from the trees. Identity changed subjectively with the times and the situation. So much depended on the need for financial, community, and cultural security, the nature and purpose of the questions asked, and who was doing the asking.

During the 1870s, a much-needed listening ear and sympathetic voice for métis interests arose in Parliament. Simon James Dawson (1818–1902),[183] an Independent in politics, envisioned the rise of a new northern province extending westward from the Sault to the present-day Manitoba boundary.[184] Until overridden by Ontario's powerful legal arguments to the contrary, Dawson cited the intermediary position of the métis and the role of French civil law as agents in fostering a distinct northern community consciousness with deep historical roots.[185] For Dawson to retain these views in the late nineteenth century was almost inconceivable to those who considered themselves more politically progressive, and not surprisingly he was dubbed an "old fossil" by the frontier press;[186] yet, when he argued that resource revenues from lands north of the Upper Great Lakes easily supported a raise in annuities to four dollars a head, in keeping with an escalation clause included in the Robinson Treaties, his Native constituents in 1875 got their desire.[187]

Triumphant from this victory, the Native community next pressed Ontario for arrears.[188] In a bid to reduce annuitant numbers to cut down on expense, Queen's Park dispatched Edward Barnes Borron (1825–1915),[189] Stipendiary Magistrate for the District of Nipissing, to the Sault. On his arrival, Borron instructed John Driver Jr. (1831–ca. 1895),[190] a Garden River band member, to conduct a series of interviews at Garden River to determine who in 1846 lived a métis lifestyle and how this form of existence "differed widely from that of the tribal life of the Indians." Those not evidencing requisite "Indian traits" in 1846 would be cut off the lists.

By 1893, the Sault social climate had changed yet again; between the mid-1860s and 1890, several métis families had risen to political and social prominence. The names of Joachim, Charles and Alexis Biron, William Bell, Frank Belanger, Harriett Boissoneau, Joseph Boissoneau, Charles and Joseph Davieau, Frank Daigle, John Driver, Henry Dubois

Sr. and Jr., Antoine Fortin, Charles and Annie Ironside, Etienne Jollineau
Sr. and Jr., Louis and Raymond Miron, Charles and William McKay,
Lawrence Patreau, John, Edward and Henry Sayers—owing to their gender and property qualifications—were on either the municipal or provincial voters' lists of 1888. Occupational diversification had occurred within
métis ranks, with several persons holding positions of community importance. By 1863, Joachim Biron was operating a regular ferry service across
the St. Mary's channel, which he inherited, but greatly expanded, from
his father. In 1881, Hyacinthe Davieau and his sons Joseph and Charles
were all listed on the census as "lighthouse keepers," as were members
of the Biron and Nolin families. Former postman Louis Miron Jr. became
the first lighthouse keeper at Gargantua Harbour in 1889, and the occupation would remain in the Miron family for three generations, until
1917. A few of the McKay clan moved to Thunder Bay where they too
engaged in the lonely profession on the isolated islands along Lake Superior's northern coast. Metcalfe Jollineau was also working in Thunder Bay
as an "engineer." Both Joachim Biron (1821–1903) and Joseph Boissoneau Jr. (1819–1914) were founding members of the Sault Ste. Marie
fire department in 1896, along with William Hearst (1864–1941) as chief
(he would later become Conservative premier of Ontario [1914–1919].
Within the Roman Catholic community at Sault Ste. Marie, Joachim
Biron's position was paramount as its leading layman. He had given the
land for the church and school, his daughter had been chosen and trained
in Paris as a nun, and he lived his life (at least in his outward appearance)
"as a model of a good living and religious man and a gentleman in every
way."[191] To raise the ire of such a person would be a political faux pas.
The annuity lists would remain as they were.

Their political astuteness honed in the challenging era between
1860 and 1880, persons of recognized métis ancestry assumed increasingly prominent roles in local band politics. In 1901, Charles Cadotte,
probably the grandson of the Charles Cadotte (1795–1865) enumerated by Vidal in 1846, became the first person not belonging to the line
of traditional Native leaders at Garden River to be elected a chief.[192] He
would be followed by another able leader of métis background, Aimable
"Mab" Boissoneau (1870–1960), elected for two separate terms: from
1931 to 1934 and 1942 to 1946. In his person and heritage, Mab Boissoneau represents the culmination of the Ojibwe-métis cultural experience at Sault Ste. Marie.[193] His father-in-law, Edward Sayers (1829–
1915), Nebenaigooching's son, provided able leadership for the
Batchawana band for many years.[194] Over time, many métis individuals

have carved important political niches for themselves not only in the Sault vicinity, but on the national political scene.

That Emery Boissoneau (1837–1931)[195] and Raymond Miron Jr. (1848–1925)[196] would be founding members of the Sault Ste. Marie Historical Society in 1921 provides proof that métis families retained a lively interest in their distinctive heritage. While today, for many, métis identity is still nurtured mainly in private, public acknowledgment is becoming more widespread as one's ability to trace métis ancestry gains new and fashionable respectability.[197] The Native community[198] also recognizes distinctions between individuals who consider themselves predominately Ojibwe and those who retain some knowledge of the French language,[199] as well as a penchant for wood carving, fiddle playing and step-dancing. At Garden River, jokes are told that play on hypothetical differences between "French" and "Indians."[200] Those associated with the traditional line of chiefs at Garden River remain Anglican and Ojibwe-speaking, with no particular aptitude for speaking French; yet all Garden River and Batchawana reserve residents evince a reticence to speak too highly or proudly of their ancestry, in keeping with the Ojibwe logic that one keeps what one truly values until the correct time for its appearance.[201]

## Conclusion

Métis history has been dominated by the idea that all roads lead to Red River. Insufficient attention has been paid to fact that between 1815 and the late 1840s there was a major backwash of people from the western frontier to a "retirement colony" at the rapids of the St. Mary's. Furthermore, what happened at the Canadian Sault cannot be seen simply as a unidirectional flow of former métis into enclaves that vested them with a new ethnic identity. The process was far more complex. Although some members of métis families eventually became leading citizens and voted in municipal, provincial, or federal elections, they also remained on band lists. Their property qualifications enabled them to retain dual identities.

Even today, the métis presence has not disappeared at the Sault. The conservative métis group at the rapids changed over time, and underwent considerable revitalization by the mid-1840s. Its preservation depended on strong, independent women as well as men, for women from early fur-trade times performed in intermediary roles as competently as men. In interacting and merging with the Ojibwe, moreover, the métis were not wholly at the mercy of undirected processes, but guided by well-thought-out choices made by individuals and families who had alternatives extended to them by local chiefs. Others progressively assimilated into White society, drawing on options open to them as individuals. What ensued within the Native community was a structured blending of resilient cultural traditions, with the métis having a major impact on the nature of the Ojibwe society. The result, especially in the early 1850s before legal constraints effectively silenced the legacy of intermediary roles inherited from the older Upper Great Lakes cultural "middle ground," was an economically and socially vital Native presence, capable of constructing its wooden houses, building its own boats, seeking its own markets, and organizing its own mineral and timber operations—much to the dismay of local officials wanting to control these resources for their own purposes. The resultant community might not have been the one that Nebenaigooching and Little Pine had envisioned with revenues issuing from fishing, minerals, and timber, but it was one that drew on two strong cultural traditions to beat the formidable odds as best it could after 1855.

Further investigations, undoubtedly, will reveal more of the structured nature of processes that affected métis communities north of lakes Huron and Superior, since north shore Ojibwe chiefs united in extending invitations to their métis kin. While considerable research has been undertaken on métis communities south of the border, the Algoma region is one area that needs more attention. Here, the old middle ground declined, then became stronger, and finally, under external pressure, collapsed into a new matrix, albeit a resilient one. In re-identifying themselves within various crucibles of change at the Sault, the formerly independent métis community ultimately lost little culturally, since they have recourse to vital oral traditions and histories written by, or about, many of their antecedents. In drawing upon such sources, scholars increasingly can refine their understanding of the processes of change and ethno-genesis north of the Upper Great Lakes.

# "THOSE FREEBOOTERS WOULD SHOOT ME LIKE A DOG"

## American Terrorists and Homeland Security in the Journals of Ezhaaswe (William A. Elias [1856–1929])

DAVID T. MCNAB

## Introduction

Since at least 1670, Walpole Island has been at the intersection of European, American, and Canadian empires and especially the "empire of nature" in which Europeans attempted to conquer nature and everything in it on Turtle Island as they had done in the Old World. The Aboriginal people who have lived there for many thousands of years have had to pay the price for it. Imperialism has been defined (and this is the definition I will use in this chapter) as "more than a set of economic, political and military phenomena. It was a habit of mind, a dominant idea in the era of European world supremacy which had widespread intellectual, cultural and technical expressions."[1] European empires define themselves by drawing imaginary lines on maps and then proceed to try to imprint them on Nature. Not recognizing the power of Nature and natural laws, sometimes in the long term, they fail to implement these borders or boundaries. The result is that these empires collapse internally as a result of their windigo mentality in relation to natural resource use. This is precisely what is happening to the current American empire as a result of its invasion of Afghanistan and of Iraq for its oil reserves.[2]

I have written elsewhere, from the oral and the written traditions, how the Peace of Paris of 1783—an internal British imperial war—lacking Indigenous knowledge, set out a nonsensical definition of a boundary through the Great Lakes using the concept of the "middle thread." In the process, the presence of islands as sacred Places and as meeting grounds was ignored. This boundary was surveyed in very different places at the expense of First Nations after the War of 1812–1814 under Article VI of the Treaty of Ghent. That survey was agreed upon by the British and American empires in 1822 in spite of the resistance of the Walpole Island First Nation and others, such as those at Akwesasne, the Place where the partridge drums, where the survey began in 1816. At Akwesasne, when the European and American scientists discovered that they did not know where to begin the survey, the Mohawks showed them by using a log and their knowledge of the local water currents of the St. Lawrence River.

In fact, by the summer of 1821, the British imperial government had to send in the 68th Regiment of Light Infantry from Montreal by water to put down the Walpole Island First Nation's resistance in order to complete the survey. However, that international boundary was never authorized, as was the case with the other boundaries both east and west of the Great Lakes, by either the American or the British or Canadian governments thereafter. It remains an imperial fiction—so much for homeland security. When European and other empires collapse, the first thing that goes are borders. Borders are frail things indeed when they are not consistent or consonant with Nature. So the watershed boundaries of the Three Fires Confederacy have remained to this day in spite of the imperial paper boundary through the Great Lakes. Nature is always much more powerful and will trump empires.[3]

I want to turn to the history of the international boundary through Lake St. Clair after its survey. Not until after the Second World War did the boundary become an issue for the First Nation's citizens, as it was applied to them in terms of enforcement on Walpole Island. The many promises made by the British imperial government to protect the right to pass and repass across it were kept until they were forgotten by the mid-twentieth century. These included the Jay Treaty of 1794, the St. Anne Island Treaty of 1796, the Treaty of St. Anne Island of 1815, and the Treaty of Amherstburg of 1821.[4] The real issue initially was that, since the border was not secure, American "freebooters," defined as piratical adventurers, also known as nineteenth-century American terrorists, were a constant threat to the First Nation's homeland, robbing and pillaging its citizens while the federal government did nothing. Homeland security was not provided by non-Aboriginal governments in the context of the international boundary.

Homeland security was not enforced because it was too expensive for non-Aboriginal governments to do so. This is a cautionary story today for both the Canadian and American governments in the aftermath of

9/11. For example, it was only in 1903 that the federal government engineered the taking of Reserve land, through a leasing arrangement with Mrs. Joshua Greenbird, for a customs house on Walpole Island. This lease later became an outright expropriation of Reserve land against the wishes of the Walpole Island First Nation. The presence of the customs house was a response to the growing tourist traffic between Canada and the United States. The federal government's purpose in having the customs house on Walpole Island was ostensibly to regulate non-Aboriginal people crossing between Canada and the United States. Initially, it was not to regulate the citizens of Walpole Island. The customs house was also put in that location as a result of geography. It provided a ready access to the mainland by a road on the Walpole Island Reserve. The main road on Walpole Island from the Chenail Ecarte (now known as the Syne River) to the St. Clair River had been constructed by the Walpole Island First Nation many years prior to 1850. It was a private and not a public road although it came to be used as such by non-Aboriginal people and their governments, who have continued to use it without paying for it or for its use and maintenance as a public road.

In 1910, Chief Joseph White and his Councillors challenged the Department of Indian Affairs over the alleged rights of the Customs Department to charge Aboriginal people duty on provisions brought from Michigan for personal use. They were also annoyed by the habits of Mr. Himugan, the first customs officer, who attempted to stop the people of Bkejwanong from bringing over any goods at all after 6:00 p.m. The customs officer's actions were a clear violation of the St. Anne Island Treaty of 1796 and the other treaties.

In May 1913, the chiefs and councils of Walpole Island First Nation resolved against selling or valuing the one acre of land on which the customs house was located. In spite the fact that Himugan and the Department of Indian Affairs were fully aware of the locatee's resistance to the continued presence of the customs house, Himugan encouraged the Department of Indian Affairs to let him purchase the one-acre lot outright. The Department of Indian Affairs did so, for $300, in June of that year, expropriating the land under section 46 of the Indian Act when it could not obtain the First Nations' consent. On 31 July 1913, the federal Department of Indian Affairs took $300 out of the trust fund accounts of the Chippewa ($225) and the Potawatomi ($75) in the form of a cheque (#2261) listed in the trust fund accounts of the Chippewa and Potawatomi First Nations (#9 and #31) as "Payt. for land" to pay Mrs. Joshua Greenbird for the one acre of land. This action was taken without any independent valuation of the lands in question. Mrs. Joshua Greenbird effectively received her own monies plus that of other First Nations' citizens to pay for her, and their own, lands.

The Walpole Island First Nation citizens continued to resist these incursions and trespasses. In the 1930s, the Walpole Island First Nation resolved in council "that we ... do herein ask the Indian Department *not* to give a deed on the customs Department lot of one acre, and that the sale be *not made to any one outside the members of the reserve.*" Nevertheless, the federal government shortly sold the acre of land on which the customs house was situated to John Collier, a non-Aboriginal person. Shortly thereafter, the Walpole Island First Nation forcefully objected to the continuing presence of the presence of the customs house on their unceded territory. That resistance has continued to this day. The federal government never paid for the taking of the land for the customs house. Other First Nations and Métis communities who have been impacted by the fiction of the international boundary have similar, although diverse, stories to tell about their own community experiences. Some of these stories are told in the TV Ontario film, *Legend and Memory: Ontario's First Nations* (2002).

It is significant to recognize how recent the enforcement of "Homeland Security" by the Canadian and American empires has been; it cannot be relegated to a long-forgotten colonial and racist past. This paper suggests that it would be worthwhile to link up the "borders of knowledge" of the intersection of community-based oral traditions with the written records left behind by Aboriginal people and by non-Aboriginal governments. This can now, at least in part, be done through the discovery, late in September 2003, of the journals of the Ezhaaswe (Never gone there), who was also known as the Reverend William A. Elias (1856–1929).[5] These journals span the period from 1884 to 1928 and offer an unusual, if not a unique, opportunity to see what everyday life was like in some Aboriginal communities in both Northern and Southern Ontario and across the international paper boundary.

## Who Was Ezhaaswe (William A. Elias)?

On Sunday, 2 December 1923, after preaching at a missionary service at Parry Island, Ezhaaswe wrote the following entry in his journal:

> The class meeting was well attended and enjoyed the testimonies given to the honor of God through our Lord Jesus Christ. Our dinner at James Walker's home well enjoyed: it was prepared with skilled hands:

seldom excelled with the neatness for she has learned the art of cooking in the Boarding Houses. While many of our women has not the
training at home will be trained in this art by working outside. With
the exception of my wife, who was trained this art at home, her mother
being the first Indian Lady who was educated Indian Boarding Institution, at Aldervill—Also her mother being brought up in the
Methodist minister's home. Likewise become the wife of Chief H.H.
Madwayosh, Saugeen Reservation. There my wife became the daughter of an Indian Chief: we made our acquaintance to each other while
attending the Mount Elgin Industrial Institution at Muncey, Ont.
Caradoc. Co. Middlesex, Ont. And we were married in the month of
August 22, 1876, in January 1877 engaged to teach school at cape Croker, Co,. Bruce Ontario for 15 months. Taught school at Saugeen Reser-
vation 3 mos. April, May, and June 1878. In July came to Parry Island
as Native Assistant Missionary for 5 years. 1883 Thence to Christian
Island 4 years as Missionary became a probationer for the Methodist
Ministry. In 1887 Went to Victoria College at Cobourg Ont. In 1889
was ordained as Minister of the gospel Went to Walpole Island Co
Kent Ont. In 1899, went into evangelical work both in Canada and in
the State of Michigan United States lived in the town of Sarnia Ont.
In 1904 was invited to be engaged in the Missionary Work in connec-
tion with the Michigan Conference Methodist Episcopal Church of
United States for 3 years. Under the Traverse City District. Petowsky,
Charlevoix, and Kewadin Missions along the shores of Grand Traverse
Bay.

In 1907 was invited to return to Canada, wintered in the Saugeen
Reservation, In 1908 I entered into teaching the Indian School at
Shawanaga Reservation till 1911. I resigned the school.

I rested and located 200 acres of Crown Land in the township of
Shawanaga Parry Sound District Ontario, in lots 10, con. 5th and 6th.
Built a house 24 X 28 dimension, and some out buildings.

Some times engaged selling Indian medicines which I studied since
I was old enough to learn the herbs and roots under my grand mother
teaching me and for forty years among the Indians I studied the art of
being an Indian Doctor [since 1871], which no other man ever learned,
then I became a assistant Missionary in the month of July 1920 for three
years was under the superintendent 1923 in September, I began to
take the superintendency at Mission Parry Island and North shore:
God gave the success in this Ministry.

Here I am preaching the gospel in Parry Island: this Church I
undertake to build in the year of 1883. Now God has appointed me
to minister in this Church in this later years to begin the work over
again. I see some great wonderful results in the hands of God, since,

assuming the responsibility on this charge; thanks be unto the Father, unto the Son, and unto the Holy Spirit for the success to gather the souls unto the fold of Christ the Savior of the World.[6]

Ezhaaswe (William A. Elias) was a significant figure in late nine-teenth-century Aboriginal history. His Ojibwa name in English means "never gone there" or "the longest way."[7] His English name comes from a variation of the name of the Hebrew prophet, Elijah. An Odawa likely of the Bear Clan, his father was Medweskug (or Jonas Elias), who had come to Walpole Island from Grand Traverse Bay in present-day Michigan in the early nineteenth century. Elias was also the grandnephew of the hereditary chief of the Bkejwanong First Nations (Chief Peter-wegeshick [In Between Dawn] [ca. 1817–ca. 1926]) at the Walpole Island Reserve in present-day southwestern Ontario.

His only uncle was Ash qua geezhig (Esquageeshig, also called James Elgin) (ca. 1831–ca. 1910), also a prominent islander who was appointed secretary and interpreter for the Walpole Island Council on 25 August 1882.[8] His younger brother Waldron Elias was also a teacher, interpreter, Methodist missionary, and secretary to the council at the Saugeen Reserve for many years.[9] A teacher, interpreter, and a Wesleyan Methodist missionary, Elias was one of the first Aboriginal people educated at Victoria College, Cobourg (which subsequently moved to Toronto), University of Toronto, where he was educated as a Methodist minister.[10] His adopted daughter, Mildred G. Elias (1917–1982), married Emerson Sands (1912–1991) at Walpole Island, and they had twelve children.

Elias married Eleanor A. Madwayosh, daughter of Chief Madwayosh from the Saugeen Reserve, in Saugeen Township on 22 August 1876.[11] They met when both were students at the Mount Elgin Institute, a residential school,[12] and were married thereafter. They had four daughters, Dorothea Florence (b. 1884?), who perhaps died in childbirth, Lizzie (b. 1885), and Beatrice (b. 1891), and adopted one daughter, Mildred G. Elias (Sands) (1917–1982). A wonderful story about their relationship appears in Elias's Journal of 1885. In August that year, while residing at the Christian Island Reserve, William asked Eleanor whether he could go to Parry Sound for two weeks. At first, he recorded, she did not reply to him. When he asked again, he got an earful. This was, he said, the first harsh word that she had spoken to him since their marriage. He did not put down the swear word or words, likely in the English language, she had used. He confessed that he was at fault and that he hoped that their perfect union in the eyes of God would be restored. The next day, he wrote that they had reconciled. On 25 August 1885, he wrote that the local Ojibwa midwives, Mrs. George Monague and the "Widow Ka de ge gwan" had come to their place and that all was ready for the birth of his second child, Elizabeth (Lizzie), who was born at 9:00 a.m. the next day.[13] I am not sure what the moral of this lesson was for Elias, although it appears he learned it the hard way.

His career included primary stops working as a teacher and a missionary at the Parry Island mission (which included Cape Croker) (1878–1887), Henvey Inlet, French River, and Grumbling Point (Point Grondine) (July 1876–1884), Christian Island (1884–1885), Victoria College, Cobourg (1884–1890), Walpole Island (1888–1898, 1914–1918), Mount Pleasant, Michigan (1899–1903), Petowsky (1903–1908), and Parry Sound, Shawanaga (1908–1913, 1918–1929), where he passed away in July 1929. Elias was educated in the traditional way as a medicine person sometime between 1914 and 1918. There are no diaries for the war years, and, since he was likely too old to serve in the Canadian Armed Forces (he was fifty-eight in 1914), this may have been when he became a medicine person. He also played a significant and pivotal role in the Methodist Church in Ontario and nationally, and helped to bring the church into its union as the United Church of Canada at its key meeting in Sundridge, Ontario, in 1928.

Elias's English name reflects the meaning of his Ojibwe name "Never gone there." In his life, he always went where others had "never gone there" before. His English name comes from the nineteenth-century Christian tradition of the Wesleyan Methodist Church. Elias is an English version of the Old Testament name for Elijah the prophet. Elijah was also known as the "troubler"—one who continually told truths that no one wanted to hear but whose prophecies came true.[14] I suspect that Elias was an Anishinabe of the Bear clan, since he was also a medicine man who probably learned his craft early in the twentieth century from a medicine person from Walpole Island, perhaps one of the Shognoshs. In his own life, Elias was a "troubler" in a political sense, since he was the first Aboriginal person to request enfranchisement under Duncan Campbell Scott's revised Indian Acts of the 1920s.[15] He raised issues of integration and modernism by the very actions of his life. The Department of Indian Affairs, after he became enfranchised, took monies from the Walpole Island trust fund accounts and paid him his share and also gave him his lot on the reserve without first making a treaty, thereby alienating part of the reserve. This remains a black hole in the unceded reserve to this day.

To date, nothing has been written about Elias, perhaps because he was an Aboriginal person and was thus seen not to be a part of the written history of Canada. Other than his recently discovered journals, he left behind only a brief reminiscence of his life, which is located in the United Church Archives in Toronto. He is not referred to in any of the standard studies of the history of Methodism in Canada (e.g., my colleague William Westfall's *Two Worlds: The Protestant Culture of Nineteenth-Century Ontario*, 1989; and Neil Semple, *The Lord's Dominion: The History of Canadian Methodism*, 1996), nor is there any reference to him, much less any separate biography, in the most recently published volume of the *Dictionary of Canadian Biography* (in which he would have appeared, since he passed on in 1929). Semple, in his official history of the Methodist Church, states incorrectly that Aboriginal people disappeared as ministers of the Methodist church in the 1860s, and thereafter.[16] Such was clearly not the case.

## Provenance of the Elias Journals

Elias's journals came to me in 2003 through my community-based research at Shawanaga First Nation and by the First Nation's oral traditions, which are embedded in their family histories. They remain the property of the First Nation. They were given by his daughter, Mrs. George Sharkey, to her friend, Lucy Adelaide Clark, who taught at the Shawanaga School at the end of the Second World War. Her friend's daughter returned them to the Shawanaga First Nation in the summer of 2003. These twenty-five journals cover various years between 1884 and 1928 and consist of more than four thousand pages of journal entries. Some of them bear the marks of living in the bush for many years, having porcupine teeth marks on the margins. They begin when Elias was at Victoria College in Cobourg in the mid-to-late 1880s. They provide a fascinating glimpse of what an Aboriginal person thought about college life and his training as a Methodist minister in the 1880s. They also provide information about the individuals who were then teaching at the college.

## Context and Content

Above all, however, these journals contain a plethora of detail about First Nations communities. Elias had a keen eye for detail and his almost daily entries give us an insider's portrait of these communities on such topics as politics, the landscape, the weather, and, above all, the names—both English and Ojibwa—of the community members. The entries are not humdrum observations. He was a natural storyteller. He describes the people and the land, and the stories that came from the land. Since he knew English well, Elias acted as the recording secretary for the Chief and Council, and he often clashed with the Indian agents who consistently manipulated the written records that were sent to Ottawa. Sometimes the journals contain the only written record of what happened during these meetings.

Fraud, White speculators, and corrupt Indian agents were the everyday order of things, and Elias was not exaggerating; his comments have been borne out by ongoing Treaty and Land Rights research over the last three decades.[17] His journals recall Louise Erdrich's definition of Anishinabe Heaven, in her stories in *The Last Report on the Miracles at Little No Horse*, as a Place where there is always "plenty to eat and no government agents."[18] On 7 January 1898, Elias recorded the following portrait of the state of affairs on Walpole Island at the end of the nineteenth century:

> Nearly five years have elapsed since the above was penned and many variegated experiences have taken place since. Once who were ["once" stroked out] members of the Methodist Church have taken offence just by the earnestness of the preacher who had gone to a conclusion to reform the place or the Islanders who have manifested in every way that they are being duped by the speculators of the adjoining white people[. O]f course it would naturally be expected to see the missionary appointed on the Island and that who undertakes to do in the reformation of the Indians[. O]f course the speculators will suffer loss because they were before tolerated to defraud the Indians on the Island by making advances on the ponies and on the cattle[. A]nd half of the stock standing on the Island were owned by the white speculators paying in this way very little money on the cattle and on the ponies[. F]or when the Indians failed to pay the money advanced the creditors would claim the stock. And thus the Indians had no chance to sell their[s] but they were borrowing money on this basis, knowing no other way to obtain money. When a person obtains a loan in this way, he was made liable to pay 120 per cent interest on the money loaned[. A]n outrageous piece of business. Thus when you borrow ten dollars $10.00 cash, he was made to pay the sum of one dollar on it for one month. When an Indian was not able to pay the interest nor the principal amount loaned him say in the course of six months, he was made to give two of one yearling cattle one of 3 or 4 year cattle. There was many a cattle and a pony was owned and would be allowed to feed or pasture on the reserve say all summer or all winter without the owner paying a cent on the pasturage. Not an Indian had any

idea the meaning of the Indian Act was being violated when the cattle and the ponies were being allowed to pasture on the reserve without the permission of the authorities that be.

And another phasis of the fraudulence being perpetrated ["during" stroked out] upon the Indians was bringing sewing machines on the Island—and also farming utensils when they ["whe" stroked out] paid for so much. The Agents would forfeit the machines or the farming utensils.

And removing them from one home to another when the payments of such were almost completed so in this manner the Indians were not making any progress upon their farm industry. And were consequently without any farm implements and scarcely any vehicles of any description. [T]he roads were in very poor condition[. N]ot many ventures to go among the Indians but now since I went to work to hazard my own life in the discouragement of those who had been carrying this morbid love of fraudulent perpetration by degrees. I had this thing removed from this community by a constant application[. M]y influence against such fraudulent transactions with the Indians.

Still another phasis of disrobing this Indian community was the selling of liquor to the Indians by traders on the International boundary[. O]r if I would style them as freebooters would almost fill the true character of such traders for I know in one instance, who in such trading completely stripped a family of all their stock and fowls they possessed. The unfortunate father and mother were strongly to drink when they were once controlled by the liquor sellors.

While in the state of stupor by the influence of liquor the yoke of oxen they had and domestic fowls were all carried away by these freebooters over to the American side[. T]his freebooting took place before the [William (1843–1901), twenty-fifth president of the United States] McKinley Bill [the high tariff of 1890] was introduced on the United States when cattle and horses were entering ["into" stroked out] the States without any fee[. S]uch traders, freebooters, or poachers as they might be characterized would bring liquor and the Indians would indulge collectively drinking carousals when it would often be dangerous ["al" stroked out] to go along the river shore[. C]ertain locations infested by these freebooters or poachers for pilaging [pillaging] was going on, chickens, ducks, geese, and turkeys and some time the pigs will be minus in the possession of the Indian families without any one to protect the community. I was at this time worried that my life was in danger if I persisted to use my influence against wicked acts at one time when remonstrating against the selling of liquor to the Indians. That those freebooters would shoot me like a dog, but I was not to be frightened by such threats.[19]

He was in fact driven out of his community by Alexander McKelvey, then the Indian agent. The latter wrote as follows on 12 November 1901:

> Elias the Dismissed and discredited Missionary who was the leader in all acts of Insubordination and is at the end of his rope was on the Island last week, but could not get anything to hold of except a young "lady." Sister of [illegible] who he accused of making his Chief between his family and her Brother, and right before her Mother he took hold of her and used her roughly, and when her brother took hold of her and undertook to stop him, he took hold of him and used him much more roughly than he did his sister, this happened in the garden and in the house on Arthur Miskokomon[']s own place. Arthur came and told me about it. And I told him if he saw fit to lay an Information against him I see if could not prevent a recurrence of such an invasion. Arthur did not like to do it as his wife is a Daughter of Elias but he said he not allow that to stop him if the thing occurred again. These two (Joe White and Elias) constantly make much trouble and frighten and deter the Indians from acting as they would if left to themselves so that at this time if it could be avoided it be better not to bring anything that would cause a split among the Council or the Rank and file to come.[20]

The journals also provide commentary on the various spiritual practices—Christian or otherwise—of community members. Although primarily written in English, the journal's contain some of Elias's sermons written in Ojibwa and some of his drawings of the places in which he resided, such as Bay Mills when he first visited that place in 1903. Elias was fluent in Ojibwa and preached his sermons in his own language. The journals will be of great interest to the current members of these communities because of his loving portraits of the individuals in them, including his portrait of his grand-uncle, of the hereditary Chief "Petwekeshig" (Elias's misspelling) at Walpole Island, who is one of the best sources for both the oral and the written history of the community in the nineteenth century. His journal entry of Tuesday, 20 October 1891, is particularly striking, especially since the former chief was then seventy-four years old:

> The storm is a good sized one[. O]n returning home I called on grand uncle Petwekeshig who was at home. He was glad to see me once more in his old fashioned shanty[. A] wooden chimney at the one end of the house, a bright fire was before him, a big wooden pipe in his left hand and a piece of sliffer (sliver) in his right hand reaching down to

the fire apparently to the interest of lighting his pipe. When I commended his piece of workmanship on that rustic chimney of his a bright happy smile lit his sallowed face. [T]o describe his furniture would not be much. [B]ut would readily be understood by those who have visited the poor Indian home with a careful eye[. O]n the right hand side of the shanty two logs laid cross-wise on which some planks are resting almost reaching the whole height of that home, constituting a bed on which five or six blankets were lying strewn in every shape to suit the careless living[. S]ome cooking utensils were carelessly laid on a place near the fire, left there apparently in readiness for their use—On the left hand corner near the door a board was fastly nailed diagonally, so into that enclosure, three or four different kinds of apples, which holds about five or six bushels, were stored, ready for their consumption. [A] square little box was pointed to me for a seat on which I gladly rested to begin a good old chat. This aged friend was one time a great man of the island—who was head chief of the place for a long time—and was the wealthiest Indian of the place. But my dear reader what brought him into this most dismal little home? [I]t was, I will answer the question through that demon drink of alcohol, which dragged this poor old soul to such sad circumstances.[21]

While not denying the impact of alcoholism, we may question such moral judgements when the person is more than 90 years old and will survive to about 116. Elias did have his biased Wesleyan Methodist blinkers on even when he was in the presence of greatness.

## William A. Elias and the Imaginary Boundary

The Elias journals show that on an everyday basis he was not at all troubled about crossing the imaginary international boundary at any time between 1884 and 1928, even though he resided on both sides of it and travelled frequently within the Great Lakes and across it. In this time period, it is fairly evident that neither the American nor the Canadian governments chose to enforce the boundary as it pertained to Aboriginal people. Stronger border control is a relatively recent occurrence dating from the mid-twentieth century. Before that time, the real issue was the presence of American terrorists—the freebooters—who crossed the fictional boundary at will to sell their liquor and to rob the citizens of Walpole Island undisturbed by either Canadian or American border officials, notwithstanding the presence of the Royal Canadian Mounted Police (RCMP) station on the Island. Aboriginal citizens required homeland security for themselves and their Aboriginal land and treaty rights. This situation was noted in Dean M. Jacobs's report on land rights regarding Walpole Island in 1976, in the context of the Jay Treaty of 1794:

> The Treaty of Amity, Commerce and Navigation commonly known as the Jay Treaty was concluded November 19, 1794. It was proclaimed February 29, 1796 by the United States.
>
> The Canadian Parliament never enacted the Jay Treaty into legislation. There have been several court cases involving the Jay Treaty and North American Indians. Article 111 of the Jay Treaty is the cause of most Indian claims. Article 111 deals with commerce and navigation duties. It is the contention of many North American Indians that the Jay Treaty provides Indian people free access between the United States and Canada for themselves and their person[al] goods, duty free.
>
> The most recent decision by the Supreme Court of Canada, in 1956, ruled that the Jay Treaty was not a treaty of peace and could only be implemented by Parliament Legislation. As it now stands the Jay Treaty is not recognized within Canada. The proximity of the International Boundary Line to Walpole Island makes this issue more acute than to other Indian Reserves.
>
> It has always been taken for granted that the Walpole Island Indians had unrestricted rights when crossing the border line. The Walpole Indians never thought of themselves being confined to the Reserve boundaries. It can be documented that the Walpole Island Indians have always contended and practiced their hunting and fishing rights wherever game could be found, including the United States.
>
> The imaginary International border line historically did not stop the Walpole Island Indians from passage nor from returning with their goods.
>
> The Walpole Island Council may wish to support the efforts of National Indian Brotherhood, to have the Jay Treaty legislated by Parliament.
>
> The Walpole Island Council should examine the Jay Treaty very carefully as it pertains to the basic Indian right of freedom of movement.
>
> The following statement issued February 14, 1974 by the Association of Iroquois and Allied Indians should be reviewed and then supported or redrafted.
>
> P.O. Box 1506, c/o Mohawk Institute, Brantford, Ontario (519) 759–5052 N3T 5V6
>
> February 14, 1974
> ATTENTION; Honorable Robert Andras
> Reference: Proposed Green Paper to be discussed in the Spring of 1974

This Association is requesting the Federal Government, to enact legislation, to allow Indian people more liberal access at the border, dividing Canada and the United States.

It has been repeatedly brought to the attention of the Federal Civil Servants, manning the customs offices on this border, that Indian people are not required to register as immigrants, or submit themselves to the laws governing the members of Canadian society. This freedom of travel is an Aboriginal Right, of the Native inhabitants residing on both sides of the Canada–United States border.

This right has been repeatedly brought to the attention of elected officials, reminding them that there is a treaty (the Jay Treaty) which was originally recognized by all people living on this continent. The Treaty of Ghent of 1814 re-enforces the articles within the original Jay Treaty that allows Indian people free access of personal belongings and themselves to either country.

Since the time that Indian people have been recognized as Allies of Canada, we have participated in all defenses necessary to maintain Canada, as an independent government, this included in many cases, the entire male population of Indian Reserves, being transported to France and other countries during what is known as the First World War, and also the Second World War.

Prior to this activity by Indian people, we were not allowed to participate in Provincial or Federal Elections and we did not have a voice in the making of legislation that did indeed affect the lives of the entire Indian population in Canada. Upon the returning of the servicemen home, (those who were still living) they were then recognized by the Government, as persons entitled to vote for Members of Parliament. After this date we have become more interested in governing ourselves, and are attempting with all effort, and co-operation of Non-Indian Society, to become a self sustaining group, and do not wish to be a burden financially, on the other members of Canadian Society.

One of the items that will begin to give self-confidence to us, is a recognition by surrounding society that Indian people do have rights, that are somewhat different as compared to the general public

This change in legislation should probably be made in the Immigration Act, and a revision also to the Federal Indian Act, although in the latter case a complete revision is in the process of being recommended by this 250,000 member organization.

This one small change shall be a step, made by the legislators showing us that Governments are indeed attempting, to obey the wishes of the Canadian Indian public.

The policy of the Federal Government has been, as far as we are aware, one that allows for a claim of loss of rights, to successful economic development. This, of course, shall require heavy initial financial commitments by the public, to assist this development, but in all likelihood will not require any changes in Immigration Policy.

We note by your statement of September 17, 1973 that Canada is considering the possibility of a much heavier flow of immigrants from other members of the Commonwealth and spreading the financial burden of settling Native Claims over a wider area, shall be a much lighter burden to each individual in their contributions to Government.

Those in charge of manpower availability and immigration possibility should consider to a much greater degree, Indian manpower already hammering on the door, and wishing to make contributions to the economic stability of this country.

The educational system in Canada is training more and more Indian people and encouraging them to continue on to higher academic levels and these people must be put into positions of responsibility, to allow them to make decisions in the proper places, for the use of Indian human resource. It has been found that Indian people working under the direction of Indian people with equal financial reward, as surrounding society will mobilize themselves to other areas in the country where human resource is needed.

In reviewing immigration legislation there must be more consideration as changes must involve men, women and children to be acceptable and not only children. By this letter, we are requesting the support of all the people in Canada, to put into law, a practice that has been exercised by us continually since inhabiting North America. As we know, laws are nothing more that [sic] habit—more than Legislation.

Your co-operation at the earliest opportunity shall be appreciated.

A copy of the relevant part of the Jay Treaty of 1794 was attached to this document.[22]

Eventually, after the Indian agent was removed from the Island in 1965, the RCMP left the Reserve, and their station, still standing, is used by the First Nation's police force. A relatively new Customs Office is still standing along the St. Clair River, and some of its officers are First Nations citizens. The federal government continues to resist living up to its solemn promises, made at the St. Anne Island Treaty of 1796 some 212 years ago. Nevertheless, the Walpole Island citizens continue to pass and re-pass freely across this fictional international boundary. Eventually, the citizens of Walpole Island will have their own Homeland Security to protect their Territory and themselves from American, and other, terrorists.

# SHIFTING BOUNDARIES AND
# THE BALDOON MYSTERIES

—•— ▬◊▬ —•—

LISA PHILIPS
ALLAN K. MCDOUGALL

Once Britain and the United States had agreed to the extent of their sovereign domains, a border between them was drawn across the Great Lakes by the Treaty of Paris of 1763. However, unresolved issues, such as compensation for losses suffered by the United Empire Loyalists, left the old Northwest in dispute. Once those differences had been resolved, the border was imposed across the Great Lakes in 1796. A legal system that permitted ownership of land under state jurisdiction followed. "Acceptable" settlers were encouraged to occupy the borderlands of the new sovereign domains, often for the strategic purposes of state security. At the same time, land speculators negotiated with authorities for the right to establish settlements, which allowed them to sell land to settlers. The Baldoon settlement was one such settlement, a project of Lord Selkirk. He acquired a block of land on the northeastern shore of Lake St. Clair, on which he planned to locate dispossessed Scots. In return for building the settlement, he would be granted an extensive block of land by the British government.

In 1804, the Baldoon settlers arrived and attempted to set up farms on marshlands at the western boundary of Upper Canada. The land, however, was home for many Aboriginal peoples. In 1796, just a few years prior to the arrival of the Selkirk settlers, the British government had promised to establish a homeland for First Nations people who had been members of the Native Confederacy, which had controlled the old Northwest. That land base was to be held in perpetuity by First Nations dispossessed from lands that were now on the American side of the newly imposed border. The large region promised to the First Nations was adjacent to that granted to Lord Selkirk. However, the commitment to providing a land base for the First Nations allies was unknown to, or forgotten by, the Selkirk settlers.

This chapter focusses on a set of events that occurred sometime between 1821 and 1823 in the region of the Baldoon settlement. By that time, the colonial government of Upper Canada had surveyed townships and actively opened land along the border to encourage settlement; it had, however, utterly ignored the 1796 treaty. Members of the Baldoon community moved north of the original Selkirk settlement to purchase better land. The movement of settlers onto First Nations land led to the series of events that became known as the Baldoon Mystery. The events included stones flying through the air, fires combusting spontaneously, a soup ladle chasing a dog, and the death of livestock. This series of events spawned the definitive "Anglo-Canadian folktale";[1] but, as the story evolved through a century and a half, it also reflected the social transformations of the region. Just as the physical boundary of the state precipitated land ownership, so shifting metaphysical boundaries have framed the subsequent versions of the Baldoon mystery and the (re)construction of those events.

## The Physical Context

When the governments of Britain and the United States set the border across the Great Lakes in 1796, it posed a serious problem for First Nations who had been the allies of Britain during and after the American Revolution. The First Nations had not been consulted during the negotiations. Because most had homelands on the American side of the border, there was considerable concern about how they would be treated by Americans, who saw them as enemies. Alexander McKee, the superintendent of Indian Affairs, responded to their concerns on behalf the British government, promising a homeland on the British side of the border.[2] The land would be situated on the border and on the shore of the Great Lakes to facilitate travel and links to other communities north and south of the border. This homeland became known as Shawanese (see map 1).[3]

However, after the War of 1812, the colonial government apparently forgot or ignored the treaty, and in the survey of townships prior to settling land, the area was (re)named Sombra Township (see map 2). The township was opened to settlement in 1821, and lots were purchased over

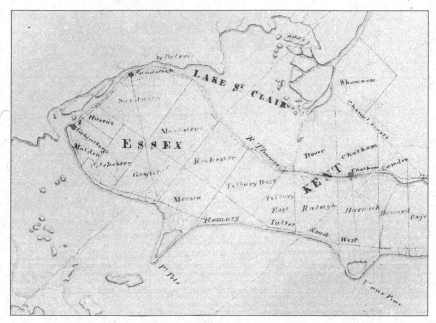

**Map 1.** Portion of Robert Pilkington's "A Map of the Western Part of the Province or Upper Canada," 1818 (Record 4817, National Map Collection, LAC).

the next two years. Some Baldoon settlers from the Selkirk settlement, which was located just south of the new township, bought land in Sombra when it became available. The Baldoon mystery was situated on that land, in the southwest corner of Sombra Township, just north of the old Baldoon settlement.

Settlement of the border and making money from land sales were priorities for the colonial government. In a time of fiscal constraint, land became a necessary resource for the colony. At the imperial level, the settlement of acceptable settlers along the border was seen to offer a defence from the "Americanization" of the frontier. Both priorities eclipsed the colonial memory's commitment to the First Nations dispossessed initially by the imposition of the border and later from the refuge they had been promised. This geographic context with its multiple boundaries is central to interpreting the iterations of the Baldoon mystery and to illustrating how stories that spoke to the First Nations' connections with the land were eventually erased and replaced with stories of Euro-Canadian frontier struggles and with social reconstructions that fit with increasingly insular contemporary Euro-Canadian assumptions. The occupation of the land by settlers frames the Baldoon mystery, while the

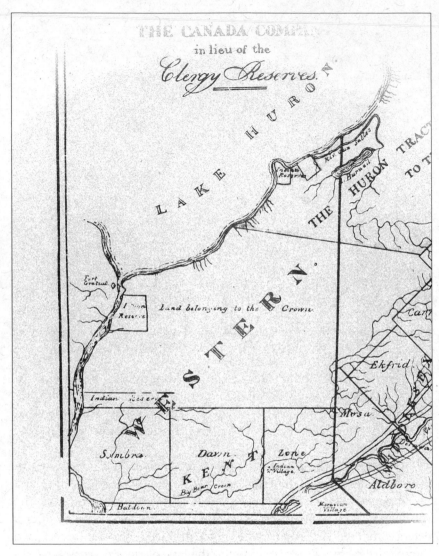

**Map 2.** Portion of "Map of the Province of Upper Canada ...", 1828 (Record 0002849, National Map Collection, LAC).

various stories, in turn, represent a clash of cultural responses. As the society in the borderlands changed, the folktale evolved. The Baldoon mystery and its significance as a folktale became a commentary on the social evolution of this borderland settlement.

## Transgressing Physical and Metaphysical Boundaries: The First Version

The importance of borders and boundaries was evident in the first pub-lished version of what later became known as the Baldoon mystery. The initial rendition appeared in the 1861 volume by Reverend Peter Jones (Kahkewaquonaby) under his section on "Fairies—Waindegoos, or Giants—Indian Names ...," where he recounted a story about "fairies on the River St Clair" and their "visitations" in 1824 "to a Scotch fam-ily living on the St. Clair."[4] Jones outlined some of the events that had been reported, which included the death of the farmer's poultry, cat-tle, pigs, and horses, stones and pieces of lead breaking the windows and entering the house, pots and kettles moved from their places with-out apparent human agency, and finally live coals found "wrapped in tow and rags" throughout the house, which eventually burned it to the ground.

According to Jones's account: "It was finally declared to be the work of witchcraft. Accordingly, a celebrated witch doctor, by the name of Troyer, residing near Niagara Falls, was sent for, to expel all the witches and wizards from the premises."[5] After meeting Mr. Troyer on the road as he returned from the St. Clair, Reverend Jones inquired after the incident:

> [Mr. Troyer] then positively stated that he knew the whole affair was witchcraft, and that he would soon make a finish of the witches. I was afterwards informed that he began to expel them by firing off guns loaded with silver bullets, which he stated were the only kind of weapons which could take effect upon a witch. Whilst he was in the midst of his manœuvring, the neighbouring magistrate, hearing of what was going on, issued a warrant to take him into custody. The great doctor ... quickly made his escape to his own quiet home. Thus ended the whole affair of the supposed witches and fairies.[6]

However, when Jones asked the "noted pow-wow chief, Pashegeegheg-waskum of Walpool [*sic*] Island" about the "strange occurrences among the white people," the chief responded:

> The place on which the white man's house now stands was the former residence of the Mamagwasewug, or fairies. Our forefathers used to see them on the bank of the river.... When the white man came and pitched his wigwam on the spot where they lived, they removed back to the poplar grove, where they have been lying for several years. Last

spring this white man went and cleared and burnt this grove, and the fairies have again been obliged to remove;… they felt indignant at such treatment, and were venting their vengeance at the white man by destroying his property.[7]

## Moral Boundaries Redefined

Folklorists have long addressed the importance of tellings and retellings of a story, as a means of structuring experience and as a means of socialization into a community.[8] The initial clue to the "teller" and the presumed "audience" is found in the framing of the story.[9] Each of the versions of the Baldoon Mystery was produced in a given context for an assumed audience. The means of framing the version indexes the teller/author's stance, or standpoint, and what was assumed to be shared knowledge. For example, Reverend Jones's story was part of his larger work outlining the *History of the Ojebway Indians…* in which his original audience was presumed to be non-Native, Christian, and literate in English. Jones's descriptions outlined and explained a world view that was assumed to be foreign to the reader. The focus of Jones's story of "the incidents on the St. Clair River" was to highlight and to explain the otherness of the world of the "heathen Indians." Jones presented his duality as a knowledgeable member of the community and as an outsider by his use of evidentials, in phrases such as "the old Indians say" (156) or "the Indians supposed." His focus on what "they believe" distanced him from the beliefs while at the same time demonstrating his knowledge of those beliefs. In Jones's words, "The heathen Indians all believe in the existence of those imaginary little folks called Fairies. The Ojebways call them Mamagwasewug, the hidden or covered beings. They believe them to be invisible, but possessed of the power of showing themselves. Many old Indians affirm that they have both seen and talked with them."[10]

Another rhetorical device Jones used to demonstrate this insider/outsider status was the use of the passive voice, as in the introductory sentence: "The following story *is related* of fairies on the River St. Clair."[11] He used the same device later when he wrote of other fairies reported to live close to his home community: "Another tribe of fairies *were said* to have formerly resided on the east bank of the River Credit, about a mile from the lake, where they often showed themselves."[12]

Tellers/authors often directly report their own relationship to the information they convey. In Jones's case, he explicitly denied personal interaction with Mamagwasewug: "In all my travels through the wilderness I have never been favoured with a visit from these invisible beings,"[13] he states, further separating his experience as a Christian Ojibwe from that of the "old" or "heathen" Indians. At the same time, and in a manner that echoed his use of the passive voice, Jones's presentation of the Ojibwe term, Mamagwasewug, and his detailed accounts of the beings that inhabit the Ojibwe world indexed him as an expert and insider in the Ojibwe community.

## Shifting World Views

The second version of the story was originally published as a newspaper series, reportedly as early as 1871 (just ten years after Jones's book was published), or as late as 1896. The text of this version comprised twenty pages followed by an additional twenty-two pages of "statements" or testimonials from people who had witnessed, or who were related to first-hand observers of, the events. The earliest versions, under the title "The Belledoon Mystery: An O'er True Story," were credited to Neil T. McDonald, apparently a direct descendant of the "Scotch" family who had been burned out so many years earlier. Authorship of later versions, with the title "The Baldoon Mystery," was sometimes credited to the story's publisher, William Colwell, founder of the *Wallaceburg News*, who published a version serially in 1895. Another copy, attributed to Colwell-Cowan, was apparently reprinted in the *Globe and Mail* in 1986, and the 1915 version, the one most commonly cited, has no author specified.

Unlike later versions of the Baldoon mystery, McDonald's rendition was not a retelling or reframing of Jones's earlier narrative. Many elements in his story appear to mirror those in Jones's, but there are significant differences in detail. For example, both stories mention Troyer by name. In Jones's version, Dr. Troyer was an ineffective witch hunter, but in McDonald's story the Reverend Father Troyer of Longwoods was a Catholic priest who stayed with the (Baptist) McDonalds for a week before making the ineffective suggestion that the difficulties "might be a visitation of God for some crime committed by old McDonald or some member of the family before coming to this country." Once the McDonalds assured him "that there was no evil deed to atone for," he returned to his charge "much disappointed at having been unable to afford the McDonalds relief."[14] Incidents such as pots and kettles moving on their own, and stones and bits of shot repeatedly "thrown" through the windows and walls of the McDonald farmhouse, were found in both Jones's and McDonald's stories, albeit with some significant differences. However, despite the similarities in the versions, it is clear that McDonald's was not based on Jones's.

The similarities in Jones's and McDonald's stories were undoubtedly due to the entextualization of the same events. However, the differences speak to the imposition of new metaphysical boundaries between the world Jones addressed and that created by McDonald. McDonald's story indexed a very different teller and audience, as well as a different reason for the telling. While Jones's story about the Mamagwasewug incident(s) on the River St. Clair was recounted to give evidence of the existence of such beings, McDonald's tale, *The Belledoon Mysteries: An O'er True Story*, focussed on the "truth" of "mysterious" happenings.

McDonald worked very hard to build a space for his audience to accept the truth value of the story as he told it, as he stated in his introduction to the appendix:

> The facts already set forth in this work we must admit are liable in this unsuperstitious age to be met with no small amount of incredulity. It would make no difference with the reading public should I assert the truthfulness of the foregoing facts; but, to disbelieve the following statements of some of our best and most reliable citizens would be to entirely revolutionize the popular opinion as regards their moral standing in the communities of which they are respected members.[15]

McDonald's statement presented powerful clues to his temporal and social context. His remark about "this unsuperstitious age" echoed an earlier statement in the text of his story that spoke of an earlier standard: "Most men's minds were more or less imbued with superstitious ideas in those days before people had become so dreadfully scientific or so properly orthodox as they are now."[16] The audience that was assumed by McDonald needed more than his assertions of "the truthfulness of the foregoing facts"; indeed, that audience needed statements from "the best and most reliable," "respected" citizens who had good "moral standing in their communities." In the testimonials, the descriptions of John T. McDonald, the owner of the house at Baldoon, almost uniformly declared him to be "honest," "hard-working," "in good standing with the Baptist Church," and/or "respectable," all factors that were consistent with the demands for accepting a source as truthful or reliable to other members of society at the turn of the twentieth century in southwestern Ontario.

While McDonald's story referred to the same events as those found in Jones's rendition, the divergent interpretation of those events revealed a shift in understanding of boundaries—the boundaries of possibilities, of cause and effect, between the natural and supernatural worlds, and between First Nations and settlers. The changes in the world views are absolute: in Jones's version, the story revolved around the transgression on the Mamagwasewug's last refuge, after having been moved by newcomers into, and then burned out of, the farthest reaches of their territory. McDonald's narrative, which focussed exclusively on the activities of European settlers, presented an entirely new epistemology surrounding the events and the region.[17] As McDonald set the stage in his first chapter for the "Belledoon Mystery," he included the following evaluative statement that indicated why this story was worth telling to his audience, presumably members of similar European settler communities: "There are fewer points of history more fraught with interest to the thinking minds than the stories of the first European settlers in this Western World, whether we peruse the adventures of a vast body like the wandering Hugenots [*sic*] or the daily experience of a family of roving emigrants, the tale of human fortitude, endurance and successful encounter of difficulties is ever new to us."[18]

As we compare Jones (1861) and McDonald (ca. 1871/1905), we find how complete the shift in epistemology was: the only overlaps that remained were the location of the event(s), the farmer's/settler's ancestry, and some of the specific occurrences, including similarities between those who tried to aid the McDonalds:

| Versions: | Jones 1861 | McDonald ca. 1871/1905 |
|---|---|---|
| Rationale for events: | Clearing the last haven for the Mamagwasewug | Refusing to sell a portion of land to a "covetous" neighbour |
| Perpetrator: | Fairies/Mamagwasewug | Woman in the long, low log house |
| Solution: | After the house burned down, nothing further happened | Shot shape-shifting woman/goose with silver bullet |
| Moral/conclusion: | Crowding Beings off their land results in retribution | "Inappropriate" desire for upright settler's land results in retribution |

Throughout McDonald's text, the world view of the McDonalds and their ilk was explicitly outlined and discussed: "They were strict Baptists of the old Coventish character, determined, steady and little likely to be lead away by freaks of the imagination," McDonald claims, adding, "McDonald [had been] impregnated from childhood by such old world lore that seems part of the Caldonian constitution." These passages provide metanarrative cues for understanding the world view of those in the story.[19] They point to a certain type of relationship between the events that occurred on the farm and the presumed cause and perpetrator of those events.

The climax to McDonald's story was precipitated by a terrifying visit to Longwoods to seek counsel with the fifteen-year-old daughter of an unnamed doctor, who had the "gift of second-sight."[20] Within moments after McDonald and the young woman met, and without any apparent prompting, the young seer asked McDonald about trouble with a piece of land: "Did not some of your neighbors desire to purchase a portion of your land, and did you not refuse them?"[21] When McDonald confirmed that the statements were true, the young woman responded with "I see [pause] a Long, Low, Log House" and then described the inhabitants. After her subsequent three-hour session with a moonstone, she emerged from her chamber and declared that a stray goose in McDonald's flock was "the destroyer of your peace. Taking the shape of that bird is your enemy."[22] Immediately after returning home, McDonald, on the advice of the young woman, shot the stray goose with a silver bullet, wounding it in the wing. According to the author,

> Whether John McDonald was right in his conjectures or not, it is not the compiler's duty to decide, certain it is that he and all his friends attributed all his troubles to the agency of the woman at the Long, Low, Log house. One thing seemed to corroborate this belief. From the time that the [stray goose] was shot and the woman wounded no spiritual manifestations were ever heard of in the McDonald family, and peace reigned supreme in the woody slopes of Belledoon.[23]

The text of the 1915 version remained identical to the one of 1905, but the title and the illustrations changed dramatically, indexing a further epistemological shift. Illustrations are key to the framing of the 1915 version of the story as they present yet another channel for cues to the interpretation (see fig. 1). In the shared text of the stories, the events were described as "mysterious," "ghostly," or as "a haunting"; they were presented as the product of an "unseen hand," "spirits," "an evil agency" and "supernatural agencies," but the term "witchcraft" was never explicitly mentioned as a cause. Despite skirting the issue, except in a humorous aside about British authorities, "witchcraft" became the obvious culprit behind the events in the 1915 version.[24] A comparison of the title pages of the two versions graphically illustrates the shifting interpretations. The 1905 version highlighted McDonald's Scottish heritage. This was repeated throughout the tale in evaluative comments such as the one referring to McDonald's "Caledonian constitution."

With the changes in the title and the illustrations, the 1915 version moved from one of Scottish fortitude and "old world" beliefs, to an

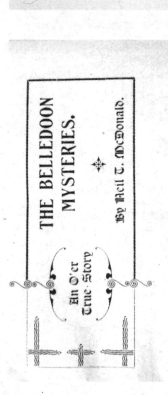

## THE BELLEDOON MYSTERIES.

### By Neil T. McDonald.

An O'er True Story

"Come roam with me the unsettled forest through
Where scenes sublime shall meet your wandering
The settler's farm with blazing fires o'er spread;
The hunter's cabin and the Indian's shed;
The log-built hamlet, deep in wilds embraced;
The awful silence of the unpeopled waste."—An.

#### CHAPTER I

THE broad and beautiful river St. Clair sweeps with majestic force between the great inland seas, lake Huron and lake St. Clair, and at about thirty miles from its source a tributary stream called by the early French settlers Channel Ecarte winds its way into a low-lying tract of country which at the period of which I write was a desolate region of marsh and forest, with here and there a cleared settlement.

In 1803 the philanthropic, but unfortunate Lord Selkirk, racked by home troubles and inspired with visions of the establishment of a second Eutopia, resolved to found a second colony that should be the means of restoring his own shattered fortunes and at the same time he be a blessing to his dependants, whose lots as in common in many old English and Scottish families, were bound up in their lord's interests.

Actuated by these motives, he set out on an exploring expedition through Canada, and, after various

## The Baldoon Mystery

### By Neil T. McDonald

"Come roam with me the unsettled forest through
Where scenes sublime shall meet your wandering view
The settler's farm with blazing fires o'erspread;
The hunter's cabin and the Indian's shed;
The log built hamlet, deep in wilds embraced;
The awful silence of the unpeopled waste."—Anon.

THE broad and beautiful river St. Clair sweeps with majestic force between the great inland seas, Lake Huron, and Lake St. Clair, and at about 30 miles from its source, a tributary stream called by the early French settlers, Channel Ecarte, winds its way into a low-lying tract of country which at the period of which I write, was a desolate region of marsh and forest, with here and there a cleared settlement.

In 1803 the philanthropic, but unfortunate Lord Selkirk, racked by home troubles and inspired with visions of the establishment of a second Eutopia, resolved to found a second colony that should be the means of restoring his own

**Figure 1.** Comparison of illustrations and title (Neil T. McDonald, *Belledoon Mysteries* [Wallaceburg: Wallaceburg News Book and Job Print, 1905]; Anonymous, *Baldoon Mystery* [Wallaceburg: Wallaceburg Press, 1915]).

obvious case of witchcraft, as attested by the image of the hag emerging from between "The Baldoon" and "Mystery" in the title. The jig-dancing Scotsman of the earlier version was replaced by a child fishing, moving the narrative genre from a story outlining the strange facts surrounding a Scotsman's misfortunes in Baldoon to a fairytale that might be heard in the halcyon days of childhood. While the hag of the 1915 version was taken directly from an old-world imagination, it had been incorporated as the prototypical explanation of the "supernatural" events in the new world that defied other interpretations, once again attesting to the absolute change in world view between Jones's version and even the 1905 McDonald version.[25]

The shifts in world view were indexed through the references to First Nations, as well. In the (shared) text of the 1905 and 1915 versions, First Nations people were only introduced twice, first in the reference to an "Indian knife" (6) with a ten-inch blade, which was dashed against a window frame by an invisible agent, and then in an espisode about an abortive effort by an "Indian Medicine Man" (15) to stop the annoyances. McDonald's assessment of this person illustrates how distant the local settler community had become from their First Nations neighbours: "The Indian, however, never put in an appearance. Perhaps he had lost the secret [to the ceremony], or probably he was not quite prepared to quit the certainties of this humdrum life, even for an eternity of buffalos and innumerable scalps."[26] The stereotyped Indian of McDonald's story certainly did not match the members of the neighbouring community of Walpole Island addressed by Jones. However, McDonald did include two testimonials from First Nations men among the twenty-eight "statements of some of our best and most reliable citizens."[27] These two statements presented very similar explanations of the events. One testimonial from "ReReNahSewa," explained,

> The trouble was caused in this way—J.T. McDonald purchased a piece of land which the disturbers wanted to purchase, and these are the steps they took to have revenge on him.... We called them wild Indians in our language and we believe they made their abode in the prairies Southeast of the house on the same farm.[28]

The other First Nations observer agreed:

> We are satisfied that what you call witchcraft we call wild Indians, and that they had their abode in a small prairie on the same farm, but they could not be seen at any time.... We are satisfied that the cause

of all this trouble was that John T. McDonald purchased the same farm that the wild Indians wanted, and to have revenge on him they took these steps to destroy his property.[29]

Although the statements were prominently displayed in the appendix, in second and third position, respectively, the interpretation offered in both, that a new-world witchcraft or what "we call wild Indians" was behind the troubles, does not appear to have been incorporated into the broader narrative. ReReNahSewa's comment that "We were aware of their doings and tried to tell him what we knew about them, but we could not understand each other's language" remained accurate some fifty years after the original event.[30] The events matched referentially but the interpretations were based on very different world views.

Finally, when we examine the definitions of boundaries in the 1869 and 1905/1915 versions, we see how fundamentally divergent the worlds of Jones and McDonald were. In Jones's narrative, the farmer on the St. Clair had "pitched his wigwam on the spot where [the Mamag-wasewug] lived" forcing them to remove to a poplar grove, which grove was cleared and burned a couple of years later. This statement presented a very clear parallel to First Nations memory of the region. As shown earlier in map 1, the Shawanese Township (now known as Sombra Township) was located just north of the Baldoon settlement. Set up by Alexander McKee in a 1796 treaty, this area was to be a refuge for those First Nations who had been forced out of their homelands in the United States and Upper Canada. The pressure of immigrant squatters and others seeking land forced the First Nations out of that area. In his assessment of what precipitated the troubles at the McDonald farm, Chief Pashegeeghegwaskum of Walpole Island was true to the understanding of the world around him: settlers encroached and those beings who were Aboriginal to the land were forced off—and subsequent troubles were to be expected. In his and Jones's discussions of the events, there was no mention of states, state boundaries, or state officials. The boundaries were set by (traditional) land occupancy, and it was those boundaries that were transgressed.

In McDonald's version, the land was assumed to belong to John T. McDonald, son of one of the original Baldoon settlers. Indeed, it was the younger McDonald's prerogative to sell—or not—the portion of land that was under dispute. Throughout this story, John T. McDonald was declared to be utterly right and righteous, except for the episode when he put his faith in the "Indian Medicine Man."[31]

McDonald's story began with a two-page history of the settlement at Baldoon, outlining the importance of various European states and colonies to the emigration to the "vast waste land though which this Channel Ecarté flowed." The boundaries mentioned in the story included the implicit bounds of McDonald's land ownership and the explicitly noted boundaries between Canada and the United States. This latter boundary appeared surprisingly often, and in some of the more humorous episodes, as when Mrs. McDonald "gave a favorite dog the mush pot to lick out": "Hardly had the unfortunate beast taken one good honest mouthful when the ladle flew out of the pot and began of its own accord to belabor the poor animal, which ran out yelping into the field. The ladle returned to its pristine duties, but the dog we are told disappeared for several days. It was found some time afterwards in Michigan, and nothing could ever induce it to return to the Canadian shores again."[32]

Other references to the border include the case of the schoolmaster who had been sent to prison in Windsor for his efforts to exorcise spirits from the home. After being let out of prison after some six months confinement, "Mr. Barker went to the Eastern States to repair his broken fortunes and has never since been heard of by his western friends."[33] Throughout McDonald's story, anyone who was not obviously from Canada was designated by citizenship ("French settlers," "old English and Scottish families," "European settlers," "good natured Scot," "British authorities," "an officer in the British army," and "a stranger from New York"),[34] another means of reinforcing social and political boundaries that were salient to the late nineteenth-century emigrant community in southwestern Ontario.

## Shifting Genres: Transgressing Borders

In 1900, the "Mystery at Baldoon House" appeared in chapter five of *Baldoon*, a novel by LeRoy Hooker. Because the book was fictional, there was little attempt to locate the historicity of the events at Baldoon in a larger scale, although within the context of the novel, there was considerable effort to establish the likelihood of its being "true," or at least possible. The main character of the larger novel, George M'Garriger, along with his a wife and three unmarried daughters, became the victims of the now familiar events when they moved into the "long-abandoned" Baldoon House. As the narrator noted, "Of course we had all heard the ghostly traditions of the house when it was inhabited by the original builder, Mactavish. But that belonged to the distant past."[35] Because the purchase of the Baldoon House in the novel was used to illustrate George M'Garriger's turn towards miserliness and his ultimate downfall, the validation of the events at Baldoon was given to Mrs. M'Garriger. According to the narrator of the story, he encouraged Mrs. M'Garriger to detail the "strange happenings": "I want to put it on record, just here, that I believe any statement made by Mary M'Garriger as I believe the verities of the multiplication table. I record this because I could not accept the views of some who were inclined to discount her understandings of the things she described on grounds of her supposed leaning toward old-world superstitions, and the influence of fear upon her mind."[36]

The events in this fictional version mirrored those found in McDonald and Jones: strange lights at night, the sound of a flail on the floor, bullets thrown through the window, beds being lifted and dropped, a kettle upending and then righting itself, dishes rattling and breaking, and spontaneous fires throughout the house. The focus, again, was on the interpretation of those events. In Hooker, there were two possible interpretations: one was supernatural and the other was "material," involving smugglers working the border between the United States and Canada: "The house is no more accursed than you are, Tom.... I believe that smuggling has been carried on in this quarter since before Mactavish and his clansmen built their first house."[37] The supernatural interpretation was attributed to Mrs. M'Garriger, whose strong Scottish accent indexed her connections with the old world and the "Caledonian constitution" referred to by McDonald.[38] The material explanation was proposed by young men trying to aid the M'Garrigers: one was a local suitor for one of M'Garriger's daughters, and the other was a newly appointed Collector of Customs.

The novel, like the stories related by Jones and McDonald, was set in a very specific, identifiable location. Hooker wove local references throughout his story, melding facts of the original stories of the farm with the activities of the fictional M'Garrigers. In many respects, Hooker was more attentive to the Baldoon setting than McDonald had been, inserting references to features of the landscape such as the "little lagoon that connects at one end with the North Branch, and at the other with Channel E'Carte and the St. Clair River" and to the scant six-mile distance between Baldoon and Walpole Island.[39] When the young customs' collector proposed his material solution—that is, that all the problems were caused by smugglers—the descriptions were couched in terms that would have been instantly recognizable to an audience of southwestern Ontario readers who shared stereotypes of the local populations.

According to the young man, the smugglers were "four men of shady reputation—Peewee, the Potawatomie Indian, of Walpole Island, Black Dick Douglas, Tonc Le Roux, and an American supposed to be confederate with these, named Julius Heyward, whose home was on the Michigan side of the St. Clair River, near Algonac."[40] This declaration presented a remarkably detailed look into the region, both in the delineation of established groups (Potawatomies, Scots, French, and Americans) and in highlighting the importance of the border as a liminal, and dangerous, zone. Unlike McDonald, who referred to Canadians in his story only by the name of their individual hometowns, Hooker built an explicit distinction between Americans and Canadians: "Before to-morrow night I shall have the *two Canadians* in hand—for I will sweat Peewee until he will be glad to tell me where they may be found."[41] The border was explicit in the material explanation, but in the alternative one the only border was between the natural and the supernatural.

## Rewriting History to Establish a Loyalist Homeland

The final version of the Baldoon mystery addressed in this paper was written by Victor Lauriston in 1952 as part of a larger work, *Romantic Kent: More Than Three Centuries of History, 1626–1952*. Lauriston's book began with "Part One: Out of the Wilderness; Chapter 1: The Days of the Attawandarons." It presented the following framing: "The year 1950 marked the completion of a century of municipal self-government for Kent. Yet this was not all the county's history. Before our municipal system was established … there had been, in Kent, more than six decades of white pioneering. To understand the condition those pioneers confronted, it is needful to go yet farther back."[42]

Like Neil T. McDonald some seventy-five years earlier, Lauriston established the region as a "vast waste land," and, also like McDonald, Lauriston focussed on the conditions of the "white pioneers." This focus was so narrowly defined that, at the beginning of chapter two, Lauriston went so far as to declare, "After the downfall of the Attawandarons, *their country became a land without a history*"[43] (emphasis added). His assertions built a new kind of boundary around southwestern Ontario, clearing away the prior claims of First Nations to create a haven for those who had remained true to the British government, for those with a God-given right to the land, the United Empire Loyalists:

A rich land, *empty of people*, it thus remained through more than a century after 1651, waiting for those who in God's good time would seek homes here.

The American Revolution changed the entire picture. *The land nobody wanted* became instantly a tremendous asset to the British government, confronted with the problem of finding new homes for the Loyalists, most of whom had sacrificed their all for the Mother land.[44]

While Lauriston admitted that there were some Algonquian people in the area, he cast doubt on their claim to the area throughout his first two chapters: "In time, wandering Ojibway tribes, particularly the Mississaugas, drifted in from the north; and *though they never settled the land to any great extent*, by the time of the American Revolutionary War they had established *some sort of title* to the territory between the Ottawa and Detroit which the British authorities, for purposes of purchase, recognized as valid."[45] Lauriston further demoted—and denied—the existing First Nations communities in his discussion of the land and the treaties: "The former Attawandaron country was fertile—and empty. But before the home government could utilize it, a legal title of some sort must be secured. The British tradition of just dealing with the Indians, the meticulous British regard for the forms of law, demanded this."[46] Given the explicit task of writing a pioneer history, it is no surprise that First Nation (Ojibwe or otherwise) peoples or beings were entirely excluded from Lauriston's account, which so closely followed McDonald's story that it used its title, *The Belledoon Mystery*.

Lauriston's version was, according to the author, "greatly abridged but retaining [the] main essentials"[47] of McDonald's story. He followed McDonald's narrative backbone quite closely and concluded with the shooting of the stray goose and the end of persecutions, followed by the coda "Thenceforth the McDonalds throve and prospered," constructing the settlers' history and prosperity as the point of the story.[48]

In recounting the story of the Baldoon mystery, Lauriston necessarily indexed the prevailing epistemologies. Following the conclusion, he included three metanarrative paragraphs in which he assessed the authenticity and veracity of the McDonald narrative. These paragraphs illustrated the categorical shift in mid-twentieth-century historiography to a scientific model, where documentary evidence and eye-witness accounts—the types of evidence privileged in the courtroom—provided the only legitimate epistemology. To discount the earlier version(s), Lauriston explicitly questioned McDonald's motives and methods:

> The narrative itself is supplemented by detailed statements of numerous eye-witnesses; *giving the impression* that the material had been gathered at first hand from old people who had witnessed the episodes. The preliminary narrative dealing with Lord Selkirk and the founding of the settlement, the only portion *that can be checked with independent authorities,* is in many respects inaccurate, due possibly to the compiler depending on local word-of-mouth tradition rather than on *contemporary records.*[49]

After rejecting the historical accuracy of the story, Lauriston presented it as a piece of folklore, the first time it was framed as such: "whatever its origin, the tale has become Kent's supreme bit of folk lore."[50] In this statement, Lauriston wrote the story out of the "scientific" history of the region. However, such an assessment then reflected back on his own rewriting of the history of southwestern Ontario prior to the Loyalists' entry: by demoting the Baldoon mystery to a folktale, Lauriston promoted his own history of the region as appropriately documented and unassailably accurate. Lauriston's declarations of how to read and evaluate history redefined the region, rejecting the boundaries set by treaties as evidence of the foolishness of the British "meticulous regard for the forms of law"! In Lauriston's history, the primordial act was the settling of the area by the self-sacrificing Loyalists.

## Documenting Social Change

While the Baldoon mystery continues to be told, the First Nations connections to the land and its inhabitants have been eclipsed by stories of pioneer fortitude and, most recently, by stories of historic paranormal activity to encourage the tourist trade.[51] Also lost are stories of the Alexander McKee 1796 treaty reserving the land of the Chenail Écarté for displaced First Nations from both sides of the newly imposed US–Canada border and the subsequent non-recognition of that treaty when the land was coveted by "acceptable" settlers. This disjunction between land and people was entrenched by Lauriston, who rewrote the history entirely so as to allow the settlers to move into his imagined, ahistorical, unpopulated "wilderness."

In this examination of the earliest versions of the Baldoon mystery, we found that such stories work both to instruct and to comprehend social and natural environments, but they function also to document changes in the comprehension of those social and natural environments. They index shifts in both metaphysical and physical boundaries. For example, by tracing the "perpetrators" in each of the stories, we find key differences in what would or could be the cause of the McDonalds' troubles. In the earliest version found in Jones (1861), the only two possible perpetrators were the Mamagwasewug and the witches being hunted by Mr. Troyer. Later, McDonald and Lauriston presented an "unneighbourly" old (witch) woman as the prototypical antagonist, while in Hooker's novel the antagonists were fringe members of the society: Potawatomies, French, and/or Americans.

In all versions, Anglo-Canadian males were portrayed as victims, as ineffectual helpers or, in their most useful roles, as guides to finding help for the McDonalds. Mr. Troyer was the witch doctor in Jones's account but was transformed into the father of the efficacious seer in McDonald's 1905 version. This was despite the fact that, in the first of McDonald's appended statements, the interviewee gave credit for the second sight directly to Dr. Troyer. Perhaps by the late 1800s it was not appropriate to have an adult male as a seer, whereas women, young and infirm or old and covetous, were considered more likely to have a connection to otherworldly activities.

Through time, the state and its boundaries became more and more central to the telling of the Baldoon story. While they were not mentioned in Jones's version, European states and New World national boundaries intruded into McDonald's narrative. Hooker placed the cause of the frightening events squarely on the US–Canada border and on those marginal people who took advantage of the lines across the water to run a smuggling operation. In Lauriston's account, the border functioned to legitimate his rewriting of the history of southwestern Ontario, where the only boundaries of importance were those that created the Loyalists and the "wastelands" that had been "emptied" by divine providence to allow them a safe haven.

The elements that united all the versions of the story were the location of the Baldoon farm and many of the otherworldly events that occurred there. The Euro-Canadian authors could not hear explanations such as those given by Chief Pashigeeghegwaskum, who proposed that the Mamagwasewug[52] "were venting their vengeance at the white man for destroying his property," or those of ReReNahSewa and Solomon Partar-sung who both stated that it was "wild Indians" ("what you call witchcraft"), and who declared that "we knew about them, but could not understand each other's language."[53] While such explanations were unhearable by the Euro-Canadian audience, the events documented in all accounts were consistent with disgruntled powers in the Ojibwe world.

The shape-shifters so familiar to the Ojibwe people were documented in all renditions of this story as a dark-headed goose or as a black dog or both, but they were associated in McDonald and Lauriston with the old, unneighbourly woman who took on the characteristics of a witch that one might meet in lore from the British Isles. That this might be someone, Mamagwasi or other, resisting the encroachment of the settlers was unthinkable in versions by non-Natives. Throughout the stories, the items that were moved, thrown, or otherwise displaced "by an unseen hand" were, in Ojibwe, grammatically animate. For example, stones, shot, kettles, and ladles are all animate, capable of agency. Spontaneous fires are still the sign of bad feelings in a community. While the referents of the events were similar in all the versions, the understanding of what those events signified differed according to the social expectations and norms of the storyteller and audience, whoever these were in a given era. As we watch the epistemological shifts evident in the narratives, we also see evidence of other boundaries and borders, which were continually imposed and reified through time. Jones's 1861 story presented both settler and Ojibwe understandings of the events on the St. Clair, with the Ojibwe explanations presented as the more sensible of the two. McDonald's (ca. 1871) version made sense in an Old World understanding of envy and revenge. An Aboriginal explanation may have existed in ReReNahSewa and Par-tar-sung's testimonials, but it was not capable of being heard.[54] Hooker (1900) gave alternatives between a supernatural explanation, through the Scottish-accented voice of a recent immigrant woman, or a "material" one, involving First Nation, French, and American outlaws. Lauriston rejected the occurrences outright, relegating them to a folktale from a bygone era.

The Baldoon Mystery offers yet another profound mystery to the reader. As the story evolved, it indexed transformations in and of the world of certainties. The shifts in ascribed meaning document how truths that were self-evident in one time may be utterly transformed by changing physical and epistemological boundaries. Privileging the latest interpretation as the one that holds the truth and applying that interpretation retroactively to write out prior understandings is the key turn in the evolution of hegemonic reality. By examining the retellings of the Baldoon story, we are able to trace the evolution of a hegemonic discourse that necessarily discounts other discourses. These other discourses continue to be spoken and yet become more and more unhearable to adherents of the dominant elements of the contemporary society.

# THE BALDOON SETTLEMENT
## *Rethinking Sustainability*

RICK FEHR

> If you want to share with us, as a visitor to Turtle Island, you must make an effort to understand us and our ways and our stories—Gin Das Winan—which is our way of knowing and understanding our history.[1]
> —Community researcher and former chief Dean Jacobs

The words spoken by Dean Jacobs of Walpole Island First Nation have become significant to this Wallaceburg researcher. Significant, as having been born and raised on the traditional territories of the Anishinaabe, I have realized that the current paths toward environmental, economic, political, and social sustainability are illusory. They are guided and controlled by outside powers located far away, in locations such as Ottawa and Washington, and in multinational boardrooms by people with no personal stake in what happens at the local level. As a research study, then, this chapter raises questions about how this economic and political process of managing from the "top-down" and the "outside-in" has impacted the capabilities of Wallaceburg and Walpole Island to maintain environmental, economic, political, and social sustainability. As a means of addressing the impact of hierarchical structures on communities like Wallaceburg and Walpole Island, some consideration must be given to the metaphysical borders imposed on the region. These borders were used to justify land occupation by colonial powers, to reinforce European superiority over colonial subjects and Indigenous peoples, and ultimately to accomplish the physical shaping of the land and waterways into the agricultural and rural–urban landscape. The shaping of the Southern Ontario landscape and its peoples into subjects of empire has long been the antithesis of sustainability. To reconsider the processes that drastically altered the region is to reconsider environmental and social sustainability. To do this, practices and beliefs that articulate sustainability beyond the colonial imperative of domination and positivism must be given priority. The potential of going beyond this approach offers the interesting possibility of developing a hybrid land ethics approach to sustainability that respects Indigenous and precolonial European ways of knowing. This form of environmental and social sustainability is born of the land and waterways and based on traditions and histories of both the Indigenous and settler cultures of Bkejwanong Territory.

To develop an understanding of how the regional wetland, Carolinian forest, oak savannah, and freshwater Great Lake ecosystems are under threat, it is important to understand the historical context of colonial history and the epistemological divisions between Anishinaabe and settler culture. The massive undertaking that would drain the wetlands along the Canadian side of Lake St. Clair in the early twentieth century opened up thousands of acres for cash-crop production. The effort to convert the tumultuous waterscape of the lower Sydenham drainage basin was a vision first brought to the area by settlers of the Baldoon community, one of the first non-Indigenous settlements in the area. That vision, although supported by the British colonial government, would encounter a host of logistical problems that were complicated by numerous factors, including administrative disagreements between the Scottish site founder Lord Selkirk and the Highlander farm manager Alexander McDonnell, as well as little to no site planning and American raids during the War of 1812.

The disruption of Anishinaabe autonomy came by way of the power dynamics illustrated above, the top-down, outside-in approach that had little if any sensual knowledge of the place that it governed. This process of colonial rule stood as a direct affront to Anishinaabe traditional ecological knowledge and practices of environmental sustainability. This process of colonial rule, lacking the local knowledge required to live in that place, also left the settlers unprepared for the situations that arose. One of the difficulties in articulating a hybrid ethic is the continuation of this process of rule, as it continuously dictates the terms of political, economic, environmental, and cultural engagement. The conflicts that result, at the community level, are also mediated by the broader pan-Canadian cultural baggage that often considers engagement in terms of resource consumption, industrial development, and federalism.

The experience of the Baldoon settlement, of its eventual failure and abandonment within three decades, as well as the utopian vision that required the defeat of unique ecological rhythms, serve as a template for studying successive social and environmental problems along the watershed areas that feed and are fed from Lake St. Clair. The lived experiences that embody traditional ecological knowledge of the Ojibwe, Potawatami, and Ottawa of Bkejwanong Territory (which includes Baldoon and Wallaceburg) provide this study with a foundation for pursuing an appropriate land ethic for the present and future. The forms of traditional knowledge do not call for the defeat or dominance of Nature but rather are built and are dependent on Anishinaabe knowledge of nature that emphasize balance, mutuality, and respect. As Anishinaabe teachings are grounded in place, so too will be any hybrid land ethics that arise from this study. A hybrid ethics approach will be one that is consistent with Anishinaabe ways of knowing and interacting with the regional environment, while at the same time respecting forms of traditional European land ethics to find a sustainable way of living in southwestern Ontario. Following the primacy of place for the development of this hybrid ethic, the histories and stories from the people of that place serve a fundamental role in guiding this ethic, as they all come from within and are not dictated by outside forces.

## Colonial Currents

In Simon Schama's *Landscape and Memory*,[2] landscape is described as the way in which humans interact with, perceive, and articulate their relationship to the land where they live. This being the case, waterscape is an interchangeable definition for this study, as the ways in which humans interact with the Great Lakes region, and in particular the St. Clair River, the Chenail Ecarté (now called the Snye), and the lower Sydenham drainage basin are of primary interest here. Currently, the main waterways define the point at which Canada ends at its southernmost point and the American Midwest begins. Beyond this, the waterways bear the marks of industries in Sarnia and the chemical valley to the north, and Detroit to the south of Bkejwanong Territory. The primary point of engagement and participation with the waterways is one mediated by border patrols and pollution.

Prior to the geopolitical and industrial control of the region, however, engaging and participating in both the development and sustainability of the waterscape existed outside this framework, with an emphasis on mutuality and reciprocity instead of domination. These acts were undertaken subjectively through the day-to-day experiences and interactions of Indigenous peoples throughout North America. Historian David McNab picks up on Schama's line of thinking, expands on it, and then applies it to the idea of reciprocity embodied by the Anishinaabe when he says, "In their oral traditions, the landscape, or Mother Earth, is seen as inseparable from their memory of that landscape."[3] In the documentary *Legend and Memory*, Jacobs highlights this as he looks over a stretch of wetland and comments that the process of living in the Great Lakes region over thousands of years has been one in which the lands and waterways were actively altered by the community to support the regional economy.[4] However, this was consciously done in ways that would support both the human economy and the wetland ecology over a period of many generations. Any act of separating the self or community from the waterscape could only be achieved through a process pursued by a people without a history grounded in that specific place or land, as their attachment to it is transient and divorced from the unique rhythms, traditions, and stories of that place. This relationship (or lack thereof) is counterintuitive to Indigenous epistemology, or as Joe Sheridan and Dan Roronhiake:wen Longboat suggest, "Where one *is* has everything to do with *what one thinks*."[5] Perhaps one of the greatest currents running against this Indigenous line of thinking came to popularity with the European enlightenment. René Descartes famously asserted in *Discourse on Method* that the best city is one that is built on a vast and open plain,[6] in a place completely divorced from history, which lacks any natural characteristics beyond the control of humanity. Of course, there is no such place, but this did not stop such perceptions and relationships in the colonial enterprise.

Neil T. McDonald, a second-generation descendant of the Baldoon settlers, offers a glimpse of how the settlers may have perceived their environment in the opening lines of a popular regional ghost story collectively referred to as the Baldoon mystery:[7] "Come roam with me the unsettled forest through/ Where scenes sublime shall meet your wandering view/ The settler's farm with blazing fires o'erspread;/ The hunter's cabin and the Indian's shed;/ The log built hamlet, deep in wilds embraced;/ The awful silence of the unpeopled waste."[8] The hostile wilderness that defeats the settlers in the *Belledoon Mystery* is not dissimilar to the state of Nature that leads to rationalism and Nature's ultimate taming or defeat. Environmental educator Jonathan Bate suggests that the perception of Nature that separates humanity from its environs is one that leads to a schizophrenic relationship: "Rousseau said that 'conscience' was the 'voice of nature' working within us. Most of us do seem, at least sometimes, to feel either guilt or fear about what the advance of 'civilization' has done, and continues to do with ever more drastic consequences, to nature. We value nature for the very reason we are destroying it; the more we 'tame' nature in our everyday lives, the more we value 'wild' nature in our leisure time."[9] This separation between self/community and place, and its effects on the land and waterscapes of the Great Lakes, became a symptom of the Euro-Canadian-colonial conquest, exploitation, distribution, and appropriation of all exploitable natural resources that in turn fuelled the French, and then the British Empire's colonial projects and outposts.[10]

The history of the Baldoon settlement exemplifies this separation between self/community and place, as it placed a group of landless Scottish Highlanders into the tide of the British colonial projects that sought to secure land at strategic points before the fledgling United States claimed it.[11] Much has been written on the desire to secure land for military and economic purposes, including the colonial desire to secure the land between Lake Huron and Lake St. Clair, which had been a centre of commerce for the Anishinaabe in the centuries leading up to the apex of British and Canadian colonialism.[12] In the early nineteenth century, the desire to secure land for these colonial projects was equally matched by Lord Selkirk's desire to relocate landless Scottish families to North America.[13] The settlers, chosen from the Scottish Inner Hebrides islands of Mull and Tyree in Argyll County, were selected by Selkirk as a first line of defense against the fledgling United States. Historian Lucille Campey highlights the emerging sense of cultural difference between America and the loyal colonies as central to Selkirk's decision: "in his view, Highlanders would be the best colonizers of such areas since their Gaelic language and distinctive culture made them less 'Disposed to coalesce' with any Americans."[14] Given that Selkirk was not on the site and various administrative problems kept the settlement impoverished, it proved easy prey to American occupation in the War of 1812. Throughout the duration of the war, the site was subject to numerous American raids, one of which resulted in the theft of a herd of cattle, close to a thousand sheep, and enough grain, flour, and other belongings to fill eleven boats.[15]

From the time of the 1804 arrival to well past the War of 1812, the Baldoon Scots had been victims of the colonial project. The immediate problem facing the settlers had been the site itself; as Wallaceburg-born historian Doug MacKenzie has noted, Selkirk toured the lands in the summers of 1803 and 1804, noting the rich dark soils that seemed perfect for crop production and pasture lands.[16] If, however, Selkirk toured the site in either spring or fall, he might have been knee deep in freezing water. As misfortune would have it, the fifteen Highland families who moved to the site in September 1804 did so following a summer of torrential rainstorms that halted nearly all work on their homes, forcing the families to winter in tents.[17] The lack of any basic infrastructure compounded a number of other problems that the settlement never fully recovered from. Within the first year, twenty-two settlers died of malaria and exposure, including eight of the fifteen family patriarchs.[18] A number of disagreements over how the settlement should be run ensued between Selkirk, who had returned to Britain, and his farm manager Alexander McDonnell, who operated out of York (Toronto), leaving the settlement in administrative chaos.[19]

Had the settlement been semi-autonomous, or even provided the basic necessities from the beginning, a more sustainable community may have emerged. Had outside political forces not been fighting tooth and claw for an international border at the settlement doorstep, appropriate cultural exchange could have been a possibility with both the Americans and the Anishinaabe. Instead, the physical landscape came to be seen as another obstacle in the way of developing a sustainable community. Aside from the political tensions and unique ecological rhythms of the region, it is important to consider that each of the settlers had been indentured to Lord Selkirk until such time as they could repay the debt of their passage.[20] As Maori scholar Linda Tuhiwai Smith has noted about indentured colonial European populations, "It was not just indigenous populations who had to be subjugated [by the colonial class system]. Europeans also needed to be kept under control, in service to the greater imperial enterprise."[21] Regardless of whether the settlers could find solutions to the problems offered by these new waterscapes, they were bound to the settlement by their place in a hierarchical class system.

In his study of Christopher Columbus, historical geographer Frederick Turner has said, "The more we come to know of history, the more it reveals itself to be symbolic, as the discrete events, artifacts, and personages tend to lose something of their individualities and to become increasingly representative."[22] Such could be said for men like Selkirk, who represented a colonial system that by its very nature was oppressive toward racialized others and those of a lower social class. Selkirk noted with nostalgia in the summer of 1803 that the site reminded him of growing up on his family's Baldoon estate in Scotland.[23] However, the symbolic act of importing his fond childhood memories onto a foreign waterscape would prove disastrous for the Scots, who were already marginalized following the battle of Culloden in 1746, as they faced increased rents, land severances, and foreign ownership of their land in Scotland. The wetlands of southwestern Ontario would not match his desire, nor would they match the desires of the class system that sought to cast its image on this waterscape. In the end, it would be the settlers who suffered, as the colonial mentality that marginalized them would follow the settlers as they founded Wallaceburg, repeating itself in a series of patterns that have continued to this day.

Directly across the Chenail Ecarté from Baldoon, the Anishinaabe of Bkejwanong Territory had also suffered from the weight of colonialism. However, the Anishinaabe were not necessarily victims of their environment as the settlers had been. Colonization came in the form of marginalization from the same political and economic system that created Baldoon and the international border through their territory. In 1796, a historic treaty was signed on St. Anne Island, enshrining, among other things, the protection of Bkejwanong Territory through the establishment of the Chenail Ecarté Reserve,[24] just east of Walpole Island and north of what would become the Baldoon settlement nearly a decade later. The key negotiator for the Crown at the time, Colonel Alexander McKee, in acting as the nominal head of the Indian Department, can be considered, like Selkirk, to be a man who represented the broader system of colonization. Having been the signatory of the 1790 McKee treaty, and as witness and participant in a number of other treaties, McKee was respected as an authority figure by both the British and the Anishinaabe (being of mixed Scottish and Shawnee descent no doubt helped). In considering both of these treaties, McNab has pointed out the gross inconsistencies reflected in McKee's written summation of the discussions and the oral history that was passed down from the Anishinaabe negotiators.[25] The result of the written misrepresentations drafted by McKee in 1790 and 1796 appear to be ones that make way for increased British settlements like Baldoon throughout the Bkejwanong Territory.

In 1790, the Three Fires Council of the Ojibwe, Ottawa, and Potawatami allowed settlement along a one-kilometre stretch on either side of the Thames River, with the Anishinaabe living in the area maintaining the rights to hunt, fish, and plant and harvest corn throughout the stretch. The treaty was not a surrender of land or water rights, but the McKee documents say the exact opposite, suggesting a complete cessation of Aboriginal title and rights to land across a large portion of southwestern Ontario.[26] A similar pattern reappeared following the 1796 St. Anne's Island treaty that was to establish the Chenail Ecarté Reserve in what is now a part of Sombra Township and the northern part of Chatham–Kent that includes Wallaceburg, as McNab states: "Not only was [the treaty] silent on the many significant promises made by McKee, such as free trade and border-crossing rights, it misrepresented the Chenail Ecarté Reserve as a cessation or surrender of lands, when in fact, McKee had agreed to protect the land forever and to retain it as a Reserve for the Native Nations."[27] It is little wonder the Anishinaabe did not welcome the Baldoon settlers when they arrived in 1804 on or immediately adjacent to land that had been reserved for Bkejwanong Territory. Having seen increased settlement along the St. Clair River, and what could have been construction on the Baldoon farmhouses in the summer of 1804—albeit construction that would be halted because of the torrential rains that summer—Chippewa Chief Wetawninse[28] of Walpole Island was told in fairly explicit terms that all of the land across the Chenail Ecarté would be for White settlers only.[29] During this encounter, it was suggested to Chief Wetawninse that the land reserved for the Anishinaabe was somewhere off to the west.

## Waves of Degradation

In charting this land ethic, it is important to bear in mind that these acts of colonial oppression are not isolated incidents. They are symbolic microcosms of broader patterns, just as Selkirk and Colonel McKee are symbolic of colonialist and imperialist systems of power that operate from the top down, usually from outside the community, and almost always with the system's interests being served first. Considering that these acts of oppression happened throughout the British Empire, it is easier to understand that many international communities and nations faced dire circumstances similar to those faced by the Scots and Anishinaabe. For both groups, borders were rigidly constructed around them and competed for by outside political forces. Symptomatic of these forces at the community level is the transforming of cultural differences into political ones, giving rise to racism as a means to justify marginalization. Another symptom of this destructive paradigm is the import of an alien land ethic that reflects patterns of colonization enacted on the lower classes and Indigenous peoples. This is reflected in natural borders being subsumed and/or defeated by an ethic that dreams of massive agricultural (and subsequently industrial) settlements. These patterns of oppression are not confined to any particular time period, but rather have a way of repeating themselves over and over throughout the years in communities like Wallaceburg.

Historians have noted that patterns of oppression are reflected in their repetition from one generation to the next. In charting the displacement of British lower-class farm workers and the rise of the upper class, historian Raymond Williams conceded he could find no beginning to the patterns of colonization that displaced men like his father. There will always be a "good old days"[30] to draw on, as far back as the Garden of Eden; yet each successive epoch brings with it new waves of displacement and marginalization, so nostalgia for the "good old days" is not the best model to assail the problems of the present. Instead, drawing on traditions, poetry, and literature of the past assists in questioning the problems of the present, in this case environmental and social problems, while at the same time providing a blueprint for how people conducted themselves ethically at an earlier point in history.

Hints of this blueprint can be found in the history of the area, as the documents reflect the ways in which the people of Walpole Island and Wallaceburg responded *proactively* and *reactively* to their environments. The ways in which the three communities in question react to and articulate the lessons learned from the process of colonization ultimately reveal how one community would survive (Walpole Island), one would collapse (Baldoon), and a third reach its present economic crisis (Wallaceburg). Therefore, in considering sustainability, a review of the area's environmental and social issues is in order. The fundamentally different ways that the people of Walpole Island and Baldoon perceived and interacted with their environments reflect the difficulties in forming an ethic of sustainability.

## Borders of the Settler Mind

Through the imagination and interaction with landscape, it is quite evident that Selkirk's primary goal was to create an agricultural utopia on the wetlands. As MacKenzie comments, almost all of the elements were present to transport a specifically European perception of land use onto the foreign landscape: "The proposed settlement appeared destined for full development because the site apparently offered the necessary environment for exploitation. Through planned settlement based on family indenture, Selkirk believed he could minimize hardships and trouble, and assure the settlement's success. Human problems could be surmounted: however, nature was to provide the one intractable obstacle."[31]

This importing of Western European epistemology, which viewed land as a resource to be exploited by human labour, was not a new trend. It was merely a reflection of the broader British Empire's doctrine of subduing and exploiting all resources—a doctrine that allowed the empire to flourish. Nature, not easily submitting to the desires of empire, becomes the enemy. Pitting Nature against humanity (and in this case the settlement against the waterways) prevented a dialogue from forming between the settlement and the regional environment, as well as between the Scots and the Anishinaabe. This dialogue would have required a completely transformative mode of thinking that would have cast off the European epistemologies that sought to draw their own lines on the land and water. To adapt to this new environment, however, would have required fundamental ontological, epistemological, and axiological[32] shifts that the settlers may not have been ready to make, considering the political forces that controlled the settlement. Consequently, the dialogue that did take place flowed only one way, from the settlers to the waterscape, with little meaningful exchange with either the Anishinaabe or the waterscape.

When considering dialogue in a literal sense, two points worthy of consideration are language and connection to place. In the Anishinaabe world view, language and the connection to place are foundational elements of identity. In his exploration of the relationship between Indigeneity and colonialism, postcolonial theorist Jace Weaver states that one of the primary problems facing settlers on their arrival to North America was a language system that was not "of the land" they settled.[33] Weaver's argument corresponds quite nicely with Ojibwe author Louise Erdrich's belief that the Anishinaabe, having been on Turtle Island since the time of Creation, are biophysically formed cell by cell by the lands and waters of their ancestors.[34] This being the case, language too could be said to have formed in relationship to the lands and waters of the Anishinaabe, as it is the territory that traditionally dictates how people think about it and interact with it, thus ultimately guiding them in their day-to-day lives. Erdich's statement locates the presence of the Anishinaabe in their territories as transcending linear time and going straight to Creation; she states of a companion, "His people were of the lake, and the lake was them."[35] In other words, "where one *is*" literally becomes "*what one thinks.*"[36] Jacobs, in his counter-argument to historical accounts by colonial intruders that describe Walpole Island as a pestilent wasteland, says, "we know our lands and waters."[37] This statement transcends the empirical knowledge of knowing where one is, say, by looking at a map, and goes straight to the primacy of place, through which language and story are the articulation of that knowledge. In situating Anishinaabe world views, Theresa Smith compares the godchild of the enlightenment, scientific thought, to the primacy of knowing land and water: "The scientist might accurately describe the facts of the storm through reference to meteorological observation and theories but she will not experience it as an Ojibwe storm. Neither the 'hyletic' data nor the index supplied by meteorology prepares us for the visits of Thunderbirds and the baggage of symbolism and meaning which they convey with them as they move across the Anishinaabe sky."[38]

On Walpole Island specifically, this knowledge of the land and water is articulated both through the language and in empirical knowledge, revealing the ultimate hybrid use of both traditional and scientific epistemologies. To know the land and waters on Walpole Island is to know the great dangers that are too often considered by-products of industrial progress. In the Walpole Island Heritage Centre's publication, *E-Niizaanag Wii-Ngoshkaag Maampii Bkejwanong—Species at Risk on the Walpole Island First Nation*, the knowledge that humans are composed of their environment goes one step further by physically connecting the Anishinaabe to wetland environments. This expression in English is secondary to the primacy of the Nishnaabemwin language, which, when expressed, acts as the cultural foundation for this connection:

> Gaawii dibishko aanind dnizwinan, niw nibiiwkaanan giiyak gezhimnayaamgag e-pkaankin e-bimaadziimgag miinwaa e-zaak'kiig miyaamgag niw niibna biin'naagdoon e-miigwemgag. Nibiiwkaanan giibi-zhi-gnawaabjigaadenoon naasaab giw doonkwoziwag. Nibiiwkaanan miinwaa doonkwoziwag neniizh naadmaagemgadoon nbiish e-zhijiwang miinwaa biintoonaawaa iw nikeyaa. Shki'ewziwning niw nibiiwkaanan wii-aanj-toong e-miijimwang aawan wiinwaa niizaanziwag maampii kina maamwi e-zhi-nokiimigag ki.

> Unlike most other habitats, wetlands directly improve other ecosystems by their many cleansing benefits. Wetlands have been compared to kidneys. Wetlands and kidneys both help control water flow and cleanse the system. The ability of wetlands to recycle nutrients makes them critical in the overall functioning of the earth.[39]

Empirical knowledge of the water is mediated by the understanding that whatever happens to the environment is not a by-product at all. Rather, environmental knowledge is situated in a way that identifies immediate spiritual and physical consequences of the destruction of wetland habitats. Through this awareness, the spiritual and physical consequences are not abstract, say as a city built on a vast and open plain. The consequences are ultimately felt by the people who live in and have knowledge of the land and water as they are intimately connected to place. The knowledge of this presence and the primacy of place is asserted in the *Species at Risk* philosophical statement:

> Giinwi, gaa-ntami-yaajig maampii Bkejwanong Nishinaabekaaning pane ngii-bi-dnizmi maa nanda kiin bi-shki-kikendamang. E-bi-ko-yaayaang ngii-bi-zhigiizhiwemi enweyaang, gaa-naadiziyaang miin-waa e-gchi-nendaak'kin … gaa-zhi-miingooziyaang ow Gzhe-mnidoo, bimaadzhijig miinwa e-nendaagoziying. Maanda dash e-zhi-nawendiying, niinwi ndibendaanaanin niw zhi-giiyak-zhichigewnan wii-kendamaang waa-ni-zhaayaang weweni. Nga-ni-miwdoonaanin nanda zhichigewinan gaa-bi-zhi-miingoyaangin nda Gzhe-mnidoominaa, miinwaa gitziimnaanig, miinwa ji-ni-zhiwebag niigaan ge-ni-yaajig ga-miinaanaanig nanda e-gchi-twaawendaak'kin naakonigewinan.

> We, the First Nations of Walpole Island Indian Territory, have inhabited these lands since the beginning of time. With this occupation we have developed our language, heritage and values … in accordance with the Creator, mankind and nature. Through this relationship, we possess the rights and freedom to determine our own path. We shall carry on these responsibilities as handed down to us by our Creator, and our elders, and ensure that future generations shall be entrusted with these sacred obligations.[40]

The connection expressed by the Elders, language keepers, and community researchers at Walpole Island is not expressed as a superficial nor abstract relationship. Instead, the relationship between the Anishinaabe and the waterscapes is deeply embedded in Creation, the sovereignty of which is traditionally expressed through language, cultural practices, and day-to-day living. Outside forms of rule cannot know the territory in the long-standing and deeply embedded way the Anishinaabe understand the territory. European systems of understanding could not offer "a sensible and cohesive alternative"[41] to the traditional ways of understanding the world; instead, these systems required that the land and waters not be considered "biophysical" components of the self and community. The same uprootedness that moved settlers from Europe to the shore of the Chenail Ecarté had been rigidly enforced through the colonial reading of treaties. Later, this uprootedness transcended to all dealings with the Anishinaabe, from the philosophy and enforcement of the Indian Act to the introduction and prominence of residential schools. The ways in which colonization dictated the terms of relationship to the land and water were similarly dictated not in languages that developed within the territory, but through languages that developed across the ocean.

When a language has a hard time interpreting and articulating the ecological rhythms of a particular area (as in the case of the transplanted languages of the Baldoon settlers), trouble arises. As Weaver quotes from Bill Ashcroft, Gareth Griffiths, and Helen Tiffin's postcolonial reader, *The Empire Writes back*,[42] "where mistranslation could not be overlooked it was the land or the season which was 'wrong.'"[43] The settlers' problem was not being able to translate what their "new world" was saying. Further, two factors complicated matters. The first was the construction of imaginary borders in their minds that further separated them from Nature (reinforcing the notions they imported to North America); this act is extended to the level of Empire through the construction of imaginary borders through Bkejwanong Territory, making "Where the Waters Divide" for the Anishinaabe a place "Where the land is divided" for settler society. The second factor (a consequence of the first) involved the great effort to shape what they believed to be a malcontent Nature to conform to a distinctly agriculturalist ethic (which would then shift, through the following two centuries, to an agriculturalist-colonial-imperialist mindset, and then to the contemporary industrialist and capitalist ethic).

Turner argues that the imaginary borders are not based solely on the desires of empire but also in the epistemological underpinnings of Christianity and pre-Christian civilizations that developed in the Middle East, all of which were retained and imported to the wetlands of Southern Ontario. He contends that this act of severing civilization from attentiveness to the rhythms of the rest of its environs effectively divorced the Western world from the rest of Creation.[44] The result of this was a completely insular way of looking at the world and an entirely narcissistic form of anthropocentrism where the sole emphasis is on the nature of humans instead of on the nature of Nature.[45] This insular way of viewing the world prevented the settlers from understanding or respecting the waterscape's natural borders, borders that were articulated every spring and fall by rising water levels.

Lynn White Jr., in his now classical challenge to Western society, echoes Turner's criticism of Western Christianity when he discusses how

Christianity became a practice of hierarchies, in which humans, and in particular men, became the fulcrum of power relations:

> By gradual stages a loving and all-powerful God had created light and darkness, the heavenly bodies, the earth and all its plants, animals, birds, and fishes. Finally, God had created Adam and, as an after-thought, Eve to keep man from being lonely. Man named all the animals, thus establishing his dominance over them. God planned all of this explicitly for man's benefit and rule: no item in the physical creation had any purpose save to serve man's purposes. And, although man's body is made of clay, he is not simply part of nature: he is made in God's image.[46]

Furthering the investigation into this ethic of sustainability, we will return to Lynn White Jr. a little later, as his call to the Western world to reimagine sustainability is one that requires spiritual dimensions that are not often considered.

The colonial mindset embodying the European agricultural settlement thus perceived and interacted with land and water in hierarchical terms. Many environmentalists and social scientists have long been warning about its dangers. Environmental educator Joe Sheridan warns that once primacy is given to developing only the land, and the other elements are ignored, the idea of settlement itself is bound for failure: "the most utilitarian element, cultivated land is so deceptively simple for us understand and manipulate that it has become culturally habitual to ignore it. Yet, land enthralls visions of stability contrary to air, water, time, and fire's shape shifting lessons."[47] The lessons from Baldoon could be lessons drawn from water, lessons the Anishinaabe know quite well through their experiences in the region, which temporal dimensions and literal history do not account for. If the European settlers were to even scratch the surface of life on the Great Lakes and the Chenail Ecarté, it would require a transformative mode of thinking that places the primacy not just on segments of the environment such as the land, but on Nature as a whole.

This transformative mode of thinking would have required listening and openness to change. Listening to the Anishinaabe of Bkejwanong Territory could have saved the fledgling community a lot of heartache and anguish, as the Anishinaabe had thousands of years of experience with the waterscape. Instead of attempting to transform the land into a European landscape for cash-crop farming and pasture, the settlers might have learned some valuable lessons about subsistence farming, gathering, and hunting that the Anishinaabe developed in tandem with the water boundaries and rhythms over successive generations. Selkirk, however, bound the settlement to the terms of indenture, and so Selkirk had all the power, regardless of how far away he was stationed.

Maintaining this idea of control, and the desire to change the landscape and drain the waterscape to create an agricultural utopia, the settlers were bound to beat back the borders articulated by the water; just as the British government was bound to beat back the borders articulated by treaties with the Anishinaabe that express mutual sharing and not dominion. This victory over the lands and waters (if it can be called that) would come nearly a century after the abandonment of the Baldoon Settlement, in the form of the industrialized drainage technologies. The advent of improved drainage-pump technologies, tiling systems, and construction techniques that allowed the building of dyke systems at the height of the industrial revolution accommodated the desire to penetrate and drain the wetlands to make room for more stable cash-crop production.[48] Firm settlement of the wetlands was pursued non-stop throughout the twentieth century, once industrial capacity could adequately confine the Snye and Sydenham rivers. The new man-made borders created from this technology are presently marked by a landscape dotted by field after field in Dover and Sombra townships with ribbons of rural roads, reinforcing the metaphysical borders between humans and technology and their environment. This was done through an act of pacification that amounted to industrial rape of the land, scarring it and changing what was supposed to be a European dream into an Indigenous nightmare.

On the chain of islands that form Walpole, however, the borders are still marked and dictated by the waters, reinforcing the significance of Bkejwanong as the place "Where the Waters Divide." On Walpole Island, the boundaries are marked by diverse wetland ecosystems, tallgrass prairie, and Carolinian forested islands that continue to support the traditional economies of hunting, trapping, and farming, all the while being balancing the participation of its citizens in the capitalist economy on their terms. In welcoming the Earth, Water, Air and Fire Conference to Walpole Island in 1994, Jacobs emphasized why there is a marked difference between the indigenous and settler societies in southwestern Ontario: "The citizens of the Walpole Island First Nation, also known as the Council of Three Fires, the Ojibwa, Potawatami and Ottawa Nations, have protected and conserved Bkejwanong since time immemorial. This is understood, and told, from the perspective of the First Nation, by our

Elders. They tell us who we are and, in spiritual terms, what the land means to our people."[49] This marks a significant difference in epistemologies. The predominant European epistemology is informed by governments and economies that are often controlled from a distance. The Anishinaabe model, however, is informed through ancestral knowledge that articulates appropriate land ethics.

While more will be said about agriculture, and how it too is being replaced by agribusiness, a brief accounting of how the area's waterscapes are suffering from environmental degradation will be given. The rise of economic imperialism has so far posed the greatest threat to sustainability in Bkejwanong Territory. In her critique of Western-based economies and the process of colonization in the South Pacific, Dominque Temple argues in "The Policy of the 'Severed Flower'" that the vast differences between formal economies (systems based on fixed markets of exchange and resource exploitation) and substantive economies (systems based on gift-giving and reciprocity) will always place colonial markets in a position of power over Indigenous peoples.[50] The effects, she argues, are loss of culture, loss of land, loss of environment, and loss of governance as the formal exchange economies are guided solely by the private interests of colonial powers, whereas gift-giving economies are guided by mutuality, alliance building, and reciprocity.

Consider for a moment that in the 1790 McKee treaty the Anishinaabe actually had an alliance-building strategy in mind when they granted Europeans the right to settle on vast tracts of land along the Thames River instead of just outright giving up everything they had known. It makes no sense for the Anishinaabe to surrender that much land when in 1796 land was being set aside for the Shawnee and other warriors allied to the Crown. The offering of land by the Anishinaabe was not a mutually exclusive separation of peoples but was meant to be a process of inclusive sharing of resources among allies. The act of "giving" this land for British settlement reveals that the Anishinaabe were actually more powerful than popular history normally acknowledges, as it reveals a common theme among substantive economies, the giving of gifts (in this case land) as a form of prestige. This also reveals a social fabric that extends beyond the Anishinaabe as it entertains the idea that settlers were received and cared for as guests by their Anishinaabe hosts. Through the giving of land, and by setting land aside for the southern allied nations, the Anishinaabe proved to be a very powerful bargaining force in the decades following the American Revolution and in the struggle for a clearly defined border. However, the act of giving as a display of power can only go so far when it involves a party who displays power through the act of taking. In the example of Bkejwanong Territory, this clash of values is evident in the misrepresentation of the McKee Treaty and the St. Anne Island Treaty. Despite his cultural alliances with the Anishinaabe, by acting as a representative of the Crown, McKee could interpret the treaties only as surrenders, in accordance with the imperative of accumulating enough wealth to ensure a foothold for the British Empire on the frontier in the face of American northerly expansion.

The effects of this paternalistic mentality have given little consideration to the Anishinaabe, and even less to the waterscapes of southwestern Ontario. This is evidenced by the collapse of the Great Lakes fisheries in the early twentieth century, Detroit's industrial toxic-waste dump on Zug Island, the deep-water dredging of the St. Clair River, the frequent sewage spills from lakeside septic pools, the introduction of zebra mussels from ship ballasts, factory hog operations, the emergence of Sarnia's chemical valley, and the dumping of treated pond water by chemical companies into the St. Clair River. Each of these environmental issues impacts the social fabric of life both on Walpole Island and in Wallaceburg. These concerns have served as common ground between the communities, and, even more, they have served to buttress the metaphysical borders first constructed by colonialist mentality. This will be discussed further through a consideration of the racialization of the Anishinaabe, but first the further agricultural and economic marginalization of both the landscape and the settlers of the area will be explored.

The agri-"culture" that has developed throughout the region over the past century has been a balance between local ownership and industrial ownership. However, just as globalization further removes power from localities and relocates power in urban centres, so too has it sought to remove the "culture" from agriculture, replacing it with "agribusiness." As agribusiness becomes the new norm across North America, local farmers in southwestern Ontario are once again facing the dislocation or loss of control that the Baldoon settlers faced on their arrival. Wendall Berry, in charting the militarization of agriculture in *The Unsettling of America*, notes the same repetitive pattern that continuously displaces settler society and prevents it forming a definitive connection with the land:

> Generation after generation, those who intended to remain and prosper where they were have been dispossessed and driven out, or subverted and exploited where they were, by those who were carrying out some version of the search for El Dorado. Time after time, in place

after place, these conquerors have fragmented and demolished traditional communities, the beginnings of domestic cultures. They have
always said that what they destroyed was outdated, provincial, and
contemptible. And with alarming frequency they have been believed
and trusted by their victims, especially when their victims were other
white people.[51]

This displacement has been occurring at an alarming rate in Wallaceburg.

In the 1830s, the Baldoon settlers had nearly all moved about five
kilometres up the Sydenham River to "Athe Forks," where they became
the founders of Wallaceburg. Like most southwestern Ontario towns,
Wallaceburg prospered from its agricultural economy in the latter nineteenth century and from the industrial economy in the twentieth century. However, both location and free trade may be reversing this trend,
as the town has experienced a substantial economic drain over the past
decade. The past ten years have seen the town's flagship industries
leave, including Wallaceburg Plastics, Libbey Foods, and the town's
largest employer, the Glass Factory. The ripple effect has led to the clo-
sure of an IGA grocer and a Zellers-anchored shopping mall. Com-
pounding these closures is an ongoing shortage of doctors and nurses
at the Sydenham District Hospital and the amalgamation of Wallaceburg
as a political entity into the broader Chatham–Kent municipality, effectively reducing the position of mayor and council to two council representatives at the regional municipal level. Subsequently, both the
provincial and federal electoral boundaries have been expanded, placing Wallaceburg in the corner of a riding the size of the Atlantic province
of Prince Edward Island.

Losing the ability to sustain itself economically while having its
political voice muted, Wallaceburg has become a town with increasingly
vacant storefronts and empty factory floors. The reasons for this may
be many, but the immediate concerns could be attributed to Wallaceburg's distance from the highway 401 and 402 corridors (making towns
like Chatham and Sarnia more favourable for employment), as well as
increased labour outsourcing to the US and Mexico because of the
North American Free Trade Agreement. Social sustainability is therefore at best tenuous and at worst an illusion as families in the community struggle financially, wondering when the next lay-off might occur,
if the next contract will have legitimacy, and if there will even be a job
the next day.

The economy that has driven Wallaceburg to prosperity and to its current slump is comparable to that of Baldoon, as both have been or are controlled by outside forces that ultimately bear no responsibility for sustaining the community. These forces are similar to the colonialist enterprise that operated from a distance. Just as power is not placed at the local level, but operates outside of it, so too are the people at the local level prevented from developing a sense of place where they live, as the necessity to move to where the work is remains a constant threat and a common reality. This was the same emerging sense at Baldoon, where economic insecurity, poor site location, and control from the outside prevented a dynamic sense of a sustainable community from developing.

There is, however, a marked difference in how Walpole Island, facing the same pressures, incorporates itself into the marketplace. Control by outside forces has long been a danger in Bkejwanong Territory, where the Indian Act and accompanying Indian agents (the last of whom was evicted in the 1965) were never invited in. Control is formed from inside the community at the grassroots level, as informed by citizens, Elders, and traditions; it is subsequently expressed through the Walpole Island Heritage Committee (Nin Da Waab Jig, or "Those who seek to find"), which then guides the band council. The immediate difference is how decisions and actions are informed by place.

The idea of sustainability should not be framed in reference to the idea of the "good old days," which conceptualizes the past, traditional ways of doing things, and Indigenous cultural practices as being idyllic, the ultimate solution to the world's problems, and the way to a utopian future. Indeed, any ethic of sustainability that seeks to develop a dialogue between Anishinaabe and Euro-Canadian ways of knowing must take into account the colonialist mentalities that conflict with sustainability. While efforts to achieve sustainability may be grounded in the past, and they may be community based and driven as they are on Walpole Island, the environmental problems cited earlier are only compounded by the racialization of Walpole Island. This resides in the many tired stereotypes filtered throughout southwestern Ontario, which reinforce the marginalization faced by people on Walpole Island. This racism, expressed as the belief that Native peoples are nothing but lazy and alcoholic, illustrates the same social problems faced by some of the economically depressed citizens of Wallaceburg. The oppressed becomes the oppressor, and acts of racism reinforce the metaphysical borders that were drawn over two hundred years ago. As a result, any attempt to develop a sense of sustainability that involves Walpole Island or incorporates forms of Indigenous Ecological Knowledge will have to be fully aware of the colonial history and the role non-Indigenous peoples have in either perpetuating it or putting an end to it.

## Rising Waters of Sustainability

When Lynn White Jr. challenged the Western world to think about environmental sustainability in spiritual terms, he did so by saying that the fundamental aspects of Western Christianity that divorced humanity from Nature have led to the birth of scientific inquiry, which thus considers problems of environmental sustainability in solely positivist and objective terms. A large part of the environmental movement operates on models of environmental sustainability inherited from the same epistemology that created the ecological problems in the first place. This being said, two points of interest should be considered when proposing a hybrid ethic. First, when the idea of subjective experience and the spiritual dimensions of environmental sustainability are discussed, it is often assumed that this is a dialogue solely for Indigenous peoples to engage in, while non-Indigenous peoples find solutions through abstract methodologies that place the self outside of personal engagement with the environment. Indigenous peoples cannot and should not shoulder this burden alone. The idea that Indigenous peoples are the sole speakers for environmental spirituality results in tokenism and leaves little room for dialogue, reinforcing the idea that non-Indigenous peoples can think about environments only objectively, as if "environments" exist only in petri dishes. Second, any dialogue between Western and Anishinaabe ways of knowing ecology must not be intrusive and must not repeat the patterns of the colonization that seek to appropriate "embodied"[52] ways of knowing and then claim this epistemology as their own, or frame it as the token knowledge shared by spiritual leaders.

Environmental sustainability is not something fashioned from empirical thought by Western environmentalists to solve the present environmental and social problems. Environmental sustainability is as old as humanity itself, and it has existed as a way of being in particular ecosystems for particular civilizations. It is grounded both in place and history. For the Anishinaabe of Bkejwanong Territory, sustainability is expressed philosophically through *mino-bimaadiziwin*, or "the way of the good life," and is exercised through community action. Anishinaabe educator Lawrence Gross, in accounting for the ethic as a unifying concept in contemporary Anishinaabe epistemology states that *bimaadiziwin*, or "the good life," is evident from birth to death in all Anishinaabe, serving as "religious blessing, moral teaching, value system, and life goal."[53] The way of expressing this through practice, the day-to-day living of the Anishinaabe, as Gross says, is "helping the Anishinaabe[g] to reconstruct their worlds in the postapocalyptic period."[54] The "apocalypse" Gross refers to here is the end of *a* world brought about by colonialism, not necessarily the end of all people or their civilization. The principles in restructuring these worlds are inherently spiritual, and speak more to efforts of sustainability than most scientifically objective models that generally seek to understand environmental and social problems as they are occurring, or in a worst-case scenario, after the fact.

Presently, on Bkejwanong Territory, the "way of the good life" is continuously confronted through all of the means of colonization discussed thus far, and it is through community action that principles of respect, mutuality, and self-determination are exercised. This community action is not a romanticizing of "the good old days" but is more akin to Gross's reconstruction of identity in a post-apocalyptic world where the threat of chemical spills into the community's drinking water and resource base is a daily threat. It is a community action that utilizes the way of the good life to engage with technology and alliance building with non-Indigenous peoples. Environmental researcher and advocate Robert Van Wynsberghe says of the Walpole Island Heritage Centre's frame of collective community action, "Having a sustainable community involves working toward equitable social, economic, cultural, and technological betterment in a way that does not pollute ecosystems and irrevocably deplete natural resources."[55] This represents an entirely dynamic form of environmental and social sustainability that draws on the place, histories, and traditions that defy objective models of environmental sustainability; but it is also one that is not static or exclusive. As Jacobs has said, environmental sustainability must be inclusive of different ways of seeing the world: "The juxtaposition of Aboriginal Knowledge and knowledge systems with mainstream European-based science is likely to enrich the world views of all."[56]

This way of living responsibly has been fundamental to sustaining all forms of life, from the individual to the community, and to the "other than human" community.[57] On Walpole Island, as in all Anishinaabe Territory, this form of traditional knowledge has been practised from about the time of Creation or the beginning of life on Turtle Island. Perhaps this provides some indication of why the people of Bkejwanong Territory are still there, while Baldoon has come and gone, and why

Wallaceburg is suffering the way it is. Here are two communities, one controlled by outside forces, continuously submitting to them, and increasingly suffering as a result. The other community, despite centuries of marginalization and outside efforts to exert control, has continuously resisted colonization through mobilization based on history, traditions, and sense of belonging to place. If, then, Wallaceburg were to respond to Jacobs when he says, "as a visitor to Turtle Island, you must make an effort to understand us and our ways and our stories,"[58] the response would have to originate from inside its own histories, its own attachment to place, and its own form of sustainability that reflects a "way of the good life."

The first step in responding to Jacobs, and in charting a path toward a sustainable land ethics, might circle back to Christianity. By looking first at Christianity, the act of thinking through the process of sustainability is not something imported from outside of Wallaceburg, as Christianity is the predominant religion of the community and has traditionally been a strong source of social sustainability. What then can be said of Christianity if it is, as White says, "the root of our present ecological crisis"?[59] In his response to the criticisms levelled against Western Christianity, theologian Willis Jenkins admits that a large portion of Western Christian epistemology has its roots in St. Thomas Aquinas's chain of being, and this reinforces the male-centred hierarchies that champion rationality and dominate the subjective.[60] Rather than stop the critique there, however, Jenkins does something rather interesting. Instead of further assailing the Thomist construction, he meditates on it and asks if it can offer a different ontological frame for people who identify in nature something that is entirely spiritual.[61] To this end, Jenkins says that to know in its diversity that all of Creation is an extension of God is not to think of it as a "gift" for the wealthy, or as building blocks for our own construction and consumption, but rather as a manifestation of the holy spirit, and failure to address this and act to preserve it is a failure to attain salvation in the Christian sense.[62] If this is the case in Christian ontology, then everything from a blade of grass to a drop of water can been seen as God, or as an exercise in divine being.

This framework, which couches the preservation of biodiversity in Christian discourse, gives its ultimate consideration to the question of responsibility and ethics. Jenkins asks of technology and of what we construct from Nature, "Do they make visible the harmony of created differences that can point us toward God, or do they stop the gaze in homogeneity, making opaque God's availability in the world?"[63] The effect of this transformative mode of thought presents an ontological state of being that cannot deny the animacy of Creation, as every living and potentially non-living thing contains a sacred energy, or in Christian discourse, the spirit of Creation. As a result, the ways in which people interact within their environments drastically change, as polluting the environment in a sense would be the equivalent of sin.

The question now becomes what a proper ethic of living on the lands and waters in a cross-cultural society and in a climate of economic disparity would be. While it was outside the aims of this chapter to offer solutions, it does point to some possible directions to begin the process of achieving an appropriate land ethic that focusses on place, history, and the stories that emerge from the communities there. For the Anishinaabe of Bkejwanong Territory, this land ethic is understood as emerging from the practices and traditions that predate the arrival of Europeans. Following the apocalypse of the settlers' arrival, the reintegration of these practices and traditions in Anishinaabe territory—while standing in direct opposition to colonial governments—may prove to be a starting point for the settler community of nearby Wallaceburg in developing a hybrid framework of land ethics. This framework must come from within and not from without. Only when the sense of place, and the histories and stories of that place, are seen as a blueprint to move forward can sustainability be pursued with a good spirit.

# NATIVISM'S BASTARD
## Neolin, Tenskwatawa, and the
## Anishinabeg Methodist Movement

‣ ⚍◊⚎ ‣

### CATHERINE MURTON STOEHR

The story of the Anishinabeg and the Loyalist settlers in Upper Canada (now Ontario) has been told without its beginning. Few places could benefit more from reorienting historical analyses, from a perspective shaped by borders to one in search of borderlands between empires.[1] The phenomenon of Anishinabeg people, who for two centuries showed no interest in the various Christian missionaries who visited them, suddenly becoming very interested in the earnest exhortations of immigrant American preachers, cannot be understood without knowledge of the immediate historical source of that interest. Unfortunately, the events that shaped the Upper Canada Anishinabeg response took place south of the Canada–United States border and have been overlooked in discussions of Anishinabe Methodism.[2] Before meeting the American Methodist missionaries in the nineteenth century, the Anishinabeg from north of the Great Lakes encountered the eighteenth-century First Nations Nativist prophets Neolin and Tenskwatawa.[3] Through their experiences fighting alongside Nativist prophets and warriors, the Anishinabeg learned that many people believed that the only safe way to respond to European settlers was through resistance supported by the spirit world. However, the vastness of Anishinabeg territory north of the Great Lakes offered the tantalizing promise of enough room to make a tentative peace with European settlers without resorting to the extremes of armed resistance. In combination, Nativism and the land of Upper Canada produced the most unlikely of offspring. While in the United States Nativists often set themselves up as the antagonists of First Nations Christian groups, in Upper

Canada, where awareness of Nativist teachings preceded intense Christian proselytizing, the anti-colonial Nativist impulse fused with apocalyptic Christian teachings in the First Nations Methodist movement. The hybrid movement drew on the Nativists' "truly radical message that Indians were one people" and on the Nativists' contention that new ceremonies could restore lost spirit power, but argued that such improvements could only be brought about through the ethical actions of First Nations people—that is, the revival promised by the Methodists existed in the future, rather than as a recognition of biological unity dependant on genetics.[4]

In the eighteenth and early nineteenth centuries, a First Nations alliance straddled the Great Lakes, operating in the shadows cast by battling colonial empires. The Ottawa, Ojibwa, and Pottawattamie nations collaborated in a long-standing defensive alliance.[5] While not restrictive, the ties between the Ottawa, Ojibwa, and Pottawattamie extended beyond defence to information sharing and cultural collaboration.[6] Villages within the three groups traded religious and social practices freely. During the colonial era, First Nations defensive military alliances facilitated the movement of cultural ideas between individual villages and nations. When the British took over French forts after the Seven Years' War, the Anishinabeg alliance joined with more far-flung First Nations to follow the Ottawa war leader Pontiac and the Delaware prophet Neolin in a resistance movement against British dominance commonly known as Pontiac's Rebellion. After the rebellion, Neolin's ideas returned north with the Anishinabeg warriors. Twenty years later, when the American settlers ended British control of the Thirteen Colonies, Americans hurried to take over the so-called "Indian lands" of the Ohio Valley that British diplomacy had long forbidden them. The Ohio First Nations, among whom anti- settler feeling was already high, united to offer a military resistance to American land stealing. News of the events in the Ohio Valley, which was then known as the "Northwest," reached north as far as Lake Superior. Members of the Anishinabeg alliance travelled to Ohio to help local Delawares, Shawnees, and Mingos fight the settlers.[7] When the Anishinabeg returned to their homes north of the Great Lakes, they brought with them knowledge of how North American settlers would behave if unconstrained by the British. Finally, some sections of the Anishinabeg alliance joined with the British to resist the American assault on Upper Canada in the War of 1812, which brought them into direct contact with Tenskwatawa, the Shawnee prophet, and his radical anti-British and anti-American teachings.

Each time that the Anishinabeg living south of the Great Lakes defended their land from the colonial invaders—Pontiac's Rebellion, the Northwest War, and the War of 1812—Anishinabeg living north of the Great Lakes travelled hundreds of miles to support them. Participation in colonial conflicts focussed the northern Anishinabeg's attention on land rights and exposed them to the racialized teachings of Neolin and Tenskwatawa, the so-called "Nativist" prophets. When faced with European settlement on their own territory, the northern Anishinabeg's experiences inclined them to concentrate on how settlement would affect their own use of land and to conceptualize their own land rights in the terms of apocalyptic spirituality. This chapter argues two points: first, that the Anishinabeg belief in the primacy of land issues, lack of trust in the British, desperate poverty, alcoholism, and disease shaped the cautious welcome they offered the settlers who moved to their territory; and, second, that although they rejected the racially exclusivist aspects of the Nativists' teachings, the northern Anishinabeg's experiences with the followers of the prophets Neolin and Tenskwatawa convinced many of them of the need for a revival of spiritual power, which predisposed them to embrace the apocalyptic teachings of American Methodist preachers in the nineteenth century. When British and American settlers arrived in British North America, the first thing the Anishinabeg wanted to learn about them was the extent to which those settlers threatened their land. It soon became clear that the farmers, while willing to fight American aggression alongside the Anishinabeg, would take the land for themselves. Missionaries, or at least the American Methodist missionaries, were eager to defend the Anishinabeg's right to their land, both against Americans and against loyal British subjects. Further, the American Methodists offered a strategy of divinely mandated social reform, designed to renew individual spirit power and community wealth, that echoed the teachings of the Nativist prophets. As a result, large numbers of Anishinabeg people in communities across Upper Canada adopted Methodist practices and terminology in the 1830s.

A recent work by British Columbian geographer Cole Harris suggests a way that historians might usefully think about the relationship between European settlement in the United States and later settlement in what is now Canada. Harris suggests that cultural analyses of colonialism have distanced actual colonial encounters from their representation in today's academic debates by failing to contextualize such encounters in their particular military and economic circumstances.[8] Cultural studies illuminate one aspect of the colonial project but obscure the practical realities of land stealing. Harris notes that "The initial ability [of colonial powers] to dispossess rested primarily on physical power and the supporting infrastructure of the state."[9] Indeed, historians have concluded that the Anishinabeg in Upper Canada supported the British against the Americans in the War of 1812 because their fear of American expansionism outweighed whatever hesitancy they might have had to join a colonial war—that is, they feared American violence.[10] However, the precise origin of that fear, where it was gained and how it was manipulated, has slipped through the cracks between Canadian and American historiography. Further, while historians have noted that, despite their alliance, manipulation and violence characterized the relationship between the British and the Anishinabeg in the settlement era, they focus on small-scale incidents of abuse and murder, ignoring the most significant way in which the British used violence.[11] The British used the threat of American aggression to secure land treaties in Upper Canada, thereby directly benefitting from the violence that the Americans were enacting. As Harris has pointed out, "Once the power of violence had been demonstrated, the threat of it was often sufficient [to dispossess people of land]."[12] In the case of the Upper Canadian land treaties, the British adopted the language of alliance and diplomacy while letting the Americans violence in the Ohio Valley speak for itself and thus create the conditions under which the British could dispossess the Anishinabeg of Southern Ontario.

If the British were manipulating international events to take over Anishinabeg territory, how can we characterize the Anishinabeg's response to their attempts? American studies that focus on intertribal relations tend to categorize particular villages or even entire nations in terms of their attitude toward colonization. In *A Spirited Resistance*, Gregory Dowd categorizes moments of agreement between parties that he labels "accommodationist" and "Nativist" as alliances of convenience between groups of people possessed of fixed, inimical political strategies who temporarily shared a single goal.[13] According to the accommodationist/Nativist binary, the northern Anishinabeg who adopted Methodism were accommodating with colonial culture and were "accommodationists." In reality, the Anishinabeg living north of the Great Lakes had been engaged in aggressive military conflicts with Europeans for over a generation when settlers arrived in their territory. As often as the Anishinabeg accommodated Europeans, they travelled long distances to take up arms. In each new colonial encounter, they evaluated their circumstance and acted according to ethical dictates far older and more complex than acceptance or rejection of a particular foreign practice. Depending on the size of an army or the actions of a settler, yesterday's Nativist could become tomorrow's accommodationist. It is unnecessary to assume that individual First Nations leaders' actions in a particular instance implied allegiance to a political philosophy limited by its position with respect to European powers. When the Anishinabeg leaders in Upper Canada decided to ally themselves with European Methodist ministers from the United States, they did so knowing how the Nativist movement had played out south of the border because they had been a part of it. Indeed, yesterday's Nativist became Upper Canada's accommodationist.

Having proposed, then, that a military struggle in the United States shaped the Upper Canada land treaties and the ensuing religious character of many Anishinabe communities, the question arises: Why have the American colonial wars figured so small in Canadian history? The answer can be found in one of the stranger consequences of colonialism. It is a truism to say that the borders between nation-states are political fictions; however, those fictions have been turned into Western fact by the national orientation of historical inquiry. Not only did the lines that the Europeans drew upon the waters of the Great Lakes divide the once-united Anishinabeg into the categories of American and Canadian, and subjugate the divided peoples to the policies of different colonial powers, but the lines that separated the water of the Great Lakes also separated the stories retold in Western scholarship. As a result, the internal logic of First Nations responses to French, British, and American colonialism has been lost to non-Native scholars. The Canadian literature does not use the American literature to help explain the development of the British colonial state in Upper Canada. Most notably, the ways in which participating in the colonial resistance to the south shaped the Anishinabeg attitude toward the settlers has been overlooked.

The First Nations Nativist movement in the United States came to prominence in Pontiac's Rebellion, which followed the Seven Years' War. As early as 1737, First Nations prophets claimed that spiritual beings were angry with the First Nations people for trading with Europeans.[14] Other prophets condemned alcohol use, materialist greed, and Christian theology as affronts to Indigenous deities.[15] By the time of the Seven Years' War, such anti-European ideas in the Ohio territory had coalesced into a popular belief that the spirits had created humans in three distinct racial groups.[16] In the mid-eighteenth century, Nativist ideas were not so segregationist as to prevent a military alliance between the Ohio First Nations (Shawnee, Delaware, and Mingos) and the French during the Seven Years' War. However, when the French defeat was imminent, the

Lenape (Delaware), Shawnee, and Mingos organized an all-Native resistance to the coming British dominance.[17] The resistance, known as Pontiac's Rebellion, relied on the strong spiritual leadership of Neolin, the Delaware prophet, who deployed the racially exclusivist, Nativist teachings popular at the time to shape a cultural movement out of military resistance.[18]

Before the Seven Years' War, the Delaware prophet Neolin told his community that a spiritual being had told him that the First Nations must renounce the cultural influences of European society and return to traditional forms of subsistence living if they wished to achieve prosperity and health. Further, Neolin's visitor informed him that the Great Spirit was angry with the Delawares for allowing non-Natives to live on their land.[19] Neolin explained that he had received this teaching one evening when he himself had been thinking about the "evil ways he saw prevailing among the Indians."[20] The stranger gave Neolin a representation of a path that his Delaware ancestors had walked through life to reach happiness. However, Neolin's map showed bars blocking the way to happiness. Those bars, Neolin learned, and later taught, were the vices that Europeans had introduced into Native societies, of which alcohol was the most destructive. In order to break through the bars and reach happiness, Neolin instructed his followers to stop using alcohol, to work toward breaking off trade with Europeans, and to observe new rituals of purification.[21] Neolin's message convinced people to take up the rituals he taught and to resist the cultural influences of their European neighbours. Neolin's teachings began to travel far when the Ottawa chief, Pontiac, accepted them. The Ottawa occupied a central position in First Nations trade networks, and cultural changes within the Ottawa affected far-flung nations. Neolin wove resistance and religious revival together when he predicted a coming war through which the newly purified First Nations would finally effect complete isolation and independence from European society.

The military actions of Pontiac's Rebellion began when the French abandoned their forts in North America. Anishinabeg warriors from what became Upper Canada got involved when British soldiers took up residence in the abandoned French forts. The northern Anishinabeg expected British officers to take over forts south of the Great Lakes, but when the British occupied Fort Detroit the Anishinabeg grew concerned. In 1761, Anishinabeg elders from the north shore of Lake Ontario, sometimes called the Mississauga, met with the British government representative William Johnson to ask him why the British were reprovisioning the old French forts with new cannons even though their enemies, the French, had departed.[22] Johnson soothed the Mississaugas with gifts of weapons, meat, and rum; however, the Anishinabeg even farther north, who had closer ties to the western Anishinabeg in Michigan, were also unhappy with the British presence at the French forts and, unlike the Mississauga Anishinabeg, the western Anishinabeg did not receive goodwill gifts. Troubled by Britain's expanded power, many warriors from north of the Great Lakes joined the southern First Nations in calling for an armed resistance against the now-unchallenged British military.

In 1763, Anishinabeg warriors journeyed from as far north as Georgian Bay to join with the Ohio Valley alliance to reassert First Nations authority in the political life of North America, and Pontiac's Rebellion began. Chiefs from three of the four major Anishinabeg communities north of the Great Lakes committed warriors to attack British forts around the Great Lakes.[23] Not all Anishinabeg villages in Upper Canada agreed on the importance of resisting a British trade monopoly in North America. The villages closer to Lake Ontario, such as those on the River Credit and Rice and Mud lakes, objected to a full-scale offensive against the British. Wabbicomicott, a chief from the Toronto area who had close personal ties to William Johnson, exposed a planned attack to British authorities at York, so convinced was he that supporting the English was in his interest.[24] Canadian historian Peter Schmaltz credits Wabbicomicott's attitude to the Lake Ontario (or Mississauga) communities' close relations with French and British traders. The more isolated villages at the Saugeen River on Lake Huron, Coldwater at Georgian Bay, and Cape Croker in the Bruce Peninsula supported Pontiac's Rebellion more fervently.[25] Concrete numbers are hard to come by, but it is known that a community on the Thames River sent 170 warriors south to support Pontiac.[26]

Historical interpretation of Pontiac's Rebellion has suffered from the Nativist/accommodationist binary. Since the First Nations received no significant land gains after the conflict, Pontiac's Rebellion has generally been seen as a Native defeat. However, during the rebellion, the Native alliance successfully captured eight forts: St. Joseph, Miami, Michilimackinac, Green Bay, Presqu'isle, Le Boer, Sandusky, and Venago. The assumption that the Natives were defeated in Pontiac's uprising rests on the belief that their aim was the Nativist goal of eradicating the British presence in North America; however, a more measured interpretation suggests that, having lost the working social equilibrium that they had achieved with their French allies, First Nations warriors wished to re-establish similar terms with the English.[27] As long as the English believed that the First Nations posed no military threat, they had no motivation to offer the Natives the favourable trading prices and generous presents that the French had used to maintain their preferential trading status. Pontiac's Rebellion afforded the English a powerful motivation to attend to Native demands in the future. In the short term, as leaders like Wabbicommicot and the other Lake Ontario chiefs feared, First Nation's military resistance hurt trade with the British.[28] In the end, however, with French forts remaining in English hands, the resistance shown by the First Nations alliance helped them to maintain a strong position in their future dealings with the English.[29] Even the more radical Anishinabeg leaders continued to trade with the British after the rebellion. Full-scale military resistance, of the kind promoted by radical Nativists, could serve the ends of First Nations–European cooperation.

The British set out their post–French era policy toward the North American First Nations in the Royal Proclamation of 1763. The Proclamation forbade individual settlers to purchase First Nations' land that had not first been ceded to the British government in a legal international treaty (according to British law) between the colonial authorities and the Native leaders of the area in question. The proclamation indicated the British government's commitment to limiting settler expansionism by disallowing private land purchases. Further, the proclamation tacitly confirmed the sovereignty of the First Nations communities by suggesting that non-Native private individuals could not form legal relationships with Native people in the absence of international treaties. Whether or not the Anishinabeg cared about their status as a nation-state under British law, they valued having the British military stand between them and aggressive American settlers.[30] When Pontiac's Rebellion was over, the northern Anishinabeg, who had fought alongside Pontiac, rejected the more extreme elements of the Prophet Neolin's teaching and returned north, preferring to maintain a military alliance and a trading relationship with the British rather than relying on an all–First Nations alliance network to protect them against settler expansion.

The northern Anishinabeg had not left the Ohio Valley permanently. They returned to support their southern allies in the so-called Northwest Indian War. When American settlers rose in defiance of the colonial government in 1775, in part because of the settlement restrictions of the Royal Proclamation, many of the same First Nations who had allied with Pontiac and the Ottawa now allied themselves with British forces. In some cases, warriors organized under the leadership of officers of the

British Indian Department.[31] Freed from the calculated restraint of British settler policy, the victorious Americans swarmed onto the Ohio territories. Faced with such behaviour, First Nations moderates gave way to the arguments of the militants and supported warrior raids into settler towns. In 1785, warriors from across the Northwest gathered at Detroit to organize a confederacy to force the United States to control their citizens. The militants' calls for resistance were answered by local leaders, the Shawnee Chief Blue Jacket, and the Miami Chief Little Turtle, who led the defence of the Ohio territories, and also by northern warriors from the Saugeen territory near Georgian Bay.[32] Led by the Saugeen warriors and accompanied by British troops, the Anishinabeg of Upper Canada sent hundreds of warriors to join the fight.[33]

The confederacy pursued its ends by raiding American settlements. The United States sent federal and state militias on retaliatory raids into Shawnee communities. In 1790, the Americans organized larger war parties that suffered defeat at the hands of the confederacy in 1790 and 1791. In 1794, the First Nations Confederacy suffered a devastating defeat: the combined First Nations force foundered when American General Anthony Wayne's troops defeated their forces at the Battle of Fallen Timbers in September. The Anishinabe warriors returned to the north with deep animosity for American settlers.

As the warriors fought, their own homelands were changing to mirror conditions to the south. The demographic composition of the northern Anishinabe territory changed dramatically. Exiles, Native and non-Native, from the revolutionary war swarmed north to find new homes. In July 1784 the first Euro-American settlers arrived and settled north of the Great Lakes. Just under four thousand people arrived in the first wave of settlers.[34] The total population of the Lake Ontario Anishinabeg at the time was under two thousand. In one month, the resident First Nations of Upper Canada changed from being spectators of settler conflicts in the south to being a minority population in their own land. The British negotiated treaties with the Anishinabeg living north of the Great Lakes before handing out land to the new settlers in order to honour the terms of the Proclamation of 1763. The treaties took place in three stages. The first treaties were conducted between 1781 and 1806 and recorded land transfers along the shores of lakes Ontario, Erie, and St. Clair, as well as the rivers that connected those lakes. The early treaties suited both parties because while the British wanted farmland for their loyal soldiers, the Anishinabeg, whose land intensive hunting took place in the interior of the area, needed only small plots of land with water access for their summer villages. When the northern Anishinabeg signed their earliest treaties with the British, they were well versed in colonial diplomatic relations and they had had first-hand experience with the aggressiveness of American settlers.

While the northern Anishinabe made a fragile peace with their new tenants, the southern confederacy's resistance to the American government's incursions continued. A young warrior named Tecumseh, who had stood on the field at the Battle of Fallen Timbers, started a third, more radical, incarnation of the intertribal resistance. In a bid to stop American settlement in the northern Ohio valley and in the northwestern states, Tecumseh, who was a Shawnee, and his brother Tenskwatawa, participated in ongoing skirmishes with state militias. Tecumseh built his military resistance on the spiritual teachings that Tenskwatawa received from visions. Like Pontiac and Neolin before them, Tecumseh and Tenskwatawa led an intertribal resistance that aimed to recreate their communities and take back their land in accordance with an ethical vision of the future that reflected, but did not mimic, the past.[35]

Tenskwatawa experienced a dramatic vision of the future of his people. Tenskwatawa reported that when his dream vision began he had been sitting at his fire thinking about how the people in his community behaved improperly. In his dream, Tenskwatawa stood on a road facing a fork that led off in two directions. Along one of the forks, he could see many houses filled with demons torturing people. In one of the houses, spirits urged their victims to drink from steaming cups, all the while reminding them of how much they had enjoyed whiskey in life. When they did drink, molten lead poured into their mouths and destroyed their stomachs. Tenskwatawa reported that he saw many people walking down the road toward the tortures.[36] The other fork in the road led to a verdant place where food abounded. Tenskwatawa concluded from the dream that alcohol was destroying his people and would bring them further destruction after death. He taught his followers to renounce alcohol and the violence that it bred. He also taught that First Nations people should avoid using European technology whenever they could. He instituted new ceremonies symbolizing turning away from European strength and ingenuity and returning to older Indigenous knowledge. Tenskwatawa used the ritual of the new fire, which required followers to extinguish the family fire that had likely been lit using a European manufactured tinderbox and start a new fire using indigenous techniques. The new fire was not extinguished for a year, and burned day and night as a symbol of the enduring power of Native life.[37]

Tenskwatawa's anti-European teachings rested on the cosmological assertion that what he called "the Whites" were the children of the Bad Spirit (also known as the Great Serpent) and not of the Great Spirit as were all other human societies.[38] Although he wanted to distance his people from the corruption he perceived in European culture, Tenskwatawa's reforms were not intended to return the Shawnee to their pre-contact state. Tenskwatawa wanted the Shawnee to find their power again so that they could live more prosperously and in peace with each other. To that end, he condemned whatever aspects of his own tradition he believed to be divisive. He condemned the shamans and the use of medicine bundles. He called for an end to all dances that included alcohol use and established new ones. He actively pursued intertribal unity by sending out messengers to spread his vision to neighbouring First Nations to encourage them to also give up harmful practices.[39] Tenskwatawa's missionaries went north to the Great Lakes region and east to the Iroquois still living in New York. Tecumseh himself travelled for several years after 1808 to spread his message and to bolster resistance to European settlements in the Ohio territory. His messengers taught the new rituals to all who wanted them.[40]

Anger at Native chiefs who had signed treaties with the American government fuelled Tenskwatawa's followers. Tecumseh and Tenskwatawa openly criticized leaders who they believed had sold out their communities. The tensions that the brothers created so disturbed their own community that they were forced to start a new one. In order to geographically act out their vision of a new Native world, they established their home in exile at Greenville, Ohio, where their own chiefs had signed a contentious land surrender.[41] Calling their new village Prophetstown, the brothers welcomed all First Nations people to visit them to learn Tenskwatawa's teachings. Native messengers travelled from throughout the northwest to stay at Prophetstown.[42]

A delegation of Anishinabeg from Northern Michigan spent more than a year with the Prophetstown community. An epidemic of smallpox hit the community in 1808, and the Anishinabeg delegation returned home unconvinced that the Prophet had enough power to protect his own people.[43] When Prophetstown was destroyed by the American army, and Tecumseh and Tenskwatawa were forced to flee to British protection at Amherstburg, their reputation as powerful warriors blessed by strong spirit protectors further declined. However, the Anishinabeg's discouragement at the brothers' waning spiritual power did not indicate a lack of support for their political commitments. Tenskwatawa's movement upheld the same political goals of pan-tribal organization and renewed local strength through revitalized rituals that Neolin and Pontiac had supported, and their purchase was broad and deep on First Nations in the Great Lakes area.

The British at Amherstburg welcomed Tecumseh and Tenskwatawa, finding themselves once again in need of an ally against the Americans. The British had angered the Americans by intercepting their trading ships on the high seas. In 1811, the Americans were preparing to invade Upper Canada as a way to punish the British for boarding American ships. Tecumseh's arrival at Amherstburg coincided with this sudden decline in US–British relations. The British welcomed Tecumseh's significant military expertise, not to mention his warriors, to help in planning strategy in case of an American attack. For the Anishinabeg of Upper Canada, Tecumseh's presence at Amherstburg ensured that his message of First Nations unity and ceremonial revival through cleansing was reinforced among the communities of St. Clair and the Thames, and through them the rest of the territory.

Even during this period, however, Tenskwatawa's influence with the Anishinabeg was muted by his polemical positions on shamans and accommodating chiefs. He condemned the Anishinabeg medicine society the Midewiwin, which was especially widespread among the Anishinabeg immigrants from the United States, and the use of medicine bags, which many Anishinabeg, Midewiwin or not, used.[44] Tenskwatawa's criticisms took on a sinister appearance when, one year after his move to Amherstburg, rumours spread that he or his followers had poisoned First Nations people from other communities who opposed them. Some of Tenskwatawa's followers were subsequently murdered in Amherstburgh.[45]

When the war with the Americans broke out in late summer of 1812, Tecumseh and his warriors supported the British as allies, inspired by a British promise that seemed to support Tenskwatawa's vision of a coming victory for the First Nations people. Britain promised their new allies assistance in the fight for a greater share of the Ohio territory. Anishinabeg warriors also fought alongside the Shawnee alliance and the British in the War of 1812. Many of the Anishinabeg leaders who would shape Native–British relations in Upper Canada for the first half of the nineteenth century fought side by side with British officers during the conflict. On the battlefield, the British–Native alliance had early success, taking control of the American forts at Michilimackinac and Detroit. The fighting then turned to the Niagara peninsula between lakes Ontario and Erie. At the Battle of Queenston Heights on 13 October 1812, Tecumseh took a fatal wound and died, and the Prophet Tenskwatawa escaped. The First Nations alliance fought on for a year and a half until the mutual capitulation ended the war. The British broke their promise to Tecumseh by failing to secure any land for the First Nations from the Americans in the Treaty of Ghent. The Americans refused to grant the requested territory because settlers had already moved onto it. The Ohio Territory that the Shawnee-led confederacy had fought so hard for went unprotected from further American settlement, and Tecumseh's warriors remained in Upper Canada. This was another defeat for the prophet and for those who counselled radical forms of resistance.

When the fighting was over and the northern Anishinabeg returned to their homes, their relations with the new British settlers in their territory had changed. A new political and cultural movement developed in Upper Canada when the fighting was over. Led by warriors who had returned from fighting the United States, the movement was characterized by a call for broadened and deepened alliances among northern First Nations communities, active critique and resistance of British, attempts to ignore treaties, and the promotion of cleansing rituals designed to promote community strength. The key difference between this movement and the Nativist movements that preceded it was that, in the newest incarnation, European technology and wisdom were not identified among the contagions plaguing Native society. Yellowhead, head chief, or *ogimaa*, of the Anishinabeg at Lake Simcoe, participated in the defence of York in 1813 and was shot in the mouth by a musket. Yellowhead's son, also named Yellowhead, became one of the leading promoters of the new movement. An important chief who negotiated several treaties with the colonial government, Yellowhead the younger also presided over the Lake Simcoe community's first attempts at farming. In his vision of cultural reform, incorporating farming into his community would strengthen their chances to achieve prosperity. He did not believe that the manitous would punish them for farming. Indeed, he also convinced his community to adopt Methodism because he believed that the Methodist god would give his community spiritual strength. While earlier Nativists believed that their people's suffering resulted from a manitou's punishment, Yellowhead believed that, while no spirit was punishing his community, their lot could be bettered if a new spirit blessed them. Not content to introduce his own community to the Methodists' deity, Yellowhead followed the Shawnee prophet's practice of travelling and sending out missionaries to spread his teachings. In a dance speech before leaders from nearby communities, Yellowhead claimed that becoming a Christian fulfilled the cultural mandate of a warrior. In the seventeenth century, Anishinabeg and Iroquois warriors fought over hunting territory borders. Warriors protected their community's means to sustain themselves through the fur trade. According to Yellowhead, adopting Christianity could protect communities, and therefore warriors were obliged to adopt it. Yellowhead's dance balanced the very stability of the village on the warriors' willingness to be, in Yellowhead's words, "determined to live or die" for the Lord Jesus Christ.[46] In leaders like Yellowhead, Christianity mixed with farming and three of the major tenets of Nativism to form a new strategy of colonial engagement.

One decade after the conclusion of the War of 1812, in the third generation after European immigration to Upper Canada, an Anishinabe warrior by the name of Shawundais attended a Methodist church service. Our account of his experience exists in the form of a conversion narrative that Shawundais, known in English as John Sunday, shared with audiences in sermons. Although he framed his talk to encourage other First Nations people to become Methodists themselves, the rhetorical structure of his story retains his own understanding of the significance and meaning of his spiritual journey in terms of the particular history of the Anishinabeg of Upper Canada.

Sunday was invited to hear a sermon in a nearby town. The preacher took for his text the Gospel of Matthew, chapter 7, verses 13–14: "Enter through the narrow gate; for the gate is wide and the road is easy that leads to destruction, and there are many who take it. For the gate is narrow and the road is hard that leads to life, and there are few who find it."[47] Sunday understood this teaching, as the preacher likely intended him to do, as an affirmation that after death some humans go to a place of destruction while others find life. So far the minister's words affirmed prophecies from Neolin and Tenskwatawa. However, when Sunday retold the story later, he framed the insight in racial terms of colonial relations: "all the wicked white men, and wicked Indians, and drunkards, shall go there; [to the place of destruction] but the good white people shall go in the narrow way; but if the Indians also become good and serve the Lord, they can go in that narrow way."[48] Sunday went on to say "my parents taught me that all the Indians shall go where sun set, but the white people shall go in the Ishpeming [above]." Sunday's parents had given him the Nativist teaching about the afterlife. Sunday had grown up believing that First Nations people and Europeans lived in distinct metaphysical universes presided over by separate Manitous. When they died, their souls would each go to a separate afterlife, much as the prophets Neolin and Tenskwatawa had taught. A non-Native author who interviewed Anishinabeg people about their spiritual beliefs in the 1830s concluded that most Anishinabeg people believed that one god created all humans; however, people known as prophets were teaching that separate gods made and ruled the First Nations people and the Europeans.[49] Clearly, Sunday's family followed one of the prophets who taught that different ethnic groups had different deities. However, according to his account, the experience at the Methodist meeting convinced Sunday otherwise.

When Sunday told this story to audiences in Europe, they likely assumed that his experience was a happy discovery that he was going to be let in on an inheritance that he had never thought to hope for. From their point of view, an Aboriginal from the colonies might well be pleased to learn that he had a share in the future blessings that the invisible spirits had prepared for Europeans. Reform-minded Methodists in England, who felt shame over how the British had treated Aboriginal people, longed to hear that the Aboriginals themselves could use the Christian comfort of the promise of heaven as a shield against the indignities and dangers of their lives as colonial subjects. First Nations audiences in Upper Canada, acutely concerned about their own futures in the colonial state of Upper Canada, likely heard more than a promise of otherworldly comfort in Sunday's words. Having seen the repeated failure of the military Nativist alliances, and unable to trust their futures to the good intentions of colonial officials, the First Nations people of Upper Canada heard Sunday's account as a declaration of a new philosophy of colonial engagement, building on the strengths of Nativism but allowing greater freedom in using European sources of power. Further, when people like John Sunday expressed anxiety about not being able to enter heaven, it was not because they doubted their own virtue; rather, they had listened to the Nativist prophets' teachings about separate gods for separate nations and separate heavens for each.

John Sunday and Chief Yellowhead realigned the boundaries of the old Nativist alliance from racial into ethical terms. According to Sunday, "Good Whites" and "Good Indians" would share a single afterlife, while "Bad Whites and Bad Indians" would share punishment in the afterlife. Sunday and Yellowhead believed that the Methodists supported the Nativists' political goals. Although Sunday, Chief Yellowhead, and others like them rejected the racial categories orthodox to Nativist movements by forming this alliance with the Methodists, they maintained the other goals of the movement: unity between all First Nations communities; the creation of healthy, economically independent communities; rejection of spiritual or economic practices that created dependence on Europeans; condemnation of alcohol use; and most importantly, the protection of Indigenous land. Believing that the non-Native Methodists in Upper Canada supported each of these goals, the Anishinabeg Methodists pragmatically modified Nativist teachings to include them as allies at a time when the large Pan-Indian confederacies were spent. Thus the insights and strategies of the Anishinabeg Methodist leaders who shaped their communities' earliest policies for dealing with settlers owed more to their knowledge and experiences of Nativism than they did to the advice and encouragement of either British political officials or Methodist missionaries.

The growing popularity of borderlands studies will likely do much to unite the First Nations communities who lived north and south of the Great Lakes in historiography just as they are united in history. American historians Jeremy Adelman and Stephen Aron have defined borderlands as "contested boundaries between colonial domains" distinguishable from the political fiction of international "borders."[50] As such, the term "borderlands" refers directly to physical space and indirectly to people in that space. The significance of such a concept for First Nations history lies in its repudiation of any form of analysis that takes international borders at face value. By terminating at the forty-ninth parallel, the historiographies of both Canadian and American First Nations have suffered from doing just that. Clearly there were significant differences between how First Nations on either side of the Great Lakes experienced colonialism—when settlers arrived in what later became Upper Canada, they announced themselves with treaties backed by presents, leaving the threat of unchecked American aggression to loom silently in the background. In the United States, settlers announced themselves by building fences that they defended with muskets. However, differences in the colonization of the two areas within the Great Lakes borderlands are not the whole story. The two stories are different, not because they are unrelated, but rather because the relationship between them is generational, the Canadian story born out of the experiences of their neighbours to the south.

# BORDERS WITHIN
## *Anthropology and the Six*
## *Nations of the Grand River*

➤━━ ⊠✦⊠ ━━➤

MICHELLE A. HAMILTON

Among the nineteenth-century records of the Ontario Historical Society is a curious postcard once mailed to David Boyle, the secretary of the society and the curator of the Ontario Provincial Museum in Toronto. Addressed from John Ojijatekha Brant-Sero, a Kanien'ke:haka (Mohawk) of the Six Nations of the Grand River, this card advertised an evening's entertainment of songs and recitations by the Brant-Sero family, who would be costumed in "old English lace and Indian Bead Work." At such sessions, his wife played the piano and Brant-Sero explained the origins of the Haudenosaunee (Six Nations) Confederacy, delivered an address from Shakespeare's *Othello* in both the Kanien'ke:haka and English languages, performed "Mohawk yells," and presented anthropological information that he helped gather during Boyle's fieldwork at the Grand River reserve.[1] Like other nineteenth-century Indigenous individuals who actively engaged in anthropology, Brant-Sero mediated between Indigenous and Euro-Canadian worlds.

Extending the borderlands concept of a zone of cultural interaction from a geographical place to an intellectual one allows the examination of such negotiations of identity within the discipline of anthropology. Several studies of First Nations anthropologists indicate that their motives and activities were affected by their multiple or shifting cultural identities, which had been shaped by familial ties, religion, the influence of anthropological mentors, and political beliefs.[2] While the Haudenosaunee have been indeed physically divided by international and provincial boundaries, they have also been affected by metaphysical borders often created by colonial pressures of assimilation, competing forms of spirituality, governance, education, and upbringing, and the transmission and preservation of traditional knowledge and the material culture associated with this knowledge. As Hele notes in the introduction to this volume, however, these competing forms are not simply Native versus non-Native; they occurred between the colonizer and the colonized, and within First Nations communities. As they struggled to deal with colonial policies, Native individuals accepted, rejected, and merged different parts of these metaphysical elements; this created a highly variable response to anthropological activity, as shown by the participation in, opposition to and manipulation of this discipline by sisters E. Pauline and Evelyn H. C. Johnson, by John O. Brant-Sero, and by the Haudenosaunee traditional council at the Six Nations of the Grand River.[3]

The anthropological endeavours of E. Pauline and Eliza H. C. Johnson were influenced by their upbringing in both a Native and a non-Native Victorian world. They were the daughters of a Mohawk father, George Henry Martin Johnson, and a British mother, Emily Howells, and the granddaughters of Helen Martin and John Smoke Johnson. The family was involved in several ways with the Six Nations governmental structure; in addition to the Anglican church, the Superintendent of Indian Affairs employed George Johnson as an interpreter, John Smoke Johnson acted as a Pine Tree chief and speaker of the Confederacy Council, and Helen Martin was a clan matron influential in choosing chiefs. The family lived on the edge of the Grand River reserve, and later in the nearby town of Brantford after the death of George Johnson.[4] By 1896, E. Pauline Johnson, the famed poetess, performer, and "Mohawk princess," had met David Boyle, curator of the Ontario Provincial Museum in Toronto, and that year she sold a mask originally owned by an Onondaga chief to him. In 1898, Boyle purchased a "medicine" mask, a turtleshell rattle, a belt of wampum, and another of dentalium shells from Johnson.[5] She appears to have shared or at least understood Boyle's greater valuation of "authentic" objects, that is those that were old, of traditional origin, and used in non-Christian ceremonies, an emphasis common to nineteenth-century collectors. Before selling a sacred False Face mask to Boyle, Johnson asked noted anthropologist and family friend Horatio Hale to vouch that it was a "genuine ceremonial mask," and to formulate a certificate of authenticity to accompany the sale of her masks in general.[6] She also expected that one of her masks would fetch a high price because it was so ancient that it was crumbling.[7] Later, Johnson played upon Boyle's partiality for "pure" or "traditional" artifacts when she described several items as once belonging to "our most blue-blooded Onondagas."[8] In advertising a wampum belt, she told Boyle it was one of the oldest of all belts, and suggested it was the Hiawatha belt that marked the formation of the Confederacy of the Five Nations.[9] Really, this wampum was not the Hiawatha belt, but Johnson may have been attempting to emphasize the age and traditionality of this item, or perhaps she designated all wampum belts as "Hiawatha" in reference to their use by the confederacy in politics and diplomacy. Later, writing to naturalist Ernest Thompson Seton in order to sell a belt, she again suggested that she possessed the Hiawatha treaty belt.[10]

Religious differences within the Haudenosaunee community may also explain why Johnson sold sacred items such as False Face masks and turtleshell rattles, and why the Johnson family possessed these items to begin with. An Anglican and an interpreter for the Anglican church, Pauline's father, George H. M. Johnson, destroyed or confiscated False Face masks owned by others.[11] Similarly, when Johnson visited a Delaware community on the Six Nations reserve, which was feasting and dancing around an "idol" carved from wood in the shape of a woman, Johnson struck off its head with an axe and split the statue. The Delaware chief had agreed to this, apparently because he had converted to Christianity himself although his people had not. Johnson threw the head on top of a shed at the Anglican parsonage, but when the family moved to their Chiefswood estate, the carving was taken too. For several years, the head was displayed in her father's study and later stored underneath their parlour table.[12] Afterwards, Evelyn Johnson remembered that children broke off its nose by playing football with it.[13]

Clearly, the Johnson family did not follow some of the traditional Haudenosaunee protocol concerning non-Christian spiritual objects. Besides games with the head of the Delaware "idol," and her sale of sacred items, Pauline Johnson and her brother decorated their residences with a collection. Pauline even transported numerous items to London and Vancouver during her trips. In the 1890s during a tour in England, for example, Johnson exhibited a False Face mask on her mantelpiece and at least one of her recitals included the display of a mask on the platform upon which she performed.[14] Information collected by anthropologists would suggest that traditionalists found such treatment of these items offensive and dangerous, and further, collectors such as David Boyle and John Brant-Sero had met with reluctance and opposition in the sale of similar masks.[15]

False Face masks, which cure illness in humans and control crop-destroying winds, are considered sentient beings by traditional Haudenosaunee. They also require care; the keeper of a mask maintains the spirit's life through offerings of corn mush and tobacco. Only to be viewed at certain ritual times of the year, masks are not to be reproduced through photography, drawing, or any other aesthetic means. When not in use, a mask can be hung out of general view in one's lodging but is more likely to be wrapped up with the accompanying turtle rattle. After the keeper's death, a mask is usually destroyed or buried, or transferred to another individual, though it must be someone within the False Face society. Grave repercussions, such as sickness and death, follow the disrespect, ill treatment, or neglect of the powerful entities that are represented by the masks.[16]

Biographers have deemed Johnson a profligate spender, and her economic state may partially explain her sale of such ethnographic items.[17] In 1897, she wrote to Boyle that "I am at a standstill, and alas! my treasures must go for money must be had at all costs."[18] In 1905, she requested the aid of naturalist and writer Ernest Thompson Seton to find a buyer for a wampum belt; she told him that she was "compelled to part with it" if she was to tour again in England. She calculated it to be worth $1,600 but was willing to accept a lesser amount.[19] One year later, Johnson sold this belt and another mask to prolific American collector George Gustav Heye for $550 but asked that she have the opportunity to redeem the belt within the next two years at a rate of 6 percent interest.[20] Similarly, in 1907, Johnson offered to Montreal lawyer and collector William Lighthall a turtleshell rattle, two "ceremonial stones," a silver medal presented to her father by King Edward in 1860, and a piece of quill and moosehair embroidery given to her mother as a wedding present, as security for a $100 loan.[21]

Her treatment and sale of ceremonial and spiritual items may not be so straightforward, however. In her writings, she claimed to be both Christian and "pagan," and it is unclear whether these identities changed over time, were a form of religious hybridization, or were mere rhetoric.[22] It is possible that the public display of False Face masks became less common as missionaries pressed the Haudenosaunee to convert to Christianity, and thus perhaps religious items came to be used more secretly. In this sense, Johnson's public use of the masks may represent an earlier traditional protocol. Anthropologist William Fenton's twentieth-century informants also distinguished between types of masks: those that visited an individual in a dream and were carved especially for the keeper as guardians were considered to be more inviolate, while extra masks could be lent to others or even sold.[23] Some contemporary community members from Grand River also suggest that Johnson's father's destruction of the Delaware idol was more posturing for the missionary, who accompanied Johnson in some versions of the story, and for his employers the Anglican church and the superintendent of Indian Affairs, than it was personal belief. Horatio Hale's telling of the story characterized Johnson as a fervent Christian who went to the Delaware ceremony alone because he believed their religion to be "monstrous"; but in her interpretation, Pauline Johnson suggested that while her father was Christian, he distinguished between those who worshipped the Great Spirit, such as his ancestral Mohawks, and those who were idolatrous like the Delawares. The Mohawks were "pagans" but not "heathen."[24]

As two of her biographers noted, Pauline Johnson's writings may also reflect guilt about the sale of such objects. For example, her 1911 short story "Hoolool of the Totem Poles" describes a West Coast Native woman who adamantly refuses to part with a family pole despite her poverty. One night, her son dreams of many small totems. The mother interprets this as a sign that she should carve tiny replicas for sale and protect the original pole. Hence, the family could be prosperous and yet preserve their culture.[25] Johnson also expressed regret over the disposal of most of the Haudenosaunee Confederacy belts, which validated Six Nations' sovereignty and recorded important treaties, because "it destroy[ed] Our Archives"; yet she had relinquished at least three of these belts herself.[26] She later appealed to David Boyle for the return of a wampum belt she had sold to him, although it was only because she required it as a prop for her lectures rather than wishing to restore it to the Six Nations community, despite the fact that the Grand River Confederacy chiefs were desperately seeking the return of all belts at this time.[27]

Her sister Eliza H. C. Johnson (known as Evelyn) turned to museums to preserve Native material culture. After Pauline's death in 1913, Evelyn Johnson donated numerous items owned by her sister to the Brantford Historical Society, and later, she willed seven False Face masks to their museum.[28] Concerned about American collecting expeditions, which often targeted wampum belts, she tried to convince the Six Nations Confederacy Council at the Grand River to entrust four remaining belts to a museum for safekeeping, but the chiefs insisted that their council house was the suitable place for their storage. In the 1920s, however, Evelyn Johnson somehow obtained these four belts and six strings of wampum and transferred them to Charles Trick Currelly of the Royal

Ontario Museum in Toronto. She stipulated that her name was never to be connected with these items, and that the objects were not to be exhibited until after her death. If the belts were still retained by the museum at this time, then ownership was to be transferred to the Royal Ontario Museum, a provision that eventually occurred.[29] It is unclear if Evelyn Johnson shared the common nineteenth-century presumption that material culture was best preserved by museums, rather than by First Nations communities, or if she feared the motives of a few individuals at the Grand River who had sold belts before. After the death of the wampum-keeper, John Buck, in 1893, the belts began to be sold by his children. Joshua Buck had sold four belts to David Boyle, but action by some of the Confederacy chiefs persuaded Boyle to return them to the council. In 1893, the council also tried in vain to retain custody of all the belts in the possession of the Buck family. In 1899, eleven belts were sold to American dealer T. R. Roddy, by the Bucks or by Chief James Jamieson. George G. Heye eventually purchased these from Roddy. Several attempts by chiefs and by the Canadian government to have these belts returned in the early twentieth century were unsuccessful.[30]

Evelyn Johnson also protested against the activities of some anthropologists. She expressed bitterness over the treatment of her grandfather John Smoke Johnson, once the keeper of a rare copy of the traditional "Book of Rites," by American anthropologist Erminnie A. Smith. She had purchased this manuscript, which described Confederacy procedures, for only $10, turning a generous profit of a few hundred dollars upon its sale to the Smithsonian Institution in the United States. The family had tried to repatriate the item, to no avail.[31] Johnson also objected to unflattering portions of David Boyle's fieldwork reports and attacked his focus on traditional Native culture. She had addressed Boyle personally about this matter, who had suggested that she write a correction to his report. Instead, in an angry letter to Richard Harcourt, the minister of Education who funded Boyle's research, Evelyn Johnson accused Boyle of presenting a distorted impression of the Six Nations since he focussed upon traditionalists and their Longhouse ceremonies. According to Johnson, he "seldom was seen among the more educated Indians," nor were there any photographs of brick homes, churches, or "accomplished" people, those who showed "advancement" and "civilization."[32] Unlike her sister, who in her writings often emphasized the Haudenosaunee past and traditional values, Evelyn Johnson seemed to prefer that anthropologists study those individuals who appeared, at least outwardly, to have assimilated into the non-Native culture.

Compared to the Johnston sisters, John Ojijatekha Brant-Sero was much more involved in anthropology. Although he was an actor, a "show Indian," and a journalist, Brant-Sero wished he could dedicate his career to research. Working as a machine-hand in Toronto in the late 1880s, he pursued employment and scholarship as a historian or anthropologist. Studying the Haudenosaunee was his "Life work," he said, and he desired opportunities to "ripen" his "scholarship."[33] He probably met David Boyle through his membership in the Ontario Historical Society (OHS) or in the pre-eminent provincial scientific society, the Canadian Institute in Toronto, and seems to have been inspired by his fieldwork; indeed, after Boyle's death, he suggested that a memorial should be created in his honour, possibly a research fund to sponsor ethnographic studies.[34] Brant-Sero also joined the Anthropological Institute of Great Britain and Ireland, the York Pioneers, the Hamilton Association for the Advancement of Science, Art and Literature, and the Wentworth Historical Society, and he assumed the second vice-presidency of the Ontario Historical Society between 1898 and 1900. Brant-Sero and his wife were also collectors, gathering pieces from the Six Nations of the Grand River and the Siksika and Kainai reserves on the prairies. They displayed these artifacts in the "Indian Exhibit" of the celebrated 1899 Canadian Exhibition, which was organized by the Women's Canadian Historical Society of Toronto and the OHS.[35]

As a historian, in 1899 Brant-Sero attempted to have documents concerning the Haudenosaunee Confederacy published, enlisting the support of David Boyle and James H. Coyne, another prominent member of the Ontario Historical Society. He also suggested that the Six Nations Confederacy Council might agree to underwrite a portion of the publication costs. By the fall of that year, however, he had dismissed the idea, reporting that there was considerable "friction" in the community over the issue.[36] Continuing his studies during 1899 and 1900, Brant-Sero researched "Pagan Rites," songs, and Mohawk genealogies. Unsponsored, he asked Boyle to solicit money from the Minister of Education, who agreed to pay Brant-Sero twenty-four dollars to conduct his research. In the end, though, Brant-Sero submitted only one manuscript concerning genealogy to Boyle.[37]

In 1900, Brant-Sero moved to the United States, where he hoped to find a better market for his talents.[38] While writing for the Chicago *Evening Post*, he continued to study the Haudenosaunee and conduct his lecture tour, which was primarily based upon Boyle's ethnographic fieldwork at Six Nations of the Grand River in 1898, during which he had acted as an informant. He wished, however, to be fully employed as an anthropologist. He had previously corresponded with Major J. W. Powell of the Bureau of American Ethnology, offering legends and traditions for sale. In 1900, he unsuccessfully appealed to Powell for employment at the Bureau.[39] He also targeted the American Museum of Natural History in New York and asked James Mooney of the Bureau and Reuben G. Thwaites of the State Historical Society of Wisconsin to contact anthropologist Franz Boas with references. Boas was unable to offer him a position at the Museum of Natural History, but suggested that it might be possible at a later date. By July 1900, Brant-Sero had left the country to lecture in England; yet he still held out hope of working for Boas, and suggested that he could attend the Midwinter Ceremonials the next year at Six Nations of the Grand River or at the Cattaraugus reservation in New York.[40]

Like Pauline Johnson, Brant-Sero emphasized the more traditional and historical side of Haudenosaunee culture. For example, in 1899, he agreed to procure a False Face mask, a turtle rattle and a complete set of corn-processing tools, including a pounder and winnowing baskets, for Janet Carnochan, president of the Niagara Historical Society. He noted that he could obtain a new pounder much easier than an old one but he assumed that Carnochan "would value an old pounder much more."[41] In a prospectus entitled "An Iroquoian Proposal" for the American Museum of Natural History, he suggested that the rituals of the Seneca and the Onondaga should be studied because these were the nations who had preserved their old ways most solidly. In this proposal, Brant-Sero advised the documentation of the uses and beliefs of herbs and roots, food preparation and taboos, and the collection of food preparation tools, clothing, and silver ornaments.[42] He considered the documentation of this traditional information to be fairly urgent. Using the common nineteenth-century salvage anthropology paradigm, which argued that Native cultures were becoming extinct or rapidly assimilated, he suggested that "No time should be lost ... before the old people die. Changes will rapidly take place over these people."[43]

Also typical of the nineteenth-century interpretations of Indigenous culture, he emphasized a romantic view of the Haudenosaunee through the noble savage stereotype, calling them the "Romans of the West ... unequalled by any other barbaric power in the new world," and describing them as a people who were famed for their once-powerful control of a massive territory.[44] They had possessed an "important sway" over a large part of North America and were proficient on the "War-path."[45] Although he used this noble savage stereotype in his writings, he vehemently opposed the image of the barbaric savage to explain Native culture. For example, speaking during his lecture tour in Germany, he attacked the authors of popular dime novels who portrayed Natives through this stereotype as "blood-thirsty scalpers and horse thieves."[46]

Until his death from meningitis in 1914, Brant-Sero continued to lecture throughout Britain and Europe, but he never received the recognition he desired as an independent anthropologist. In contrast, some of the Six Nations Confederacy Council Chiefs from the Grand River reserve employed history, anthropology, and their practitioners for political reasons. According to Gerald Killan, his biographer, David Boyle's "friends along the Grand River appreciated his attempts to reconstruct Iroquoian prehistory and his efforts to preserve their cultural heritage." Killan cited Boyle's adoption and naming as Ra'-ri-wah-ka-noh'-nis or "an ambassador" by the Mohawk in 1892 as proof of their gratitude.[47] Brant-Sero believed Boyle's adoption honoured his research as well as his role as the "voice between races."[48] This suggested significance of his adoption, however, may have been overemphasized, as it occurred several years before the bulk of his ethnological work at the Grand River reserve and the subsequent building of community relationships. Further, Boyle was not the only individual to receive this name upon adoption. In an 1896 ceremony performed by Chief William Wage, the Six Nations conferred the name "Ra-vi-wa-non-neh," or "ambassador," upon William Wilson, the County Master of the Orange Order, and declared him an honourary member of their people.[49] In this light, one wonders whether Boyle's adoption was simply part of a wider system of recognition. As well, current scholarship on adoption has suggested alternative meanings for this ritual, including the creation of political allies and their use to educate the public against stereotypes.[50] Anthropologist Sally Weaver has suggested that the Six Nations cooperation with historical societies and anthropologists stemmed from their quest for federal government recognition of their sovereignty.[51]

Indeed, Boyle's fieldwork at the Six Nations of the Grand River occurred at a politically tenuous time for the Haudenosaunee. Throughout the late nineteenth century, the Haudenosaunee Council fought against fresh restrictions and forced assimilation under the Indian Act, and also protested the transfer of the Indian Affairs administration from the British to the Dominion government after Canadian Confederation in 1867. Historically, the Haudenosaunee relationship with the British Crown had been as independent military allies who possessed political bargaining power, but within Canada they were considered to be wards of the government. The federal government also blocked several attempts by the Six Nations of the Grand River to appeal to the Crown, and this loss of communication with England symbolically and literally represented a loss of leverage.

These problems may have been further complicated by spiritual and political differences within the Six Nations of the Grand River community itself. As early as the 1860s, Haudenosaunee Council members followed both Christianity and the Longhouse religion. According to anthropologist Sally Weaver, the Mohawk, Oneida, and Tuscarora nations were more likely to follow some form of Christianity, while the Seneca, Onondaga, and Cayuga nations sustained their traditional spirituality.[52] Council members both regarded the Council as part of their founding spiritual doctrines and as a secular political body. As well, although all sought the preservation of their sovereignty, some Council chiefs promoted political reform while others supported more traditional procedures. The Seneca, Onondaga, and Cayuga mostly preferred the traditional Council, while some members of the Mohawk, Oneida, and Tuscarora nations desired a measure of governmental reform, including the possibility of an elected council. These latter nations believed that they could protect the autonomy of their government by a pragmatic transformation of the council into a local government. In contrast, the traditional element protested what they saw as any relinquishment of power.[53]

According to Weaver, in the 1890s, the pro-reform body maintained the majority of Council and acted as the administrators and interpreters. Another group, known as the Progressive Warriors, unsuccessfully petitioned the Canadian government to institute an elected council at Six Nations, while a conservative faction continued to seek federal recognition of Haudenosaunee sovereignty. In 1906, the Progressive Warriors reorganized as the Indian Rights Association and appealed to the Canadian government for an elected council in 1907 and 1910, supported by a small number of the Mohawk, Cayuga, Tuscarora, Seneca, and Delaware nations.[54] While the seriousness of the splits within the Council and the impact on its political effectiveness have been recently questioned by Indigenous scholars, even minimal support for an elected council and the dispersal of the wampum belts that validated Haudenosaunee sovereignty and treaty rights could be exploited by the Dominion government, particularly after the Indian Act of 1869 and the Indian Advancement Act of 1884, which promoted elective councils, an eventuality finally imposed upon the Grand River in 1924.

Aside from the consequences of the "factionalism" on the reserve, it does seem clear that, under pressure from the federal government and the Department of Indian Affairs, the Six Nations of the Grand River community attempted to maintain autonomy in their own political affairs. Consequently, part of the Six Nations Council may have looked to groups such as the Ontario Historical Society and prominent individuals such as David Boyle to validate their claims to be independent founders of Ontario, in equality with the United Empire Loyalists, rather than child-like wards of the Dominion government. Recognition of the Six Nations as Loyalists was tied to the idea that they were allied with Britain during the American Revolution, and thus were a sovereign nation. In 1897, the Haudenosaunee affiliated with the Ontario Historical Society, and consequently they were allowed to form their own society and appoint one delegate with voting powers for each nation. Invited to hold the 1898 Ontario Historical Society annual meeting on the reserve at Ohsweken, eighty society members and several hundred Haudenosaunee gathered at the Six Nations Council House in June.[55] Chiefs A. G. Smith, John Gibson, Alexander Hill, Nicodemus Porter, Benjamin Carpenter, and Richard Hill acted as representatives to the Ontario Historical Society, one for each of the nations, in addition to Nelles Monture of the Delaware.

In his 1898 address to the Society, Delaware Chief Nelles Monture emphasized the loyalty of the Six Nations to the British Crown, a theme repeated by Indian Affairs Superintendent E. D. Cameron. Strategically using language similar to the Loyalist myth, Chief A. G. Smith welcomed the society's members "as brothers whose fore-fathers fought side by side with ours ... in defence of our country—as brothers whose fathers were devoted and loyal through many dangers and difficulties, privations and sorrows to this land and country, and to the throne of Great Britain ... brothers who are with us still in loyalty and love to the same flag under which our fathers fought and fell." Both Monture and Smith stressed the "civilized" and "advanced" nature of the Haudenosaunee. Monture also stated his hope that the Ontario Historical Society would educate the public about the Six Nations' "progress," and suggested that they were ready to govern their own affairs, especially by having a representative in the Canadian parliament.[56]

The image of the Haudenosaunee as equal to United Empire Loyalists had been presented before, and during the late nineteenth century it was a powerful tactic because the United Empire Loyalists were feted by historians, museums, and the public, and the loyalty and military power of the Six Nations, in particular during the founding of English

Canada, had been lauded numerous times by Canadians. For example, at the 1884 Loyalist centennial celebrations, the organizing committee recognized Haudenosaunee loyalty and the progress in the "civilization" of their society.[57] In 1897, during Queen Victoria's Jubilee celebration, they had been deemed "ever-loyal" by the Toronto *Globe* in its description of the party of 600 Haudenosaunee hosted by John Brant-Sero and his wife at their Hamilton home. At this gathering, the *Globe* reported that the Brant-Seros flew banners reading "Welcome Loyal Indians" and "God Bless Our Queen," and prominently displayed a large picture of the Queen. At this celebration, Chief and Deputy-Speaker David Thomas emphasized the untarnished "chain of friendship" between the Confederacy and the Queen, and their continuing faithfulness to Britain. After a feast, the Six Nations celebrants patriotically marched into Hamilton before returning to the Brant-Sero home for tea.[58] The following year, at a United Empire Loyalist Association meeting, Honourary Secretary-Treasurer W. Hamilton Merritt stated that without the Six Nations, Canada would have fallen to the United States, and then he awarded a medal to War of 1812 veteran John Smoke Johnson and instated him as an honourary vice-president.[59] At this same meeting, Brant-Sero advocated for a separate Indian Act for the Six Nations because they possessed "superior intelligence," the same message he had delivered earlier in 1897 to the Women's Historical Society of Toronto.[60]

The Six Nations never did form their own historical society as the Ontario Historical Society suggested, and it was not until 1909 that the Haudenosaunee Council made another overture. That year, the Council invited the OHS to speak at their celebration of King Edward's birthday on Victoria Day. Again they emphasized their loyalty and service as military allies; Council Secretary Josiah Hill suggested to Ontario Historical Society officials that their address should discuss the participation and dedication of the Haudenosaunee during the French and British wars in colonial North America, battles that led to the fall of French Canada and the beginning of the rule of the British in Canada. The invitatory letter from Hill arrived too late, however, for the Society to attend this event.[61]

In 1911, the Haudenosaunee again sought recognition from the Ontario Historical Society for their status as joint founders of Upper Canada. During the annual meeting held in Brantford, members of the Ontario Historical Society travelled to the Council house in Ohsweken. Here, Chief John W. M. Elliott addressed the gathering, emphasizing the longevity of their traditional government and the significant role of the Haudenosaunee as British allies in the French colonial wars and in the

American Revolution. He pointed out the incongruity of their new rank as minors under the Canadian government and, as descendants of the United Empire Loyalists, requested the help of the OHS to influence the federal government to reinstate their rights and privileges as a sovereign people.[62] In response, President David Williams referred their appeal to the Ontario Historical Society council for consideration. This body, however, decided against supporting the Six Nations' claim, based upon a clause in the OHS constitution, which stated that it would not discuss politics.[63]

Although many Canadians recognized the Six Nations as loyal allies who indeed aided the founding of British Canada, the Confederacy Council chiefs were unsuccessful in obtaining the support of the Ontario Historical Society and its officers in their bid for recognition of their autonomy; but their activities reveal that they believed history or anthropology and its practitioners could be useful political tools. While John Brant-Sero also attempted to use Haudenosaunee history to bolster sovereignty claims, he was mostly concerned with building his career as an independent anthropologist, partly modelled after David Boyle's scholarship. E. Pauline and Evelyn H. C. Johnson, though involved in anthropology to a lesser degree, also contributed to the development of the discipline in nineteenth-century Canada, and in particular to the dispersal of some significant political and spiritual material culture. Such individuals have been often "anthropologized" as informants, a role that too often suggests anonymous or passive participation in conjunction with noted scholars. As Scott Michaelsen has suggested, however, such individuals should be considered active "auto-anthropologists" and "anti-anthropologists."[64] Within Victorian anthropology, a web of metaphysical borders of familial, religious, political, and educational experiences underlay Indigenous motives, resulting in a mixed response to its practitioners.

# THE GRAND GENERAL INDIAN COUNCIL OF ONTARIO AND INDIAN STATUS LEGISLATION

⊷ ⊠◊⊠ ⊶

NORMAN SHIELDS

Beginning in 1869, Canadian Indian status legislation discriminated against Aboriginal women on the basis of gender. Women who married outside their band, as defined by the Indian Act, were subjected to varying negative consequences, including loss of Indian status if they married non-Aboriginal men or Aboriginal men without Indian status, called "non-treaty Indians." Owing in large part to an Aboriginal women's movement that coalesced in the 1970s and 1980s, Canadian legislators repealed the more overtly discriminatory aspects of Indian status legislation in 1985 and enacted remedial legislation that made it possible to reinstate those women and their descendants who had lost their Indian status because of the earlier legislation. Male-dominated provincial and national Indian political organizations failed to assist women in their struggle against discrimination. Indeed, Aboriginal women considered them obstructions. Several researchers have explained the apparent political schism between Aboriginal women and their male counterparts by arguing that, whereas Aboriginal leaders in Ontario initially "strongly opposed" the discriminatory legislation, many Aboriginal men in the 1970s had internalized the patriarchal or sexist practices of the Canadian state.[1]

It is certainly true that the Six Nations in Ontario consistently rejected the legislation from its inception; the Anishinabek, in contrast, never succeeded in reaching consensus on "Indian status" at the Grand General Indian Council of Ontario. By failing to take notice that Indian status legislation divided Anishinabek political leaders, scholars have obscured an injustice perpetrated against Britain's Anishinabek allies, especially the Potawatomi, who settled in Upper Canada rather than submit to the United States' removal policy of the middle decades of the nineteenth century. Analysis of Ontario Anishinabek responses regarding discriminatory Indian status legislation complicates existing scholarship on the subject and reveals sensitive historic and demographic issues, rather than the internalization of patriarchy per se, as explanations for the Grand Council's inaction on the legislation in the late nineteenth and early twentieth centuries.

The Grand General Indian Council of Ontario, a council of autonomous Anishinabek First Nations in Ontario that convened under that name between 1870 and 1936, and that initially included the Six Nations as well, frequently discussed Indian status legislation.[2] Once the Six Nations and Anishinabek parted political company in 1882, the Grand Council largely approved Indian status legislation relating to women's marriage to non-Aboriginal men. Women's marriage to non-treaty Indians, however, proved to be a sensitive and divisive issue. When a woman out-married an Aboriginal man, Indian status legislation stipulated that she should be severed from her birth community and transferred to her husband's band, the "patrilineal principle." Their children would be members of the husband's band. Early formulations of the legislation clearly assumed membership in an Indian Act band, which in Southern Ontario was a false assumption. Anishinabek who emigrated from the United States formed a large minority of the Algonquian-speaking people in the province. Despite expressly inviting them to settle in British-controlled territory, neither Britain nor Canada entered into treaty with their (for lack of a better term) "immigrant" allies, depriving them a secure land base, annuity, and Indian status. Thus, Indian status legislation eventually provided for marriages to non-treaty Indians as well. The law relating to marriage to non-treaty Indians produced two opposing movements among the Anishinabek of Southern Ontario: in the Georgian Bay and Lake Huron region, Anishinabek felt a sense of duty to an immigrant population with whom delegates had strong historic and kinship connections; in the interior of the province, the people were committed to protecting an increasingly circumscribed First Nations land and resource base. Women's marriage to non-treaty Indians kept Indian status legislation on the Grand Council's agenda and the council itself divided.

Colonial legislators began defining who had Indian status in the middle of nineteenth century in the context of managing First Nations lands. One historian has remarked that the wider significance of early Indian status formulas, which were fairly innocuous, was the implicit principle that the colonial government, not First Nations, would determine who was an Indian and a member of a band.[3] After Confederation, Canadian legislators adopted a uniform definition of Indian status. Persons of "Indian blood," their descendants, and any woman married to such individuals had Indian status. Non-Aboriginal male spouses were denied Indian status. In 1869, Canada consummated its commitment to the patrilineal principle. If a woman married a status Indian from another band, she was severed from her birth community and transferred to her spouse's band. If she married a non-Aboriginal man, she lost her Indian status altogether, but retained her claim to an equal share of her former band's capital assets, subject to being bought out at ten years' purchase. The legislation neglected to provide for marriage to non-status Indians, an oversight that legislators addressed in 1876 and 1880 Indian Act amendments. After 1880, a woman who married a non-status Indian, like her counterparts who married non-Aboriginal men, lost her Indian status but retained her right to her share of the capital accounts of her former band, subject to being bought out at ten years' purchase.[4] Indian status legislation remained essentially unchanged until after the Second World War, when new amendments actually made Indian status legislation more onerous for women.[5]

In her pioneering study of Aboriginal women and the law in Canada, Kathleen Jamieson noted that Aboriginal women suffered economically, socially, and psychologically under the discriminatory Indian status legislation. From an economic point of view, Aboriginal women were unable to inherit reserve property from their parents or to own property in their own right in their birth communities. As for social costs, loss of Indian status meant Aboriginal women and their children could not make use of educational and other social programs provided to status Indians; admittedly, such programs have been more significant in recent years than in the nineteenth century. Finally, the psychological effects of loss of Indian status could be enormous. As Jamieson explained, women and their children who had lost Indian status found "themselves with identity problems, culturally different and often socially rejected by white society, yet [unable to] participate with family and relatives in the life of their former communities."[6] The "disruption and misery" caused by the "invidious distinction" of Indian status legislation, wrote Jamieson, were "profound and impossible to measure."[7] A recent study suggests that, in some cases, women who had lost their Indian status but chose to maintain links to their birth communities were able and expected to do so, thus alleviating some of the psychological, to say nothing of the economic or social, impact of Indian status legislation.[8]

In the early 1970s, with the support of a growing Aboriginal women's movement in Canada, Jeannette Lavell and Yvonne Bedard, Ojibwa and Six Nations women respectively, sought to challenge Indian status legislation in the courts on the grounds of sexual discrimination. Incredibly, the Supreme Court of Canada ruled against them.[9] What is important to note is that these two women faced not only the federal government in their legal challenge, but also the various Aboriginal provincial and national political organizations, many of whom offered testimony and submissions to refute the women's legal arguments.[10] The political organizations' opposition to Lavell and Bedard arose from distinctly political purposes. Prominent Aboriginal political leaders of the 1970s admitted that women were discriminated against by Indian status legislation, but they were anxious to retain the Indian Act in its entirety as a "lever" against the federal government. They feared that a successful legal challenge of Indian status legislation on the basis of the Canadian Bill of Rights would jeopardize their aim to achieve a thorough, consultative overhaul of the Indian Act. Thus, male-dominated political organizations were all too willing to sacrifice the immediate redress of women's legitimate and pressing grievances for other ends.[11]

Not surprisingly, feminist scholars have roundly criticized their decision. Jamieson, for example, argued that after the Lavell and Bedard imbroglio, it "became clear to most Native women for the first time that there was a connection between their personal situation and the structure of power and privilege from which they had been systematically excluded, first by Europeans and now unexpectedly by many Native men."[12] Another historian noted that the legal challenges mounted by Aboriginal women in the 1970s "proved that Indian women could hope for little support from Indian men," and added that the National Indian Brotherhood "more or less interpreted 'Indian rights' to mean rights to which only status Indian men were entitled."[13] Considering that by the end of 1987 96,000 people had applied for reinstatement, the willingness of male Aboriginal leaders to sacrifice to the larger project the grievances of women and their descendants who were denied Indian status is indeed troubling.[14] In addition to its interference in the Lavell and Bedard legal challenge, the National Indian Brotherhood continually refused throughout the 1970s and early 1980s to accord First Nations women's organizations an equal voice in negotiations with the federal government. The situation deteriorated to such an extent that, in 1978, a Native Women's Association of Canada newsletter editorial blamed both the federal government and male Aboriginal political leaders for the slow progress of their fight against discrimination.[15]

Perhaps to highlight the apparent patriarchal attitudes of male Aboriginal political leaders of the 1970s, Jamieson wrote that their nineteenth-century counterparts had "strongly opposed" the discriminatory Indian status legislation.[16] That claim is true, but only to a certain extent. Delegates to the Grand Council did indeed oppose the legislation soon after its enactment in 1869. The patrilineal principle inherent in Indian status legislation particularly concerned Six Nations delegates. They took pains to explain to Anishinabek delegates that federal definitions of Indian status must address matrilineal descent and matrilocal settlement, the traditional social organization of the Six Nations. A Grand Council committee of the whole enumerated four reasons to reject the legislation. Delegates concluded that the 1869 formula was unjust in depriving women of their birthright; they noted that the legislation was inconsistent with earlier definitions of Indian status; they pointed out that the patrilineal and patrilocal principles of the legislation contravened "ancient and acknowledged" Aboriginal customs; and they argued that the legislation promoted among Aboriginal women an "immoral tendency" to live with their partners outside wedlock in order to circumvent the legal repercussions of Indian status legislation.[17]

The fact that Grand Council delegates remarked on what may be called women's common-law marriage strategy only a year after the implementation of the discriminatory Indian status legislation suggests that the Six Nations and Anishinabek First Nations in Ontario understood at an early date the implications of federal legislation. Indeed, in the early 1870s Ojibwa chiefs from the Canadian side of Sault Ste. Marie (see Map 1) opposed the removal of women from their band lists from the moment their names were struck off. According to ethnohistorian Janet Chute, when chiefs from the Sault Ste. Marie region learned of the deletions in 1872, they immediately dispatched a letter to Ottawa asking that the women removed from their band lists be "reclaimed," and that the Indian status legislation of 1869 "be repealed."[18] Needless to say, legislators did not repeal the Indian status legislation. Accordingly, like other communities, First Nations in the Sault Ste. Marie region "adopted" their women's husbands into their band. Their strategy did not always work. In 1884, Augustine Shingwauk of Garden River complained to the Grand Council that women whose husbands had been adopted into his

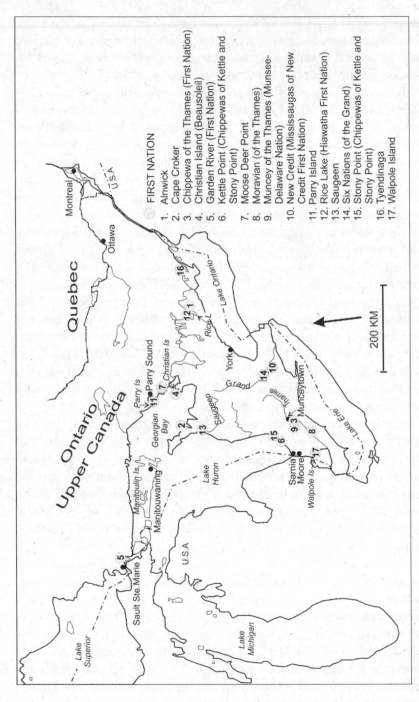

**Map 1: Selected First Nations in Upper Canada**

band were not receiving their annuity.[19] Parry Island launched the same complaint in 1889 after members of the Moose Deer Point First Nation, who did not have Indian status by virtue of their having entered into treaty with neither Britain nor the Government of Canada, were struck from its band list, despite having been adopted.[20]

The Six Nations and the Anishinabek parted political company in 1882. With the departure of the Six Nations from the Grand Council, opposing Anishinabek opinions on Indian status legislation come into sharper focus. One or all of its aspects were discussed in 1884, 1894, 1900, 1910, and 1917.[21] Some of the minutes for the period 1886 to 1898 are missing, and status may very well have been discussed on other occasions during that period, but the pattern apparent at the 1884 and 1894 councils is sufficient for analysis.[22] The legislative discrimination against women who married non-Aboriginal men caused little sensation. The attitude of the male Anishinabek delegates towards non-Aboriginal, "White," husbands is unmistakable. Grand Council delegates regarded non-Aboriginal husbands with equal parts suspicion and dread. As a prominent Chippewa of the Thames delegate explained to the Grand Council in 1894, "intermarriage of the women with whites was a source of trouble to his band by which they had lost many hundred dollars. Their best timber was taken and their best land used by them. These people," he continued, "came there and took every advantage they could and they could not be driven away. They made use of what did not belong to them and it was time that proceedings of the kind was stopped."[23] Is it possible that in addition to the economic and social threat associated with non-Aboriginal husbands, delegates also feared that if they permitted them to reside in the community, they would necessarily be entitled to sit in council and therefore represent a political threat as well?

In any case, very few delegates thought that non-Aboriginal husbands should be admitted to band membership, or even reserve residency, by virtue of having married an Aboriginal woman. Exceptional non-Aboriginal husbands merited consideration, and delegates appeared to think that for them adoption techniques, or simple non-compliance, would suffice to alleviate the most pernicious aspects of non-membership, namely, permission to settle with the band. Thus, the opinion of a prominent Walpole Island Ojibwa that all Aboriginal women, regardless of their marriage choice, "in addition to their annuity should also retain their landed property to be handed down to [their] children," received no discernable support from other delegates, however impressive the principle. A New Credit delegate expressed regret that a widowed out-married woman became "a stranger, a hanger on outside with no place of shelter," while the wives of Aboriginal men enjoyed their new-found band privileges for life; but one Cape Croker delegate spoke for a large majority when he remarked that if a woman wanted to marry a non-Aboriginal man, she "had full liberty to go and follow her husband, a white man who could support her. She was aware of the consequences and let her abide by them." As for concerns of the Chippewa of the Thames about "being cramped by people who had no rights on the reserve," the Cape Croker delegate thought they "had no one to blame but [themselves] for it. Why not take the law and drive these people away?" he asked. Kathleen Jamieson has argued that "even if the Indians of Ontario and Quebec did not like white men on the reserves they certainly did not approve of the government remedy and ... they saw this as an attack not only on female Indians but on all Indians."[24] It seems clear that Jamieson has reduced the opinions of "Indians of Ontario and Quebec" to those held by the Six Nations, a matrilineal society. As the Grand Council's deliberations attest, at least some Anishinabek did believe that Indian status legislation could, and should, be used to prevent non-Aboriginal husbands from settling in Aboriginal communities.

Whereas most Anishinabek delegates to the Grand Council thought the law relating to women's marriage to non-Aboriginal men ought to be retained, intermarriage between women and non-treaty Indians divided the council. Opposing Anishinabek attitudes toward non-treaty husbands are amply documented in the minutes of the Grand Council's deliberations on Indian status legislation. In 1884, one Cape Croker delegate thought depriving "an Indian woman (marrying outside of the tribe) of her rights with regard to the share of the land was improper," and he "urge[d] upon the delegates to recommend that the section be altered so that she should enjoy the privilege of land ownership." Meanwhile, Peter Edmund Jones of New Credit argued that "the legal points of the question" should be considered: "the landed property should descend [through] the male population of the Tribe.... If the section was altered there would be danger of breaking up the tribal relation."[25] The minutes record eleven delegates representing Cape Croker, New Credit, the Munceys of the Thames, Garden River, Alnwick, and the Chippewas of the Thames speaking to the issue or advancing motions. New Credit's Peter Edmund Jones, as is evident, favoured retaining the Indian status legislation without amendment. The Muncey, Alnwick, and two of the four Chippewa of the Thames delegates concurred. When an Alnwick chief remarked that although the legislation appeared "hard at first sight," he thought it was "framed for the protection of the Indians," the Cape Croker delegate replied, "it was more of a punishment than protection," and again expressed his strong support for amending the legislation. Garden River's Buhg-we-ne-ne also spoke unambiguously, and unopposed by the Georgian Bay and Lake Huron region delegates, in favour of according normal band privileges to women married to non-treaty Indians. By way of contrast, only two delegates from the interior of the province spoke in favour of extending normal band privileges to women married to non-treaty Indians.[26]

The 1894 Grand Council confirmed the pattern that emerged in 1884. Georgian Bay and Lake Huron First Nations were more willing to accord band privileges to women out-married to non-treaty Indians than were their counterparts in the interior of the province. Delegates discussed the Indian status legislation in a short but revealing evening session, which resumed the following morning and carried over into the afternoon. After several attempts to state the consensus of the group failed, the council abandoned its attempt to reach common ground. On this occasion, women's marriage to non-Aboriginal men prompted the discussion, but delegates soon turned to non-treaty Indians. Chippewa of the Thames delegates emphatically endorsed the existing Indian status formula, and relentlessly chastised both non-treaty and non-Aboriginal husbands. Speaking to both classes of spouses, a Chippewa of the Thames delegate stated bluntly, "[treaty Indians] as owners of the soil should be protected in their holdings and not crowded out by the children of our women marrying outside, to men generally of low character." One of the two Chippewa of the Thames delegates that opposed the legislation in 1884 now said that "too many whites and non-treaty Indians who had married Indian women had through good nature been permitted to retain their land too long, and now with their rising families were becoming very troublesome." Another Chippewa of the Thames delegate, as he had in 1884, made a "powerful speech" in favour of the legislation. Referring to non-treaty Indians, he remarked that, "This kind of people kept roving over the country without any aim in view to bother themselves; they went were [*sic*] they were not welcome, but from charitable motives were not sent away; they stopped where they made the easiest living." Leaving aside his open contempt, he also argued that non-treaty Indians "should not be supported by our bands," which in any case "had no land to spare. Let these people call on the government for help."[27]

The suggestion that the non-treaty Indians of Ontario call upon the federal government for assistance certainly had some merit, and others shared that view. In George Paudash's oral history, "The Coming of the Mississaugas," the hereditary chief from Rice Lake recalled meeting non-treaty Potawatomi from Moose Deer Point, near Parry Sound, who had fought with Tecumseh in the War of 1812 and "did not dare go back" to the United States. They had war medals, but no land or annuity. He echoed the suggestion that non-treaty Indians should approach the government for assistance. Said Paudash, "I am sure that if their case was presented to the Government they would get either land or annuity like ourselves."[28]

The Moose Deer Point case is a little unusual because it falls in between two distinct "waves" of Aboriginal immigration to British North America. The first wave consisted of some of Britain's Aboriginal allies during the American Revolutionary War, including the Six Nations who settled at Grand River and Tyendinaga, and the Moravian and traditional Munsees who settled along the Thames River in southwestern Ontario. The second wave of immigration began in the late 1830s before slowing to a trickle less than a decade later, and included a number of different tribal groups, but Potawatomi immigrants were by far the most numerous. Many of the 1830s emigrants had travelled annually to Canada to receive presents and renew their alliance with Britain. Playing upon their stated desire to emigrate to British North America as an alternative to "removal" in the United States, Sir Francis Bond Head, Upper Canada's worst lieutenant-governor,[29] encouraged his American Aboriginal allies, through his chief superintendent of the Indian department, to settle in British territory. He promised that Britain could thus meet its obligations to them, by which he meant deliver presents and reaffirm its friendship and alliance.[30] In private however, Bond Head told the Colonial Office that he expected few to emigrate and that those who did would soon be on their way. He confidently declared that when Britain discontinued distributing presents to "visiting Indians" in 1840, a deadline that was eventually extended to 1843, the treasury could expect to save some £4000 on presents formerly distributed to Britain's American Aboriginal allies.[31]

Bond Head's duplicity explains ethnohistorian James A. Clifton's observation that the colonial government had not made preparations nor set aside money for the settlement of their American Aboriginal allies. Some second-wave immigrants, like those encountered by Paudash, came a little earlier than Bond Head's "invitation." Odawa in Ohio, for example, requested permission to settle in British North America in 1829, and received a warm welcome on Manitoulin Island.[32] As the

Moose Deer Point example attests, some War of 1812 allies also chose to reside in British North America rather than return to the United States. The bulk of the immigration, however, occurred after Bond Head's invitation, receding in scope by 1843. Although historians agree that Potawatomi immigrants were the most numerous, their precise numbers remains something of a mystery. According to Clifton, more than 3,000 Potawatomi chose to emigrate to Canada, of whom about 3,000 chose to stay.[33] Historian Anthony J. Hall considers that figure to be too high.[34] The difficulty arises from the fact that colonial officials almost always enumerated the American Aboriginal allies together with their Ojibwa or Odawa hosts. If Clifton's calculations are correct, the immigrant Potawatomi accounted for around 20 percent of the Algonquian-speaking population of Upper Canada in the middle of the nineteenth century. Assuming only half of Clifton's estimated 3,000 Potawatomi entered the province at Sarnia, the principal of two immigration routes, they would have filled five average Ojibwa reserves in Upper Canada. According to Schmalz, the American Aboriginal allies outnumbered the native population at Saugeen by a margin of six to one shortly after mid-century. Thus, although the influx of 3,000, or perhaps somewhat less, Potawatomi may seem insignificant in a province whose population had surpassed 400,000 by 1840, their presence in Upper Canadian Aboriginal communities would have been palpable.[35]

A number of motivations, some yet unknown, influenced Potawatomi decisions to leave the United States. According to Clifton, familiarity with and preference for the Great Lakes environment, a manifest antipathy to the United States, a "romantic vision" of British alliance, proximity to British traders and distribution points for presents, the offer of settlement in 1837, and the possibility of acquiring new land were all potential motivations to emigrate. Clifton also emphasized the traditionalism of the immigrant Potawatomi, who anticipated "greater respect for their culture and customs" than could be expected in the United States.[36] Instead, British authorities wanted the Potawatomi to submit to the "civilization" program then underway throughout Upper Canada. "By avoiding the American policy of removal and segregation," Clifton observed wryly, "the migrant Potawatomi had to confront and adapt to the British policy of supervised settlement," of "forced acculturation and assimilation."[37] More than four hundred Potawatomi eventually settled in a separate village on Walpole Island, where they were slightly outnumbered by the Ojibwa already residing there. Repulsed by the thought of an intertribal village, which they were trying to avoid in the first place,

only a few Potawatomi settled at the village under construction at Manitowaning on Manitoulin Island. The rest of the Potawatomi found shelter in Ojibwa and Odawa communities from west of Lake Ontario to the
north shore of Lake Huron and perhaps beyond. Besides Walpole Island,
important early American Aboriginal allies' destinations in Upper Canada
included Kettle Point, Stony Point, Saugeen, Cape Croker, Christian
Island, Munceytown, and Moore, each of which, with the exception of
Munceytown, were situated in the Georgian Bay and Lake Huron region.
At every destination, the Potawatomi initially formed separate communities, some of which persisted into the twentieth century, but they ultimately integrated with their hosts. In short, the Ojibwa and Odawa
residing in the Georgian Bay and Lake Huron region bore the brunt of
second-wave Potawatomi emigration.[38]

One of the factors that distinguished Potawatomi immigrants from
other Algonquian-speaking immigrant groups was that there were no
Potawatomi settlements in Canada to which to turn, and they were initially received coolly. Schmalz identified cultural criteria as the principal
factor determining how the Saugeen and Cape Croker First Nations
received different immigrant populations, but he also cited religion and
level of acculturation as contributing factors. Saugeen and Cape Croker
preferred Ojibwa immigrants, while other Algonquians, mostly Potawatomi, were "integrated." Non-Algonquians were "isolated." Moreover,
Potawatomi familiarity with horticulture aroused jealousy among "the
more conservative Ojibway who found it difficult giving up their hunting and gathering economy," and religious differences exacerbated those
feelings.[39] For Clifton, Potawatomi traditionalism accounted for the initial resistance they encoutered. From Walpole Island, the Potawatomi
were reported to be "rovers averse to settling." Sarnia considered the
Potawatomi's wandering habits a bad influence for the rising generation, and at Saugeen the Potawatomi were reported to be "indolent and
improvident." Soon after their arrival in the province, the Mississauga
Methodist missionary, Peter Jones, remarked that the Potawatomi were
"heathens and wandering," and "in a most deplorable state of poverty and
degradation."[40] Clifton also noted that the absence of annuity meant the
Potawatomi were "cash poor" and thus a burden on their hosts' assets,
and, moreover, "were in open competition with those Indians already
resident in Canada for an increasingly restricted land base."[41] Nevertheless, there did exist some sympathy for the Potawatomi, who together
with the Ojibwa and Odawa formed the historic Three Fires Confederacy, and who had initially been one people. Thus, despite early difficul-

ties, Clifton characterized the immigration into Southern Ontario as successful, noting that hostility proved to be the exception rather than the rule.

Gradually, either because they were pressured to move along, or because they were seeking to escape the advance of non-Aboriginal settlement, the Potawatomi unable to find stable settlement in Southern Ontario began to drift northward. According to Clifton, those Potawatomi were "more successful in moving in with small Odawa and Ojibwe communities."[42] Clifton's discussion on that point is significant for considering Indian status legislation. "Mixed local communities," wrote Clifton,

> began assimilating together, not to a Euro-Canadian model, but to a nascent "Canadian Indian" model. One of the mechanisms involved in this assimilative process was inter-marriage, the familiar and traditional device of exchanging women between village communities. Certainly, the frequency of inter-marriage between Potawatomi and Canadian Indians with treaty rights to reserves opened doors to Potawatomi settlement which might have remained closed had they remained strictly endogamous.[43]

The Grand Council's recurring deliberations on the subject of women's marriage to non-treaty Indians suggests that by the late nineteenth century a similar "assimilative process" operated in the more southerly destinations as well. Additionally, Grand Council deliberations on Indian status legislation qualifies Clifton's theory that intermarriage "opened doors" to settlement "which might have remained closed" otherwise. If intermarriage opened doors, Indian status legislation worked to close them.[44]

To return to the Grand Council, the delegates from the Ojibwa bands in the Georgian Bay and Lake Huron region that had "integrated" the Potawatomi emigrants, and who had therefore intermarried the most, generally did not share contempt for non-treaty Indians expressed by the Chippewa of the Thames. Saugeen is exemplary. Speaking of non-treaty Potawatomi who had resided on the Saugeen tract for nearly sixty years, a Saugeen spokesman remarked that "he did not want to drive such people away; they were of his own kind." Similarly, Cape Croker delegates, as they had in 1884, appeared willing to suffer non-treaty husbands in the community, not as full-fledged members, but at least on the basis of hospitality.[45] The gap in the points of view between the Georgian Bay and Lake Huron region on the one hand, and the interior of the province on the other, proved irreconcilable, and discussions in 1900,

1910, and 1917, the last year the Grand Council specifically discussed Indian status legislation, ended in stalemate.[46]

Although many Anishinabek bands were "strongly opposed" to some, or all, aspects of the discriminatory Indian status legislation, after 1870 that opposition was not unanimous. For the next forty-five years, Anishinabek delegates to the Grand Council could seldom agree on a remedy for the Indian status formula, or even that a remedy was needed. Different combinations of several considerations account for the council's inaction. Some delegates, and the band councils they represented, may have begun to internalize the patriarchal attitudes of Canadian legislators, including the notion that property ownership was a distinctly male domain. Resistance to "unscrupulous" and "quarrelsome" non-Aboriginal men of dubious character was a prevalent concern. Conservation of limited band resources in the face of an influx of non-treaty Indians was another important consideration. Finally, Anishinabek delegates to the Grand Council were committed to consensus decision-making, especially on controversial issues, and Indian status legislation certainly qualified as controversial; indeed, it may have been the most controversial of all the difficult legislation delegates discussed between Canadian Confederation and the First World War. The differing demographic circumstances faced by the Georgian Bay and Lake Huron region and the interior of the province of Ontario ensured that the Grand Council would never reach consensus on Indian status legislation as it pertained to non-treaty Indians. More research on local conditions, especially through oral history, will cast more light on Anishinabek men's attitudes towards Indian status legislation, and women generally, in the late nineteenth century. It seems clear, however, that their inaction on women's Indian status cannot be merely reduced to the internalization of patriarchal or sexist attitudes. That said, as was the case in the 1970s, some male First Nations leaders in the nineteenth century did appear to be willing to sacrifice women's interests for a larger project.

# "THIS IS A PIPE AND I KNOW HASH"
## Louise Erdrich and the Lines Drawn
## upon the Waters and the Lands

━◆━

UTE LISCHKE

## Introduction

Lines drawn both on the water and on the land bisect and serve to divide
Native American communities. In response, Native Americans in their
stories and literatures have resisted these borders throughout their territories. Themes dealing with borders, border crossings, and borderlands
are not new to Native American literature. Most borderland stories in
North America are centred on the actual physical borderland in the
southern United States, for example, the Texas–U.S. Southwest–Mexico
border. Some Canadian authors have written about the borderland, too,
mainly the Canada–US border in the north; most notably, the
Greek–Cherokee writer Thomas King's short story "Borders" is considered to be one of the most humorous and striking examples of the relationship of Native people to the "political" border between Canada and
the US.[1] However, most literary commentators have ignored the themes
of borders and borderlands as portrayed in Native American orature.
Many Aboriginal writers, such as King, Tomson Highway, and Drew Hay-
den Taylor, portray certain events as "funny" even though they are serious, since "traditional Aboriginal oral stories have their own conventions
of expression and structure."[2]

Native writers living in Canada and the United States, especially in
the borderlands areas between these two countries, have a different perspective on conceptualizing "mixed" Native identity within their geographic borders, given the "differences between identity legislation and

colonization histories in Canada and the United States."[3] These differences are exacerbated for Aboriginal people such as Louise Erdrich who reside in borderland areas between both countries and who frequently travel within their homelands, yet cross international geographic borders. In fact, Erdrich has ancestors and relatives within her homeland in both Canada and the United States. This situation highlights the fluidity of Aboriginal identities.

In the context of globalization and transnationalism, geographic borders of nineteenth-century nation-states that were drawn by European empires will gradually become obsolete, especially in terms of the market economy and multinational corporations, even in a post-9/11 context. However, Aboriginal people and their homelands have always transcended these national borders. For Erdrich, an international writer, homeland security has played and will continue to play a role, especially living in the borderlands of Canada and the US. This fact has become an important aspect in her life and writings.

It has been suggested that borderlands are physically present wherever two or more nations/cultures meet each other, where people of different nationalities and cultures occupy the same territory.[4] In Native North American territories, however, artificial borders do not exist; there are natural watersheds, which they share out of mutual respect. First Nations have resided in their territories, which are referred to geographically as Turtle Island or North America, since time immemorial. For them, the linear borders are but a recent and wholly artificial construct. In many of the stories that have been written by native people, borders are represented as political artifacts that need to be dismantled or subverted, as in King's "Borders," in order to overcome cultural ignorance. This chapter will be structured around stories of resistance to the lines drawn upon the lands and the waters of Turtle Island, focussing primarily on the Native writer Louise Erdrich.

For Native Americans, writing about borders and borderlands is complex, since their former territories were structured in very different ethno-geographical ways from present-day borders; but some have written about the difficulties they confront when crossing the forty-ninth parallel. Rather than belonging to a pan-Canadian Aboriginal nation, most Native people have forged links with national and continental Aboriginal communities, regarding themselves "an international body of Indigenous peoples, sometimes referred to as the 'Fourth World.'"[5] Louise Erdrich comes from the borderland of Turtle Mountain Reservation. She now lives in Minneapolis, Minnesota, and has written extensively about the borderlands that surround the Great Lakes. As she demonstrates in her writings, cultural and political identities are socio-political constructs, and as such can evolve, building on internal diversities and perspectives.

In many of her writings, Erdrich reveals her characters' uneasy relationship to the "international border," including her own experiences at various border crossings. Most commentators have not seen her as a "Canadian" as well as an "American" writer even though her homeland of Turtle Mountain is on both sides of the international border. This uneasy relationship to the border is explored in several of her novels, especially the border's representation in her works published prior to 11 September 2001, with a particular focus on *The Blue Jay's Dance: A Birth Year* (1995), *Route 2* (1991), *The Bingo Palace* (1994), and her post-9/11 dealing with border guards in *Books and Islands in Ojibwe Country* (2003).

"The truth about stories is that that's all we are," King tells us at the beginning of *The Truth about Stories: A Native Narrative*, the Massey lectures he delivered in 2003.[6] In his fiction, essays, and poetry about Native characters and communities in North America, King has explored the complications of this deceptively simple statement. For him as for many other Native writers, the borderland is not only a geographic location but a psychological space that inhibits and discourages cooperation among different cultures and nations. Their stories highlight the ways in which political, social, and cultural conflicts across borders might shape the discourse on identity and authority. In many instances, boundaries divide physically and geographically, but they might also help to transcend differences, enable interaction, and generate understanding between cultures, perhaps even serving to establish new identities.

## Story #1: *The Blue Jay's Dance: A Birth Year*

Erdrich was born in Little Falls, Minnesota, in June 1954, of Cree-Métis-Chippewa (also known among the people as Anishinabe and by anthropologists/linguists as Ojibwa) descent on her mother's side, and German, Jewish, and Catholic heritage on her father's side.[7] She is of the Bird and Bear clans from the Turtle Mountain Reservation in North Dakota, west of the Great Lakes watershed and just south of the international border that divides Canada and the US. The Chippewa Nation has resided since time immemorial in birchbark country—the country along the Great Lakes and connecting waterways of northeastern North America, now as far west as present-day North Dakota and Manitoba.[8] The Cree

Nation—both the Plains and the Swampy Cree—continue to reside in the Prairie provinces and Northern Ontario and Quebec in Canada, as well as in the northwestern states of the US. Erdrich's family, then, is from Canada as well as the US. Their presence predates the wholly artificial international boundary (now only 183 years old) by many thousands of years.[9]

Erdrich tells stories—indeed, her life story is one of testing, trial, and stress—to find her own sense of self, her place, and her spirituality. *The Blue Jay's Dance* is Erdrich's autobiography of a birth year, a composite of her experiences from her diary of the birth of her children in the early 1990s during her marriage with Michael Dorris (1945–1997). The book is seasonal in structure, beginning in the winter, the time for telling stories after the first snow has fallen for the year, and ending in the fall. Lyrical and haunting, it is a series of thematically connected stories about her family, time, and the birth of her children. Canada figures in this work, especially as it provides clues to her Canadian heritage. Her great-grandmother on her mother's side was a "pure Canadian" named Virginia Grandbois—literally Virginia of the large forest.[10] Erdich reports in her family history that, in 1782, "All land west of the Appalachians was still Indian territory and the people from whom I am descended on my mother's side, the Ojibwa or Anishinabe, lived lightly upon it, leaving few traces of their complicated passage other than their own teeth and bones. They levered no stones from the earth. Their houses, made of sapling frames and birchbark rolls, were not meant to last."[11] There was no international border between Canada and the US.

By 1882, things had been altered: "The last of the Indian treaties were signed, opening up the West. Most of the Anishinabe were concentrated on smallholdings of land in the territory West of the Great Lakes. The Turtle Mountain people wore trousers and calico dresses, drove wagons, spoke their own language, but also attended Holy Mass."[12] More than one hundred years later, her maternal grandfather, Tribal Chairman Patrick Gourneau, passed away. In *Blue Jay's Dance*, Erdrich goes home to Turtle Mountain—always border country inhabited by the Anishinabe, Cree, and Métis—for the funeral at St. Ann's Church: "The graves of Ojibwa, Cree, and Mitchif Catholics, guarded by statutes of cast concrete and plastic, march up a windy hill. Our Catholic great-great-grandparents are buried behind the church, and the pagans, the traditionals, lie yet in another graveyard, where the uneven markers are crowded by sage and wild prairie rose."[13] In the section entitled "Three Photographs," she provides a brief glimpse of the richness of the mother's family history: "Mary Lefavor, my grandmother—Ojibwa, French, and Scots [and certainty Cree], perhaps a descendant of the Selkirkers of Rudolph's land—stands beside a fellow first communicant."[14] Her maternal family is from Turtle Mountain, as well as from "Rudolph's Land"—Canada—the home of the Great White North and the North Pole.

## Story #2: *The Bingo Palace* (1994)

In this collection of stories, which takes place in the 1970s, Erdrich once again focusses on mixed-blood families, especially Lipsha Morrissey and Gerry Nanapush. The best example and most extended treatment of Canada and the borderlands occurs when Lipsha and Shawnee Ray decide to go on a date to Ho Wun's Chinese Restaurant just across the border in Manitoba, Canada; the restaurant is described as a "romantic place, the walls covered in red paper patterned with flocked lanterns, signs for happiness, benevolence, and luck."[15] Black bean sauce shrimp, dumplings, and flower petal soup are all on the menu, as well as lots of rich foods and exotic vegetables. In June Morrissey's blue Firebird, they head into the black north along a new stretch of highway, "eventually reaching the lighted building next to the highway, the checkpoint people from the reservation always breezed through when they went up to Canada."[16] Canada is depicted as a place where government officials, including border guards, openly practise racism against Aboriginal people:

> Lispsha rolled down his window to answer the usual questions, but here's where it started, that little wrinkle in destiny which he somehow came to believe that Zelda might have arranged. The incident grew out of nothing more than a border guard's dark mood, or maybe an unfilled quota, or just a fit of thoroughness. The guard, an elderly clean-cut type with a deep crisp voice, asked Lipsha to step out of the car. Lipsha turned off the ignition and did so. The officer reached to the dash-board and gently removed the ashtray and brought it beneath the floodlit awning to examine. Lipsha got back into the driver's seat, tried to smile confidently at Shawnee, but she wasn't looking at him. The guard took a long time poking through the ashes with a ballpoint pen before he came up with something. He walked back, leaned down to the car window.
>
> "I have bad news," he said, holding between his thumb and forefinger what looked like a tiny seed. His voice was formal and neutral. "I am compelled to search this vehicle."[17]

After searching the vehicle, the border guard returns with the "small, foil-wrapped brick of Zelda's old-time pemmican fruitcake resting in the open palm of one hand. In the other, he carried the elaborate bag that contained the sacred pipe that had once belonged to Nector Kashpaw."[18] The pipe was originally from Resounding Sky, Nector's father, and it had been smoked when the treaty was signed with the American government in the nineteenth century, at which time the Pillagers, like Big Bear's people, refused to sign the treaty. The guard tells Lipsha and Shawnee that they are in federal protective custody until he can get a "lab analysis"; he adds, "I've heard it all and I've seen it all. But this is a pipe and I know hash."[19] He then puts down the fruit bread, opens the quill bag, and takes out the bowl of the pipe and the long, carved stem. He holds out his hands and there, as they watch, under the strong lights, he looks from one piece to the other and decides to connect the pipe as one:

> So many things would happen in the next months, soon after, that Lipsha wouldn't have time to take in or understand. But always, he would think back to that action, which seemed to happen slowly and to last for timeless moments. It seemed, on thinking back, that there, in the little border station, in the hands of the first non-Indian who ever attached that pipe together, sky would crash to the earth.
> 
> "Please, don't," Lipsha whispered.
> 
> But the frowning man carefully and methodically pressed the carved stem to the bowl and began to turn it and jam it until the two sections locked into place. The eagle feather hung down, the old trade beads clicked against each other three times. Then there was silence, except for the buzzing lights. The guard turned to make his phone call, walked counterclockwise, around the room and desk. The pipe hung from his hand, backwards, casual as a bat. The eagle feather dragged lower, lower, until it finally touched the floor.[20]

Lyman Lamartine, Lipsha's uncle, rescues them from the Canadian border guard by explaining the significance of the pipe to him, at which point the latter "straightens with an air of discovery" and lets them all go back to the reservation.[21] They never do get to Ho Wun's for Chinese food. What had been a very routine crossing of the border for food and entertainment becomes an ordeal for Lipshaw, who begins to understand the enormous significance of his Native heritage. At the other extreme is the border guard's intense lack of understanding of Native traditions and cultures. By not understanding the rituals surrounding sacred pipes, and especially by putting the pipe together, the border guard insults Native people and, at least in this instance, discourages them from crossing the lines drawn upon the land.

## Story #3: *Route 2* (1991)

Border crossing was less complicated for Louise Erdrich and Michael Dorris in the summer of 1985 in their crossings between Canada and the United States. In the privately published book *Route 2*, Erdrich and Dorris describe the journey they undertook that year along Highway or Route 2, also known as the Theodore Roosevelt Highway. They set out in a Dodge Caravan. Son Abel has been sent to Outward Bound somewhere in Northern Ontario, and the rest of the family, including four children, set out to reach the Pacific in ten days with many relatives to visit. The book is divided into two sections, "West" and "East." In the first section, Erdrich describes the drive to Spokane, Washington, where they will visit family. As the family reaches Grand Forks, close to the Canadian border, a city known for its mall, the billboards lure drivers into the city: "We like Canadians."[22] Because of the strength of the Canadian dollar at that time, Canadians were welcomed to cross the border for shopping trips.

The family also travels north to Dunseith, where they stop at the International Peace Garden, a shrine to harmony straddling the US–Canada border. The International Peace Garden was the dream of a Canadian horticulturist, Henry Moore, who wanted to establish a "garden" in 1928 somewhere along the international boundary between Canada and the United States that would recognize and commemorate the peace and goodwill between these two countries. In 1931, Manitoba and North Dakota offered adjoining tracts of land free of cost in the scenic Turtle Mountains, Erdrich's Homeland. She comments, "Strolling through its manicured flowerbeds, we are battered by juxtaposition: celebrations of amicability vying with the nests of jets and bombs capable of world destruction [Minot Airforce Base to the south], the abiding resonance of Indian tribes subsisting on their ancestral lands or the small family farms of Russian and Norwegian emigrants crowded by conglomerate-owned agribusinesses. On Route 2 the ironies seem especially jumbled and striking, unavoidably troubling."[23]

From here, roads extend north/south between Canada and US. In Wolf Point, the family shops at the tribally chartered craft store for next year's family Christmas gifts: hand-painted Sioux pottery, flowing beaded earrings, a shawl decorated with ribbon work, and abalone shells. These items are not declared later at the Canadian border. Erdrich remarks:

"Canada is a big country. It takes four large packages of powdered milk to keep two babies marginally content in their car seats from British Columbia to Ontario and at least one water slide a day to subdue older children gone stir crazy in their futile attempts to complete travel bingo cards."[24] There are also "stretches of hundreds of miles in British Columbia, Alberta, Saskatchewan and Manitoba with nary a dry cleaner shop, a moving van, or a roadside picnic table to check off and when a featured item does at last appear, the competition to claim it can make the quest for the holy grail look tame by comparison."[25] The last major stop for the family is Manitoulin Island, "a mythic place of origin, the starting point for the tribe to which Louise belongs."[26] For Erdrich, Manitoulin figures as "a haven where Anishinabec language and custom is forever cherished and revitalized, where a new spirit of optimism and delight constantly is re-formed. Even in myth, it is a place where people come to gain a glimpse of a world in balance, a world as it could be, a world of beauty governed and reflected by art."[27] It is a place that Erdrich visits often and where she finds spiritual renewal. The artificial lines that are drawn upon the waters of the Great Lakes cannot erase the spiritual connection of Native peoples to a meeting place that has been significant for them since time immemorial. The sheer spirituality of the place will continue to draw Native people to return. It is also for this reason that Erdrich will return to the Lake of the Woods to explore the origins of her people and continue her quest to seek Native spirituality.

## Story #4: *Books and Islands in Ojibwe Country* (2003)

In *Books and Islands*, an autobiographical work published by the National Geographical Society in 2003, Erdrich explores the relationship between books and islands, which she argues function in disparate but similar cross-cultural ways. Most of the book, almost 125 of 143 pages, takes place in Canada in the summer of 2002. Along with *The Blue Jay's Dance* and *Route 2*, this work is significant in terms of our understanding of Erdrich and her writings. Autobiographical works by Aboriginal people are always of importance in increasing our understanding of their lives, since they are spiritual as well as confessional in nature and illustrate the character of dreams and stories.[28] *Books and Islands* is certainly no exception. It is dedicated to her daughter, Kiishikok, also known as Kiish, who was born in 2000 and whose name in English is Sky Woman, "and [to] her brothers and sisters." It is beautifully illustrated by Erdrich's drawings, which serve to highlight the fact that books are not new; they predate the first European contacts. As she remarks at the outset, the "Ojibwe people were great writers from way back and synthesized the oral and written tradition by keeping mnemonic scrolls of inscribed birchbark. The first paper, the first books."[29]

The purpose of the trip to Canada was both ceremonial and spiritual. The book was written to describe Erdrich's travels to the islands in the Lake of the Sand Hills (Lake of the Woods) to show Kiish where her ancestors (specifically, her namesake, who is her paternal grandmother) came from. Her father is Tobasonakwut, also known as Peter Kelly Kinew, of the Big George family, Lynx clan, from the Onegaming Reserve; he was born on Big Island and raised on Garden Island. At the outset, Erdrich clearly reveals the theme of her work:

> My travels have become so focused on books and islands that the two have merged for me. Books, islands. Islands, books. Lake of the Woods in Ontario and Minnesota has 14,000 islands. Some of them are painted islands, the rocks bearing signs ranging from a few hundred to more than a thousand years old. So these islands, which I'm longing to read, are books in themselves. And then there is a special island on Rainy Lake that is home to thousands of rare books ranging from crumbling copies of Erasmus in the French and Heloise's letters to Abelard dated MDCCXXIII (1723), to first editions of Mark Twain (signed) to a magnificent collection of ethnographic works on the Ojibwe that might help explain the book-islands of Lake of the Woods.[30]

Erdrich and Kiish reach Canada and the southeastern shore of the Lake of the Woods near Morson and the Big Grassy Reserve.

The islands in Lake of the Woods, as books, take her back to the very foundation of things, to a time when the stones howled. They also enable her to highlight the significance of reading, which comes before writing and the language, which come from Mother Earth. Erdrich recalls her visit to Manitoulin Island in 1985 and being impressed by the significance then of the Ojibwe language.[31] She tells the story of the meaning of the language for Peter, who "delights in the language, his first language. He loves to delineate the sources and origins of words, keeps lists of new words, and creates them himself. Yet, as with many of his generation, he endured tremendous punishment for this love. He remembers singing his father's song to comfort himself as he was driven to a residential school at age eleven. The priest who was driving stopped the car, made him get out, and savagely beat him."[32] For Erdrich, not a fluent speaker, the Ojibwe language is adapted to the land as no other language can possibly be. Its philosophy is bound up with the northern earth, lakes, rivers, forests, and plains. Its origins pertain to the animals and their particular habits, to the shades of meaning in the very placement of stones. Many of the names and songs associated with these places were revealed to people in dreams and songs—it is a language that most directly reflects a human involvement with the spirit of the land itself. It is a language of the paintings that seem to glow from within the rocks.[33]

After visiting the islands and rock paintings, Erdrich and Kiish then leave the Lake of the Sand Hills and Peter, driving east towards Rainy Lake and Ernest Oberholtzer's (Ober's) Island, which is filled with the many books Oberholtzer collected. They stop for the night at a dingy, creepy place called the Skylark Motel, which comes "without the Skylarks" in room 33. Such ambiguous places "always inspire uneasy nights and sometimes spectacular and even numinous dreams."[34] This experience takes her back to her German heritage as well.

*Austerlitz* was written by W. G. Sebald (1944–2001), a German writer well known for developing a new form of writing as a response to the human tragedy he refers to as the holocaust "industry," an official culture of mourning and remembering; the book "is about the near dissolution of a man's personality during the reconstruction of his memory. Austerlitz, who has forgotten most of his early childhood, follows threads of history, traceries of his own consciousness; he digs through lists of deportees and examines photographs and propaganda movies to find the truth of his origins."[35] Erdrich enters the world of dreams and prophecies:

> The books we bring to strange places become guides and prevailing metaphors, catch-alls, lenses for new experience. As I read late into the night, moths whirling at the spotted shade, this book speaks to me with melancholy prescience, anticipating 9/11 in the first pages when Austerlitz speaks of how the smallest buildings—cottages, little pavilions—bring us peace, while we contemplate vast buildings, overdone buildings, with a wonder which is also dawning horror "for somehow we know by instinct that outsize buildings cast the shadow of their own destruction before them, and are designed from the first with an eye to their later existence as ruins."[36]

This image reminds her of the destruction of the islands in the Lake of the Woods and of the drowning of the wild rice in its waters.[37]

To reach Ober's Island (which is actually three islands), Erdrich has to cross into the US from Fort Frances to International Falls. She admits that she is "nervous":

> I am carrying those eagle spikes and although I have a right to carry them and I have my band enrollment card, I hate the questioning, the scrutiny, the suspicious nature of the border guards. What I don't expect is that the man, my age, very trim and professional looking in his blue uniform, will question me about my baby.
> "Do you have any proof that you're her mother?"
> I stare at him in shock, it is such a strange question. I have to think.
> "Well," I say, "I can nurse her."
> He stares back at me. Gestures to the side of the building.
> "Pull over."

Erdrich is extremely worried and wonders if she will be asked to nurse her baby publicly to prove that she is the mother.

> I pull over, wishing that I had a copy of the Jay Treaty, which guarantees Native People the right to cross the Canadian–U.S. border without hassle. A woman meets me. I undergo more questioning. I start to grip Kiizhikok a little harder, in alarm, I suppose, and in response she holds onto me tightly. The guard asks a series of easy questions and then, suddenly, as though to trip me up, shoots the question, "And who is this?" at me, indicating Kiizhikok. Each time, grasping the strategy, I shoot right back, "My daughter!" Each time, Kiizhikok grips me even tighter. I'm so glad she isn't going through one of those mother-rejecting stages, or branching out adventurously, or growling at me, as she likes to do as a joke, right now. Eventually the sharp-eyed woman clears us. We've passed some mother/daughter test. But when I get into the van I find that I'm actually shaken. For the first time in quite a while I'm surprised to find that I crave a stiff drink. Yes, I do. A straight shot of really good whiskey. And a cigarette.[38]

After finally crossing the border, they take a boat to Ober's Island, which is today run by a trust because Oberholtzer, of German descent, was a close friend of the Ojibwe. Erdrich's experience while crossing the borders in the summer of 2002 is very similar to Lipshaw's experience in *The Bingo Palace*. Only circumstances have changed. The border guards are not concerned about "ceremonial" feathers or other Native objects of spirituality. Indeed, after the incident of 9/11, security has become a much more significant issue. Here is a mother, alone with her child, and being questioned about proof of her own motherhood. This line of questioning is, quite naturally, a shock for Erdrich.

Erdrich's borderland story is especially significant because of her mixed heritage—and here the political border between Canada and the US is especially significant. There is a big difference between American Indians and Native Canadians of mixed heritage—their corporate identity in terms of the federal laws of the US and Canada is different. Living in Minnesota as a member of the Turtle Mountain reservation in North Dakota, Erdrich is considered a "registered" Indian. Were she to live just one hundred kilometres farther north, she would be classified as a Métis and not a status or a treaty Indian. To complicate matters, Erdrich does not "look Indian," although she is culturally a Native; but her young daughter looks more "Indian," like her father (who is not of mixed descent), which complicates the identity and motherhood issues. For this reason, each border crossing for Erdrich and her young daughter is fraught with challenges to Erdrich's identity as an Aboriginal person even though she is a registered tribal member at the Turtle Mountain reservation. Canadian border guards would treat sacred pipes and feathers as illegal contraband. The dark baby without an "Indian" father is a "stolen" baby that cannot possibly be hers. These are borderland experiences that only mixed-heritage people understand.

## Retrospect

Books transcend the borders of modern nation-states and empires. Borders and homeland security are a significant aspect of Louise Erdrich's life and writings. The Canadian connection continues to be a significant aspect of Erdrich's life and writings. In the end, what is significant is the spirit of the songs, and the stories that connect Aboriginal people to Nature and the environment. The boundaries are natural and shared, based on the configuration of the lands and waters in each Aboriginal territory. These spirits of Aboriginal orature are real and tangible and not illusory; moreover, as Erdrich's writings indicate, they are powerful, representing peace and not war. Critics must take note that, as Native writers in North America are beginning to network with Aboriginals from around the globe, they are also reaching a global readership, transcending all borders.

What is the real message of 9/11 for Erdrich? The Aboriginal structure of Turtle Island is predicated on watersheds as borders between Aboriginal nations, which reflect their Homelands, and not on the linear lines drawn upon the lands and the waters based on non-geograph-ical assumptions of European and North American empires and nation-states. As borders begin to disappear in the wake of 9/11, we will begin to see with greater clarity the survival and presence of the Anishinabe/Cree/Métis names and places on the landscape of the twenty-first cen-tury as they have been for thousands of years past and for the future as homelands. For Erdrich, this is the real lesson of 9/11—a message of peace rather than war and places with natural borders and small buildings.

# NOTES

## Introduction, by Karl S. Hele

1 Throughout this volume, the reader will encounter different spellings of Aboriginal nomenclature. As editor, I have elected not to alter the various spellings. These reflect regional dialects, preferred names and spellings, and common usage on either side of the international border. For instance, Anishinabeg is also rendered Anishinabe, Anishinabek, and Anishnaabeg, and the European-derived Ojibwa, Saulteur, Ojibway, Chippewa, and Chippeway are also used to refer to the same people.

2 Mary Louise Pratt, *Imperial Eyes: Travel Writing and Transculturation* (London: Routledge, 1992), 1–11; Andrew R. L. Cayton and Fredrika J. Teute, "Introduction: On the Connection of Frontiers," in *Contact Points: American Frontiers from the Mohawk Valley to the Mississippi, 1750–1830*, ed. Andrew R. L. Cayton and Fredrika J. Teute (Chapel Hill: University of North Carolina Press for the Omohundro Institute of Early American History and Culture, 1998), 1–2; James O. Gump, *The Dust Rose Like Smoke: The Subjugation of the Zulu and the Sioux* (Lincoln: University of Nebraska Press, 1994). Here Gump is essentially repeating Robert F. Berkhofer's conclusions in "The North American Frontier as Process and Context," in *The Frontier in History: North American and South Africa Compared*, ed. Howard Lamar and Leonard Thompson (New Haven, CT: Yale University Press, 1981), 43–75. Jeremy Adelman and Stephen Aron, "From Borderland to Borders: Empires, Nation-States, and the Peoples in Between in North American History," *American Historical Review* 104, no. 3 (1999): 814–41. See also Evan Haefeli, "A Note on the Use of North American Borderlands," John E. Wunder and Pekka Hamalainen, "Of Lethal Places and Lethal Essays," and Adelman and Aron, "Of Lively Exchanges and Larger Perspectives," all in *American Historical Review* 104 (October 1999): 1222–25, 1229–34, 1235–39. The quotation from Haefeli is found on page 1224.

3 Herbert Eugene Bolton, *The Spanish Borderlands: A Chronicle of Old Florida and the Southwest* (New Haven, CT: Yale University Press, 1921); and Frederick

Jackson Turner, *The Frontier in American History* (1920; reprint, New York: Dover Publications, 1996), 1–38. For an example of Bolton's work, see Bolton and Ross, *The Debatable Land*. For discussions of Bolton's legacy, see Weber, "Turner, the Boltonians, and the Borderlands"; and Klein, *Frontiers of the Historical Imagination*, 191, 205, 262.

4 See, for example, Bolton, *The Spanish Borderlands*; Herbert E. Bolton and Mary Ross, *The Debatable Land: A Sketch of the Anglo-Spanish Contest for the Georgia Country* (New York: Russell and Russell, 1968); David J. Weber, "Turner, the Boltonians, and the Borderlands," *American Historical Review* 91 (February 1986): 66–81; Kerwin Lee Klein, *Frontiers of the Historical Imagination: Narrating the European Conquest of Native America, 1890–1990* (Berkeley: University of California Press, 1999); Philip Curtis Bellfy, "Division and Unity, Dispersal and Permanence: The Anishnabeg of the Lake Huron Borderlands" (PhD diss., Michigan State University, 1995); Paul Andrew Demers, "The Formation and Maintenance of the Canada–United States Border in the St. Mary's River and Lake Huron Borderlands, 1780–1860" (PhD diss., Michigan State University, 2001); and James Brooks, *Captives and Cousins: Slavery, Kinship, and Community in the Southwest Borderlands* (Chapel Hill: University of North Carolina Press, 2002).

5 For the exploration of the western borderlands, see Neal McLeod, "Plains Cree Identity: Borderlands, Ambiguous Genealogies, and Narrative Irony," *Canadian Journal of Native Studies* 20, no. 2 (2000): 437–54; Randy William Widdis, "Borderland Interaction in the International Region of the Great Plains: An Historic-Geographical Perspective," *Great Plains Research* 7, no. 1 (1997): 103–37; Shelia McManus, *The Line Which Separates: Race, Gender, and the Making of the Alberta–Montana Borderlands* (Edmonton: University of Alberta Press, 2005); McManus, "Mapping the Alberta–Montana Borderlands: Race, Ethnicity and Gender in the Late Nineteenth Century," *Journal of American Ethnic History* 20, no. 3 (2001): 71–87; McManus, "'Their Own Country': Race, Gender, Landscape, and Colonization around the 49th Parallel, 1862–1900," *Agricultural History* 73, no. 2 (1999): 168–82; David G. McCrady, *Living with Strangers: The Nineteenth-Century Sioux and the Canadian–American Boderlands* (Lincoln: University of Nebraska Press, 2006); and Sterling Evans, ed., *The Borderlands of the American and Canadian Wests: Essays on Regional History of the Forty-ninth Parallel* (Lincoln: University of Nebraska Press, 2006). For explorations of the eastern borderlands, see Colin G. Calloway, "The Abenakis and the Anglo-French Borderlands," *Dublin Seminar for New England Folklife* 14 (1989): 18–27; and Stephen J. Hornsby, Victor A. Konrad, and James J. Herlan, eds., *The Northeastern Borderlands: Four Centuries of Interaction* (Fredericton: Acadiensis Press, 1989). For some recent unpublished and published studies of the Great Lakes regio, see Karl Hele, "'By the Rapids': The Anishinabeg–Missionary Encounter at Bawating (Sault Ste. Marie), c. 1821–1871" (PhD diss., McGill University, 2003); Demers, "The Formation and Maintenance of the Canada–United States Border"; Lisa Philips Valentine and Allan K. McDougall, "Imposing the Border: The Detroit River from 1786 to 1807," *Journal of Borderland Studies* 19, no. 1 (2004): 13–22; and Bellfy, "Division and Unity, Dispersal and Permanence." Finally, the *Michigan Historical Review* has announced an upcoming volume that will examine the Great Lakes borderlands in the context of Michigan's past.

6 Adelman and Aron, "From Borderlands to Borders," 814–41.

7 Adelman and Aron, "From Borderlands to Borders," 816.

8  Adelman and Aron, "From Borderlands to Borders," 817–18.
9  "Great Lakes Coast Guard Armed with Machine Guns," *Muskegon Chronicle* 17 March 2006; Julia Necheff, "U.S. to Use Air Patrols along Canadian Border," *CNEWS*, 3 February 2006; Yvonne Abraham, "Volunteers Beginning Watch near Canada Line: Minutemen See Threat in North," *Boston Globe*, 4 October 2005; Christopher Bolkcom, "Homeland Security: Unmanned Aerial Vehicles and Border Surveillance," *Congressional Research Service Reports on Homeland Security*, Federation of American Scientists, <http://www.fas.org/sgp/crs/home-sec/RS21698.pdf> (accessed 22 March 2006).
10  For instance, see Jean Comaroff and John L. Comaroff, "The Colonization of Consciousness in South Africa," *Economy and Society* 18, no. 3 (1989): 267–96.

## Chapter 1: "'We have no spirit to celebrate with you the great [1893] Columbian Fair': Aboriginal Peoples of the Great Lakes Respond to Canadian and United States Policies During the Nineteenth Century," by Edmund J. Danziger Jr.

1  Simon Pokagon, "The Red Man's Greeting," in *Talking Back to Civilization: Indian Voices from the Progressive Era*, ed. Frederick E. Hoxie (Boston: Bedford/St. Martin's, 2001), 31–35.
2  Helen Hornbeck Tanner, ed., *Atlas of Great Lakes Indian History* (Norman: University of Oklahoma Press, 1987), 182.
3  For a discussion of British and American frontier policies during this period, see J. R. Miller, *Skyscrapers Hide the Heavens: A History of Indian–White Relations in Canada* (Toronto: University of Toronto Press, 1991), chap. 4–5; Reginald Horsman, "United States Indian Policies, 1776–1815," in *History of Indian–White Relations*, vol. 4 of *Handbook of North American Indians*, ed. Wilcomb E. Washburn (Washington: Smithsonian Institution, 1988), 29–39.
4  See Francis M. Carroll, *A Good and Wise Measure: The Search for the Canadian–American Boundary, 1783–1842* (Toronto: University of Toronto Press, 2001), chapters 5 and 6 for a description of surveying the Great Lakes international boundary. Although scholars generally have focussed on the differences between Canadian and United States Indian policies and their implementation, the comparative works of two historians underscore international similarities during the last half of the nineteenth century—the focus of this essay. See C. L. Higham, *Nobel, Wretched, and Redeemable: Protestant Missionaries to the Indians in Canada and the United States, 1820–1900* (Albuquerque: University of New Mexico Press, 2000); and Roger L. Nichols, *Indians in the United States and Canada: A Comparative History* (Lincoln: University of Nebraska Press, 1998).
5  William Ashworth, *The Late, Great Lakes: An Environmental History* (Detroit: Wayne State University Press, 1987), 65.
6  For a brief review of Great Lakes Indian land cessions, removal, and the establishment of reserves, see Tanner, *Atlas*, 155–68.
7  Randall White, *Ontario, 1610–1985: A Political and Economic History* (Toronto: Dundurn Press, 1985), 110.
8  Robert Bothwell, *A Short History of Ontario* (Edmonton: Hurtig Publishers, 1986), 53, 98.
9  Edward S. Rogers, "Northern Algonquians and the Hudson's Bay Company, 1821–1890," in *Aboriginal Ontario: Historical Perspectives on the First Nations*, ed.

Edward S. Rogers and Donald Smith (Toronto: Dundurn Press, 1994), 333–35; and Kenneth Norrie and Douglas Owram, *A History of the Canadian Economy* (Toronto: Harcourt Brace and Jovanovich, 1991), 240–41.

10  James P. Barry, *Georgian Bay: The Sixth Great Lake* (Toronto: Clarke, Irwin, 1968), 75–76.

11  Pratt, "The Advantages of Mingling Indians with Whites," an extract of the Official Report of the Nineteenth Annual Conference of Charities and Correction (1892), 46–59, quoted in *Americanizing the American Indians: Writings by the "Friends of the Indian," 1880–1900*, ed. Francis Paul Prucha (Cambridge, MA: Harvard University Press, 1973), 262.

12  Charles E. Cleland, *Rites of Conquest: The History and Culture of Michigan's Native Americans* (Ann Arbor: University of Michigan Press, 1992), 234–35; Arrell M. Gibson, *The American Indian: Prehistory to the Present* (Lexington, MA: D. C. Heath, 1980), 426–28; Francis Paul Prucha, *The Great Father: The United States Government and the American Indians* (Lincoln: University of Nebraska Press, 1984), 1:580–81, 393; and Philip Weeks, *Farewell, My Nation: The American Indian and the United States, 1820–1890* (Arlington Heights, IL: Harlan Davidson, 1990), 204–5, 217–18, 232–33.

13  Hiram Price Annual Report, Commissioner of Indian Affairs, 24 October 1881, in *The American Indian and the United States: A Documentary History*, ed. Wilcomb E. Washburn (New York: Random House, 1973), 1:300; and Morgan quoted in James A. Clifton, *The Prairie People* (Lawrence: Regents Press of Kansas, 1977), 392.

14  Murray quoted in Boyce Richardson, "Kind Hearts or Forked Tongues? The Indian Ordeal: A Century of Decline," *Beaver: Exploring Canada's History*, 67 (1987), 18–23; E. Brian Titley, *A Narrow Vision: Duncan Campbell Scott and the Administration of Indian Affairs in Canada* (Vancouver: University of British Columbia Press, 1986), 201; and Royal Commission on Aboriginal Peoples (RCAP), *Volume 1: Looking Forward, Looking Back* (Ottawa: Canada Communication Group—Publishing, 1996), 188–91.

15  Canada (Province of), An Act to Encourage the Gradual Civilization of the Indian Tribes in this Province, and to Amend the Laws Respecting Indians, Statutes of the Province of Canada 1857, 20 Vict., c. 26, in *Canadian Indians and the Law: Selected Documents, 1663–1972*, ed. Derek G. Smith (Toronto: McClelland and Stewart, 1975), 50–54; Canada, An Act to Amend and Consolidate the Laws Respecting Indians (Indian Act), Statutes of Canada 1876, 39 Vict., c. 18, in *Canadian Indians and the Law*, 87–115. For a fuller discussion of British and Canadian Indian policy legislation, see the RCAP *Volume 1*, 271–73, 180–82, 267–69, 280; Nichols, *Indians in the United States and Canada*, 199–212; Richardson, "Kind Hearts or Forked Tongues?" 16–41; Indian and Northern Affairs Canada, *First Nations in Canada* (Ottawa: Queen's Printer, 1997), 73–75, 81–82; Titley, *A Narrow Vision*, 11; and Olive Patricia Dickason, *Canada's First Nations: A History of the Founding Peoples from Earliest Times* (Toronto: McClelland and Stewart, 1992), 250–319.

16  Richardson, "Kind Hearts or Forked Tongues?" 24–27.

17  Alice C. Fletcher, under direction of the Commissioner of Education, *Indian Education and Civilization*, Bureau of Education Special Report, 1988, a Report Prepared in Answer to Senate Resolution of 23 February 1885, Senate Executive Document no. 95, 48th Congress, 2nd Session (Serial 2264), 578; and Indian Affairs, Report for the Year Ended 30 June 1898, 62 Victoria, *Sessional Papers* (no. 14), 1899, 450.

18 Indian Affairs, Report for the Year Ended 30 June 1898, 62 Victoria, *Sessional Papers* (no. 14), 1899, 450.

19 For a discussion of allotment and location tickets, see Prucha, *The Great Father*, 2: chap. 26, 34; and Miller, *Skyscrapers*, 114, 190–91.

20 Edmund Jefferson Danziger, Jr., *The Chippewas of Lake Superior* (Norman: University of Oklahoma Press, 1978), 104.

21 Tanner, *Atlas*, 168.

22 James Wilson, *The Earth Shall Weep: A History of Native America* (New York: Grove Press, 1998), 310–11; and Philip Cate Huckins, "Broken Vows, Broken Arrows: An Analysis of the U.S. Government's Off-Reservation Boarding School Program, 1879–1900" (PhD diss., Boston College, 1995), 92.

23 See, for example, J. R. Miller, *Shingwauk's Vision: A History of Native Residential Schools* (Toronto: University of Toronto Press, 1996); and John S. Milloy, *"A National Crime": The Canadian Government and the Residential School System, 1879–1986* (Winnipeg: University of Manitoba Press, 1999).

24 See, for example, Sarah Shillinger, "'They Never Told Us They Wanted to Help Us': An Oral History of Saint Joseph's Indian Industrial School" (PhD diss., University of Pennsylvania, 1995).

25 Higham, *Nobel, Wretched, and Redeemable*, 208–9.

26 Joel W. Martin, *The Land Looks after Us: A History of Native American Religion* (New York: Oxford University Press, 2001), 81–82.

27 Frederick E. Hoxie, *A Final Promise: The Campaign to Assimilate the Indians, 1880–1920* (Lincoln: University of Nebraska Press, 1984), 42–52; J. R. Miller, introduction to *Aboriginal Peoples of Canada: A Short Introduction*, ed. Paul Robert Magosci (Toronto: University of Toronto Press, 2002), 32; and Philip Weeks, *Farewell, My Nation*, 217–18, 228–30.

28 L. Vankoughnet, Deputy Superintendent General of Indian Affairs, Draft Statement, 22 August, 1876, *RG* 10, vol. 1995, file 6886, Indian Affairs fonds, Red Series, Library and Archives Canada, Ottawa, ON (LAC); Deborah Anne Montgomerie, "Coming to Terms: Ngai Tahu, Roberson County Indians, and the Garden River Band of Ojibwa, 1840–1940. Three Studies of Colonialism in Action" (PhD diss., Duke University, 1993), 260–61; RCAP, *Volume 1*, 261.

29 Abbott to Superintendent General of Indian Affairs, 12 September 1894, Annual Report, Indian Affairs, 1894, 58 Victoria, *Sessional Papers* (no. 14), 1895, 9–11.

30 Sarnia Reserve Interpreter William Wawanosh to Indian Agent Adam English, 25 August 1886, Red Series, *RG* 10, vol. 2351, file 70569, Indian Affairs, LAC.

31 La Pointe Agent W. A. Mercer to Peter Phelon, 21 December 1895, La Pointe Agency, Letters Received, RG 75, National Archives and Records Administration, Washington, USA (NARA).

32 David R. M. Beck, "Siege and Survival: Menominee Responses to an Encroaching World" (PhD diss., University of Illinois at Chicago, 1994), 165–66.

33 Green Bay Agent Thomas Jennings to Commissioner of Indian Affairs, 21 February 1890, Letters Received, Green Bay Agency, RG 75, doc. no. 5844, NARA.

34 Jane Stewart, "Statement of Reconciliation," in *Gathering Strength—Canada's Aboriginal Action Plan* (Ottawa: Indian Affairs and Northern Development, 1997).

35 Kevin Gover, Assistant Secretary of the Interior–Indian Affairs, Remarks at the Ceremony Acknowledging the 175th Anniversary of the Establishment of the Bureau of Indian Affairs, 8 September 2000, www.tahtonka.com/apology .html (accessed 14 June 2005).

## Chapter 2: "Cross-border Treaty-signers: The Anishnaabeg of the Lake Huron Borderlands," by Phil Bellfy

1 Adopted from Peter Salway, *The Frontier People of Roman Britain* (London: Cambridge University Press, 1965), 1–4.

2 Salway, *Frontier People*, 4.

3 AIM (American Indian Movement), "Brief to the Committee on Indian Affairs and Northern Development of the House of Commons (Canada)," ms. (University of Regina, SK, ca. 1973), 18.

4 See *Mitchell v. MNR*, [2001] 1 S.C.R. 911, 2001 SCC 33.

5 All of the treaty data are taken from Charles J. Kappler, ed., *Indian Treaties: 1778–1883* (New York: Interland, 1972).

6 See Lewis Cass, "Governor Cass to the Secretary of War, Sault St. Marie, June 17, 1820," in *The Territory of Michigan*, vol. 11 of *The Territorial Papers of the United States*, ed. Clarence Edwin Carter (Washington: Government Printing Office, 1942), 36–37.

7 Henry Rowe Schoolcraft, *Personal Memoirs of a Residence of Thirty Years with the Indian Tribes on the American Frontiers: With Brief Notices of Passing Events, Facts, and Opinions, A.D. 1812 to A.D. 1842* (Philadelphia: Lippincott, Grambo, 1851), 248; and Penny Petrone, *First People: First Voices* (Toronto: University of Toronto Press, 1983).

8 Janet Chute, "A Century of Native Leadership: Shingwaukonse and His Heirs" (PhD diss., McMaster University, 1986), 30.

9 Schoolcraft, *Personal Memoirs*, 110.

10 For a complete discussion of these "presents distribution" patterns, see James A. Clifton, "Visiting Indians in Canada," ms. prepared for the Fort Malden National Historical Park, Parks Canada, 1979.

11 Information on Canadian treaties taken from Government of Canada, *Indian Treaties and Surrenders*, 3 vols (1891; reprint, Saskatoon: Fifth House, 1992).

12 Spelling in the text for these treaty-signers is given as it appears in the original documents.

13 Francis X. Chauvin, "Walpole Island Is Home of a Thousand Indians," *Border Cities Star* [Windsor, ON], 7 August 1929, Archives of Ontario (AO), MU 2133, Mss. Misc. Coll. 1929 #13.

14 *Indian News* 16, no. 12 (July–Sept. 1974): 1+.

15 John Price, *Native Studies: American and Canadian Indians* (Toronto: McGraw-Hill, 1978), 227.

16 Ladis K. D. Kristof, "The Nature of Frontiers and Boundaries," *Annals of the Association of American Geographers* 49, no. 1 (1959): 272.

17 Retold in Dan Smith, *The Seventh Fire: The Struggle for Aboriginal Government* (Toronto: Key Porter, 1993), 6–7.

18 Smith, *Seventh Fire*, 103, 125, 136.

19 Jack Storey, "Protest by Shopping: Indians Use International Bridge to Assert Border-crossing Rights," *Evening News* [Sault Ste. Marie, MI] (19 July 1993): 1A.

20 See Michael Janofsky, "Officials Lay Groundwork for Cleanup of Great Lakes," *New York Times*, 4 December 2004, A12.

21 John Sturm, "Farewell to the Swan Creek Chippewa," *Chronicle: The Quarterly Magazine of the Historical Society of Michigan* 21, no. 2 (1985): 20–25, 22.

22 Peter S. Schmalz, *The Ojibwa of Southern Ontario* (Toronto: University of Toronto Press, 1991), 134.

23  Chute, "Century of Native Leadership," 488n94.

24  Schmalz, *Ojibwa*, 23, 114.

25  Schoolcraft, *Personal Memories*, 658.

26  Schoolcraft, *Personal Memories*, 583.

27  Chute, "Century of Native Leadership," 489n106.

28  Chute, "Century of Native Leadership," 288.

29  Andrew J. Blackbird, *History of the Ottawa and Chippewa Indians of Michigan* (Ypsilanti, MI: Ypsilanti Job Printing House, 1887).

30  Chute, "Century of Native Leadership," 110, 138.

31  Chute, "Century of Native Leadership," 516n68.

32  Douglas Leighton, *The Historical Development of the Walpole Island Community*, Occasional Paper no. 22 (Wallaceburg, ON: Walpole Island Research Centre, 1986).

33  Schmalz, *Ojibwa*, 169.

34  John Richardson, *Tecumseh and Richardson: The Story of a Trip to Walpole Island and Port Sarnia* (Toronto: Ontario Book Co., 1924), 101.

35  Chute, "Century of Native Leadership," 118.

36  John H. Pitezel, *Lights and Shades of Missionary Life* (Cincinnati: Printed at the Western Book Concern for the author, 1857), 358.

37  Chute, "Century of Native Leadership," 489n106.

38  Robert F. Bauman, "The Migration of the Ottawa Indians from the Maumee Valley to Walpole Island," *Northwest Ohio Quarterly* 21, no. 3 (1949): 109.

39  Chute, "Century of Native Leadership," 153–54.

40  Richardson, *Tecumseh and Richardson*, 100.

41  Schmalz, *Ojibwa*, 136.

42  Richardson, *Tecumseh and Richardson*, 101.

43  "Deed of Sale; Huron Church Reserve: 11 Sep. 1800," Hiram Walker Papers, AO.

44  Bauman, "Migration of the Ottawa Indians," 109.

## Chapter 3: "From Intercolonial Messenger to 'Christian Indian': The Flemish Bastard and the Mohawk Struggle for Independence from New France and Colonial New York in the Eastern Great Lakes Borderland, 1647–1687," by Mark Meuwese

1  The most comprehensive information on the Flemish Bastard is provided by Thomas Grassman, "Flemish Bastard," *Dictionary of Canadian Biography* (*DCB*), vol. 1, 1000–1700 (Toronto: University of Toronto Press, 1966), 307–8. See also Peter Lowensteyn, "The Role of Chief Canaqueese in the Iroquois Wars," 5 November 2006, *Lowensteyn Family On-Line: Humanities*, http://lowensteyn .com/iroquois/canaqueese.html (accessed 26 December 2006). Throughout this essay, I use the French term "Flemish Bastard" because that name was recognized by both French and Anglo-Dutch officials in the 1660s. The speech by the Flemish Bastard about the political structure of the Iroquois Confederacy was mentioned most recently by William N. Fenton, *The Great Law and the Longhouse: A Political History of the Iroquois Confederacy* (Norman: University of Oklahoma Press, 1998), 273. Daniel K. Richter discusses the Flemish Bastard as war chief and negotiator in *The Ordeal of the Longhouse: The Peoples of the Iroquois League in the Era of European Colonization* (Chapel Hill: University of North

Carolina Press for the Institute of Early American History and Culture, 1992), 103–4, 120, 126. See also Matthew Dennis, *Cultivating a Landscape of Peace: Iroquois–European Encounters in Seventeenth-Century America* (Ithaca: Cornell University Press, 1993), 217. I have borrowed the term "First French–Iroquois War" from Evan Haefeli and Kevin Sweeney, *Captors and Captives: The 1704 French and Indian Raid on Deerfield* (Amherst: University of Massachusetts Press, 2003), 43. The Flemish Bastard was surprisingly not discussed by Richter in his essay "Cultural Brokers and Intercultural Politics: New York–Iroquois Relations, 1664–1701," *Journal of American History* 75, no. 1 (1988–1989): 40–67. For other recent literature on cultural brokers and negotiators, see for example James H. Merrell, *Into the American Woods: Negotiators on the Pennsylvania Frontier* (New York: Norton, 1999); Margaret Connell Szasz, ed., *Between Indian and White Worlds: The Cultural Broker* (Norman: University of Oklahoma Press, 1994); and Nancy L. Hagedorn, "Brokers of Understanding: Interpreters as Agents of Cultural Exchange in Colonial New York," *New York History* 76, no. 4 (1995): 379–408.

2  Allan Greer, ed., *The Jesuit Relations: Natives and Missionaries in Seventeenth-Century North America* (Boston: Bedford/St. Martin's, 2000), 1–19, contains a discussion on the production and the intended readership of the *Jesuit Relations*. The scanty primary sources about the Flemish Bastard have led some historians to confuse the Flemish Bastard with other prominent Mohawk leaders. In his otherwise excellent study of Mohawk Protestantism during the seventeenth and eighteenth centuries, William B. Hart incorrectly equated the Flemish Bastard with a Mohawk leader who was known under the various Iroquois and European names of Joseph Togouiroui, Athasata, Kryn, and the Great Mohawk. It is true that both the Flemish Bastard and Joseph Togouiroui were prominent Mohawks who increasingly associated with the French in the 1680s. Despite these similarities, Togouiroui was almost certainly not the Flemish Bastard. For example, Togouiroui joined a combined French–Native expedition against the Dutch colonial town of Schenectady in February 1690. Because of the Flemish Bastard's partly Dutch background and his frequent friendly visits to the Dutch communities on the Upper Hudson during the 1650s and 1660s, it is unlikely that he would have participated in the devastating attack in 1690 that killed and captured many Dutch inhabitants. See William B. Hart, "For the Good of Our Souls: Mohawk Authority, Accommodation, and Resistance to Protestant Evangelism, 1700–1780" (PhD diss., Brown University, 1998), 45. For Joseph Togouiroui, see the entry by Henri Bechard in *DCB*, vol. 1, *1000–1700*, 650–51. For the French–Native attack on Schenectady, see Thomas E. Burke Jr., *Mohawk Frontier: The Dutch Community of Schenectady, New York, 1661–1710* (Ithaca: Cornell University Press, 1991).

3  Reuben G. Thwaites, ed., *The Jesuit Relations and Allied Documents* (hereafter *JR*) (Cleveland: Burrows Brothers, 1896–1900), 35:213.

4  A. J. F. van Laer, trans. and ed., *Fort Orange and Beverwijck Records: Court Minutes, 1652–1660* (Albany: University of the State of New York, 1920–1923), 1:90–92.

5  For recent scholarship arguing for the interconnectedness of eastern North American colonies with one another and with Aboriginal peoples, see Haefeli and Sweeney, *Captors and Captives*; April Lee Hatfield, *Atlantic Virginia: Intercolonial Relations in the Seventeenth Century* (Philadelphia: University of Pennsylvania Press, 2004); Karen Ordahl Kupperman, "International at the Creation:

Early Modern American History," in *Rethinking American History in a Global Age*, ed. Thomas Bender (Berkeley: University of California Press, 2002), 103–22; and Cynthia J. Van Zandt, "Negotiating Settlement: Colonialism, Cultural Exchange, and Conflict in Early Colonial Atlantic North America, 1580–1660" (PhD diss., University of Connecticut, 1998). An early example of this approach is David B. Quinn, ed., *Early Maryland in a Wider World* (Detroit: Wayne State University Press, 1982).

6   Grassman, "Flemish Bastard," *DCB*, vol. 1, *1000–1700* (Toronto: University of Toronto Press, 1966), 307–8. Similarly, Shirley W. Dunn, *The Mohicans and Their Land, 1609–1730* (Fleischmanns, NY: Purple Mountain Press, 1994), 199, 200, 202, does not connect Smits Jan to the Flemish Bastard.

7   Jeremy Adelman and Stephen Aron, "From Borderland to Borders: Empires, Nation-States, and the Peoples in Between in North American History," *American Historical Review* 104, no. 3 (1999): 814–841; Evan Haefeli, "A Note on the Use of North American Borderlands," *American Historical Review* 104, no. 4 (1999), 1224. See also John E. Wunder and Pekka Hamalainen, "Of Lethal Places and Lethal Essays," and Adelman and Aron, "Of Lively Exchanges and Larger Perspectives," in *American Historical Review* 104, no. 4 (1999): 1229–34, and 1235–39.

8   French–Iroquois and Dutch–Iroquois relations are discussed in Richter, *Ordeal of the Longhouse*, chap. 4, 5. See also Dennis, *Cultivating a Landscape of Peace*, pt. 2; and José Antonio Brandâo, *"Your Fire Shall Burn No More": Iroquois Policy Toward New France and Its Native Allies to 1701* (Lincoln: University of Nebraska Press, 1997).

9   Daniel K. Richter, "War and Culture: The Iroquois Experience," *William and Mary Quarterly* 40 (1983): 528–59. See also Richter, "Iroquois Confederacy," in *The Encyclopedia of New York State*, ed. Peter Eisenstadt (Syracuse: Syracuse University Press, 2005), 791–94. Brandâo, *"Your Fire Shall Burn No More,"* appendix C, gives a different assessment of Iroquois demography in this period.

10   On the English conquest of New Netherland and Albany, see Richter, "Cultural Brokers and Intercultural Politics: New York–Iroquois Relations, 1664–1701," *Journal of American History* 75, no. 7 (1988–1989): 40–67; and Donna Merwick, *Possessing Albany, 1630–1710: The Dutch and English Experiences* (New York: Cambridge University Press, 1990). For French–Iroquois relations in this period, see Brandâo, *"Your Fire Shall Burn No More."*

11   Richter, *Ordeal of the Longhouse*, chap. 10, 11; J. A. Brandâo and William A. Starna, "The Treaties of 1701: A Triumph of Iroquois Diplomacy," *Ethnohistory* 43, no. 2 (1996): 209–44; and Richard Aquila, *The Iroquois Restoration: Iroquois Diplomacy on the Colonial Frontier, 1701–1754* (Lincoln: University of Nebraska Press, 1997).

12   For the ambiguities of borderlands, see Haefeli, "A Note on the Use of Borderlands," 1223. Haefeli refers to Richter's *Ordeal of the Longhouse* to make his point. See also Alan Taylor, *The Divided Ground: Indians, Settlers, and the Northern Borderland of the American Revolution* (New York: Alfred A. Knopf, 2006). The concept of borderlands is also applied to the Iroquois, albeit in a slightly different context, by David Lee Preston, "The Texture of Contact: European and Indian Settler Communities in the Iroquoian Borderlands, 1720–1780" (PhD diss., College of William and Mary, 2002). Preston focusses on everyday interactions between Iroquois and European colonists in colonial New York.

13   Govert Loockermans to Gilles Verbrugge, 21 December 1647, Stuijvesant-Rutherford Papers, folder 2: 1647, New York Historical Society (a microfilm

copy of this collection was consulted at the Amsterdam City Archive). See van den Bogaert, *A Journey into Mohawk and Oneida Country, 1634–1635: The Journal of Harmen Meyndertsz van den Bogaert*, trans. and ed. Charles T. Gehring and William A. Starna (Syracuse: Syracuse University Press, 1988).

14 Charles Gehring, director of the New Netherland Project, believes that Swist Jan is not Smits Jan. Email correspondence from Martha Dickinson Shattuck to Mark Meuwese, 1 August 2002. Based upon the circumstantial evidence, however, I believe the coincidence is too great, for Swist Jan not to be the same as Smits Jan. On Iroquois women, see Natalie Zemon Davis, "Iroquois Women, European Women," in *Women, "Race," and Writing in the Early Modern Period*, ed. Margo Hendricks and Patricia Parker (New York: Routledge, 1994), 243–58.

15 The regular Mohawk visits to Rensselaerswijck, Fort Orange, and Beverwijck are analyzed by Dennis, *Cultivating a Landscape*, pt. 2; Merwick, *Possessing Albany*.

16 van Laer, *Fort Orange and Beverwijck Records*, 1:90–92 (Flemish Bastard identified as a Mohawk by Dutch officials). For similar confusion among colonial officials about recognizing the ethnic identity of a person of Aboriginal-European descent, see James H. Merrell, "'The Cast of His Countenance': Reading Andrew Montour," in *Through a Dark Glass Darkly: Reflections on Personal Identity in Early America*, ed. Ronald Hoffman, Mechal Sobel, and Fredrika J. Teute (Chapel Hill: University of North Carolina Press, 1997), 13–39. For the mistreatment of Mohawk visitors by Dutch fur traders, see Richter, *Ordeal of the Longhouse*, 96–97; and Dennis, *Cultivating a Landscape of Peace*, pt. 2. On the family of the Flemish Bastard in 1666, see Marie de l'Incarnation, *Word from New France: The Selected Letters of Marie de l'Incarnation*, ed. Joyce Marshall (Toronto: Oxford University Press, 1967), 320.

17 For the Iroquois–Huron wars, see Richter, *Ordeal of the Longhouse*, chap. 3. On Iroquois war chiefs, see Richter, *Ordeal of the Longhouse*, 33–35. On the Flemish Bastard as war chief in 1650, see *JR* 35: 213.

18 On Iroquois tactics, see Haefeli and Sweeney, *Captors and Captives*, 58–59; and Brandâo, *"Your Fire Shall Burn No More,"* 34–35. Quotation from *JR* 35: 213.

19 Francis Jennings, *The Ambiguous Iroquois Empire: The Covenant Chain Confederation of Indian Tribes with English Colonies from Its Beginnings to the Lancaster Treaty of 1744* (New York: Norton, 1984), 104.

20 van Laer, *Fort Orange and Beverwijck Records*, 1:90–92. For a slightly different translation, see Charles T. Gehring, trans. and ed., *Fort Orange Court Minutes, 1652–1660*, vol. 16, pt. 2, New Netherland Documents Series (Syracuse: Syracuse University Press, 1990), 76–78.

21 For the Flemish Bastard's arrival, see *JR* 41: 85. For the Mohawk–French negotiations, see also Dennis, *Cultivating a Landscape of Peace*, pt. 2.

22 For the speech of the Flemish Bastard, see *JR* 41:87–89. See also Jennings, *Ambiguous Iroquois Empire*, 104–5.

23 *JR* 41:87–89.

24 Jennings, *Ambiguous Iroquois Empire*, 105–6; Dennis, *Cultivating a Landscape of Peace*, 233–41; and Daniel K. Richter, "Iroquois vs. Iroquois: Jesuit Missions and Christianity in Village Politics, 1642–1686," *Ethnohistory* 32, no. 1 (1985): 1–16.

25 On the French promise to stay out of the Iroquois wars against the Aboriginal Allies of the French, see Marie de l'Incarnation, *Word from New France*, ed. Marshall, 217–24. See also Dennis, *Cultivating a Landscape of Peace*, 233–41.

26 *JR* 42, chap. 15; Nicolas Perrot, "Memoirs on the Manners, Customs, and Religion of the Savages of North America," in Emma Helen Blair, trans. and ed., *The Indian Tribes of the Upper Mississippi Valley and Region of the Great Lakes* (Cleveland: Burrows Brothers, 1911), 157–58. Perrot's account discusses a French deserter having shot the Jesuit.

27 Richter, *Ordeal of the Longhouse*, 98–99, 108–9.

28 Richter, *Ordeal of the Longhouse*, 95–98; and Marcus Meuwese, "'For the Peace and Well-Being of the Country': Intercultural Mediators and Dutch–Indian Relations in New Netherland and Dutch Brazil, 1600–1664" (PhD diss., University of Notre Dame, 2003), 437–57.

29 Meuwese, "'For the Peace and Well-Being of the Country,'" 428. For Smits Jan's offer to ransom Dutch captives, see E. B. O'Callaghan and Berthold Fernow, eds., *Documents Relative to the Colonial History of the State of New York* (Albany: Weed, Pearsons and Company, 1856–1887), 13:261. On the Esopus Wars, see Allen W. Trelease, *Indian Affairs in Colonial New York: The Seventeenth Century* (Ithaca: Cornell University Press, 1960), 148–68.

30 O'Callaghan and Fernow, *Documents*, 13:261, 264. See also Meuwese, "'For the Peace and Well-Being of the Country,'" 428–29.

31 O'Callaghan and Fernow, *Documents*, 13:274–75, 278, 283. See also Meuwese, "'For the Peace and Well-Being of the Country,'" 429.

32 Richter, *Ordeal of the Longhouse*, 99–102.

33 O'Callaghan and Fernow, *Documents*, 3:146–48; for Nicholls's letter, see 146. For the use of Aboriginal couriers in New Netherland, see Meuwese, "'For the Peace and Well-Being of the Country,'" 334–35.

34 W. J. Eccles, *Canada under Louis XIV, 1663–1701* (Toronto: University of Toronto Press, 1964), chap. 1, 2; and Marshall, ed., *Word from New France*, 278–82.

35 Richter, *Ordeal of the Longhouse*, 102; W. J. Eccles, "Daniel de Remy de Courcelle," *DCB*, vol. 1, *1000–1700* (Toronto: University of Toronto Press, 1966), 570.

36 Richter, *Ordeal of the Longhouse*, 102–3.

37 Eccles, "Daniel de Remy de Courcelle," 570. Although Colonel Richard Nicholls suggested in letters to Albany officials that the Mohawks were subjects of the English Crown, Nicholls did not instruct his subordinates to prevent the French from invading the Iroquois nations or making a treaty with them. See O'Callaghan and Fernow, *Documents*, 3:146–48.

38 See Perrot, "Memoirs on the Manners," 199, on the Flemish Bastard at Schenectady; and Eccles, "Daniel de Remy de Courcelle," 570.

39 Perrot, "Memoirs on the Manners," 200–201; Marshall, ed., *Word from New France*, 283; *JR* 50:197. For the Mohawk wars with the Mahicans and Southern New England Algonquians, see Neal Salisbury, "Toward the Covenant Chain: Iroquois and Southern New England Algonquians, 1637–1684," in *Beyond the Covenant Chain: The Iroquois and Their Neighbors in Indian North America, 1600–1800*, ed. Daniel K. Richter and James H. Merrell (Syracuse: Syracuse University Press, 1987), 61–73.

40 See Marie de l'Incarnation, *Word from New France*, ed. Marshall, 319, on the Flemish Bastard and other Mohawks being forced to make snowshoes. On Tracy, see Leopold Lamontagne, "Alexandre de Prouville de Tracy," *DCB*, vol. 1, *1000–1700* (Toronto: University of Toronto Press, 1966), 554–57.

41 See Marie de l'Incarnation, *Word from New France*, ed. Marshall, 319–20.

42 On the French–Aboriginal expedition against the Mohawks, see Eccles, "Daniel de Remy de Courcelle," 570–71; and Lamontagne, "Alexandre de Prouville de

Tracy," 1:556. On the Flemish Bastard's warning, see Marie de l'Incarnation, *Word from New France*, ed. Marshall, 320.

43  For the Flemish Bastard's return to his people, see Marie de l'Incarnation, *Word from New France*, ed. Marshall, 327; for Tracy's order to return their captives, see *JR* 50:205. See also Richter, *Ordeal of the Longhouse*, 103–4.

44  For the Flemish Bastard's offer, see Perrot, "Memoir on the Manners," 203; *JR* 50:209; and Richter, *Ordeal of the Longhouse*, 104.

45  O'Callaghan and Fernow, *Documents*, 3:150–52. For van Curler, see Richter, *Ordeal of the Longhouse*, 24, 93–104.

46  O'Callaghan and Fernow, *Documents*, 3:148. Van Curler may have drowned or been killed by Mohawks angry at him for providing aid to the French troops at Schenectady. See Richter, *Ordeal of the Longhouse*, 104.

47  Marie de l'Incarnation, *Word from New France*, ed. Marshall, 328–33.

48  An excellent discussion of the Christian Indians and Canadian Iroquois along the St. Lawrence Valley is Haefeli and Sweeney, *Captors and Captives*, chap. 3.

49  Perrot, "Memoirs on the Manners," 203. On the religious identity of the Christian Indians, see Haefeli and Sweeney, *Captors and Captives*, chap. 3.

50  O'Callaghan and Fernow, *Documents*, 3:435. The 1687 French expedition against the Senecas is discussed in Richter, *Ordeal of the Longhouse*, 156–58.

51  For the testimony, see O' Callaghan and Fernow, *Documents*, 3:433–36. For the lack of solidarity among the Five Nations during the colonial period, see Daniel K. Richter, "Ordeals of the Longhouse: The Five Nations in Early American History," in *Beyond the Covenant Chain: The Iroquois and Their Neighbors in Indian North America*, ed. Daniel K. Richter and James H. Merrell, 11–27. See also Fenton, *Great Law and the Longhouse*, 275.

## Chapter 4: "The Anishinabeg and Métis in the Sault Ste. Marie Borderlands: Confronting a Line Drawn upon the Water," by Karl S. Hele

I would like to thank Social Science and Humanities Research Council for providing financial support for much of the research that went into this paper.

1  Reverend Abel Bingham, Annual Report for 1844, 22 August 1844, Letter Received, Office of the Indian Agent, Sault Ste. Marie subagency, 1842–1852, Office of Indian Affairs, USA, Center for Research Libraries, Chicago disbursement microfilm.

2  Carolyn Jane Harrington, quoting Selkirk, in "The Influence of Location on the Development of an Indian Community at the Rapids of the St. Mary's River" (MA thesis, University of Western Ontario, 1979), 292.

3  Jeremy Adelman and Stephen Aron, "From Borderlands to Borders: Empires, Nation-States, and the Peoples in Between in North American History," *American Historical Review* 104, no. 3 (1999): 816–18.

4  Patricia Jasen, *Wild Things: Nature, Culture, and Tourism in Ontario, 1790–1914* (Toronto: University of Toronto Press, 1995), 7–28, 86–92, 95–99. See also note 6.

5  Elizabeth Arthur, "Beyond Superior: Ontario's New-Found Land," in *Patterns of the Past: Interpreting Ontario's History*, ed. Roger Hall, William Westfall, and Laurel S. MacDowell (Toronto: Dundurn Press, 1988), 132–33.

6  For instance, see Judge John Prince's diary entry for 12 July 1861; Prince referred to the Sault region as "this *'New Siberia'*" (emphasis in original) on 14 December 1851. See R. Alan Douglas, ed., *John Prince: A Collection of Documents* (Toronto: Champlain Society, 1980), 179, 192. See also "Missionary Intelligence—Letter, J. Clark, Sault Ste. Marie, 9 November 1833," *New York Christian Advocate*, 13 December 1833; Jeremiah Porter's diary entry for 19 January, in Journal no. 3, Incidents 1832 Winter, Diaries 1831–33, Jeremiah Porter Papers, Clarke Colonial Church and School Society, Historical Library, Michigan Central University, Mt. Pleasant, MI (CHL); "Mrs. Chance, 14 Mar. (1861)," *Annual Report of the Colonial Church and School Society*, 1862, 76; Isaac Hellmuth, *The Annual Address of the Rt. Reverend I. Hellmuth, PDDCL, Bishop of Huron* (London: Evening Herald Steam Printing, 1873), v; Edward Francis Wilson, *Missionary Work among the Ojebway Indians* (New York: E. and J. B. Young, 1886), 50; Stephen H. Long, *The Northern Expeditions of Stephen H. Long: The Journals of 1817 and 1823 and Related Documents*, ed. Lucile M. Kane, June D. Holmquist, and Carolyn Gilman (St. Paul: Minnesota Historical Society, 1978), 240; and Andrea Gutsche, Barbara Chisholm, and Russel Floren, *The North Channel and St. Mary's River* (Toronto: Lynx Images, 1997), 218.

7  For a discussion of the Sault Ste. Marie Ojibwa, see Harrington, "The Influence of Location."

8  Rev. F. A. O'Meara, *Appeal on Behalf of Indian Missions in the Diocese of Toronto* (Toronto: Diocesan Church Society, 1856), 6.

9  Karl Hele, "'By the Rapids': The Anishinabeg–Missionary Encounter at Bawating (Sault Ste. Marie), c. 1821 to 1871" (PhD diss., McGill University, 2002), 171–286.

10  Article 4, *Treaty with the Chippewa, 1826*, in Charles J. Kappler, ed., *Indian Affairs: Laws and Treaties* (Washington: Government Printing Office, 1904), 2:269.

11  The final issues surrounding the border were finally resolved in 1842 when the Webster-Ashburton Treaty awarded Sugar and Neebish Islands to the US. Gutsche, Chisholm, and Floren, *The North Channel*, 246–47; and Francis M. Carroll, *A Good and Wise Measure: The Search for the Canadian–American Boundary, 1783–1842* (Toronto: University of Toronto Press, 2001), 138–40, 278–80.

12  A. C. Osborne, "The Migration of Voyageurs from Drummond Island to Penetanguishene in 1828," *Ontario Historical Society Papers and Records* 3 (1901): 123–66; S. Cook, *Drummond Island: The Story of the British Occupation, 1815–1828* (1896; reprint, Ann Arbor, MI: University of Michigan Press, 1997), 87–88; and Karen J. Travers, "The Drummond Island Voyageurs and the Search for Great Lakes Métis Identity," in *The Long Journey of a Forgotten People: Métis Identities and Family Histories*, ed. Ute Lischke and David T. McNab (Waterloo: Wilfrid Laurier University Press, 2007), 219–44.

13  Frederick Goedike, Batchiwenon, to George Gordon, Michipicoton, 11 February 1812; and Dond. McIntosh, Matagami, to George Gordon, Sault St. Maries, 19 February 1813, George Gordon Papers, Archives of Ontario (AO); and Gladys McNeice, *The Ermatinger Family of Sault Ste. Marie* (Sault Ste. Marie, ON: Creative Printing House, 1984), 43–52.

14  For a greater discussion of Indian policy for both BNA and US, see David T. McNab, "Herman Merivale and Colonial Office Indian Policy in the Mid-Nineteenth Century," in *As Long as the Sun Shines and Water Flows: A Reader in Canadian Native Studies*, ed. Ian A. L. Getty and Antoine S. Lussier (Vancouver: University of British Columbia Press, 1990), 85–103; John Milloy, "The Early

Indian Acts: Developmental Strategy and Constitutional Change," in *As Long as the Sun Shines and Water Flows*, 39–55; John L. Tobias, "Protection, Civilization, Assimilation: An Outline History of Canada's Indian Policy," in *As Long as the Sun Shines and Water Flows*, 29–38; Janet Chute, *The Legacy of Shingwaukonse: A Century of Native Leadership* (Toronto: University of Toronto Press, 1998); Brian W. Dippie, *The Vanishing American: White Attitudes and U.S. Indian Policy* (Kansas: University of Kansas Press, 1982); Francis Paul Prucha, *The Great Father: The United States Government and the American Indians*, abridged ed. (Lincoln: University of Nebraska Press, 1996); Elizabeth E. Neumeyer, "Indian Removal in Michigan, 1833–1855" (MA thesis, Central Michigan University, 1968); Roger L. Nichols, *Indians in the United States and Canada: A Comparative History* (Lincoln: University of Nebraska Press, 1998), 174–205; Olive P. Dickason, *Canada's First Nations: A History of Founding Peoples from Earliest Times* (Don Mills: Oxford University Press, 2002), 209–15; Charles E. Cleland, *Rites of Conquest: The History and Culture of Michigan's Native Americans* (Ann Arbor: University of Michigan Press, 1992), 164–263; and Robert J. Surtees, "Canadian Indian Policies," in *History of Indian–White Relations*, vol. 4 of *Handbook of North American Indians*, ed. Wilcomb E. Washburn (Washington: Smithsonian Institution, 1988), 81–95.

15  James A. Clifton, *A Place of Refuge for All Time: Migration of the American Potawatomi into Upper Canada, 1830 to 1850* (Ottawa: National Museum of Man Mercury Series, 1975), 33–35, 53–54; Nichols, *Indians in the United States and Canada*, 200; and Philip C. Bellfy, "Division and Unity, Dispersal and Permanence: The Anishinabeg of the Lake Huron Borderlands" (PhD diss., Michigan State University, 1995), 156–60. See also Bellfy's paper in this volume.

16  Upper and Lower Canada were united in 1841 in response to the 1837–38 rebellions. The new colony became known as the United Provinces of Canada.

17  Clifton, *A Place of Refuge for All Time*, 33–35.

18  Dickason, *Canada's First Nations*, 263–65, 313–14; and Bonita Lawrence, *"Real" Indians and Others: Mixed-Blood Urban Native Peoples and Indigenous Nationhood* (Vancouver: University of British Columbia Press, 2004), 14–37.

19  See *R. v. Powley*, [2003] 2 S.C.R. 207, 2003 SCC 43.

20  Robert E. Bieder, *Science Encounters the Indian, 1820–1880: The Early Years of American Ethnology* (Norman: University of Oklahoma Press, 1986) discusses the emerging classification of Indians by racial type. See also Reginald Horsman, "Scientific Racism and the American Indian in Mid-Nineteenth Century," *American Quarterly* 27 (May 1975): 152–68.

21  The usage of the term "Parole" reflects a sixteenth- and seventeenth-century ritual originating from France's presence in the region. The 1836 document, while maintaining the name parole, is a complaint with an attached list of signatures and hence closer to the modern concept of a petition.

22  Parole from Sault Ste. Marie Chippewa (carried by P. Cadotte) to Andrew Jackson, 13 November 1836, regarding 28th March 1836 Treaty payments, Letters Received, Office of Indian Affairs, Sault Ste. Marie Subagency, 1824–1841: 185–86, Records of the Michigan Superintendency, Indian Affairs, CHL; George Ermatinger, to James Ermatinger, 5 October 1836, Ermatinger Family Papers, AO; George Johnston to Schoolcraft, Superintendent of Indian Affairs, Detroit, 28 March 1837; Charlotte McMurray to Jane Schoolcraft, 3 June 1836, r24, c41, prt1: 14291, and Power of Attorney dated 7 September 1836, r25 c41 prt2: 14554, Henry Rowe Schoolcraft Papers, CHL; H. R. Schoolcraft to C. A.

Harris, Commissioner of Indian Affairs, 30 October 1837, Michigan Superintendent and Mackinac Agent Letters Sent 1836–1851, 1:351–52, CHL; Kewenzy Shawwana, Chief of the Sault; to Schoolcraft, 11 October 1836, Michigan Superintendent and the Mackinac Agency Letters, Letters Received, 1836–1851, 1: 338, CHL; Major W. V. Cobbs, subagent and fort commander, SSM, to C. A. Harris, commissioner of Indian Affairs, Washington, 13 February 1837, C224; Major Cobbs to C. A. Harris, 26 March 1837, folder 1837, A36–G129: 424–28, 431–45, C244; H. R. Schoolcraft to C. A. Harris, War Department, 24 July 1837, folder 1837, S200–S553: 701–11, S430, Records of the Michigan Superintendency of Indian Affairs (henceforth Michigan Superintendency), 1824–1831, Letters Received by the Office of Indian Affairs 1824–1881, CHL; and Marjorie Cahn Brazer, *Harps Upon the Willows: The Johnston Family of the Old Northwest* (Ann Arbor: Historical Society of Michigan, 1993), 267; Jeremy Mumford, "Mixed-Race Identity in a Nineteenth-Century Family: The Schoolcrafts of Sault Ste. Marie, 1824–27," *Michigan Historical Review* 25, no. 1 (1999): 14–15, refers to how Schoolcraft hid grants of land on Sugar Island to his wife and child by using their Ojibwa names. The US Senate eventually rejected the allocation of lands to all mixed-blood Natives.

23 Schoolcraft to C. A. Harris, Commissioner of Indian Affairs, 30 October 1837, Michigan Superintendent and Mackinac Agency Letters Sent, 1836–1851, 351–52, Michigan Superintendency, CHL; *Treaty with the Ottawa, etc., 1836*; and *Treaty with the Ottawa and Chippewa, 1855*, in Kappler, ed., *Indian Affairs* 2:726; Charles E. Cleland, *The Place of the Pike (Gnoozhekaaning): A History of the Bay Mills Indian Community* (Ann Arbor: University of Michigan Press, 2001), 26–28; Russell Magnaghi, *A Guide to the Indians of Michigan's Upper Peninsula, 1621–1900* (Marquette: Belle Fontaine Press, 1984), 55; and Janet Lewis, *The Invasion* (1932; reprint, East Lansing: Michigan State University Press, 2000), 222–25.

24 Cleland, *Place of the Pike*, 27, 35–36.

25 Chute, *Legacy*, 171, 177–78.

26 Andrew Lefebvre, "Prohibition and the Smuggling of Intoxicating Liquors Between the Two Saults," *Northern Mariner* 11, no. 3 (2001): 33–40.

27 H. R. Schoolcraft to Lewis Cass, 12 July 1822, Sault Ste. Marie Agency Records, Letters Sent: 12 July 1822–2 May 1833: 1–2, Michigan Superintendency, CHL.

28 For instance, see H. R. Schoolcraft to Lewis Cass, 18 July 1822, 5–7, and Schoolcraft to John H. Paton, Secretary of War, 7 August 1829, Letters Sent: 12 July 1822–2 May 1833: 246–48, Sault Ste. Marie Agency, Michigan Superintendency, CHL; and Cass to George Boyd, Indian Agent, Mackinac, 7 April 1822, vol. 1: 7 May 1816–1 November 1831, Letters received by the Agent at Mackinac, Michigan Superintendency, CHL.

29 Circular, H. R. Schoolcraft, Indian Agent, to George Johnston, Elijah B. Allen &c., 5 May 1823, Sault Ste. Marie Agency Records, Letters Sent, 12 July 1822–2 May 1833: 27–28, Michigan Superintendency, CHL.

30 Anna Brownell Jameson, *Winter Studies and Summer Rambles in Canada* (1838, reprint, Toronto: McClelland and Stewart, 1990), 449; Francis M. Heath, *Sault Ste. Marie: City by the Rapids; An Illustrated History* (Burlington: Windsor Publications, 1988), 36–38; and Graeme S. Mount, John Abbott, and Michael J. Mulloy, *The Border at Sault Ste. Marie* (Toronto: Dundern Press, 1995), 10–12.

31 Karl Hele, "'How to Win Friends and Influence People': Missions to Bawating, 1830–1840," in *Historical Papers, 1996: Canadian Society of Church History*, ed.

Bruce L. Guenther (Canada: Canadian Society of Church History, 1997), 162; W. McMurray, Sault Ste. Marie, to Colonel James Givens, Chief Superintendent of Indian Affairs, Toronto, 10 January 1837, 62455; McMurray to Col. Givens, 13 February 1837, 62650–53; McMurray to Col. Givens, 14 March 1837, 62828–30, Chief Superintendent's Office, Upper Canada, Correspondence, January 1837–31 March 1837, RG 10, vol. 64, Library and Archives Canada, Ottawa, ON (LAC); and Audrain to Schoolcraft, 21 June 1834, Letters Received by the Agent at Mackinac, 2:364, Michigan Superintendency, CHL.

32 For instance, see Richard E. Ruggles, "McMurray, William," in *Dictionary of Canadian Biography*, vol. 12, *1891–1900* (Toronto: University of Toronto Press, 1990), 680–81; Karl Hele, "'How to Win Friends,'" 159, and "By the Rapids," 171–86.

33 Brazer, *Harps Upon the Willows*, 294.

34 George Johnston, Reminiscence (no. 4), Box 1, George Johnston Papers, CHL; Graeme S. Mount, "Drums along the St. Mary's: Tensions on the International Border at Sault Ste. Marie," *Michigan History* 73, no. 4 (1989): 32–36; Graeme S. Mount and Michael J. Mulloy, "Rivals and Friends at the Sault," *Beaver* 70, no. 3 (1990): 48–51; and Graham A. MacDonald, "Commerce, Civility and Old Sault Ste. Marie," *Beaver* 312, no. 3 (1981): 52–59.

35 William Nourse to George Simpson, 1 September 1838, Nourse to James Keith, 24 November 1838, and Nourse to G. Simpson, 29 January 1839, Sault Ste. Marie Correspondence Book, 1838–1839: 34–35, 40, 45, B.194/b/13, Hudson's Bay Company Archives, Winnipeg, MB.

36 Mount, Abbott, and Mulloy, *Border*, 12–15.

37 Elmwood, Schoolcraft's Agency House, was the focus of the community from approximately 1827 to 1832. For an example of the intellectual curiosity at the Sault, see Philip P. Mason, ed., *Schoolcraft's Ojibwa Lodge Stories: Life on the Lake Superior Frontier* (East Lansing: Michigan State University Press, 1997).

38 Rumours circulated among the non-Natives concerning Ord's parentage. According to one story, he was the son of George IV and his mistress, Mrs. Maria Fitzherbert. While irrelevant to the overall narrative, the rumours do provide an interesting backdrop to Ord's life at the Sault from 1837 to 1849. Unfortunately, I have been unable to discover the true nature of Ord's origins. Local historians Alan Knight and James Rajnovic argue that the nineteenth-century rumours surrounding Ord were correct. Joseph and Estelle Bayliss, *Historic St. Joseph Island* (Cedar Rapids: Torch Press, 1938), 149.

39 J. Ord, sub-Agent, to H. R. Schoolcraft, 26 April 1838; Ord to Schoolcraft, 5 March 1838, 4:253, 137–41, Michigan Superintendent and Mackinac Agent, Michigan Superintendency, CHL.

40 J. Ord to H. R. Schoolcraft, 1 September 1838, 5:176, Michigan Superintendent and Mackinac Agent, Michigan Superintendency, CHL.

41 William Keating, "To the Editor of the *Chatham Chronicle*," *Chatham Chronicle*, 15 August 1849, found in the Wawanosh Family Papers, Box 4381, file no. I-1–1, Band History Correspondence, 1835–1858, J. J. Talman Regional Collection, Archives and Research Collections Centres, University of Western Ontario, London, ON; and Chute, *Legacy*, 123.

42 Chute, *Legacy*, 114–15, 138. According to Chute, there were many more parties, including the *Globe*, who claimed that the Ojibwa were squatters with no claims and that the Métis were the true agitators. See Deborah Anne Montgomerie, "Coming to Terms: Ngai Tahu, Robeson County Indians and the Gar-

den River Band of Ojibwa, 1840–1940: Three Studies of Colonialism in Action" (PhD diss., Duke University, 1993), 214; LAC, RG10 (Indian Affairs, 712) "In Council," 10 October 1845.

43 For references to the continued importance of seasonal movements, see Rev. Abel Bingham, Report for the year ending 30 September 1846, Sault Ste. Marie Agency, 1824–1852; and Charles P. Babcock, Acting Superintendent of Indian Affairs, to Luke Lea, Commissioner of Indian Affairs, Annual Report, 27 November 1850, B794, Folder 1850, B782-S515: 639, Michigan Superintendency, CHL.

44 W. A. Richard, Acting Superintendent of Indian Affairs, Detroit, to W. Medill, Commissioner of Indian Affairs, Annual Report, 22 November 1847, R102, Folder 1847, C8-R110: 225–26, Michigan Superintendency, CHL. Susan E. Gray also notes that the Indian populations in Western Michigan utilized a variety of income sources. Gray, "Limits and Possibilities: White–Indian Relations in Western Michigan in the Era of Removal," *Michigan Historic Review* 20, no. 2 (1994): 71–91.

45 *Treaty with Chippewa, 1820*, in Kappler, ed., *Indian Affairs* 2:187–88; and Cleland, *Place of the Pike*, 16–19.

46 Article Third, *Treaty with the Ottawa, etc., 1836*, in Kappler, ed., *Indian Affairs* 2:451.

47 Petition contained in H. C. Gilbert, Indian Agent for Michigan, Detroit, to G. Manypenny, 15 December 1853, G223 Folder Mackinac 1853, G176-I336: 193–95, Mackinac Agency 1828–1880, Letters Received by the Office of Indian Affairs, Michigan Superintendency, CHL.

48 Hele, "'By the Rapids,'" 372, and "James D. Cameron: Baptist and Mixed-Blood Minister at Bawating: 1831–1859," in *Papers of the 35th Algonquian Conference*, ed. H. C. Wolfart (Manitoba: University of Manitoba Press, 2004), 154–56.

49 Brackets are in the original document. See the text of the Robinson-Huron Treaty, reproduced in Canada, *Indian Treaties and Surrenders*, vol. 1, *Treaties 1–138* (1891; reprint, Saskatoon: Fifth House Publishers, 1992), 151.

50 Roman Catholics of Sault Ste. Marie, Petition to Sir John Colbourne, 12 January 1835, Catholic Archdiocesan Collection, AO.

51 Chute, *Legacy*, 160–94. Fishing was seen in a similar light. A. B[ingham] to Schoolcraft, Superintendent of Indian Affairs, 23 October 1837, Letters Received, 1836–1851, 3:383, Michigan Superintendent and Mackinac Agent, Michigan Superintendency, CHL.

52 Joseph Hill, "Bruce Mines and Garden River Missionary Anniversaries," *Christian Guardian*, 31 May 1854.

53 New England Company, "14th May 1870, Mr. Chance wrote to the Treasurer as follows," in New England Company, *History of the New England Company, from its incorporation in the seventeenth century to the present time*, 213; and P. S. Church, Diary, 9 February [1850?], Sault Ste. Marie Collection, CHL.

54 See Lister's report in New England Company, "Mr. H. J. Lister's Report (25th February, 1869)," in *History of the New England Company*, 200.

55 See "Lister's Report," New England Company, *History of the New England Company*, 200–201.

56 W. Spragge to [? illegible], 9 August 1862, Band History Correspondence, 1860–1869, Box 4381, File No I-1-2, Wawanosh Family Papers, J. J. Talman Regional Collection, Archives and Research Collections Centre, University of Western Ontario.

57  New England Company, Appendix III in *History of the New England Company*, 275.

58  New England Company, Appendix III in *History of the New England Company*, 275. Charles Biron, charged with and acquitted of inciting the Indians in 1864, may have encouraged the Ojibwa to resist government timbering restrictions. Chute states that Biron was sentenced to the penitentiary at Penetanguishene. Regardless of the outcome, the Ojibwa continued to resist non-Native usurpation of their timber rights. John Prince, Diary, 17 March and 14 June 1864, John Prince Papers, Sault Ste. Marie Public Library, Sault Ste. Marie, ON; and Chute, *Legacy*, 181.

59  Magnaghi, *A Guide to the Indians of Michigan's Upper Peninsula*, 58.

60  Dorothy M. Burrows, *Central Through the Years: Sault Ste. Marie, Ontario; A History of Our Church, 1851–1975* (Sault Ste. Marie: Central United Church, 1975), 8.

61  Chute, *Legacy*, 183, 190.

62  New England Company, "Mr. H. J. Lister's Report (25th February, 1869)," in *History of the New England Company*, 210; J. Chance to A. N. Buell, 29 April and 15 June 1868, Buell Family Papers, AO.

63  Prince, Diary, 1 October and 11 November 1861, Prince Papers.

64  Joseph Wilson, Crown Lands Agent, Sault Ste. Marie, to W. Spragge, Deputy Superintendent General of Indian Affairs, 26 December 1863, RG10, vol. 615: 315–18, Indian Affairs, LAC.

65  W. Spragge to C. Dupont, 20 February 1864, RG 10, vol. 615: 367–68, Indian Affairs, LAC; Hector Languin to William Plumber, 11 May 1869, enclosing letter Jos. Wilson to Secretary of State, 7 April 1869, RG 10, vol. 617: 132, Indian Affairs, LAC; New England Company, "Garden River Mission," in *History of the New England Company*, 212–13; See also "The other letter from Mr Chance was dated the 21st February, 1871, and was to the following effect," in New England Company, *Report on the Proceedings of the New England Company, for the Civilization and Conversion of Indians, Blacks, and Pagans in the Dominion of Canada, South Africa, and the West Indies, During the Two Years 1871–1872*, 42; and Karl S. Hele, "Conflict and Cooperation at Garden River First Nation: Missionaries, Ojibwa, and Government Interactions, 1854–1871," *Journal of the Canadian Church Historical Society* 47, no. 1 (2005): 75–117.


## Chapter 5: "In the Shadow of the Thumping Drum: The Sault Métis—The People In-Between," by Alan Knight and Janet E. Chute

1  This view has been held successively by Louise Phelps Kellogg, *The French Regime in Wisconsin and the Northwest* (Madison, WI: State Historical Society of Wisconsin, 1925); Helen Hornbeck Tanner, "The Glaize in 1792: A Composite Indian Community," *Ethnohistory* 25, no. 1 (1978): 15–39; Jacqueline Peterson, "Many Roads to Red River: Métis Genesis in the Great Lakes Region, 1680–1815," in *The New Peoples: Being and Becoming Métis in North America*, ed. Jennifer Peterson and Jennifer S. H. Brown (Winnipeg: University of Manitoba Press, 1985), 37–72; Richard White, *The Middle Ground: Indians, Empires and Republics in the Great Lakes Region, 1650–1815* (Cambridge: Cambridge University Press, 1991); and, most recently, Lucy Eldersveld Murphy, *A Gathering of Rivers: Indians, Métis, and Mining in the Western Great Lakes, 1737–1832* (Lincoln: University of Nebraska Press, 2000).

2 This distinction was first drawn by the Métis National Council in its opening statement to the United Nations Working Group on Indigenous Populations in August 1984, in Geneva. What we are aiming at is clarification and a degree of separation from the western group, not in diminishing their sense of identity by the use of the uncapitalized métis.

3 George Woodcock, *Gabriel Dumont* (Edmonton: Hurtig, 1975), 44–45.

4 "Middle ground" is a term developed by Richard White in his book by that name to define the cultural milieu that arose on the western frontier.

5 Métis society drew mainly upon French culture for its transferable European legacy, although with time métis society had to accommodate to increasing numbers of "Britons and Scotch, and Irish and Yankees." Kohl stated that these "others" sometimes inhibited the French métis, who felt less inclined, for instance, to sing traditional French songs in the presence of persons of other European nationalities. Kohl, *Kitchi-Gami: Life among the Lake Superior Ojibway* (1860; reprint, St. Paul, MN: Minnesota Historical Society Press, 1985), 113.

6 An early grant from Great Crane to the British commander at Michilimackinac, Robert Rogers, surfaced in 1847 in the possession of Mare Barhams of Port Hope, Canada West. Other grants were made by Great Crane's successors to independent Sault traders and merchants and, in 1798, to the North West Company. See "Treaty with the Northwest Company, Metosaki [Maidosagee] *et al*," 10 August 1798, Sault Ste. Marie, MS 75, Peter Russell Papers, Archives of Ontario, Toronto, ON (AO). See also "Affidavit of L. Nolin and L. Gorneau regarding Mare Barhams' claim," 1847, Alexander Vidal's Memorandum Book, Alexander Vidal Papers, J. J. Talman Regional Collection, Archives and Research Collections Centre, University of Western Ontario, London, ON. Traders often promised, orally at least, to provide the Sault band with gifts as well as feasts in the spring and fall.

7 For the Crane genealogy, see "Testimony of Mary Oboshawabawnoqua," in Major W. V. Cobbs to C. A. Harris, Commissioner of Indian Affairs, March 1837, M 234–422/422, Letters Received by the Office of Indian Affairs, 1824–1881, National Archives, Washington, DC; and Henry Rowe Schoolcraft, *Personal Memoirs of a Residence of Thirty Years with the Indian Tribes on the American Frontiers* (Philadelphia: Lippincott, Grambo, 1851), 570. A more general discussion of this subject can be found in Janet E. Chute, "Ojibwa Leadership During the Fur Trade Era at Sault Ste. Marie," in *New Faces of the Fur Trade: Selected Papers of the Seventh North American Fur Trade Conference, Halifax, Nova Scotia, 1995*, ed. JoAnne Fiske, Susan Sleeper-Smith, and William Wicken (East Lansing: Michigan State University Press, 1998), 158.

8 It has been argued that Cadotte persuaded the local Ojibwe to assist in building the palisaded fort, enclosing four houses and outbuildings, and, with the French defeat, was influential in transferring Ojibwe loyalties to the British Crown. See Clever F. Bald, *The Seigneury at Sault Ste. Marie* (Sault Ste. Marie, MI: Sault Express, 1937); David A. Armour, "Cadot (Cadotte), Jean-Baptiste," in *Dictionary of Canadian Biography* (hereafter *DCB*), vol. 5, *1801–1820* (Toronto: University of Toronto Press, 1983), 128–30; Bruce M. White, "Cadotte, Joseph," in *DCB*, 99–101; Etienne Tallemite, "Legardeur De Repentigny, Louis," in *DCB*, 447–48; and Jean-Marie Le Blanc, "Bonne de Nissegle (Misele), Louis," in *DCB*, 69–70.

9   David A. Armour, "Cadot (Cadotte), Jean Baptiste," in *DCB*, vol. 5, 128–30.
    When Cadotte's first wife died, in 1766, he married (at Detroit in 1767) Marie
    Mouet de Langlade, an Odawa woman and the reputed mother of Charles
    Langlade Jr. (according to an 1826 treaty). See Paul Trap, "Mouet de Langlade,
    Charles-Michel," *DCB*, vol. 4, 1771–1800, 563–64. Cadotte's own son of this
    second union, Joseph Marie, died young (1768–1773). Cadotte also fathered
    Joseph (born 1788), Augustin, and Charlotte Angelique by his third wife, a
    Native woman. The Cadotte girls were sent to the Notre Dame school in Mon-
    treal. The Cadotte children were baptized at Michilimackinac.

10  In 1767, Cadotte assisted Alexander Henry and his partners, Henry Bostwick
    and John and Edward Chinn, in their unsuccessful mining ventures at Copper
    Rock on the Ontonagon and northwest of the Sault. In 1775, Cadotte joined
    with a number of traders including Alexander Henry, Peter Pond, and the Fro-
    bisher brothers to explore possibilities in the western prairie trade. Their voy-
    ages took them through the Lake of the Woods, Winnipeg River, Lake Winnipeg,
    and the Saskatchewan, and some of the party even reached the Rockies. In
    1780, Cadotte and John Sayers organized and led a raiding party of Ojibwe
    from Lake Superior's south shore in an unsuccessful attack on the Spanish at
    St. Louis, Missouri, and the following year accompanied Chief Madjeckewiss
    (ca. 1735–ca. 1805) of Michilimackinac, who was sent to the Chaquamegon
    region of Lake Michigan to negotiate a peace between the Ojibwe, Fox, and
    Sioux. Again his efforts proved a failure. With Henry's financial backing,
    Cadotte was able to build up a lucrative trade in Superior's Fond du Lac region
    during the 1770s, which provided him with the resources to launch the careers
    of his two sons. By 1786, the three Cadottes were partnered in the firm of
    Messrs. Cadotte and Company, and established posts at Folle Avoine, Cour-
    tes Oreilles, Crow's Wing, and L'Anse. Gradually the sons assumed the oper-
    ational side of the business from their increasingly enfeebled father. See "Articles
    of Agreement Between Jean Baptiste Cadotte, Gentleman, and the North West
    Company," in W. S. Wallace, ed., *Documents Relating to the North West Company*
    (Toronto: Champlain Society, 1934), 90–94.

11  Piquette had been employed by Cadotte since 1762 and resided in the Amer-
    ican Sault from 1788 to 1810.

12  The document granting lands to Indians at Sault Ste. Marie, Michigan, 5 August
    1826, mentions Sangemanqua, widow of Jean Baptiste Cadotte Jr., along with
    her children: Archangel (1798), sometimes known as Julia Nolin, became the
    second wife of Louis Gournoe (1790–1863) of LaPointe, Wisconsin, in 1824;
    Louison (1802–1871) married an unknown English woman and, later, Lucy
    Godin; Sophia Johnston (1812–1880) married Thomas Edwards (Oshawano),
    widower of Mary Ann Piquette, in 1846; Edward died before 1850 and worked
    for the AFC); and Polly Johnston (1816–1891) married sailor Amos Stiles,
    widower of Catharine Ermatinger, in 1865. Each child was given one section.
    They never received their land because that part of the treaty was never rati-
    fied. Jean Baptiste Jr. and Janette Piquette were also the parents of Marie-Char-
    lotte Cadotte (1779–1807). Archange's daughter Jane Gurnoe married Chief
    John Whaiskey, nephew of John and Susan Johnston, in 1840. In 1821, Janette's
    brother-in-law, Joseph Cadotte, swore before Judge Doty that Janette Piquette
    Cadotte had lived upon her lot in Sault Ste. Marie, Michigan, since 1807 and
    during that time had cultivated and improved the front of her lot and had a con-
    siderable portion of it fenced in. Judge Doty noted that her house was very old

and stood on the western boundary of her lot. She declared her loyalty to the American government, her claim was recognized, and her name was placed on the first Chippewa County tax rolls of 1823 and 1825. Later, she sold her land, became a housekeeper for George Johnston, and lived with her brother.

13    Theresa M. Schenck, "Lewis Saurin Johnston, 1793–1825," in *The John Johnston Family of Sault Ste. Marie*, ed. Elizabeth Hambleton and Elizabeth Warren Stoutamire (Sault Ste. Marie, MI: Johnston Family Association, 1993), 27–28. Some sources state that Cadotte and Piquette were married only between the years 1797 and 1808. Another source says that they were married 15 June 1808 at the métis settlement in Deux Montagnes, Quebec. It is known that Jean Baptiste had fathered children with other women, including sons Joseph (b. 1788) and Alexis (b. 1793) Cadotte. His wife Janette Piquette Cadotte was the mother of two daughters, Sophie and Polly, by Lewis Saurin Johnston.

14    Michael's children include (1) Michael Jr. (1787–1856), who married Madeline Kwesewen (Ikwesen), or "Little Girl," daughter of Wabejejauk (White Crane) of LaPointe and sister to Nebenaigooching in 1829 and in 1840 Esther Kagwajan (Porcupine Skin), daughter of Kishkitichimen of Lac de Flambeau; (2) Marguerite (1788–1858), who married Leon St. Germain; (3) Jean Baptiste (b. 1790); (4) Augustin (1794–1872), who married Acaqugish; (5) Etienne (1796–1803); (6) Julie (1798–1835), who married Joseph Dufault; (7) Charlotte (1805–1887), who married Truman A. Warren (d. 1825) and in 1829 James Rough Ermatinger (1808–1866); (8) Marie (1797–1843), who married in 1821 Lyman M. Warren (d. 1847); (9) Angelique (1794–1885), who married Alexis Biron (1787–1866); (10) Agathe (b. 1795), who married William Perrault (1793–1875); (11) Teresa, who married Françoise LaRose (1810–1894); (12) Thomas (b. 1801); (13) Antoine (1803–1835), who married Rosalie Bourbonnet; (14) Isabelle (b. 1806); and (15) Joseph (b. 1807), who married Sophie Otawkwe. Another daughter apparently married Louis Corbiere of Penetanguishene and Beausoliel Island. Difficulties arise in numbering Michael Cadotte's children because he had children with the same name by different mothers. John Bell (1800–1872) claimed to have married a Marie Cadotte (1800–1860) and Henry Bughwujjenene (1813–1890) a Margaret Cadotte, both daughters of Michael. Michael Cadotte was a veteran of the War of 1812 and most likely received military permission to settle at Sault Ste. Marie. Charles Cadotte, Agathe Perrault, Angelique Biron, and Teresa La Rose were all at the Sault according to Vidal's survey of 1846. According to St. Mary's Roman Catholic registers (Sault Ste. Marie, MI), Michael Cadotte Sr. died of consumption in the American Sault in 1837. His son Michael Jr., who had lost an arm at the Battle of the Thames, was still living at La Pointe in 1853. William W. Warren, *History of the Ojibwa Nation* (1885; reprint, Minneapolis: Ross and Haines, 1970), 372.

15    Waubojeeg (1747–1793) was head chief of the Reindeer clan and came from Grand Portage near Chequamegon Bay. He was the son of Mamongeseda (Loon Foot), who in turn was the half-brother (through his mother) of the Dakota Chief Wahpasha. Allied with de Repentigny, Mamongeseda led the Ojibwe of western Lake Superior against the British at Quebec in 1759. The elder brother of Ogemahqua (Shingwaukonse's mother) and Obemauunoqua (Mrs. John Sayer), Waubojeeg was the father of Susan Johnston, Marie Cadotte, Waishkee, and Ahdeek, and nephew to Charlotte Ermatinger and Nancy Ashmun.

In some sources there is confusion between Waubojeeg (The White Fisher) and Waubejejauk (The White Crane).

16 John Jacob Astor (1763–1848) incorporated the American Fur Company in 1808 and planned to compete with both the NWC and the HBC. He established subsidiaries or branch plant operations: (1) the Pacific Fur Company, which was to control the Columbia River valley where Astor had built a post at Astoria, Oregon, while (2) the South West Company (SWC), formed in 1811 (where Canadian merchants participated), would operate in the Great Lakes. After foreigners were excluded by an act of Congress, Astor purchased NWC interests in the Michilimackinac Company in order to strengthen the SWC. By 1821, Astor had formed an alliance with the Chouteau interests of St. Louis, which led to the control first of the Missouri River and later the Rocky Mountains. Like a modern-day conglomerate, it grew by crushing and absorbing its opposition. When Astor withdrew in 1834 the company split and the northern branch came under the control of Ramsey Crooks (1787–1859), who moved his headquarters to La Pointe, Wisconsin. Over-extension would lead to the company's eventual bankruptcy in 1842.

17 When a twenty-one-year-old Alexander Mackenzie (1764–1820) visited the Sault in 1785, he discovered "a village formerly a place of great resort for the inhabitants of Lake Superior, and consequently of considerable trade; it is now, however, dwindled to nothing and reduced to about thirty families of the Algonquin Nation, who are one half of the year starving and the other half intoxicated, and ten or twelve Canadians who have been in the Indian country from an early period of life and intermarried with natives who have brought them families." Alexander Mackenzie, *Alexander Mackenzie's Voyages* (London: n.p., 1802), 1:47.

18 Jacqueline Peterson, "Many Roads to Red River," 59.

19 One such person was the Michilimackinac merchant Dominque Rosseau (1755–1825), although he was constantly embroiled in disputes with the North West Company. Robert Derome, "Rosseau, Dominque," in *DCB*, vol. 6, *1821–1835* (Toronto: University of Toronto Press, 1987), 663–66.

20 Sylvia Van Kirk and Jennifer Brown have shown how fur-trade Native women rose to positions of eminence in their husband's households owing to their Native domestic skills and frequent intermediary positions as interpreters or negotiators. Other scholars, such as Susan Sleeper-Smith, are beginning to trace how familial and fictive kin networks among Native and métis women sustained social and cultural continuity within Great Lakes extended families like the Chevaliers over several generations. Only recently are fur-trade women and female networks being recognized as having left major marks on the historical record, which otherwise might have been rife with cultural misunderstanding and repeatedly unnecessarily stained with bloodshed. Jennifer Brown, *Strangers in Blood: Fur Trade Families in Indian Country* (Vancouver: University of British Columbia Press, 1980); Sylvia Van Kirk, *Many Tender Ties: Women in Fur Trade Society, 1670–1879* (Winnipeg: Watson and Dwyer, 1980); Susan Sleeper-Smith, "Furs and Female Kin Networks: The World of Marie Madeleine Réaume L'Archevêque Chevalier," in *New Faces of the Fur Trade: Selected Papers of the Seventh North American Fur Trade Conference*, ed. JoAnne Fiske, Susan Sleeper-Smith, and William Wicken (East Lansing: Michigan State University Press, 1998), 53–72; and Sleeper-Smith, *Indian Women and French Men: Rethinking Cultural*

*Encounter in the Western Great Lakes* (Amherst: University of Massachusetts Press, 2001).

21  Athanasie has been called a Nipissing woman, but the description of her parentage given in the Michilimackinac registers is ambiguous. She may have been the daughter of a man named Nipissing from Saginaw, who was a close relative of Chief Madjeckewiss. Alexander Henry the Elder was present at the Ojibwe's and Odawa's capture of Michilimackinac in 1763, which occurred in the aftermath of Pontiac's rebellion. Athanasie's auspicious role would play and important part in helping her husband's trading career. Moreover, she carried on trading practices in her own right. David Armour, "Henry, Alexander," in *DCB*, vol. 6, *1821–1835* (Toronto: University of Toronto Press, 1987), 316–18; Armour, "Madjeckewiss," in *DCB*, vol. 5, *1801–1820* (Toronto: University of Toronto Press, 1983), 567–68; and Francis Parkman, *The Conspiracy of Pontiac and the Indian War After the Conquest of Canada*, vol. 1 (Boston: Little, Brown, 1883).

22  Nolin was the NWC's agent at Sault Ste. Marie from 1790 to 1800. His wife (married about 1770) was the daughter of voyageur Joseph-Victor Couvret (born 1695) and Marie Charlotte Demeurant, a métis, born at Sault Ste. Marie. Nolin had three sons and three daughters, including Adolphe, Augustin, Louis, Angelique, and Marguerite. In 1777, Nolin purchased Alexander Henry's and Jean-Baptiste Blondeau's fur post at Michipicoten for 15,000 *livres*, and in 1780 acquired 2½ acres from Jean Baptiste Barthe on the south side of the St. Mary's River and twenty-four acres on the north side, twenty-two of which were cleared, with three houses, a large dwelling house, stable, cow house, and barn. In 1819, Nolin sold his establishment to Charles Oakes Ermatinger and moved to Pembina in the Red River Valley. Donald Chaput, "Nolin, Jean-Baptiste," in *DCB*, vol. 6, *1821–1835* (Toronto: University of Toronto Press, 1987), 548.

23  David A. Armour, "Mitchell, David," in *DCB*, vol. 6, *1821–1835* (Toronto: University of Toronto Press, 1987), 508–510. Elizabeth Mitchell ran her retail business from 1816 to 1828 while her brothers were active in the fur trade in southern Michigan. During the War of 1812, her ability to recruit Native military assistance won her a commendation and a medal from the British (awarded 1814). Following the onset in 1815 of American rule on Mackinac Island, the American commander, Major Henry Puthuff, posted a notice for her to stop holding conferences with her Odawa kin. When her Native kinsfolk continued to visit, he threatened to arrest her, but she escaped by night to Drummond Island. She resumed her trade on Mackinac Island once American fears had subsided, and her salon became a social hub of the palisaded community. In 1820, the Mitchells' granddaughter, Elizabeth Ann Hamilton (1796–1858), married Thomas Gummersall Anderson (1779–1875), later Upper Canada's northern superintendent of Indian Affairs (1830–1845). Anderson's first wife was a métis daughter of James Aird of Prairie du Chene and a granddaughter of Chief Wahpasha, half-brother to Waubojeeg. Thomas Millman, "Anderson, Thomas," in *DCB*, vol. 10, *1871–1880* (Toronto: University of Toronto Press, 1972), 11–13.

24  David A. Armour, "Johnston, John," in *DCB*, vol. 6, *1821–1835* (Toronto: University of Toronto Press, 1987), 356–59; Marjorie Cahn Brazer, *Harps upon the Willows: The Johnston Family of the Old Northwest* (Ann Arbor: Historical Society

of Michigan, 1993); and Janet Lewis, *The Invasion: A Narrative of the Events Concerning the Johnston Family of the St. Mary's* (New York: Harcourt and Brace, 1932).

25  Anonymous, "General Cass at Sault Ste. Marie in 1820," *Wisconsin Historical Collections* (1869; reprint, Madison: State Historical Society of Wisconsin, 1907), 5:410–16; and Otto Fowle, *Sault Ste. Marie and Its Great Waterway* (New York: George Putnam's Sons, 1925), 312–13.

26  George Johnston, "Reminiscences by Geo. Johnston of Sault Ste. Mary's, 1815 (1), 1816 (2) and 1820 (3)," *Michigan Pioneer and Historical Collections* (hereafter *MPHC*), 12:605–9 (Lansing: Wyncoop Hallenbeck Crawford, 1887).

27  Peterson, "Many Roads to Red River," 58.

28  Lewis-Saurin Johnston (1793–1825) was named for his uncle, Lewis Saurin, bishop of Dromore in the Church of Ireland. He entered the British Indian Department with the British Indian Superintendent George Ironside Sr.'s backing. Previously he was commissioned an ensign in the British navy during the War of 1812, served on the *Queen Charlotte*, and returned home with serious wounds that resulted in his death. He carried on an extended affair with Janette Piquette Cadotte, which resulted in two children—Polly and Sophia. George Johnston (Kahmentayha) (1796–1861) married Louisa Raymond of La Pointe. He became an interpreter and agent for both the British and American Indian administrations (notably in Florida during the Second Seminole War), besides engaging in various entrepreneurial endeavours. Like George, William Miengun (Wolf) (1811–1863) found employment as an interpreter, was a sometime fur trader at the west end of Lake Superior, and ended his life as county clerk and register of deeds. William married Susan Davenport, a métis from Mackinac Island. Jane Johnston (1800–1842) married Michigan Indian agent and ethnologist Henry Rowe Schoolcraft, while her sister Eliza (1802–1883), who never married, remained close to her mother and eventually inherited the Johnston home. Charlotte Johnston (1806–1878) married Anglican clergyman William McMurray, and Anna Marie Johnston 1814–1856 married, first, James Schoolcraft, Henry Schoolcraft's brother, and, following his murder in 1846, the Reverend Oliver Taylor of Pontiac. The youngest child, John McDougall Johnston (1816–1895) also found work as an interpreter, annuities paymaster, and clerk in the sutler's store at Fort Brady. John wed Justine in 1842, niece of Janette Piquette Cadotte and the daughter of Jean Baptiste Piquette, who claimed to have been a grenadier in Napoleon's army. By her he had ten children and also fathered two children by an Ojibwe girl named Catishe: "The four boys and four girls were brought up in the mixed heritage of a bilingual household, learning how to fashion moccasins and mocuks, while they read Scott and Burke. They were devout Protestants, but conversant with the ancient lore of the Ojibways. They traveled, dressed fashionably, were literary in their written expression, and were at ease with the highborn, yet they conformed comfortably to the canoe and the campsite, understood the mysteries of nature and shared ideas with their native friends and relations. Did they, then, exemplify the highest promise of a melding of two races and two cultures? The answer, like their parentage was mixed. In terms of worldly status and achievement the women did, the men did not. The three girls who married, married well into white society, attaining dignified, and even important positions. The men never quite made it. For them, the personal conflicts of a bi-racial heritage seemed to impede advancement,

even in the relatively fluid society of nineteenth-century America." Brazer, *Harps Upon the Willows*, xv.

29  Archange Barthe's father, Charles Andre Barthe, had worked in the fur trade in the Detroit area since the 1740s.

30  Askin first married *à la façon du pays* an Odawa slave named Manette (or Monette), whom he later freed in 1766. Their children were John Jr., who married Madelein Peltier; Catherine, who married William Robertson, legislative councillor of Upper Canada, and the Hon. Robert Hamilton of Queenston; and Madeleine (d. 1811 of tuberculosis), who married Dr. Robert Richardson of the Queen's Rangers and post surgeon at Fort St. Joseph on St. Joseph's Island (1801–1802). Askin's second wife was Marie Archange Barthe (m. 21 June 1772 at Detroit). Their children were Theresa, who married Colonel Thomas McKee (1770–1814), superintendent of Indian Affairs for the Northwest Department (1796–1814); Archange, who married Colonel Merideth of the Royal Artillery; Allice (or Adelaide), who married Colonel Elijah Bruch of the Michigan militia; Charles, who became a captain of militia; Phillis Elonor, who married Captain Richard Pattison of Sandwich; and Alexander David. Archange Barthe Askin's sister Theresa (d. 1811) married (on 30 September 1774 at Detroit) Alexander Grant (1734–1813) of Detroit. Grant commanded a sloop on Lake Champlain during the Seven Years' War and was commodore of the Western Lakes, headquartered at Detroit. He served as MLA in 1792 and was administrator of the government of Upper Canada 1805–1806.

31  Jean Baptiste Barthe was born at Detroit, the son of Charles Andre Barthe and Marie Teresa Campeau. At Detroit, on 28 December 1778, he wed Geneviève Cullerier *dit* Beaubien (1761–1847), the daughter of Jean Baptiste Cullerier Marie Barrois, and she lived with him at the Sault until 1788. The Campeaus and Beaubiens were well-established fur-trading families, and Barthe's father had worked for Marie Campeau's father. Paul and Basil Beaubien were winterers for Charles Oakes Ermatinger's brother George at Fond du Lac in 1817. Barthe's establishment was located on the property John Johnston would later inhabit, and Barthe is credited with laying the original foundation for the Johnston home. His son, Jean Baptiste Jr. (1779–1812), was a lieutenant in the First Essex Militia and died in the War of 1812. The Barthes retired to Detroit but later retreated to Canada, where Jean Baptiste Sr. died on the Peck River near Sandwich. For an account of Barthe's own participation in the War of 1812, see Pierre Berton, *The Invasion of Canada, 1812–1813* (Toronto: McClelland and Stewart, 1980), 208–10.

32  The firm of John B. Barthe and Company acted as a forwarding agent to both Askin and Pierre de Rastel de Rocheblave of Montreal. Barthe's original partner in this endeavour was Jean Baptiste Cadotte Sr., who in 1778 decided to break his association with Alexander Henry and would eventually form his own company in 1786. David A. Armour, "Cadot (Cadotte), Jean Baptiste," 128–30; and Pierre DuFour and Marc Ouellet, "Pierre de Rastel de Rocheblave," *DCB*, vol. 7, *1836–1850* (Toronto: University of Toronto Press, 1988), 735–38. For a fuller account of Barthe's economic operations at the Sault, see Joseph and Estelle Bayliss, *River of Destiny: The Saint Mary's* (Detroit: Wayne State University Press, 1955), 52–54.

33  J. B. Barthe Papers, Burton Historical Collection, Barthe MS Ledger, Detroit Public Library, Detroit, MI. See also Milo Quaife, ed., *The Askin Papers* (Detroit: Detroit Public Library, Burton Historical Collection, 1928), 1:43. Whether

Shingwaukonse was the son of Jean Baptiste or Lavoine Barthe remains open to debate.

34 Lavoine Barthe continued to reside at La Pointe, Wisconsin, as late as 1830.

35 Janet E. Chute, *The Legacy of Shingwaukonse: A Century of Native Leadership* (Toronto: University of Toronto Press, 1998). The first of Shingwaukonse's four wives was his cousin, a daughter of Shingabow'ossin. His children include Thomas Ogista (1796–1883), who married Jane; Marie (b. 1796), who married Francis Grant (1785–1857); Nahwahgwaishkum "George" (1799–1840), who married Ningahbeunoqua; Augustine (1800–1890), who married Pewaundahgahsenoqua (Jane); Jean Baptiste Tegoosh (1808–1876), who married Elizabeth (or Isabelle); Peter Tegoosh (b. 1811), who married Marie Emikwan (Wasseiabanokwe); Henry Bughwujjenene (1813–1900), who married Sophie Belanger and Margaret Cadotte; Annie Shingwauk (1815–1887); Charlotte Shingwauk (1831–1881), who married Charles LaRose; John Erskine (1836–1919), who married Sagakwan and Cecile Shawan; George "Meneseno" (The Little Warrior) (1839–1923), who married Cecile Belleau; and Joseph (b. 1851). Erskine, a repeated second name in the family, recognized the Pine family's acknowledgement of their connections to the Askins. Thomas Ogista was an American and a Baptist, the Tegooshs Roman Catholic, and the rest Church of England. Augustine, Bughwujjenene, John Erskine, and George would all succeed their father as chief at Garden River. Thomas Ogista, Shingwaukonse's eldest son, remained on American soil.

36 One impediment in Shingwaukonse's transition between his métis and Ojibwe identities must have been his light-coloured skin and reputed hazel-blue eyes. Nebenaigooching was much darker in complexion.

37 "Nebenaigooching" has been said to mean "The Eclipse," but this is an extremely rough translation. The word actually refers to "He who appears [in the night sky] like the moon when it is holding water," or "when it is more noticeable on one side than the other." "Balancing on one side" is another interpretation. It is known that Nebenaigooching had a relationship with Shingwaukonse's daughter, Annie Shingwauk (1815–1887) and that on 10 August 1832 he married, in a Roman Catholic ceremony in Chippewa County, Michigan, Marie Connor (or O'Connor) (although other sources say LaBris or Brisbois), the daughter of Thomas and Susan Connor of Snake River and granddaughter of Pimegeezhigoqua (Pamidjeewung) of the American Sault; the Garden River Jesuit Burial Register confirms her name as Marie O'Connor in the record of her son Patrick Sayers's death on 17 November 1917. Nebenaigooching fathered at least ten children: Edward (1829–1915), who married Suzanne Crochieres; George (b. 1831); Julie (b. 1833), who married Robert Robertson; Suzanne (1839–1919), who married Joseph Bell; Toussaint (b. 1840); Frank; Joseph (1841–1883), who married Therisa LaRose (d. 1877); Thomas (1842–1934), who married Josephine Solomon (1847–1924); James (1849–1925), who married Sophie McKerchie; and Patrick (1851–1917). "Sayer" and "Sayers" are used interchangeably throughout the historical record to refer to the same family. Historically, "Sayer" was commonly used; the contemporary spelling of the family name is "Sayers."

38 The son of Jean Baptiste Perrault and Marie Lemaitre of Trois-Rivières, Quebec, Jean Baptiste Perrault was active in the area of the Great Lakes from the 1780s with his cousins, Joseph and Alexis Rheume, who also worked for Cadotte. He was at Red Lake in 1788, and in 1789 was an associate in the

Sandy Lake Company along with Cadotte, Sayers, John Cazelet, Joseph Rheume, and Gabriel Adina LaViolette. From 1789 to 1803, he worked on the Chippewa River, Minnesota, at Crow Wing, and on the Mississippi as an employee of the Fond du Lac Department. He was appointed master carpenter for the HBC fort at the Sault in 1812. Perrault married an Ojibwe woman by the name of Marie Ares [Harris?] (1761–1864) and fathered a number of children, including Isobell, William (1793–1875), Edward (1804–1901), and Charles of Penetanguishene. Jean Baptiste Perrault, "Narrative of the Travels and Adventures of a Merchant Voyageur in the Savage Territories of Northern America, Leaving Montreal the 28th of May, 1783 (to 1820)," *MPHC*, 37:508–619 (Lansing: Wynkoop Hallenbeck Crawford, 1909–1910). Louis-Phillippe Cormier, "Perrault, Jean-Baptiste," *DCB*, vol. 7, *1836–1850* (Toronto: University of Toronto Press, 1988), 686–87. Jean Baptiste Perrault allegedly maintained kin connections with Andagweos, or Crow's Meat, at La Pointe, father of noted chiefs Kitche Bezshike (Besheke, or Buffalo) and Mezai (Catfish). Several of Mezai's family moved to the British Sault and married into the Davieau, Biron, and Cadotte families.

39  This document, signed by Major Joseph Maramette and William McKay of the Indian Department and dated 29 June 1819, is in the possession of the Sayers family. See also "Batchawana and Garden River Indians Differ on Who Was Last Head Chief," *Sault Star*, 23 November 1939. Nebenaigooching lost his position to Shingwaukonse, who became head chief in 1835.

40  See Douglas A. Birk, "Sayer, John," *DCB*, vol. 5, *1801–1820* (Toronto: University of Toronto Press, 1983), 741–42; Birk, "John Sayer and the Fond du Lac Trade: The North West Company in Minnesota and Wisconsin," in *Rendezvous: Selected Papers of the Fourth North American Fur Trade Conference*, ed. Thomas C. Buckley (St. Paul: North American Fur Trade Conference, 1981); and Douglas A. Birk, *John Sayer's Snake River Journal, 1804–1805: A Fur Trade Diary from East Central Minnesota* (Minneapolis: Institute from Minnesota Archaeology, 1989). John Sayers married, *à la façon du pays* about 1778, Obemauunoqua, daughter of Mamongazida and a Dakota Sioux. Their children were Pierre Guillaume (b. 1779); John Charles (1780–1838); Julie (b. 1786), who married Adolphe Nolin; and William (1786–1855). The children from John Sayers's second marriage, to Elizabeth McPherson, were Henry (1796–1875), who married Marie Cameron, and Mary (Saganoshequa), who married John H. Fairbanks (1798–1880); other children from his marriage were George (b. 1803), John (b. 1805), Anna or Nancy (b. 1814), Margaret, and James.

41  "In 1849 a jury of the Quarterly Court had found Guillaume Sayer [Jr.] guilty of illegal trading in furs. Sayer had openly defied the HBC monopoly over the fur trade, but neither Assiniboi nor the Company had any means at their disposal to enforce the decision of the court and the monopoly was quietly abandoned to a *de facto* free trade." J. M. Bumstead, *The Red River Rebellion* (Winnipeg: Watson and Dwyer, 1996), 32. See also Brown, *Strangers in Blood*, 210; and Olive Patricia Dickason, *Canada's First Peoples: A History of Founding Peoples from Earliest Times* (Toronto: Oxford University Press, 1997), 238. Guillaume Sayer Jr. (b. 1803) was the son of Pierre Guillaume Sayer (b. 1779 in Leech Lake, Minnesota) and Marguerite Saulteau, who were married in 1800. They were present at Red River during the 1835 census and settled to the west of Sault Ste. Marie, according to the Minnesota Treaty of 1854. A further link between the two communities is evident in the person of Michael "Toussaint" Sayers (1820–

1884), who came to Sault Ste. Marie from Red River as a trader, boatman, and blacksmith for the HBC. Toussaint Sayer lived on the south side of Queen Street, east of East Street and along the waterfront (part of Henry Sayer's property near the present day Sault Public Library). His daughter Marguerite (1850–1934), by his first wife Philomene Biron (daughter of Alexis Xavier Biron and Angelique Cadotte), married Charles Pim (1846–1914), son of the prominent Irish merchant and postmaster David Pim (1817–1870). Charles Pim later became town treasurer for Sault Ste. Marie.

42   John Sayers's lot was three acres along the south shore of the St. Mary's River by eighty in depth. This property was bounded on the east by the Ojibwe encampment, and on the west on a plot once occupied by François and Joseph Dufour. His own agents at this time were Michael Augie and John Reed. John Reed was later killed by Natives north of Lake Superior in 1812. Henry Sayers, son of John Sayers and Elizabeth McPherson, inherited what remained of his father's business at the Sault. He claimed land in Sault Ste. Marie, Canada, in 1818 (lots 20 and 25) and used the Sault as his base of operations as a free trader from 1838 to 1845. With his marriage to Marie, the daughter of HBC Chief Factor John Dougall Cameron, he was able to play both sides of the fence; he was placed in charge of the HBC post at Whitefish River for a short time in 1830 and appointed HBC factor at Mississagi from 1845 to 1862. Nebenaigooching's son, Edward Sayers (1829–1915), inherited Henry's property in the Sault and at Mississagi upon his death in 1875. Edward Sayers became chief of the Batchawana band in 1899.

43   Myron Momryk, "Ermatinger, Charles Oakes," *DCB*, vol. 6, *1821–1835* (Toronto: University of Toronto Press, 1979), 236–37. Ermatinger also had a brother George (1770–1841) and nephew, James Rough Ermatinger (1806–1866), who lived in the American Sault. Brother George married a Shawnee and was working at Fond du Lac in 1817 with the Beaubein brothers.

44   Marjorie Wilkins Campbell, "Ogilvy, John," *DCB*, vol. 5, *1801–1820* (Toronto: University of Toronto Press, 1983), 635–36. Since 1798, Ogilvy had centred his Lake Superior base at St. Joseph's Island.

45   See George E. Thorman, "Oakes, Forrest," *DCB*, vol. 4, *1771–1800* (Toronto: University of Toronto Press, 1979), 585; and Myron Momryk, "Ermatinger, Lawrence," *DCB*, vol. 4, *1771–1800* (Toronto: University of Toronto Press, 1979), 262–63. Charles Oakes Ermatinger was a nephew to John and Edward Chinn, who had both married Ermatinger sisters. Montreal merchant Edward Chinn was connected with Jean Orillat's wholesale operations at Michilimackinac while John was a partner with Alexander Henry, Henry Bostwick, and Jean Baptiste Cadotte in their ill-fated search for copper deposits on Lake Superior in 1767. Lawrence and Jemima Ermatinger had eight children: Jemima, Ann Mary, Lawrence Jr., Frederick, Forrest, George, and Charles Oakes. Frederick, who succeeded his uncle, Edward Grey, as sheriff of Montreal, was one of the first directors of the Bank of Montreal, while brother Lawrence became an assistant commissary-general in the British army. Frederick Ermatinger acted as Charles Oakes's banker and agent in Montreal. The Ermatingers must have been an extremely adaptable family, having transformed themselves culturally and linguistically from German-Swiss to English (as evidenced by the names of the children), to English-French-Ojibwe in the space of three generations. There are also reasons to suspect that while the Ermatingers declared themselves nominally Christian they may in fact have been secular Jews. See

Gerald Tulchinsky, *Taking Root: The Origins of the Canadian Jewish Community* (Toronto: Stoddart Publishing, 1997).

46  Katawbidai was the son of Biaswah II, principal chief of the Ojibwe village at Sandy Lake near the mouth of the Savanna River in Minnesota. Katawabidai was present during the unrest at Michilimackinac in 1763 and had met Zebulon Pike during his exploratory trip to the source of the Mississippi in 1805. Katawbidai married Obenegeshipequag and fathered three sons: Mongozid (Loon's Foot) (chief at Fond du Lac, 1825–1847), Kahnindumawinjo or Kanandawwawinzo (chief at Sandy Lake, 1837–1852) and Sugutaugun (captured by the Dakota Sioux). He also had three daughters: Charlotte, who married Charles Oakes Ermatinger; a second, unnamed daughter, who married Shebagizi (Hole in the Day); and the youngest, Nancy (Keneesequa), who married Samuel Ashmun Jr. Shebagizi's son John (born in Red River; 1815–1890) was a later resident at Garden River, as were his sons John and William (1830–1903). Before 1818, it was almost mandatory for a neophyte trader to marry a daughter of a prominent chief in the district in which they wished to trade. As one trader after another entered tracts southwest of Lake Superior, and new trading fields were opened, new alliances developed.

47  Charles Oakes Sr. married Charlotte Katawabidai in Christ Church, Montreal, on 6 September 1832, after his retirement from the fur trade. The Ermatinger children included Ann (1800–1817); Charles Oakes Jr. (1802–1857); Frances (b. 1804), who married Frances Perry; George (1806–1822); Jemima, who married Captain T. C. Cameron; Frederick William (1811–1869); James (1815–1890); who married Mary Isabella Fraser; John (b. 1817); Edward; Jane (d. 1875), who married James McDonald; Annie (d. 1869), who married Carl Becherer; Lawrence; and Marguerite, who married William Aitkin. Charles Oakes Ermatinger Jr. was appointed magistrate for Lake Superior on 18 November 1849. Gladys McNeice, *The Ermatinger Family of Sault Ste. Marie* (Sault Ste. Marie, ON: Creative Printing House, 1984).

48  Bayliss and Bayliss, *River of Destiny*, 285–86. Samuel Ashman of the AFC married his wife during his posting at Lac de Flambeau in 1824. Ashmun left the AFC and was appointed justice of the peace for Chippewa County in 1831 and, over the next three decades, would hold nearly every local municipal position available including judge, sheriff, supervisor, state representative, postmaster, and census enumerator.

49  William Aitkin was the last to enter the sphere of kin alliances at Sandy Lake, with his marriage to Marguerite Ermatinger in 1818. Altogether Aitken fathered twenty-five children with two wives. Although he was born in Scotland, his Ojibwe clients called him Shagaausheence (Little Englishman). He began as an agent for the trader John Drew (who retired to the Sault around 1802) and then worked as an independent trader before taking over John Sayer's operations in 1818. Between 1824 and 1838, Aitken was in partnership with the AFC, and with their retreat from the region he returned to the independent trade. Traders with close ties to the local Native community retained an edge over their competitors even as late as the 1830s, when furs and game were disappearing from the Fond du Lac region.

50  Warren, *History of the Ojibwa*, 116–17. Warren (1825–1853) was born at La Pointe, Wisconsin, the son of Lyman Warren and Mary Cadotte. He married Mathilda Aitken, the daughter of William Aitken and his second wife, Gin-Gion-Cumig-Oke, and they had five children.

51  Alexander Henry the Elder noted that "in the family of M. Cadotte no other language than Chippewa was spoken." Alexander Henry, *Travels and Adventures in Canada and the Indian Territories Between the Years 1760 and 1776*, pt. 1 (New York: I. Riley, 1809), 38.

52  Some became members of the Grand Medicine Society, or Medewiwin, to which both men and women could belong. J. G. Kohl noted that Native women could participate in major religious rites and rarely became warriors. Kohl, *Kitchi-Gami*, 126–27.

53  D. S. Lavender, *The Fist in the Wilderness* (New York: Doubleday, 1964), 268–70.

54  In 1816, Ermatinger and John Askin Jr., in their capacity as magistrates, refused to issue warrants to arrest Nor'Westers tainted with blood after the murder of Governor Robert Semple (see note 81, below), and Ermatinger continued to forward supplies to Selkirk's Red River settlement for several years afterwards. A veteran of the era of the XY Company and NWC struggles, when faced with fur-trade disputes, he always reacted cautiously to prevent dissention within the Sault community. Seven Oakes nevertheless sent shock waves throughout the Upper Great Lakes community, and Ermatinger, determined to cloister his growing family away from any potentially tumultuous forums and ensure them wider employment prospects, retired to Montreal in 1828. The Sayers family, in contrast, found themselves more and more drawn into the conflict at Red River due to their promotion of the idea of free trade and family connections both with Red River and Pembina. See also David R. Farrell, "Askin, John," *DCB*, vol. 5, *1801–1820* (Toronto: University of Toronto Press, 1983), 37–39.

55  See Robert S. Allen, *His Majesty's Indian Allies: British Indian Policy in the Defence of Canada, 1774–1815* (Toronto: Dundurn Press, 1991); Berton, *Invasion of Canda*; Robert E. Bieder, "Sault Ste. Marie and the War of 1812: A World Turned Upside Down in the Old Northwest," *Indiana Magazine of History* 95, no. 11 (1999): 1–13; Alec R. Gilpin, *The War of 1812 in the Old Northwest* (East Lansing: Michigan State University Press, 1958); Barry Gough, *Fighting Sail on Lake Huron and Georgian Bay: The War of 1812 and Its Aftermath* (St. Catharines: Vanwell Publishing, 2002); Barry Gough, *Through Water, Ice and Fire: Schooner* Nancy *of the War of 1812* (Toronto: Dundurn Group, 2006); and Lavender, *Fist in the Wilderness*.

56  Post Journals, Michipicoten Post, 22 August 1818, MG 20, B/129/a/9/1818–1819, Hudson's Bay Company Archives, Winnipeg, MB (henceforth HBCA).

57  Gabriel Franchère wrote of Jean Baptiste Nolin's situation around 1814 that "He was an old Indian trader, and his house and furniture showed signs of his former prosperity." Gabriel Franchère, "Narrative Voyages to the Northwest Coast of America in the Years 1811, 1812, 1813 and 1814," ed. Reuben Gold Thwaites, *Early Western Travels* (1854; reprint, New York: AMS Press, 1966), 6:395. In July 1822, Henry Schoolcraft referred to the Nolin home "as a princely chateau of the once powerful lords of the North West Fur Trade." Schoolcraft, *Personal Memoirs*, 97–98.

58  Chaput, "Nolin, Jean-Baptiste," 548.

59  Ellen (1813–1860); Alexander Jr. (1815–1890s, m. Angelique Mezai); Marie (1816–ca. 1910, m. Boisvert, Louis Miron, and Frank LaRose); Xavier (b. 1817); François Joachim (1821–1903, m. Harriet Thibeault); Charles (b. 1833, m. Constance Thibeault); Pierre; and Philomene (m. Toussaint Sayers).

60  Until his death in 1866, Alexis Xavier Biron remained well respected by all seg-
    ments of the Sault community. Biron was supposedly descended from a French
    marshal and was alleged to have succeeded to the seigneury of Pierreville in
    Lower Canada. Shortly before Biron's death, the local judge, John Prince
    (1796–1870), lauded Biron for remaining a gentleman in his advanced years
    in spite of sickness and other difficulties. Prince, Diary, 3 January and 12–13
    March 1862, Hiram Walker Papers, AO.

61  John Siveright to James Hargrave, 10 May 1823, Hargrave Collection, MG
    19–A21, series 1, vol. 1, 7–8, Library and Archives Canada, Ottawa, ON (here-
    after LAC). John Siveright (1779–1856) was posted to the Sault between the
    years 1816 and 1823. In 1816, he was implicated in the massacre at Seven
    Oaks but acquitted at the York trials in 1818. Elizabeth Arthur, "Siveright,
    John," *DCB*, vol. 7, *1836–1850* (Toronto: University of Toronto Press, 1988),
    820–22.

62  Boissoneau was a native of Levis, Lower Canada, and also held his 9½ acres
    (4 acres enclosed; lot 32) by the authority of Major Winniett. He claimed res-
    idence in the Sault from 1816. According to the obituary for grandson Joseph
    Boissoneau III (d. Lansing, Michigan, 9 December 1944), the original Bois-
    soneau "left France at age 12, made two trips across the Atlantic, and by age
    18 had learned a trade as a ship's carpenter and helped build the first vessel
    on Lake Superior … [He] lived most of his life and died in Sault, Ontario, just
    east of Plummer Hospital at the corner of Leo and Queen Streets and some of
    the plum trees he planted are still there. He married at the age of 16 and after
    that continued to live at the Sault." Obituary of Joseph Boissoneau III, *Sault
    Daily Star*, December 1944.

63  Previous to the erection of Sacred Heart Church, Roman Catholic residents
    crossed the river to attend St. Mary the Virgin church in the American Sault.
    For a complete list of Roman Catholic families at the Sault in 1846, see Antoine
    Iva Rezek, *History of the Diocese of Sault Ste. Marie and Marquette* (Houghton:
    M. A. Donohue, 1907), 2:48. According to Sacred Heart parish records from
    the British Sault, a frame building was erected in 1850 under the supervision
    of Father Jean Baptiste Menet, SJ. The contractor hired to build the church
    was Joseph Boissoneau. The land on which it stood was donated by Joachim
    Biron, Alexis Xavier's son. It was granted in trust to the Crown though the deed
    for it was not obtained until 18 July 1857. The census of 1861 declares that
    the early Roman Catholic church had a value of $1,200 and would seat between
    three and four hundred persons, with a stable worth $50. The present-day
    Sacred Heart (later Precious Blood) Church was erected in 1875 from stone
    blasted out for the building of the American canal in 1855. More than one of
    the Cadotte, Boissoneau, and Biron girls became nuns. Joachim Biron's daugh-
    ter Therise was educated in Paris as a nun at the request of Father Auguste
    Kohler. According to Alexander Vidal's survey of 1846, "The Burial Ground
    [between the church and the river] claimed by the Roman Catholic Church …
    has been in use for over 50 years and has many graves in it; some old timber
    purchased years ago for building a church still lies on the ground; it has an area
    of over ¾ of an acre (Lot No. 25)." The cemetery no longer exists and the
    graves were transferred to Holy Sepulcher cemetery, north of the Sault.

64  Boissoneau's children included Joseph Jr. (1821–1914, m. Marie Ross of Red
    River); Magloire (1822–1904, m. Marguerite Biron); Narcisse Sr. (1823–1899,

m. Marie Cromote); Anna (1824–1854); Amable (1826–1846); Françoise/Frank (b. 1831, m. Charlotte LaRose); Theophile (1832–1919, m. Mary Agnes Nanki-tokikimkwe and Marie Monsomee); Emery (1838–1927, m. Angelique Biron); Lucille (1845–1872, m. Edward Lambert); Mary; and Leon (1847–1886, m. Harriet Biron).

65 Peterson discusses this proclivity in "Many Roads to Red River," 47.

66 Frederick J. Falkner, "Narrative Re: Sault Ste. Marie, Ontario," paper written for the Sault Ste. Marie Historical Society on its founding, 20 June 1921, Sault Ste. Marie Historical Society Archives, Sault Public Library, Sault Ste. Marie, ON.

67 John Johnston deplored the way Nor'Westers and petty traders at La Pointe plied Chief Mamongazida and his daughter, John Sayers's country wife Obemauunoqua, with whiskey. Journal of John Johnston, 19 June 1828, Schoolcraft Papers on microfilm at Michigan State University, East Lansing, MI. Struggles between the NWC and HBC had degenerated by the 1790s into resource-depleting vigilante warfare, detested by Sault traders such as Johnston and Nolin, who possessed a more magnanimous perspective on intercultural relations. The fact that the Sault band burned John Sayers's establishment after his return to Montreal suggests that he, as a representative of the NWC, may have offended Native custom in some way prior to his departure. Sayers left around 1807, and his holdings were burned in 1818. According to an affidavit submitted to the American government by Michael Cadotte, Sayers's establishment had been burned once before, in 1797. Cadotte, Affidavit in Report No. 42, Land Cessions in Michigan, United States Committee on Public Lands, *20th Congress, House of Representatives, 2 January 1828*, 452. The HBC, the eventual "winner" in the contest, recognized that the Great Lakes region was beyond the bounds of its 1670 charter and, due to the encroaching political and judicial presence of Upper Canada, decided after 1821 to relegate the Sault to a mere supply post. Thereafter, the company ceased to provide for the spring and fall feasts the Native population had enjoyed and come to expect under the NWC.

68 Shingabaw'ossin and Katawbidai also died in 1828, and Ermatinger retired to Montreal following the loss of his Drummond Island operations to the Americans and the news of the death of his brother, Frederick, his agent and banker in Montreal.

69 Sylvia Van Kirk, "Cameron, John Dugald," *DCB*, vol. 8, *1851–1860* (Toronto: University of Toronto Press, 1985), 121–22. Cameron's NWC and HBC postings include Nipigon 1795–1805, Bas-de-la-Riviere [Manitoba] 1811–1813 and 1832–1834, Sault Ste. Marie 1813–1818, Rainy Lake 1824–1832, Michipicoten 1836–1839, and LaCloche 1830 and 1839–1844. His wife, Marie Lesperance (Okuqwajibut, b. 1770), was of mixed Odawa–Ojibwe heritage from the region about the Sault. She and Cameron married in an Anglican ceremony at Red River on 5 June 1833.

70 See Roger Burford Mason, ed., *Travels in the Shining Island: The Story of James Evans and the Invention of the Cree Syllabary Alphabet* (Toronto: Natural Heritage Books, 1996), 26; and Alden G. Meredith, ed., "Sheriff William Botsfield Jarvis," in *Mary's Rosedale and Gossip of "Little York"* (Ottawa: Graphic Publishers, 1928), 105.

71 Although Cameron sent his sons for their education to the Reverend James West's Red River grammar school 1820–1823 and Upper Canada College, he

never attempted to impress upon them a standard for personal identity or world view. Because of this, Cameron, like Johnston and others, probably saved his children from the plunge into the psychological maelstrom experienced by other prominent métis such as James Ross of Red River, whose father expected his sons to eschew their Native cultural roots. Sylvia Van Kirk, "'What If Mama Is an Indian?': The Cultural Ambivalence of the Alexander Ross Family," in *The New Peoples: Being and Becoming Métis in North America*, ed. Jacqueline Peterson and Jennifer S. H. Brown (Winnipeg: University of Manitoba Press, 1985), 207–17; Arthur N. Thompson, "John West: A Study of the Conflict Between Civilization and the Fur Trade," *Journal of the Canadian Church Historical Society* 12, no. 3 (1970): 44–57; and Karl Hele, "James D. Cameron: Baptist and Mixed-Blood Minister at Bawating, 1831–1859," in H. C. Wolfart, ed., *Papers of the 35th Algonquin Conference* (Winnipeg: University of Manitoba Press, 2004), 137–61.

72 Reverend Dr. David Jones, HBC chaplain and missionary at Red River, Report to the Church Missionary Society, July 1833, Anglican General Synod Archives, Toronto, ON. Cameron at first was chagrined by his son's behaviour but quickly forgave him.

73 Cameron's and Shingwaukonce's first wives were sisters by different mothers. Shingwaukonce's eldest son, the American-born Thomas Ogista (1796–1883), along with Shingabaw'ossin's nephew, Henry Shegud Sr., assisted Cameron in the Baptist missions at the Tequaminon River, Naomikong on Whitefish Point, and later at Bay Mills. Thomas's son, John Ogista (1820–1907), was active with the Methodists. Following the death of his first wife and young son (John Dugald) in the influenza epidemic of 1841, Cameron married Henry Shegud's daughter, Lydia Malcolm (Kewayabunskwa, b. 1822). He fathered three children by his first wife (John, James Duncan, and Mary) and John Kiwitakighik (b. 9 November 1852) by his second.

74 The St. Mary the Virgin Roman Catholic Church marriage register in Sault Ste. Marie, Michigan, records that in 1837 William Cameron, Episcopal priest (ordained by the Anglican Bishop of Quebec in 1832), was married to Sophia Nolin, "Michael Nolin's daughter," and that the couple had a son, William. Sophia's grandparents were Adolphe and Julie (Sayers) Nolin of Penetanguishene. Sophia Nolin Cameron was a member of Oshawano's band in 1860.

75 Gustavus Anderson (1825–1896) was born on Drummond Island and was the first resident Anglican incumbent at Garden River (1848–1849). He was educated at Upper Canada College and Trinity College, Toronto. From 1850 to 1870 he was rector of the Mohawk Church at Tyendinaga on the Bay of Quinte. He concluded his ministry at Deseronto as chaplain to the Penetanguishene Reformatory.

76 See "Treaty and Schedule Referred to in Preceeding Treaty [Fond du Lac Treaty of August 5, 1826]," reproduced as an appendix in Thomas L. McKenney, *Sketches of a Tour to the Lakes* (Minneapolis: Ross and Haines, 1827), 485. Sugar Island and neighbouring smaller islands on the other side of the international border were also home to a sizable métis community. Many of these métis owned tracts obtained years before, under provisions in the American 1826 Fond du Lac Treaty granting a section of land to each son and daughter of certain prominent traders. The Johnstons were included, as were the Cadottes, the Ashmuns, the children of "the white Indian," John Tanner (who had written a well-known captivity narrative in 1830), the Aitkens, and many others.

These residents endured the watchful eye of the local Michigan Indian agent Henry Schoolcraft in many of their affairs. Not surprisingly, Schoolcraft's brother-in-law, George Johnston, spent a great deal of time in the more congenial atmosphere of the British Sault.

77  The Camerons and Johnstons were linked in a variety of economic and social endeavours. George and his native wife, Wassidgeewunoqua (Louisa Raimond of La Pointe on Madeline Island), were particular favourites. For a while, George managed his father's fur-trading post on Drummond Island, in addition to interpreting for the British Indian Department. In these capacities he represented a continuation of the old "middle ground." His brothers, William and John, similarly assumed intermediary roles as recruiters of Native military assistance, interpreters, and paymasters at treaty payments. Shortly before his death, George had been employed, under Schoolcraft's auspices, as a sub-agent at La Pointe, after which he and Thomas Ogista embarked on fishing ventures at Goulais Bay and mineral explorations east of the British Sault. By 1848, he was exploring mineral ranges around Bruce Mines with Ogista, and from 1850 to 1854 he was employed in the same area by Connecticut senator and mining entrepreneur Truman Smith. Brazer, *Harps upon the Willows*, 341.

78  Sugar Island was trapped in an international political limbo and belonged to neither Britain or the United States. It was a place of neutrality where neither country could exert its jurisdiction. Under the Webster-Asburton Treaty of 1842, it was finally awarded to the United States. Frances M. Carroll, *A Good and Wise Measure: The Search for the Canadian–American Boundary, 1783–1842* (Toronto: University of Toronto Press, 2001).

79  Possibly the son of Robert Dickson (1765–1823), Mascotapah or Red Hair Man, who commanded the Native forces that attacked Michilimackinac in 1812 and Prairie du Chein and was buried on Drummond Island. Robert Dickson had married Helen (Totowin), the daughter of the chief of the Wahpeton branch of the Santee Sioux. Robert S. Allen, "Dickson, Robert," *DCB*, vol. 6, *1821–1835* (Toronto: University of Toronto Press, 1987), 209–11.

80  Grace Lee Nute, "James Dickson: A Filibuster in Minnesota in 1836," *Mississippi Valley Historical Review* 10, no. 2 (1923): 127–39, 174–81; Elizabeth Arthur, "General Dickson and the Indian Liberating Army in the North," *Ontario History* 61, no. 3 (1970): 151–62; and Jennifer S. H. Brown, *Strangers in Blood*, 190–92. See also M. R. Montgomery, *Jefferson and the Gunmen: How the West Was Almost Lost* (New York: Crown Publishers, 2000).

81  Their reluctance may have resulted, in part, from a number of earlier experiences. See John Halkett, *Statement Respecting The Earl of Selkirk's Settlement upon the Red River in North America, its Destruction in 1815 and 1816; and the Massacre of Governor Semple and His Party* (London: John Murray, 1817); lxv. Those who testified at the trials and had a connection with Sault Ste. Marie include Kawtawabetay, John Charles Sayers, Joseph Brisbois, Louis Blondeau, Louis Nolin, F. F. Boucher, John Siveright, and Augustin Lavigne (Shingwaukonse assuming his métis identity?). John Dugald Cameron's older brother Duncan (1764–1848) was also prominent in impeding the progress of Lord Selkirk's colony while in charge of the HBC's Winnipeg Department. See also Gene M. Gressley, "Lord Selkirk and the Canadian Courts," in *Canadian History before Confederation: Essays and Interpretations*, vol. 1, ed. J. M. Bumstead (Georgetown: Irwin-Dorsey, 1972), 287–306; and F. L. Barron, "Victimizing his Lordship: Lord Selkirk and the Upper Canadian Courts," *Manitoba History* 7 (1984): 14–

22. The descendents of the old Nor'Westers feared the lack of career opportunities in the prevailing atmosphere of fur-trade company cutbacks. Their plan was to recruit an army of métis volunteers from communities between the Montreal River and the Red River—an idea that probably originated with the memories of the Voyageur Corps during the War of 1812. In the spring of 1816, Duncan Graham (d. 1847) of Mackinac engaged Eustace Roussain (b. 1783) and Roussain's brother-in-law, William Morrison (1785–1866) of Sault Ste. Marie, Michigan, as his agents, and dispatched them into Minnesota with the purpose of harassing the NWC and denying them trade. Morrison and Roussain then linked up with James Grant (a son of Peter Grant? 1764–1848), and in the summer of 1816 led a group of Ojibwe and métis warriors from the Sault to Rainy Lake and Red River to attack Selkirk's supporters. In September 1816, they were captured by Selkirk at Sandy Lake and taken as prisoners to Fort William. The following month, Grant escaped Selkirk's custody at Sault Ste. Marie and went to Washington to complain to the US government about Selkirk's presence on American soil. In December, Morrison and Roussain turned up at Fond du Lac, and Morrison was placed in charge of the Fond du Lac Department for the South West Company, a subsidiary of the newly founded AFC. Between 1826 and 1831, Roussain worked in full partnership with the AFC and William Aitken at his post on Leech Lake. Roussain married three Ojibwe sisters—Shauwunnanbanoqua, Wanwausumoqua, and Payahaubuoqua—each of whom, with their respective children, were to receive one section in Sault Ste. Marie, Michigan, in 1823, but the land never materialized since the treaty was never ratified.

82  This was evidenced by the large numbers who attended Cameron's outdoor revival services. See Karl S. Hele, "'By the Rapids': The Anishinabeg–Missionary Encounter at Bawating (Sault Ste. Marie), c. 1821 to 1871" (PhD diss., McGill University, 2002); and Alan Knight, "'A Study in Failure': The Anglican Mission at Sault Ste. Marie, 1832–1841," *Journal of the Canadian Church Historical Society* 45, no. 2 (2003): 133–224.

83  Church registers exist for a fair number of baptisms, marriages, and deaths. Death records in St. Mary's Roman Catholic Church, Sault Ste. Marie, Michigan, beginning in the 1830s, provide data pertinent to an earlier era. Later Roman Catholic, Anglican, Baptist, and Methodist church registers are also useful, as are the HBC records for the Sault area. From such sources, one can recreate a fairly clear picture of the networks of family interrelations governing the British Sault community at this time. The Belleau, Cadotte, Crochière, Desnomee, Jollineau, LaRose, LaBatte, LeSage, LeMais, LaFond, LaCharite, Mastat, Nolin, Perrault, Soulière, and Thibeault families were some of the Canadians on the St. Mary's parish roll in 1846. Rezek, *History of the Diocese*, 2:48. Despite the irregular visits of the priests, parishoners in the Roman Catholic community in the British Sault remained devoted, although, as Fritz Pannekoek noted of the Métis at Red River, while they had the reputation of devoted Catholics, "they were not slaves to the institutional church. They might listen to their clergy, but they were quite capable of making individual decisions. The influence of religion amongst the boatmen and plainsmen, in fact, depended more upon the character of individual priest." Fritz Pannekoek, "Some Comments on the Social Origins of the Riel Protest of 1869," *Historical and Scientific Society of Manitoba, Transactions* 3, nos. 34–35 (1977–1979), 46.

84  Bryant, "To the *Evening Post*, 15 August 1846, Sault Ste. Marie," in *The Letters of William Cullen Bryant, 1836–1849*, ed. William Cullen Bryant II and Thomas G. Voss (New York: Fordham University Press, 1977), 458.

85  Bryant, *Letters*, 458; and Robert J. Thomas, "Afterward," in *The New Peoples: Being and Becoming Métis in North America*, ed. Jacqueline Peterson and Jennifer S. H. Brown (University of Manitoba Press, 1985), 248.

86  Fritz Pannekoek, Arthur S. Morton, George Stanley, and others have argued that the Métis of Red River were inclined to occupy land left vacant for a period by their comrades, though this view may be coloured somewhat by a reliance on HBC records, as the company regularly derided the Métis' landholding system. Highly flexible land practices were not followed by the Sault métis community, still tinged with vestiges of old French law.

87  "Of late," wrote artist George Catlin of his visit to the Sault in 1830s, "it has been found by money-making men to be too valuable a spot for the exclusive occupancy of the savages, like hundreds of others, and has at last been filled up with adventurers who have dipped their nets till the poor Indian is styled as an intruder, and his timid bark is seen dodging about in the coves for scanty subsistence, while he scans and envies the insatiable white man filling his barrels and boats, sending them to market to be converted into money." George Catlin, *Letters and Notes on Manners, Customs and Condition of the North American Indians* (1844; reprint, New York: Dover Publications, 1973), 162. The local Ojibwe had finally come to realize that the over-exploitation of the fisheries was a threat to their way of life. This meant the second great undermining of their major resource staple (fish and furs) within a period of thirty years. Added to this was the decimation caused by successive waves of smallpox, which swept through the region between 1800 and 1835. See Graham MacDonald, "The Saulteur Fishery at Sault Ste. Marie, 1640–1920" (MA thesis, University of Waterloo, 1977); Grace Lee Nute, "The American Fur Company's Fishing Enterprises on Lake Superior," *Mississippi Vally Historical Review* 12, no. 4 (1926); and G. P. de T. Glazebrook, ed., *The Hargrave Correspondence, 1821–43* (Toronto: Champlain Society, 1938), 433.

88  The largest mercantile business on Sugar Island was owned by Philetus Swift Church (1812–1883), a native of New York State. Farmer, miller, and wholesaler (from 1845), Church's residence was located on the north side of the island at Church's Landing or Churchville, opposite Garden River on the north channel. By the 1850s, Church's Landing boasted two docks, a sawmill, dry docks, and a shipyard to provide necessary maintenance for Church's tug *The Pioneer*, which he used to haul logs, supply firewood to passing steamers, and deliver domestic supplies. He ran a raspberry jam and maple syrup business that employed thirty-five Garden River Natives (mostly women), and it has been estimated that he exported between five and twelve tons of jam, along with half a ton of maple syrup, each season.

89  John Driver to Edward Barnes Borron, 5 June 1893, Aemilius Irving Papers, MU 1465 27/32/10, AO. See also R. Matthew Bray, "Borron, Edward Barnes," *DCB*, vol. 14, *1910–1920* (Toronto: University of Toronto Press, 2001), 101–2.

90  The mouth of the Thessalon River and the Duck Islands, between Drummond and Manitoulin Island, were popular summer fishing places. George Boyd, Schoolcraft's predecessor as Indian agent, estimated in 1822 that approximately three-quarters of the Ojibwe's food supply was fish based. "George Boyd to Lewis Cass," 21 January 1822, cited by MacDonald in "The Saulteur-

Ojibway Fishery," 71. Many métis worked as coopers and were proficient in barrelling fish, which they sold to the HBC and merchants on Sugar Island, at Mackinac, and at Penetanguishene. One barrel held approximately 200 pounds of fish.

91 At Sault Ste. Marie, the two largest retail stores were at the AFC and the independent merchant Pierre Barbeau's store on the American side. The HBC had eliminated their retail operation after 1827. According to the Baylisses, Joshua Trott had "a small store at Windmill Point," and "M. Biron had one farther east as early as 1820." Bayliss and Bayliss, *River of Destiny*, 255. Available products included bread, butter, boots and shoes, buttons, calico, candles, coffee and tea, cotton and flannel cloth, castor oil, cloves, chamber pots, collar studs, combs, flour, galoshes, grind stones, hammers, haying forks, knives and cutlery, linseed oil, looking glass, tin kettles, paint, panes of glass, tobacco pipes, matches, molasses, nails and hinges, ribbon, rolled tobacco leaf and snuff, scythes, shovels, soap, sperm oil for lanterns, salt, sugar, wine and spirits, suspenders, thread, twine, gunflints, shot and powder, whitewash and brushes. American Fur Company Ledgers 1834–1838 and Peter Barbeau Lettersbooks 1844–1847, Bayliss Public Library, Sault Ste. Marie, MI. See Bernie Arbic, *City of the Rapids: Sault Ste. Marie's Heritage* (Allegan Forest, MI: Priscilla Press, 2003), 102–10.

92 In 1834, Anglican missionary William McMurray wrote of his difficulties in caring for those who had been left behind at the mission while the younger Ojibwe had gone to their winter traplines. He wrote his superiors in Toronto that "there are six or seven old widows here, who wish to join us, two of them have already done so; could you devise any plan by which they could get some yearly support? Some have children, and others grandchildren; a small sum annually would not be an assistance but a charity; they are truly poor and needy. I have given them many presents of provisions, but my means are so small, I can ill afford it." William McMurray, Fourth Annual Report to the Toronto Society, 1834, Anglican General Synod Archives, Toronto, ON.

93 Kohl, *Kitchi-Gami*, 318–20.

94 The métis first petitioned their bishop for a priest to reside permanently on the Canadian side and attend exclusively to their community's interests. Petition to the Right Reverend Alexander McDonald [*sic* Macdonell], Roman Catholic Bishop of Upper Canada, 14 September 1834, Bishop Macdonell Papers, Catholic Archdiocesan Collection, AC2402, AO. The community then wrote to Sir John Colborne for help in building the church. "To His Excellency, Sir John Colborne, K. B. Lieutenant Governor of the Province of Upper Canada, 1835," Bishop Macdonell Papers, AO.

95 Father Francis Xavier Haetscher (1784–1863) was an Austrian Redemptionist (CCCR) and McMurray a Northern Ireland Protestant. Haetscher repeatedly attempted to tweak the nose of McMurray by constructing a bark chapel not far from McMurray's residence in Ermatinger's "Old Stone House." He made a point of burning the Book of Common Prayer at the riverfront where the Anglican could plainly comprehend the priest's contempt. Bishops John Strachan and Alexander Macdonell, however, remained on fairly good terms during their episcopacies. William McMurray correspondence with Bishop Strachan, 1832–1838, Bishop John Strachan Papers, AO.

96 Angus Bethune (1783–1858) was the son of Anglican clergy John Bethune and brother of Alexander Neil Bethune, the future second bishop of Toronto. Bethune was appointed chief factor at Sault Ste. Marie (1824–1834) and was

in charge of the Lake Superior (1832–1839) and Lake Huron districts (1834 and 1837–1839). Hilary Russell, "Bethune, Angus," *DCB*, vol. 8, *1861–1870* (Toronto: University of Toronto Press, 1985), 85–86.

97  Report on the District of Sault Ste. Marie, 1835, B/194/e/8/1835, HBCA.

98  William Nourse to Louis Denis Laronde, B/194/b/9/1834–1835, HBCA.

99  Thomas G. Anderson to Captain G. Philpotts, 18 July 1835, Strachan Papers, MG35, AO.

100  Hudson's Bay Company Post Journals, Sault Ste. Marie, 30 September 1834, B/194/a/8/1834–1835, HBCA.

101  Hudson's Bay Company Post Journals, Sault Ste. Marie, 30 September 1834, B/194/a/8/1834–1835, HBCA.

102  Anderson's Journal, 1835, Anderson Papers, S29, Toronto Metropolitan Library, Toronto, ON. This was adding insult to injury. The government provided presents on the grounds that Native people had assisted the British cause in the War of 1812. Many Roman Catholic métis had offered their services to Britain at that time.

103  Anderson and his superiors were, in fact, more concerned with the general threat that Nebenaigooching presented to "the Establishment" through his involvement with illegal liquor sales and the independent trading in furs. The actions of "free traders" such as Nebenaigooching brought the government of Upper Canada into conflict with both the Americans and the HBC in an area that they were unable to properly police or control.

104  In return for services from Father Haetscher of Sault Ste. Marie, Michigan, the métis agreed to cut timber for the construction of a church on the American side. The priest would then come every third Sunday to the British side to conduct mass. Soon after beginning to haul stones and cut wood for this church, the métis requested that the Roman Catholic bishop at Kingston, Alexander Macdonell, use his influence to help them finish the church. Petition to Sir John Colborne, 24 September 1834, Catholic Archdiocesan Archives, AO. In January the next year, they complained both to Macdonell and Colborne that McMurray had prevented them from continuing to work on their project. Petition to Sir John Colborne, 12 January 1835, Catholic Archdiocesan Archives, AO.

105  Edward H. Capp, *The Story of Bow-a-ting, Being the Annals of Sault Ste. Marie, Ontario* (Sault Ste. Marie: Sault Star Press, 1904), 163.

106  Despite the fact that he had married the métis granddaughters of the Sioux chief Wahpasha, David Mitchell, and Elizabeth Bertrand.

107  B/129/e/1833–1834, HBCA.

108  "I told them the government would not purchase from them, [and] that they had now refused our offer of land at St. Joseph's which they might otherwise regret," Anderson reported angrily. Yet his words were hollow, as the removal scheme had been defeated by the métis' quick action in defence of their interests. Thomas Anderson to Captain G. Phillpots, 18 July 1835, Strachan Papers, AO.

109  John Bell to Bishop Macdonell, 8 April 1834, Catholic Archdiocesan Archives, AO.

110  Peter MacFarlane was a trader at La Cloche, owned property in the American Sault near the present-day Bayliss Library, held a mining location at Thessalon in 1847, and became a member of Oshawano's band in 1855. J. Fletcher Williams, "Memoir of William W. Warren," in Warren, *History of the Ojibway Nation*, 9–22.

111  The Bell children included Suzanne (1822–1854, m. Joseph Savard), Peter (1831–1891, m. Marie Brassard), Joseph (1833–1904, m. Suzanne Seyers [Sayers] [1839–1919]), Sophia, and Mary (b. 1841, m. Peter Jones [1841–1930]). Mary Cadotte Bell's sisters married Henry Buhwujjenene and Truman and Lyman Warren, and her niece married Michael Belleau Sr. (1819–1899). Bell later joined the Garden River band. Both John Bell and Peter McFarlane were Roman Catholics by birth. John Bell embraced Anglicanism after he began acting as Little Pine's interpreter in 1842, and he is listed as belonging to the Church of England in both the 1861 and 1871 census. He reportedly renounced this conversion and returned to the Roman Catholic Church shortly before his death.

112  T. G. Anderson to S. P. Jarvis, 23 May 1840, RG 10, Correspondence of the Northern Superintendent of Indian Affairs, vol. 124, 69819–20, LAC.

113  William and Charlotte McMurray left the rapids in 1837 when the government failed to honour its promise of houses. McMurray and his family settled at Dundas and later Niagara-on-the-Lake in Upper Canada.

114  Chute, *Legacy of Shingwaukonse*, 81. The wily Shingwaukonse also took advantage of the British government's vulnerability in the aftermath of the 1837 crisis to try to get the British to continue giving presents to the métis. Anderson to Jarvis, 23 May 1840, RG 10, vol. 124, 69712–13, LAC. Anderson, by this time, had come to wonder if métis not in receipt of the Queen's bounty might prove disloyal. RG 10, vol. 124, 69676–79, LAC.

115  As George Fulford, on finding this leader's name in an account book of the Lake Vermilion trader Vincent Roi, surmised, the chief's main purpose was not to trade. George Fulford, "The Pictographic Account Book of an Ojibwa Fur Trader," in *Papers of the Twenty-Third Algonquin Conference*, ed. William Cowan (Ottawa: Carleton University, 1992), 191–223. His actions at this time counter the assumption that the middle ground disappeared forever following the Treaty of Ghent. The alarms of 1837 resuscitated the need for Native intermediaries. The rebellions may have been transient phenomenon, but they were enough to elevate Little Pine, John Bell, George Johnston, and James Dugald Cameron to intermediary roles that provided them with far greater status than adoption of metropolitan norms. Officials such as Henry Schoolcraft and Dr. John Bigsby of the International Boundary Commission of 1823 at such times feared the métis, whom they saw as representing a militarily and commercially aggressive group. Nothing would suit young métis better, Bigsby claimed, than to embark "on a war venture at the head of their Indian friends, to kill and be killed at ten shillings a day." John Bigsby, *The Shoe and The Canoe; or Pictures of Travel in the Canadas*, vol. 1 (London: Chapman and Hall, 1850), 130.

116  J. D. Cameron to the Honorable James H. Price, Commissioner of Crown Lands, 1847, Indian File, Bruce Mines Museum, Bruce Mines, ON.

117  "Louis Cadotte gained some notoriety when, as interpreter in 1844, he accompanied Arthur Rankin [1816–1893 and John William Keating (d. 1869)] to England with two Chippewa chiefs, four young men, two women and a ten-year-old girl. All were Indians except Cadotte, who was half-Indian, using the Indian name Not-een-a-um (Strong Wind). They were dressed in the picturesque costumes of the Indians. In England, Cadotte married a refined but romantic English lady. This caused so much trouble that it broke up Rankin's business and the party immediately returned to America [although the overall venture

was considered a success, since the return was about $75,000]. Cadotte brought his English bride to the Sault, where she is said to have lived unhappily but without complaint, and died about two years later. Cadotte later married Lucy Godin, a French-Canadian woman, with whom he lived many years, dying in 1871." Bayliss and Bayliss, *River of Destiny*, 281–83. In 1860, Louison Cadotte was living in the American Sault. Warren, *History of the Ojibway Nation*, 490. See also Patrick Brode, "Rankin, Arthur," *DCB*, vol. 12, *1891–1900* (Toronto: University of Toronto Press, 1990), 884–85.

118　Similar attitudes appeared at Red River around the same time. See Irene M. Spry, "The Métis and Mixed-Bloods of Rupert's Land Before 1870," in *The New Peoples: Being and Becoming Métis in North America*, ed. Jacqueline Peterson and Jennifer S. H. Brown (University of Manitoba Press, 1985), 96–118. Henry Rowe Schoolcraft, though married into a prominent trader family and having métis in-laws, remained aloof from the ebb and flow of the Native life around him. His métis wife Jane often felt lonely and isolated. Schoolcraft's writings from the mid-1820s to the time of his departure from the Sault in 1832 stand as a revealing barometer of changing social attitudes around him as his work reflects the influence of pseudoscientific ideas filtering in from the south. In his early years at the rapids, he had speculated on the racial legacy he would engender by begetting children by his métis wife, the former Jane Johnston. Their progeny, he anticipated, would exhibit traits of what he termed the "Algic mind," governed more by feeling than reason, or so he thought, which he deemed to be solid Anglo-Saxon rationality and common sense. When these hopes were darkened by the death of his favourite son, William, Schoolcraft progressively retreated into ideological speculations on race that lacked the compassionate depth of his earlier researches. The health of his wife, meanwhile, slowly deteriorated due to a heart condition, and she turned to laudanum, dying at the early age of forty-two. Schoolcraft's dictatorial demeanour towards métis who worked for him was particularly resented. Within métis society, to be treated as a servant was viewed as a gross insult. When Schoolcraft demeaned Sophie Cadotte Johnston, Lewis Saurin Johnston's illegitimate child by Janette Piquette, by treating her worse than a domestic servant, her métis kin were enraged. The local sheriff, John Hulbert, who had married Schoolcraft's sister, found himself obliged to reprimand Schoolcraft severely for his lack of respect for the young girl. Schenck, "Lewis Saurin Johnston," 27–28. "Sophie Johnston" as she called herself, although abandoned by the early death of her father, eventually married Thomas Edwards, a son of Edward Oshawano and a grandson of Chief Oshawano. Similar protective displays were shown in the Nolin family. When Roman Catholic Bishop Joseph-Norbert Provencher urged Jean Baptiste Nolin's daughters, Angelique and Marguerite, to become school-teachers, their elderly father objected on the ground that he did not want his children to be servants. This reflected métis attitudes Jean Baptiste Nolin had brought with him from the Upper Great Lakes area. After his death, however, his two educated daughters taught at the first girls' school in western Canada, located in St. Boniface. Donald Chaput, "The Missus Nolin of Red River," *The Beaver* 306, no. 3 (1975), 14–17. The impact of prejudice, however, was evident at the Sault when James Schoolcraft was murdered in 1846. It was widely held that John Tanner (1779–1846), once a captive among the Ojibwe for thirty years, was the perpetrator. Another man, Lieutenant Tilden, later confessed that he had killed Schoolcraft. The mystery of Schoolcraft's death has never been solved. John Fierst, "Return to 'Civilization': John Tanner's Troubled Years at Sault Ste. Marie," *Minnesota History* 50, no. 1 (1986): 23–36; Tammy Stone-Gordon, "The Other Schoolcraft," *Michigan History* 78, no. 2 (1994): 24–27; and George M. Blackburn, "George Johnston: Indian Agent and Copper Hunter," *Michigan History* 54, no. 2 (1970): 108–21.

119 Extract of a Report from Lieut. Harper, RN, Commanding HMS *Experiment*, dated Penetanguishene, 1 September 1845, RG 10, vol. 10, and vol. 151, 87759–60, LAC.

120 Survey of Sault Ste. Marie 1846, RG 1 series A-1-6; Alexander Vidal Diary, 1846; and Letters Received by the Commissioner of Crown Lands, RG 1 series CB1, AO. Local métis employed by Vidal on his survey, which lasted from 20 April to 18 September, were John and Peter Bell, Charles and Michael Cadotte, Pierre Crassier [Crochieres?], La Rose, Sayers, Michael Surrette, and John Whalen as chainbearers and axemen, and Trott and Biron as cooks.

121 J. M. Higginson, Civil Secretary, to the Hon. Denis-Benjamin Papineau, Commissioner of Crown Lands, 15 October 1845, RG 1, A-1-6, AO. Vidal endeavoured to map the inhabited areas as he found them. In the first concession, containing the métis lots, he ran a baseline, which paralleled but did not account for the sinuosities of the river. Small, irregularly shaped blocks to the south of this baseline, which fronted the river and where the majority of dwellings were located, were then incorporated into the adjoining lots to the north. The lots were mostly long and narrow—the average being 2½ acres with an average frontage of 2.5 chains (one chain equals 66 feet)—although there were a few of ½ and ¾ acres: 9½ acres for Joseph Boissoneau Sr., 14½ acres for William Cameron, 10 acres for Joseph LeFond, and Ermatinger's "Old Stone House" was 26 acres. In 1846, in the first concession, 170 acres were enclosed with 10 acres retained by the Church of England and ¾ of an acre by the Roman Catholics for a burial ground. Fifty-one acres (32 percent) were owned by Joseph Wilson, William Cameron, and Joshua Trott, and 12.5 acres (8 percent) by Orkneymen John Driver and Henry Leask, leaving 96.5 acres (60 percent) in the possession of the métis. In the region north of Wellington Street, in the second and third concessions, Vidal applied the thousand-acre section survey then popular in Canada West, although he modified it somewhat. In this system, ten hundred-acre lots, each two and one half times as long as they were wide, were laid out. Five lots were supposed to exist between the cross roads and two between the concessions. Vidal cut that number from five to three, and subdivided the second and third concessions into fifty-acre lots. The fourth concession was surveyed in the traditional manner. Vidal also suggested that the townships bordering the future town be two concessions deep and six blocks wide, and conceded, on his map, 1,200 acres to the HBC west and north of the town plot. With the exception of the French settlements along the St. Clair River, Sault Ste. Marie is one of the few places in Ontario where the survey systems of both English and French Canada are combined.

122 This was a fact recognized by the community itself. In 1893, Joseph Wilson wrote that most métis' grandfathers at Sault Ste. Marie "were lower Canadian Frenchmen and old Hudson's Bay servants or employees. But most of the young men of today have Indian mothers." Joseph Wilson to John Driver, 1893, Aemilius Irving Papers, MU 1465, 27/3/9, AO.

123 These persons and their ages in 1846 were (1) Pierre Belleau, 69; (2) Samuel Black (1785–1841); (3) Joseph Boissoneau Sr., 60; (4) Michel Bouille; (5) Pierre Brassard [Bourassa], 36; (6) Jean Baptiste LeCharité, 71; (7) Jean Baptiste Contien, 45; (8) Jean Baptiste Crochières, 63; (9) John Joseph Driver, 40; (10) Michael LaBatte, 60; (11) Augustan LaRose [LaRoche], 60s; (12) Henry Leask, 34; (13) Joseph LeFond, 63; (14) Jean Baptiste Mastat Sr., 82; (15) Louis Miron Sr., 51; (16) Raymond Miron Sr., 50s; (17) Alexander Ross McKay, 47; and (18) Edward Perrault, 42. Belleau, Boissoneau, Bouille, Brassard, LeCharite, Crochières, LeFond, Mastat, and the Mirons were Frenchmen, born in Lower Canada. Contein was born at LaPointe, LaRose came from Green Bay, and McKay from Rice Lake, Wisconsin. Driver and Leask were Orkneymen. Samuel Black was born in Scotland. Black was not a local and most likely held his land for speculation. He had worked for the XY Company, the NWC, and the HBC. He was appointed chief factor in 1837. Always a combative personality, he was murdered by a disgruntled Indian at Fort Kamloops. Edward Perrault was the son of Jean Baptiste Perrault. LaBatte was born on Drummond Island and was the son of Louise Cadotte (Oh-ge-ke-quah), also known as Mother Pecon. McKay was most likely the métis son of Alexander McKay (1770–1811), of Astoria fame, who was the NWC factor at the Sault (1806–1808). William Perrault, 53, and Etienne Jollineau Sr., 83, along with his son, Pierre "Kanosh," 33, had worked for the AFC. The Jollineaus were born in the United States, and Etienne had married Françoise Du Chene, one of the original French families in the American Sault. Alexander Ross McKay married Jollineau's daughter Angelique.

124 According to Alexander Vidal's survey of 1846, Jean Baptiste Soulière, aged about 55, a Frenchman from Lower Canada, had spent some time on Drummond Island. He had occupied a lot flanking the HBC's tract for twenty-five years. A portion of Soulière's plot had been purchased by a man named Guidon, who had left the Sault prior to the survey. The next property belonged to Michel Boneau, who resided in the American side, but he allowed Pierre Mastat, 63 (son of Jean Baptiste), to reside in his house in his absence. Sixty-nine-year-old Pierre Belleau was but a relative newcomer to the British Sault and lived on a single acre beside this field. Michel Bouille had claimed possession of the next lot for twelve years. Jean Baptiste LeCharité and Augustan LaRose had held their property for twenty-five years, whereas their neighbour to the east, William Perrault, most likely just returned from his travels around the world (with John Jacob Astor), for the funeral of his father in 1844, had resided on his for only two. Alexis Biron, 31, similarly, had obtained his by purchase from Pierre Cameraire only two years previously. Lying between Biron's lot and the Old Stone House, once the residence of Charles Oakes Ermatinger, lay twelve more lots, one of which was the Roman Catholic graveyard. These lots belonged to Pierre Brassard (Bourassa), 36, who owned two separate plots, Michel LaBatte, 60, Louis Miron Sr., 51, Joseph LeFond, 63, François La Rose, 36, Alexis Xavier Biron, 59, Etienne Jollineau, 83, Charles Cadotte, 51, Joshua Trott, 58, and the Roman Catholic Church. The Englishman Trott appeared on the scene in 1840, had a mercurial temper, was a lifelong bachelor and a member of the Church of England, and, according to E. H. Capp in *The Story of Bow-a-Ting* (1904), kept "a little bark shack" store on Windmill Point. Trott died in 1872.

125  These lots, from west to east, belonged to Jean Baptiste Contien, 51; Madame [Marie] Perrault, 85 (the wife of Jean Baptiste Perrault Sr.); Raymond Mastat, 61; Henry Sayer, 50; Nebenaigooching, 38; Ambrose Surrette, 46, known as Tete Blanche or Whitehead; Jean Baptiste LeSage, 55; Jean Baptiste Crochières, 64; Joseph Boissoneau Sr., 60; Joseph Boissoneau Jr., 26; Henry Leask, 34, captain of the HBC schooner *Whitefish* who had married Catherine Surrette; Jean Baptiste Denomee, 47, who was married to Susan Jollineau; an absent owner by the name of St. Marc Martin, who had gone to St. Joseph's Island; the Episcopal clergy; William Cameron, 38, who owned two lots but preferred to reside in the United States; John Joseph Driver, 40, an Orkneyman with a Native wife who had retired from the HBC and would come to an early death in 1848; land set aside for the Church of England; and the plot belonging to Henry Sayer's sister Margaret. Vidal noted of the Anglican property that "it has an enclosure of about ten acres on which a church has been erected and within which there are a few graves; it is in possession of the Church of England though never used now, no minister having resided here for three or four years [1841]." This property simply "disappeared" during the Anglican absence from the Sault (1841–1865) and is no longer claimed as either a church or a cemetery. It was located at the top of the Pim Street hill and was on the 1859 town survey. Part of Contien's lot belonged to stepdaughter Marguerite Lafontaine, 22, who was attending school in Montreal. Contein married Marguerite's mother, Josette Jollineau, who was previously married to Lafontaine. Marguerite Lafontaine Contien later married the American-born Michael Neveau, a Native fisherman, and lived in "Frenchtown."

126  Joseph Wilson was born at Tulliallan, Perth County, Scotland, and arrived in the Sault as a lumber agent for his father George Wilson (1784–1866), a retired naval officer, as early as 1843. At that time he was living in the HBC storehouses. He was appointed preventive officer of customs at the Sault on 19 July 1845. His sixty-year-old father, a resident of Medonte township, was given the original appointment as collector of customs but turned it down in favour of his son following a summer visit. Joseph received his appointments as Crown lands agent on 25 July 1845, collector of customs on 4 March 1848, postmaster on 6 October 1848 (to 29 August 1857), justice of the peace on 29 August 1860, and judge of the court of common pleas on 22 July 1863. He served as Indian agent from 1856 to 1870, was captain (later major) of the First Volunteer Rifle Company 1849 and 1863 to 1866, and supervised the construction of the Korah township settlement road in 1867. Wilson lived with his spinster aunt, Jane March (1799–1888), until his marriage to Caroline Louisa Sherman (1841–1894) in 1866 at the age of forty-eight. They had one child, Mary Jane (1868–1903), who wed Albert Willie Penhorwood. Caroline Sherman Wilson was later declared legally insane.

127  Falkner, "Narrative Re: Sault Ste. Marie, Ontario."

128  In 1821, Nicholas Garry, a committee member of the HBC, visited the Sault and described the buildings as consisting of "a Dwelling house—a large store, a lesser one, a Shop, several small houses for Workmen these are Wooden buildings—a very excellent Stone Warehouse for Dry Goods the Roof covered with Tin Plates—and the whole considered Fireproof—and a smaller very low one, of the [blank] Character, which is called their Cellars. These Buildings have been erected since the year 1814 when this Post was entirely destroyed by the Americans. At the end of the Portage there is a well built Wooden Warehouse.

The Company have here a very extensive Farm—nearly 30 Acres and a Tract of Land 9 Miles in Length by 3 in Breadth." Nicholas Garry to William Smith, HBC Secretary, London, E/11/2/3–4, HBCA.

129   Hyacinthe Davieau married Josette Piquette and Charlotte Mezai. Charlotte Davieau's sister Angelique wed Alexis Biron Jr., and brother Francis married Angelique Cadotte. Hayacinthe Davieau Jr. married Louise Cadran, and Josette Davieu married Louis Cadran. Another daughter, Marguerite, married Francis Perrault, and Terisa lived for some time with William McKay. Pierre Brassard married Julie Mastat. Michael Boyer married Angelique LeCharité, while his sons, Michael Jr. and Benjamin, married sisters, Madeline and Julie Corbière. Daughter Madeleine married François Nolin, Pierre married Celia Grant, and Elizabeth/Isobelle married William Bell. Joseph Mousseau remained a bachelor and lived with his widowed mother, Magdalena Mousseau (1757–1852) in Sault Ste. Marie, Michigan. This branch of the McKay clan were descended from Colonel William McKay (1772–1832). Their father, and McKay's son, William McKay Jr., was the first person to be buried in the Queen Street cemetery. Robert S. Allen, "McKay, William," *DCB*, vol. 6, *1821–1835* (Toronto: University of Toronto Press, 1987), 464–65; and Jean Morrison, "McKay, Alexander," *DCB*, vol. 5, *1801–1920* (Toronto: University of Toronto Press, 1983), 532–34.

130   Frank LaRose and William Perrault probably received military patents to their property through their marriages to Agathe and Theresa, the daughters of War of 1812 veteran Michael Cadotte Jr., who claimed residence in the Sault from at least 1817. Mademoiselle St. George owned part of a lot connected with Joseph Boissoneau. She resided in Montreal and depended upon Boissoneau for the care of her property. Ermatinger had employed a Francois St. George as one of his winterers.

131   Later, the HBC at Sault Ste. Marie, despite its claim for twelve hundred acres in Vidal's survey, would itself be viewed as "a squatter" on Crown land by the Canadian government, because it was operating beyond the bounds of its 1670 charter and the amalgamation with the NWC in 1821 did not include an outright land purchase. Hartwell Bowsfield, ed., *The Letters of Charles John Brydges, 1879–1882: Hudson's Bay Company Land Commissioner* (Winnipeg: Hudson's Bay Record Society, 1977). A number of métis individuals were buried in the old HBC cemetery, located at the northeastern corner of the HBC property, and their bones were reburied under the front steps of the present-day St. John the Evangelist Anglican Church parish hall. The names, for the most part, have been lost to history, but two that are known are George Moore (1800–1865) and Kenneth Mackenzie (d. 1816). Jean Morrison, "Mackenzie, Kenneth," *DCB*, vol. 5, *1801–1820* (Toronto: University of Toronto Press, 1983), 543–44.

132   Potatoes, vegetables, and some corn had been raised at Garden River for years to supply fur-trade brigades. A small Ojibwe and métis community resided there most of the year. J. G. Kohl noted that the garden plots were known as "*deserts*—the French Canadians, accusing themselves, as it were, of being desolators of nature." Kohl, *Kitchi-Gami*, 304. Similarly, while some translate *Vieux Desert* as "the old deserted place," others believe it refers to "an old clearing under renewed cultivation."

133   The métis man whom J. G. Kohl interviewed in the mid-1850s who spoke about his mother and his wife both possessing the Crane as their totemic mark was undoubtedly a Cadotte. This man knew locations where persons of

the Grue (Crane) totem resided: La Pointe, Sault Ste. Marie; Folle Avoine [Fond du Lac District] near Detroit; and, surprisingly, also "a la baie de Hudson." Kohl, *Kitchi-Gami*, 149. His knowledge of the Cranes of Sandy and Weagamow lakes in Northern Ontario shows how broadly information travelled at this time. Edward S. Rogers and Mary Black Rogers, "Who Were the Cranes? Groups and Group Identity in Northern Ontario," *Approaches in Algonquin Archaeology: Proceedings of the Thirteenth Annual Conference of the University of Calgary Archaeological Association*, ed. Margaret Hanna (Calgary: University of Calgary Press, 1982), 247–88; Valerie Grant, "The Crane and Sucker Indians of Sandy Lake," in *Actes du quatorzieme congres des algonquinistes*, ed. William Cowan (Ottawa: Carleton University, 1983), 75–90; and Theresa Schenk, *The Voice of the Crane Echoes Afar: The Sociopolitical Organization of the Lake Superior Ojibwa, 1640–1855* (New York: Garland, 1997).

134 Members of the same totem, by tradition, did not marry, but as Little Pine had adopted the totem of the Plover (*cheechishkawae* or *tchitchwishkiway*) many of his relatives and connected kin did intermarry with the Cranes over extended generations.

135 Mezai was an Ojibwe speaker at La Pointe and evidently a brother of the noted Loon totem chief Bezhike (Buffalo). He had connections to the Perrault family and moved to Goulais Bay around 1837. Henry Schoolcraft recognized Mezai (Catfish) as a minor chief. Schoolcraft, *Personal Memoires*, 102–3. See also note 38, above.

136 The Sugar Island Native and métis community and the métis settlement at the Sault were closely interrelated. Endogamy failed to exist in the Sault region, and although priests discouraged intermarriage among Roman Catholics and Protestants, interdenominational marriage was common. Any governmental regulations meant to control residence patterns were totally disregarded. Even head chiefs, whose movements were far more regulated by the Indian agent than those of ordinary Native persons during these years, continued to disregard agency administrative boundaries in their living arrangements. For instance, Oshawana, who signed a major treaty at the American Sault in 1855 and was regarded as one of the leading chiefs, is buried in the Roman Catholic cemetery at Garden River on the British side; his tombstone reads: "Francis Shawano 1794–1884—'Chief of the Chippeways.'" The Shawanos were connected with both the Garden River and Thessalon bands through repeated marriages into the Pine family. Pierre Charette, Jean Baptiste Denome, Jean Baptiste LeSage, Charles LaRose, Augustine LaRoche, Francis Roussain, Francis and Louis Nolin, Joseph Piquette, and John Sayre received eighty acres each under American treaty of 30 September 1854 with the Chippewas of Lake Superior. Others, like the Gurnoes, Bushas (Bouchers), Ermatingers, and many of the Cadottes tended to remain with American bands.

137 Surnames include Abotasoway, Barnard, Belliveau, Boissoneau, Corbière, Crochières, Fonatiane, Gordon, Jourdreau, La Blanc, La Brae (Brown), La Coy, La Fleur, Lamorandier, La Pointe, La Sage, La Tore, Le Vasseur, Nolin, Recollet, Roi (King) Russeau, Roussain, Sayers, Solomon, and Thibeault. A. C. Osborne, "The Migration of Voyageurs from Drummond Island to Penetanguishene in 1828," *Ontario Historical Society Papers and Records* 3 (1901), 123–66.

138 Population of Sault Ste. Marie in 1849, Aemilius Irving Papers, AO.

139 When the Reverend James Beaven visited Garden River in 1845, he noted the absence of any wooden houses. James Beaven, *Recreations of a Long Vacation, or*

*a Visit to the Indian Missions of Upper Canada* (London: Society for the Preservation of the Gospel in Foreign Parts; Toronto: H. and W. Roswell, 1846), 124. When Anna Brownell Jameson visited the Sault in the 1830s, she asked why, if the Ojibwe wanted houses, could they not build them on their own? "I was told that it was impossible, that they neither *could* nor *would!*—that this sort of labour is absolutely inimical to their habits. It requires more strength than the women possess; and for men to fell the wood and carry the logs were unheard of degradation." Anna Brownell Jameson, *Winter Studies and Summer Rambles in Canada* (1838; reprint, Toronto: McClelland and Stewart, 1990), 477.

140 They were seen as valuable teachers because they practiced small-scale agriculture and animal husbandry. Métis women could weave, churn butter, and tend domestic farm animals, as well as perform tasks undertaken by Native women such as lacing snowshoes and manufacturing moccasins. The Native population also sought to draw upon lively French traditions that included traditional French songs, fiddle playing, step-dancing and special fetes. Janet E. Chute, "Preservation of Ethnic Diversity at Garden River: A Key to Olibwa Strength," *Papers of the Twenty-Eighth Algonquin Conference*, ed. David H. Pentland (Winnipeg: University of Manitoba Press, 1997), 50.

141 Chute, *Legacy of Shingwaukonse*, 106–36.

142 Doug Owram, *Promise of Eden: The Canadian Expansionist Movement and the Idea of the West, 1856–1900* (Toronto: University of Toronto Press, 1980), 36–40.

143 Chute, *Legacy of Shingwaukonse*, 21. Napoleon Joseph Charles Paul Bonaparte (1822–1891), commonly called Prince Napoleon, or Plon Plon, visited Sault Ste. Marie in 1861. He was the son of Napoleon's brother Jerome and Catherine of Wurtenburg. He was named successor to Napoleon III if the emperor remained childless. A professed liberal, he married Princess Clotilde, daughter of King Victor Emmanuel II of Italy in 1859. For his visit to Sault Ste. Marie, see Camille Ferri-Pisani, *Prince Napoleon in America, 1861: Letters from His Aide-de-Camp*, trans. George J. Joyaux (Bloomington: Indiana University Press, 1959).

144 William MacTavish to A. H. Campbell, 16 November 1849, B/194/b/15/1849–1850, HBCA. Accompanying Macdonell were his brother Angus Macdonell, also a lawyer, and a mutual friend of the Macdonell brothers, Wharton Metcalfe, a British sketchist and landscape artist. See Alan Knight and Janet E. Chute, "A Visionary on the Edge: Allan Macdonell and the Championing of Native Resource Rights," in *With Good Intentions: Euro-Canadian and Aboriginal Relations in Colonial Canada*, ed. David Nock and Celia Haig-Brown (Vancouver: University of British Columbia Press, 2006), 87–105.

145 George Catlin, *Letters and Notes on Manners, Customs, and Condition of the North American Indians* (1844; reprint, New York: Dover Publications, 1973), 2:162.

146 Those holding the same totem, even if no direct biological connection could be traced, tended to regard each other as siblings and be bound by ties of loyalty to one another.

147 These activities were part of the oral tradition at Garden River. The exact numbers cannot be determined. William MacTavish, the Sault's HBC chief factor and the main source of the information on this matter, changed the estimates. At one point he stated that fifteen Ojibwe (Chippewa) from the United States had joined the expedition instead of just three. MacTavish to James Hargrave, November 1848, Letter Book, W. MacTavish, 17 October–25 May 1849, MU 1391, AO.

148 Pierre LeSage (1819–1910) was a free trader. In 1837, he married the daughter of Raymond Mastat and later wed Teresa Tegoosh, one of Pierre Lavoine Barthe's daughters and Little Pine's granddaughter. Eustace was born in 1833 and died in 1922. The identity of Pierre and Eustace's father is unknown, but it is probable that all the LeSages born at the Sault—Jean Baptiste in 1815, Pierre in 1819, Joseph in 1828, and Eustace in 1833—were all sons of Jean Baptiste LeSarge, who had settled at the Sault in 1818 and traded at Drummond Island prior to 1827. Joseph LeSage Sr. married Henrietta McKerchie of Sugar Island and Sophie Belanger, and his son Joseph Jr. would marry Polly, the daughter of Augustin Shingwauk, while another daughter, Rosalind, wed Jesse Wells Church of Sugar Island.

149 This man was most likely the son of Michael Boyer Sr. (1805–1895) and Angelique LeCharité, which meant that Charles Boyer would have been a young man in his teens like Eustace LeSage. Charles Boyer was likely a descendent of the Charles Boyer who between 1771 and 1779 was a partner with Lawrence Ermatinger, Forrest Oakes, Joseph Fulton, and Peter Pangman in the Great Lakes fur trade out of Michilimackinac. His aunt, Margaret Boyer, married François Nolin, and his grandfather, Jean Baptiste LeCharité (1775–1849), was a retired HBC voyageur who had first signed on with the company in 1794 and was with David Thompson at Fort des Prairies in 1799.

150 In 1849, Sheriff John Hulbert and Samuel Ashmun of the American Sault had incorporated a company to enter the local fishing trade and compete with the AFC and the Northern Lake Company for the Lake Superior fishery. Fowle, *Sault Ste. Marie and Its Great Waterway*, 410.

151 An anatomy of Shingwaukonse's plan is examined in Janet E. Chute, "A Unifying Vision: Shingwaukonse's Plan for the Future of the Great Lakes Ojibwa," *Journal of the Canadian Historical Association* 7 (1996): 55–80.

152 The document with LeSage's reindeer totem on it is the Pennefather Treaty of 1858. A copy of this treaty is in the Aemilius Irving Papers, AO.

153 Little Pine's revelation of his métis background exposed him to ridicule and prejudice in the press at times. One of his detractors, John William Keating, despite Keating's marriage at the Sault in 1837 to a métis woman named Julie Paladeau, sought to undermine the chief's Native rights campaign by describing him as a métis "from the extremity of Lake Superior, shrewd and intelligent, and who has worked himself up to a prominent place, by means of the traders and missionaries, and what is vulgarly called the 'gift of the gab.'" Keating, "To the Editor of the Chatham Chronicle," *Chatham Chronicle*, 15 August 1849.

154 William Cameron alerted the authorities to the expedition's intentions. B/194/b/1-15/1824-1850/Reel 1M224, HBC Sault Ste. Marie.

155 The métis and Ojibwe persons who went with Anderson and Vidal in 1849 included Peter Bell, son of John Bell, Mezai's son Francis, Waubmama (White Pigeon), son of Muckdayoquot (Black Cloud), and Piabetassung's son, Waisangais. A. Vidal and Thomas G. Anderson, "Report on the Visit to Indians on North Shore of Lake Huron and Superior for Purpose of Investigating Their Claims to Territory Bordering on These Lakes," 1849, Aemilius Irving Papers, AO.

156 Alexander Clark (1818–1895) served "48 years as skipper on the Great Lakes" (from his gravestone in Korah cemetery at Sault Ste. Marie) under Thomas Lamphier (d. 1869) on the HBC supply ship *Whitefish*, the schooner *Napoleon*, and

as pilot on the steamer *Rescue* under Thomas Dick. He had lived at The Pic and retired to Pointe aux Pins, west of the Sault, where he earned a living as farmer, fur trader, whiskey dealer, and sometime sailor. He married Thomas Lamphier's daughter, Betsy (1821–1879). Betsy Clark's mother Jane (1791–1887) was a Scottish Cree métis from Moose Factory. See Barbara Chisholm and Andrea Gutsche, *Lake Superior: Under the Shadow of the Gods* (Toronto: Lynx Images, 1998), 198–200.

157 *British Colonist* (Toronto), 8 February 1850. The Anglican missionary, Frederick O'Meara, at Manitowaning on Manitoulin Island was even more agitated. O'Meara argued that "unquiet men" were trying to revolutionize the province and that the Native people had been duped by traitors to the Queen. Frederick O'Meara to A. H. Campbell, 12 November 1849, RG 10, vol. 612, 392–97, LAC.

158 These persons were placed on the band annuity lists, mostly under Ojibwe names, in 1850. Vouchers for payment made in respect to negotiating Indian Treaties, 1850, Aemilius Irving Papers, AO. The following métis names appear on those treaties pertaining to Garden River: John, Joseph, Peter, and William Bell; Charles, Joachim, and Joseph Biron; François, Theophile, and Thomas Boissoneau; Louison, Michel, and Charles Cadotte; Charles LaRose; Joseph LeSage; Frank Perrault; and François and Joseph Recollet. Canada, *Indian Treaties and Surrenders from 1680 to 1890* (1891; reprint, Toronto: Coles, 1971). See page xxii on Garden River treaties. For Treaty 91B see vol. I, p. 229; Treaty 111: vol. I, p. 260; Treaty 110: vol. I, p. 257; Treaty 165: vol. I, p. 63; Treaty 130: vol. I, p. 301; Treaty 140: vol. II, p. 1; Treaty 166: vol. II, p. 65; Treaty 196: vol. II, p. 119; Treaty 243: vol. II, p. 209. In return for his long-term support, John Bell was granted his own section on the extreme west end of the Garden River reserve on the Root River, which came to be known as Bell's Point. It was individually assigned land, under treaty, and, as such, was not held in common.

159 Statement of Joshua Biron of Sault Ste. Marie, included with a letter from John Driver to E. B. Borron, 5 June 1893, Aemilius Irving Papers, AO. Alexis Biron recounted that only he, his brother Joachim Biron, John Bell, Louison Cadotte, and Charles Cadotte (all with Cadottes family ties) joined Little Pine's group and "were allowed the same privileges as the Indian members of the Band." Statement of Alexis Biron, 1893, Amelius Irving Papers, AO.

160 W. L. Morton, *Manitoba: A History* (Toronto: University of Toronto Press, 1957), 78–79.

161 Nebenaigooching, Shingwaukonse, Kabaosa from Garden River, and Piabetassung, chief of the American band on Sugar Island, even requested that Ermatinger and each of his children be given land or a mineral location at the Sault, owing to Ermatinger's help in securing métis land title at the rapids. To His Excellency the Earl of Elgin and Kincardine, from Nebenaigooching et al., 10 September 1850. Upper Canada Land Petitions, "E," Bundle 6, 1847–1852, AO. RG 1, vol. 182-B, C-1892, AO. Nebenaigooching personally placed this document in chief commissioner William Robinson's hands. This constituted a radical reversal of the Ojibwe stance in 1842, when they rebuffed the Ermatinger estate's claim that had been submitted to the government on 11 August 1843. Thomas G. Anderson to James Fraser, 2 January 1842, Indian Affairs, RG 10, vol. 124, 69765–6 and vol. 124, 69765–7, LAC. (Fraser was acting as agent for Charles Oakes Ermatinger's son, William.) The Pine sent a similar petition in October 1842. Capp, *The Story of Bow-a-ting*, 175–76. In contrast, Anglican

clergy William McMurray attempted to launch a chief's claim in 1850 in the name of his son Willy (as a grandson of Waubojeeg) but was rejected personally by Shingwaukonse. Anna Johnston Schoolcraft, Dundas, to George Johnston, 23 September 1850, and William McMurray to George Johnston, Dundas, 23 October 1850, George Johnston Papers, Burton Historical Collection, Detroit Public Library, Detroit, MI.

162  The first petition, drawn up by Alexis Xavier Biron and Charles Oakes Ermatinger Jr.—heir to the Ermatinger estate at the rapids—asked that the Crown grants be given to fifty-five French and métis individuals. The second document, requesting one hundred acres be granted to the métis community, was signed by Charles Cadotte, who, though he held land at the rapids, stated he had come from Red River, along with thirty-four others. Petitions relating to land received by the Crown Lands Department, Upper Canada Land Petitions, "E," Bundle 6, 1847–1852, RG 1, L3, vol. 182-B, AO. A schedule of the inhabitants of the village and the acreages each family head occupied is included with these petitions. They show that most métis held strip farms of 1.5 acres to 3 acres along the waterfront. These allotments extended northward from the shoreline to comprise anywhere from ten to fifty acres.

163  Copy of an indenture of a gift of land from the Indians to the Roman Catholic Church at Garden River, 1850, recorded by Colloton in Ojibwe in 1953, Colloton Papers, Anglican Heritage Collection, Bishophurst, Sault Ste. Marie, ON. This piece of land was taken from the land given to Tegoosh but also near the plot designated for but never used by Joachim Biron (near the present-day Garden River Roman Catholic cemetery). In 1849, Little Pine had also leased land for a period of nine hundred years to the Anglican Church for the price of one peppercorn annually, with Allan Macdonell acting as his agent. Indenture Contract of a gift of land from Indians to Rev. G. Anderson, 1849, Thomas Anderson Papers, Baldwin Room, Toronto Metropolitan Library, Toronto, ON. St. John's Anglican Church, Garden River, would receive its grant for land under the terms of Treaty 130 in 1873.

164  "Shinguioouse, Shinguacouse or Chinguacouse Town Plot, Garden River, Algoma District—17th April, 1872. By Chippewa Indians. A block of land. To be sold to McCrae, Craig & Company, for a steam saw mill. No. 165, 63, II." Canada, *Indian Treaties and Surrenders*, 92–93.

165  Chute, *Legacy of Shingwaukonse*, 237.

166  Canada (Province of), *An Act to Make Better Provision for the Administration of Justice in the Unorganized Tracts of Country of Upper Canada*, Statutes of the Province of Canada 1853, 16 Vict, c. 56.

167  Joseph Wilson was appointed Indian agent from 1856 to 1870. He could be caustically racist in his remarks towards métis individuals, particularly if he felt they had contravened resource laws or in some other way proved disruptive. In 1856, for instance, he arrested three métis whom he considered unruly and sent them north, as deserters, with the HBC, an action that caught the notice of the national press. Executive Council Minutes, 28 June 1856, Canada State Book Q 350, MS9, Executive Council Records, AO. At the same time, certain settlers held Wilson in considerable esteem. Frederick Falkner described him as a "friend, the very best," to all the métis and Ojibwe, as well as being a good (unlicensed) doctor to them. Edward Capp, rector of St. Luke's Anglican Church in Sault Ste. Marie, was the clergyman who would eventually preside at Wilson's funeral in 1904. As the guardian and caretaker of his now-lost

diaries Capp praised Wilson and referred to him as "a virtual patriarch and father to the inhabitants." Capp, *Story*, 174. In Medonte township, Wilson was the childhood friend of Sir Samuel Benfield Steele, who later became the first commissioner of the North West Mounted Police. Their fathers were both retired naval officers and functioned as the local Medonte magistrates. Ronald J. Stagg, "Elmes Yelverton Steele," *DCB*, vol. 9, *1861–1870* (Toronto: University of Toronto Press, 1976), 743–44; and Sam Steele, *Forty Years in Canada* (1915; reprint, Toronto: Prospero, 2000).

168 According to Edward Capp, "Philetus S. Church (living on Sugar Island at the upper end of Lake George) an American citizen, had been cutting timber on the Canadian side and that Major [*sic*] Wilson promptly attached the timber. On March 18, 1846, the major crossed to the American side on business and was arrested and thrown into jail. No explanation was offered in response to his enquiries until another officer appeared with a paper, on signing which he was told he would be released. The document was authority for Church to remove the timber he had cut. Major Wilson indignantly refused to sign, saying he would rather starve than to be a party to such rascality. He was left in jail until March 20th, when the authorities, becoming alarmed at what had been done, released him. On returning home, he found the town, and especially his own family in a state of great alarm, for none knew his whereabouts. Major Wilson complained to headquarters and in due time Washington apologized for the action of his persecutors." Capp quoted in Bayliss and Bayliss, *River of Destiny*, 255–56.

169 George Ironside Jr. is buried on the northwest corner of the Queen Street cemetery in the Sault. He was the son of George Ironside Sr. (1760–1830), also in the Indian Department. His mother was a Wyndotte and a relative of the Prophet (Tenkwatewa). George Jr. married Annie Symington (1810–1902). Two of their daughters, Annie (1832–1874) and Eliza (1829–1910), would marry the last HBC chief factor at Sault Ste. Marie, Wemyss Simpson (1825–1894). Ironside's son Charles (1844–1898) married Joachim Biron's daughter, Alphonsine (1846–1907), while his namesake, George Ironside III (b. 1840), wed Joseph Wilson's niece, Caroline Buchanan, in 1879. Another son, Alexander McGregor Ironside, served as a clerk and interpreter in the Indian Department at Manitowaning in the 1860s and 1870s and briefly succeeded his father as northern superintendent. Wemyss Simpson was first cousin and brother-in-law to HBC governor Sir George Simpson. The Simpsons and Ironsides were known as staunch Anglicans. Simpson donated the land for Bishophurst, the residence of the Bishop of Algoma, and there is a memorial to Charles Ironside, one-time diocesan treasurer, in St. Luke's Anglican Cathedral. In the opinion of Douglas Leighton, George Ironside Jr. was "conscientious, humane and knowledgeable" and "in many ways represented the best type of Indian Department employee." Dennis Carter-Edwards, "Ironside, George," *DCB*, vol. 6, *1821–1835* (Toronto: University of Toronto Press, 1987), 340; and Douglas Leighton, "Ironside, George [Jr.]," *DCB*, vol. 9, *1861–1970* (Toronto: University of Toronto Press, 1976), 407–8.

170 Driver to Borron, 4 March 1893, Aemilius Irving Papers, AO. Driver stressed that it was around the time of the Pennefather Treaties (1859) that the métis "all left the Soo and went to live on the Garden River Indian Reserve, and to my own recollection that only after ... they had been included as Members of the Bands and that the Birons came back to the Soo ..."

171 William Cameron to Robert Pennefather, 8 July 1858, RG 10, vol. 235, 139547-50, Indian Affairs, LAC.

172 Native and métis alike were fined, even jailed, for taking timber from an Indian reserve. Joachim Biron's younger brother Charles, an educated member of the Garden River band, was apprehended in 1864 for taking six pine planks from Garden River and imprisoned in the Penetanguishene penitentiary. William Spragge to Charles Dupont, 26 April 1864, RG 10, vol. 615, 434, Indian Affairs, LAC. Charles had been arrested before, in 1857, when he took six pine planks from the Elliot mining location, situated in the midst of the Garden River reserve. Joseph Wilson, as timber agent, complained that métis such as Biron who were permitted to receive Indian presents, partake of annuities, and reside on reserves plundered valuable resources. His allegations that most offenders were métis was contradicted, however, by his repeated punishments of Ojibwe "offenders" as well, many of whom left for the United States in consequence. Joseph Wilson to Robert Pennefather, 8 July 1857, RG 10, vol. 235, 139452-4, Indian Affairs, LAC.

173 In 1862, Judge John Prince, who hired members of the Davieau, Denomee, and Jollineau family as farm labourers, shooting companions, and guides, and purchased his fish from the Bells, mused that a good many métis "had annuity paid to them by Capt. Ironside." Prince, Diary, 21 October 1862, AO.

174 George Ironside to Robert Bruce, 27 March 1858, RG 10, vol. 241, 14326, Indian Affairs, LAC. At this time, Nebenaigooching was endeavouring to gain the political influence of Bishop Frederick Baraga of Marquette and frequently acted as his personal guide as he visited his widespread diocese and often crossed into Canada.

175 Copy of accounts of payments to Indians under Robinson Treaties, 1850–1892, Aemilius Irving Papers, AO. Much of the information for the years 1850 to 1859 was collected by George Johnston and John William Keating. Surveyors Letters Received, vol. 66, 233, Crown Land Papers, A 1-1, AO. "The United States government also give to the Chief Oshawwanwno, for his own use in fee simple, a small island in the River St. Mary's adjacent to the camping ground hereby surrendered, being the same island on which he is now encamped and said to contain less than half an acre provided that the same has not been heretofore otherwise appropriated or disposed of, and in such case this grant is to be void and no consideration is to be claimed by said chief or any of the Indian parties, hereto, in lieu thereof." Article 3, Treaty with the Chippewa of Sault Ste. Marie, 1855, in Charles J. Kappler, ed., *Indian Affairs: Laws and Treaties* (Washington, DC: Government Printing Office, 1904), 732.

176 John Stoughton Dennis (1820–1885), Public Land Surveyor (PLS), was responsible for the survey and Dennis township (1859) was named after him. For Dennis's later encounters with Métis during the survey of Red River in 1869, see Bumstead, *Red River Rebellion*, 274.

177 Goulais Bay was principally a fishing community that had grown up around a Roman Catholic church (Our Lady of Sorrows) established by Father Auguste Kohler in 1847. Many of the métis from the Sault's "Frenchtown" later joined Nebenaigooching's band at Goulais Bay. In 1893, Indian agent William Van Abbott reported on behalf of the Batchawana band that "Chief Nebenaigooching ... resides on the Garden River Reserve with a great many of his people.... This band do not participate in any of the work or profit of this reserve, they have a small reserve of the their own at St. Mary's Rapids [Whitefish

Island] occupied by a few families. The members are all scattered, some living at Goulais Bay where they have farms of their own others at Batchawana,
Agawa River, Lizard Island, Lake Superior. These mostly earn their living by
fishing in the summer, hunting and lumbering in the winter." Dominion of
Canada, Annual Report of the Department of Indian Affairs for the Year Ended
30th June 1893 (Ottawa: S. E. Dawson, 1894), 9, <http://www.collections
canada.gc.ca/indianaffairs/020010-119.01-e.php?page_id_nbr=8794&PHPSES-
SID=et4hc0a2c0vvs6o33fpingmpc5> (cited 23 November 2007).

178 Joseph Wilson to Charles Dupont, 20 January 1864, RG 10, vol. 615, 621–23,
    Indian Affairs, LAC.

179 This is revealed by a comparison of information drawn from the 1846 town plot
    survey with material from the Sault registry of deeds and land transactions for
    the 1860s. It is also doubtful, given the nature of the data available, that any
    more than a handful of métis were issued official government land patents. Only
    half a dozen métis families were able to retain their properties at the Sault
    into the late nineteenth century.

180 The métis who did retain land at the Sault after 1871 experienced drastic
    reductions in the size of their plots due to the size of standard municipal lots,
    probably owing to the demands of taxation.

181 Sault Ste. Marie Village Minutes, 22 January 1872. Of the fifty-two volunteers (in
    a population of 304) on the regimental list of the Sault Ste. Marie Infantry Mili-
    tia from 1863 to 1866, only eleven were métis: Neil and Daniel McKay, Raymond
    Miron, Hyacinthe Davieau, William Grant, "Balles" Mastat, John Boissoneau,
    Joseph LaFond Jr., Joseph LaBatt, Louis Miron Jr., and Joseph Dubois. There were
    no Natives—a great change from the time of the War of 1812—and the métis
    were gradually dropped from the roll after the Fenian threat of June 1866.

182 Sault Ste. Marie Village Minutes, 12 February 1872, Sault Ste. Marie City Hall.
    In the 1871 census, the following families informed enumerator John Carney,
    the local tavernkeeper and brother of the sheriff, that their "racial origin" was
    "French": Belleau, Biron, Boissoneau, Bourassa, Boyer, Brassard, Cadotte, Cor-
    bière, Daveau, Denomée, Dubois, Fortin, Jollineau, LaFond, Lefleur, LeBatt,
    LaRose, LeMais, LeSage, Mayville, Mastat, Miron, "Watap" Nolin, Perrault,
    Portero, Recollett, Soulière, Surrette, Sayers, Thibeault, and Tremblay. The
    Bell, Driver, Grant, Ironside, McKay, Moore, and Robertson families were clas-
    sified as "Scottish." John Whalen called himself "Irish." The Shingwauks,
    Nebenaigooching (recorded as Joseph Sayer), Cadottes, Clarks, Joneses,
    Neveaus, Solomons, Thompsons, and others with obvious Ojibwe names were
    all "Indians." Census of Canada, 1871, microfilm. Sault Ste. Marie's popula-
    tion was 879.

183 Dawson sat as a Conservative in the Ontario Legislature from 1875 to 1878
    and as an Independent in the federal Parliament from 1878 to 1891, although
    he usually voted with John A. Macdonald's Conservatives and was an unoffi-
    cial member of their caucus (13 February 1879 to 3 February 1891). See Janet E.
    Chute and Alan Knight, "Taking Up the Torch: Simon J. Dawson and the Upper
    Great Lake's Native Resource Campaign of the 1860s, 1870s and 1880s," *With
    Good Intentions: Euro-Canadian & Aboriginal Relations in Colonial Canada*, ed. Celia
    Haig-Brown and David Nock (Vancouver: University of British Columbia Press,
    2006), 106–31.

184 Dawson's biographer, Elizabeth Arthur, noted that Dawson's eastern bound-
    aries for his cherished province remained ambiguous and that it was highly

unlikely that Ontario would countenance any diminution of its control over the territory from the Sault to Thunder Bay. Elizabeth Arthur, *Simon J. Dawson, C. E.* (Thunder Bay: Thunder Bay Historical Museum Society, 1987), 21.

185 Dawson, for instance, called for recognition of a right for métis to cut trees along the shores of Lake Huron and Superior in order to construct overnight shelters during their travels.

186 See, for instance, the Rat Portage *News* of 1 February 1889, cited in Arthur, *Simon J. Dawson*, 27.

187 Vidal first suggested a clause be inserted of this nature. A. Vidal and T. G. Anderson, Report, 1849, Aemilius Irving Papers, AO.

188 Of the 5,231 Native annuitants registered on band lists in 1890, 2,894 were questioned as being of doubtful status. It was argued that while the number of "Indians" had remained about the same since 1850, métis numbers had escalated to six times the original number on the treaty lists. It was claimed that William Benjamin Robinson had noted only eighty-four métis for Lake Superior and two hundred on Lake Huron, and that between 1850 and 1890 the number of métis had increased from 284 to 1,710. Information derived from various sources in the Aemilius Irving Papers, AO.

189 A native of Staffordshire, England, and a graduate in engineering from the University of Edinburgh, Borron was a former mine foreman at Bruce Mines (1852–1868), mining inspector for the Lake Superior region (1868–1873) and Reform member of the federal Parliament for Algoma (1874–1878). He was appointed stipendiary magistrate in 1879 with orders to report on agricultural, mineral, and forest values in Northern Ontario as requested by the provincial government.

190 John Driver was the perfect assistant for such a task since he straddled three worlds as (1) a métis (he was listed on the 1861 census as a boatbuilder), (2) a member of the Garden River band, and (3) a man who had held political office on the Sault Ste. Marie municipal council. A lifelong bachelor, he was the son of John Joseph Driver (1806–1848), an employee of the HBC, and Marie (1811–1861), "a Native of Upper Canada." His sister, Catherine, married Antoine Biron, and another sister, Jane, wed Jarvis Pine (1838–1898), who was previously married to Marie Abotassoway of Manitoulin Island. Jarvis Pine was Little Pine's grandson, a Roman Catholic and chief at Garden River (1897–1898).

191 Obituary of Joachim Biron, *Sault Express* (Sault Ste. Marie, MI), 10 July 1903. Shortly before his death, Biron was personally sought out as a leading Liberal supporter and greeted by Wilfrid Laurier on the prime minister's trip to the west in 1903. There is a photograph in the Sault Ste. Marie museum of the two men standing in the sunshine on the verandah of the Algonquin Hotel, on the northeast corner of Queen and Pim Streets, once a part of Biron's original property. Pallbearers at Biron's funeral included Mayor William Plummer, Judge O'Connor, Crown Attorney J. J. Kehoe, Police Chief John Dawson, Joseph Morin, and Theodore Roy. Joachim Biron's grave was destroyed in the 1980s, when the Garden River flooded and his coffin crumbled and was washed away.

192 One of the younger sons of Little Pine, George Shingwauk (1839–1923) (The Little Warrior) was defeated in the 1902 band election by Charles Cadotte (1868–1907). Charles Cadotte was a relative of the wives of John Bell, Bughwujjenene and Mrs. George Shingwauk's mother. His great-grandfather was likely Michael Cadotte Sr. of La Pointe, Wisconsin. George Shingwauk was

married to Cecile Belleau, the daughter of Margaret Cadotte and Michael Belleau Sr., who had originally come from the Keeweenaw Peninsula on Lake Superior's south shore. Charles Cadotte, although a shrewd negotiator with the logging companies, was defeated himself the following year by George Shingwauk. The sudden death of Cadotte's main supporter, Joachim Biron, in the midst of the 1903 election meeting, undoubtedly impeded Cadotte's cause. Janet E. Chute, "Shingwauk, George (Menissino, Menissinowini, also known as George Pine)," *DCB*, vol. 15, *1921–1930* (Toronto: University of Toronto Press, 2005), 1095–97.

193 Aimable Boissoneau married Margaret, the daughter of Edward Sayers, and granddaughter of Nebenaigooching. They adopted three children from a variety of backgrounds. He was the son of Frank Boissoneau (1836–1872) and Charlotte LaRose (1835–1872), who died when he was a child. He was raised by his grandparents, Frank LaRose (1810–1894) and Marie Biron Boisvert Miron (1816–1910). His grandfather's first wife was Theresa Cadotte, a daughter of Le Grande Michel, and his great-uncle, Charles LaRose (1820–1880), was married to Charlotte Shingwauk (1831–1881). Mab was fluent in French, English, and Ojibwe.

194 During his lifetime, Edward Sayers was a boatman, farmer, fur trader, free trader, liquor salesman, police constable (1860–1875), and chief of the Batchawana band (1899–1915). From his "uncle" Henry he had inherited seven lots in the centre of Sault Ste. Marie, which he sold in 1887. That year, he also owned a forty-acre plot of land in Tarentorus township, "only three miles distant from the Sault." As a métis, he was an independent entrepreneur who never quite succeeded. He married Suzanne Crochières, the daughter of Jean Baptiste Crochières (1782–1877), of Sault Ste. Marie and Sugar Island, and Genevieve Tabor, and they had a large family.

195 Emery Boissoneau was the son of Joseph Boissoneau Sr. He was an HBC carpenter and boatman, was a member of the Sault Volunteer Infantry in 1866, and went west with Colonel Garnet Wolseley in 1870. He married twice: Angelique Biron (1846–1870), a daughter of Alexander Biron Jr. and Angelique Mazai, and Angelique Belleville (1856–1933), and fathered eleven children. Emery Boissoneau died in Sepparton, British Columbia. The divisions among the métis community in defining identity and the identity of others in their own ethnic group is evident in Emery Boissoneau's personal history, where he defines himself as a "Frenchman" and the Birons, or at least some of the Birons, as "halfbreeds." In response to an enquiry from fellow historical society member Henry C. Hamilton concerning the annuity moneys received from the Batchawana band by his two daughters, Angelique (1864–1895) and Mary (b. 1867), Emery wrote, "I was married to a half breed woman by the name of Angelique Biron and thru Chief Sayers he put me on the list and thru his son's jealousy my treaty money was stopped so I figured between Mr [William Van] Abbot [the Indian agent] and Sayers it was hushed up that about 50 years ago." Both of Emery's daughters continued to receive annuities even after they had married white men.

196 Raymond Miron was the son of Louis Miron Sr. (1812–1858) and Joachim, Alexis, and Charles Biron's older sister Marie (1816–1910). Raymond married Jane Nolin. His widowed mother, Marie, had first married a Boisvert and then, following Louris Miron's death, Frank LaRose, who joined with Louis Riel at Pembina in 1875. She returned to the Sault following LaRose's death in

1894. Raymond worked as a labourer and boatman for the HBC, was a member of the Sault Volunteer Militia in 1866, and, though retired by 1924, was listed in the city directory as a night watchman at the ship canal.

197   The phenomenon of "passing White" existed at the Sault until recent years. During our interviews, we encountered a number of "Whites" bearing the same surnames as métis persons who had occupied lots along the waterfront in 1846. They denied repeatedly that their ancestry was anything but pure French or that they were in any way related to band members holding similar surnames, when in fact genealogical records would prove that they were linked by kinship.

198   This refers to members of the Garden River and Batchawana First Nations. In the 1930s, the Batchawana First Nation purchased the old Rankin mining location (1,537 hectares) for $17,000. The Rankin Location was wedged in between the eastern boundary of the Municipality of Sault Ste. Marie and the western line of the Garden River Reserve, and was declared a reserve in 1951. In 1991, the Batchawana First Nation claimed a population of 446 individuals, and Garden River claimed 901 persons.

199   Garden River contains a stretch of shoreline along the St. Mary's River known as Frenchman's Bay.

200   The division today is between "Ojibwe" and "French." The term "Anishinabeg" or "the people" covers both. The terms "half-breed," "mixed blood," or "métis" were not used in the authors' presence. One joke, told in the 1980s by a man, a descendent of Little Pine, who considered himself more Ojibwe than French, went like this: "How do you tell the difference between a Frenchman and an Indian? By the way they show you a stone in a river. You're going down a river in a pointer and the Ojibwe says, "Look! There's a stone." The Frenchman goes, "Bang! There's a stone." Interview with Fred Pine Jr., Garden River, 10 June 1982. The jest was to be taken wholly in good fun, for the speaker recognized that Ojibwe and métis were equally competent in river running.

201   Chute, *Legacy of Shingwaukonse*, 16–18.

## Chapter 6: "'Those freebooters would shoot me like a dog': American Terrorists and Homeland Security in the Journals of Ezhaaswe (William A. Elias [1856–1929])," by David T. McNab

1   John M. Mackenzie, *The Empire of Nature: Hunting, Conservation and British Imperialism* (Manchester: Manchester University Press, 1988), ix; and Mackenzie, *Empires of Nature and the Nature of Empires: Imperialism, Scotland and the Environment* (East Linton: Tuckwell Press, 1997), 1–30, 70–86.

2   Mackenzie, *Empire of Nature*. See also the chapters on the history of the Bkejwanong Territory in David McNab, *Circles of Time: Aboriginal Land Rights and Resistance in Ontario* (Waterloo: Wilfrid Laurier University Press, 1999), 147–85; and David McNab, ed., *Earth, Water, Air and Fire: Studies in Canadian Ethnohistory* (Waterloo: Wilfrid Laurier University Press, 1998), 35–64.

3   David McNab, "Borders of Water and Fire: Islands as Sacred Places and as Meeting Grounds," in *Aboriginal Cultural Landscapes*, ed. Jill Oakes, Rick Riewe, et al. (Winnipeg: Aboriginal Issues Press, 2004), 39–44.

4   McNab, *Circles of Time*, 203–8.

5  I am grateful for this information on Elias's name, which was provided to me by the linguistic/cultural experts at a meeting at Nin.Da.Waab.Jig (Walpole Island Heritage Centre) on 26 April 2005: Jennie Greenbird, Elizabeth Isaac, Elaine Jacobs, and Reta Sands. Elias's journals are held at the Shawanaga First Nation Archives and Resources.

6  Elias, Journals, #11, 2 December 1923, 1921–1923. Shawanaga First Nation Archives and Resources.

7  I would like to thank Elder and former Chief Donald Keeshig of Cape Croker for this information, which he told me in a conversation with him on 9 August 2005 at Keeshigonong, the Place of the Sky, at Cape Croker.

8  Ebenezer Watson, Indian Superintendent, Sarnia, to Sir John A. Macdonald, Prime Minister and Superintendent General of Indian Affairs, 25 August 1882, Binder on "Charles Jacobs Family Tree," Reference no. 1672, Nin.Da.Waab.Jig. Files, Bkejwanong (Walpole Island) First Nation.

9  Elias, Journals, #8, 1921–1922. Shawanaga First Nation Archives and Resources.

10  In the Victoria University Archives in Toronto, there is no evidence that Elias ever graduated with a degree from Victoria College. I would like to thank Christine Grandy for this information.

11  Ontario Marriage Index, Saugeen Township, 22 August 1876, Microfilm 19, Registration #001369, http://www.archives.gov.on.ca/english/interload/marriage _rec.htm (accessed 4 April 2006), Archives of Ontario (AO).

12  Elizabeth Graham, comp., *The Mush Hole: Life at Two Indian Residential Schools* (Waterloo, ON: Heffle Publishing, 1997). This school was originally called the Wesleyan Ojibway Industrial School, Mount Elgin, which was named after the Governor General in 1849—Lord Elgin.

13  Elias, Journals, #1, entry of 25 August 1885, #2, 1885–1887. Shawanaga First Nation Archives and Resources.

14  See 2 Kings in the Old Testament. This name fits with Elias's life as a Methodist missionary.

15  Sharon Helen Venne, ed., *Indian Acts and Amendments 1865–1975: An Indexed Collection* (Saskatoon: Native Law Centre, University of Saskatchewan, 1981).

16  Neil Semple, *The Lord's Dominion: The History of Canadian Methodism* (Montreal: McGill-Queen's University Press, 1996), 178; see also William Westfall, *Two Worlds: The Protestant Culture of Nineteenth-Century Ontario* (Montreal: McGill-Queen's University Press, 1989).

17  McNab, "Borders of Water and Fire," 44–45. See, for example, the following reference to Americans fishing: Vankoughnet wrote to his counterpart, Major John Tilton, then the federal deputy minister of Fisheries, on 8 July 1885 regarding the marshes and fishing in Lake St. Clair, as follows: "On the occasion of an interview which I had recently with Mr. C.H., Gooderham Esq., and Mr. Bright, of Toronto, who, with others, have a Shooting lease from the Dept. for part of Walpole Island & its marshes, these gentlemen informed me that American fishermen cast their nets near the northern mouth of the streams running through Walpole Island. They do not violate the law exactly by throwing their nets across the streams, but they have them sufficiently far out on each side of the mouth of the streams to impede effectively the passage of the fish up the streams. These gentlemen stated that the streams are ["therefore in consequence" stroked out] consequently almost completely depleted of fish & that the Indians are suffering as a consequence. I feel convinced that I have only to bring this matter under your notice to cause you to have the

proper remedy applied." There was no reply from the deputy minister of Fisheries to this letter. Vankoughnet to Tilton, RG 10, vol. 2118, file 22610, part 1, Indian Affairs, Library and Archives Canada, Ottawa, ON (LAC).

18 Louise Erdrich, *The Last Report on the Miracles at Little No Horse* (New York: HarperCollins, 2001), 294.

19 Elias, Journals, 26 May 1888–3 December 1913. Shawanaga First Nation Archives and Resources.

20 McKelvey to J. D. McLean, 12 November 1901, RG 10, C-15,861, vol. 6975, file 471, Indian Affairs, LAC. I am grateful to Rick Fehr, PhD candidate in the Faculty of Environmental Studies at York University, who discovered this letter and shared it with me.

21 Elias, "Pocket Journal Cobourg 1887."

22 Dean M. Jacobs, "Land Claims Research Paper Walpole Island Reserve," unpublished paper for the Association of Iroquois and Allied Indians (1976), 156–62.

## Chapter 7: "Shifting Boundaries and the Baldoon Mysteries," by Lisa Philips and Allan K. McDougall

The authors wish to thank SSHRC for its support of our grant documenting the impact of the imposition of the USA–British border in the period 1763–1830.

1 A very brief rendition of the story is located in *The Canadian Encyclopedia Online*, Junior version, under the entry "Folktales," at <www.thecanadianencyclopedia.com> (accessed 7 September 2007).

2 For a discussion of the reasons for the loss of this potential refuge for First Nations from across the old Northwest, see Lisa Philips Valentine and Allan K. McDougall, "Imposing the Border: The Detroit River from 1786 to 1807," *Journal of Borderland Studies* 19, no. 1 (2004): 13–22.

3 This area is labelled the "Shawanees Township" by Smith and Stout on their 1813 map, Record 4827, Map Collection, Library and Archives Canada, Ottawa, ON (LAC).

4 Peter Jones (Kahkewaquonaby), *History of the Ojebway Indians* (London: Houlston and Wright, 1861), 158.

5 Jones, *History*, 158.

6 Jones, *History*, 159.

7 Jones, *History*, 159.

8 "[Ruth] Benedict argued that symbolic form 'reflected' the 'context of situation.' ... In her discussion of folklore, she wrote: 'Peoples' folk tales ... are their autobiography and the clearest mirror on their life.... Behavior and attitudes became more articulate in folklore than in any other cultural trait, and folklore then tends to crystallize and perpetuate the forms of culture that it has made articulate.'" Benedict from entry on "Folklore" in *Encyclopedia of Social Sciences*, 6:291, quoted in Hugh Dalziel Duncan, *Symbols and Social Theory* (New York: Oxford University Press, 1969), 169. Dell Hymes argues that "in cultures where the telling of stories was a major way of understanding, explaining and dealing with experience, experience was put into the form of personal or culturally shared narrative ... instead of a chaos of events, experience was organized into sometimes subtle patterns," in *Ethnography, Linguistics, Narrative Inequality* (London: Taylor and Francis, 1996), 136. See Bronislaw Malinowski, *Malinowski and the Work of Myth* (Princeton, NJ: Princeton University Press,

1992); Richard Bauman, *Verbal Art as Performance* (Prospect Heights, IL: Waveland Press, 1984); and Ruth Benedict, *Zuni Mythology* (New York: AMS Press, 1969).

9  Erving Goffman, *Frame Analysis: An Essay on the Organization of Experience* (New York: Harper and Row, 1974); and Lisa Philips Valentine, *Making It Their Own: Severn Ojibwe Communicative Practices* (Toronto: University of Toronto Press, 1995).

10  Jones, *History*, 156.

11  Jones, *History*, 157.

12  Jones, *History*, 157.

13  Jones, *History*, 157.

14  Neil T. McDonald, *The Belledoon Mysteries: An O'er True Story* (1871, 1895; reprint, Wallaceburg, ON: Wallaceburg News Book and Job Print, 1905), 14.

15  McDonald, *Belledoon Mysteries*, 21.

16  McDonald, *Belledoon Mysteries*, 15.

17  William Labov and J. Waletzky, "Narrative Analysis," in *Essays on the Verbal and Visual Arts*, ed. J. Helm (Seattle: University of Washington Press, 1967), 12–44; and William Labov, "Transformation of Experience in Narrative Syntax," in *Language in the Inner City*, ed. William Labov (Philadelphia: University of Pennsylvania Press, 1972), 354–96.

18  McDonald, *Belledoon Mysteries*, 2.

19  McDonald, *Belledoon Mysteries*, 3, 15.

20  This was not Dr. Troyer, who was a Catholic priest from Longwoods in McDonald's version of the story.

21  McDonald, *Belledoon Mysteries*, 17.

22  McDonald, *Belledoon Mysteries*, 17.

23  McDonald, *Belledoon Mysteries*, 20.

24  "Poor Mr. Barker's exorcisms had no apparent effect on the spirits, but they succeeded in rousing the ire of the British authorities, who since they gave up the amiable practice of burning old women by act of parliament have had the strongest objection to the luxury of witchcraft being indulged in by the people." McDonald, *Belledoon Mysteries*, 14; Anonymous, *The Baldoon Mystery*.

25  See Rick Fehr, "The Baldoon Settlement—Re-Thinking Sustainability," chap. 8 in this volume.

26  McDonald, *Belledoon Mysteries*, 15.

27  McDonald, *Belledoon Mysteries*, 21. McDonald's appendix, comprising twenty-eight statements by witnesses or relatives of witnesses, presented another clue to his presumptions about his audience. While there is no indication whether McDonald conducted the interviews that comprised the appendix, they all followed a similar format. These statements began with a metanarrative frame that included the speaker or author's entitlement to tell the story, whether through first-hand knowledge or having heard the story or stories from close relatives. These initial statements typically were followed by a recount of events, which varied greatly in their elaboration from one speaker to the next, and closed with either a testimonial about the character of John T. McDonald or a testimonial about the character of the person from whom the speaker/author received his or her knowledge.

28  ReReNahSewa, in McDonald, *Belledoon Mysteries*, 24.

29  McDonald, *Belledoon Mysteries*, 25.

30  McDonald, *Belledoon Mysteries*, 24.

31 "So, though almost worn to death with their persecutions the McDonalds were doomed at last to err towards the end of their afflictions." McDonald, *Belledoon Mysteries*, 15.

32 McDonald, *Belledoon Mysteries*, 7.

33 McDonald, *Belledoon Mysteries*, 14.

34 By 1905, significant components of the author's social mosaic were included in the text: "French settlers" (1), "old English and Scottish families" (1), "European settlers" (2), and "wandering Hugenots" (2). In addition to state or national affiliation, old world religious categories were used to show the range of religious affiliations attesting to the phenomenon. Examples include a Methodist class leader (7), Catholic friends (14), and members of the Baldoon community who were described as strict Baptists (3).

35 LeRoy Hooker, *Baldoon* (Toronto: Poole Publishing, 1900), 119–20.

36 Hooker, *Baldoon*, 123–24.

37 Hooker, *Baldoon*, 141.

38 A sample of this eye-dialect, or written accent, illustrates how Mrs. M'Garriger's Scottish roots were so clearly indexed: "Yill belive it noo, Tom, that we're bein' pairsecutit in thes hoose frae the bottomless pit; for the hand's that tippit the muckle pot wes no veessible tae mortal een; an' they'll be tae be weel acquent wi' fire, tae reach intil't like yon, an' tak' plenty time tae ward their meeschief." Hooker, *Baldoon*, 139.

39 Hooker, *Baldoon*, 142.

40 Hooker, *Baldoon*, 144.

41 Hooker, *Baldoon*, 144–45; italics added.

42 Victor Lauriston, *Romantic Kent: More Than Three Centuries of History, 1626–1952* (Chatham: Shepherd Printing, 1952), 11.

43 Laurison, *Romantic Kent*, 20; italics added.

44 Laurison, *Romantic Kent*, 20; italics added.

45 Laurison, *Romantic Kent*, 19; italics added.

46 Laurison, *Romantic Kent*, 20.

47 Laurison, *Romantic Kent*, 470.

48 Laurison, *Romantic Kent*, 470.

49 Laurison, *Romantic Kent*, 470; italics added.

50 Laurison, *Romantic Kent*, 470.

51 John Columbo, "The Baldoon Mystery," in *Ghost Stories of Ontario* (Toronto: Hounslow Press, 1996), 25–27; and Sue Darroch, Poltergeist of Baldoon," 2005, *Ontario Ghosts and Hauntings Research Society*, <http://www.torontoghosts.org/chathamkent/baldoon1.htm> (cited 8 April 2007).

52 "Mamagwasewug" is the plural form of "Mamagwasi." The latter, incidentally, is a variant of "maamagwaasi," from the 1976 play *Baldoon*, by James Reaney and C. H. Gervais.

53 Jones, *History*, 159; Barry Milliken, in collaboration with Rachel Shawkence, *Annie Rachel: Mshkikiikwe; Stories from an Elder of the Kettle and Stony Point First Nation* (London: Centre for Research and Teaching of Canadian Native Languages, 1996), 103.

54 For those who have had the privilege to live in Algonquian communities, the spontaneous fires are a very familiar response to disrespectful displays towards powerful others. The types of "pranks" played on the McDonalds are typical of those performed by shaman. A. Irving Hallowell, *Role of Conjuring in Saulteaux Society* (Philadelphia: University of Pennsylvania Press, 1942).

## Chapter 8: "The Baldoon Settlement: Rethinking Sustainability," by Rick Fehr

1 Dean Jacobs, "Bkejwanong—'The Place Where the Waters Divide': A Perspective on Earth, Water, Air and Fire," in *Earth, Water, Air and Fire: Studies in Canadian Ethnohistory*, ed. David T. McNab (Waterloo: Wilfrid Laurier University Press, 1998), 9.
2 Simon Schama, *Landscape and Memory* (New York: Random House, 1996), 10.
3 David McNab, *Circles of Time: Aboriginal Land Rights and Resistance in Ontario* (Waterloo: Wilfrid Laurier University Press, 1999), 3.
4 *Legend and Memory: Ontario's First Nations*, prod. David Hawkins and Daniel Kitts (TV Ontario, 2002).
5 Joe Sheridan and Dan Roronhiake:wen Longboat, "The Haudenosaunee Imagination and Ecology of the Sacred," *Space and Culture* 9, no. 4 (2006): 369.
6 René Descartes, *A Discourse on Method* (1637), Project Gutenberg, <http://www.gutenberg.org/dirs/etext93/dcart10.txt> (accessed 25 August 2006).
7 McDonald's account of his family's encounter with the supernatural has become a campfire story told throughout the region. See Neil T. McDonald, *The Belledoon Mysteries: An O'er True Story* (1871, 1895; reprint, Wallaceburg: Wallaceburg News Book and Job Print, 1905).
8 McDonald, *Belledoon Mysteries*, 3.
9 Jonathan Bate, *The Song of the Earth* (London, UK: Pan Macmillan, 2000), 35.
10 Linda Tuhiwai Smith, *Decolonizing Methodologies: Research and Indigenous Peoples* (New York: Zed Books, 1999), 23.
11 Lucille H. Campey, *The Silver Chief: Lord Selkirk and the Scottish Pioneers of Belfast, Baldoon and Red River* (Toronto: Natural Heritage Books, 2003), 52.
12 David McNab, Bruce Hodgins, and Dale Standen offer a historical perspective on the importance of the canoe in securing the Lake St. Clair region for the Anishinaabe, and subsequently how land, not the water, played a pivotal role in the negotiating of treaties to secure the region for Britain. See McNab, Hodgins, and Standen, "'Black with Canoes': Aboriginal Resistance and the Canoe: Diplomacy, Trade and Warfare in the Meeting Grounds of Northeastern North America, 1600–1821," in *Technology, Disease and Colonial Conquests, Sixteenth to Eighteenth Centuries: Essays Reappraising the Guns and Germs Theories*, ed. George Raudzens (Brill International: Leiden, The Netherlands, 2001), 254–55.
13 A. E. D. MacKenzie, *Baldoon, Lord Selkirk in Upper Canada* (London, ON: Phelps Publishing, 1978), 20–27.
14 Campey, *Silver Chief*, 53.
15 MacKenzie, *Baldoon*, 55.
16 MacKenzie, *Baldoon*, 41.
17 MacKenzie, *Baldoon*, 45.
18 MacKenzie, *Baldoon*, 10.
19 MacKenzie, *Baldoon*, 47.
20 MacKenzie, *Baldoon*, 27.
21 L. T. Smith, *Decolonizing Methodologies*, 23.
22 Frederick Turner, *Beyond Geography: The Western Spirit Against the Wilderness* (New York: Viking Press, 1980), 118.
23 James Lloyd Clark, The Baldoon Settlement Lands: The Effects of Changing Drainage technology, 1804 B 1967 (MA thesis, University of Western Ontario, 1970), 4.

24 David McNab, "Borders of Water and Fire: Islands as Sacred Places and as Meeting Grounds," in *Aboriginal Cultural Landscapes*, ed. Jill Oakes et al. (Winnipeg: Aboriginal Issues Press, 2004), 36–38.

25 McNab, *Circles of Time*, 154–56; and McNab, "Borders of Water and Fire," 9–10.

26 McNab, "Borders of Water and Fire," 9.

27 McNab, "Borders of Water and Fire," 10.

28 Identified as Wittaness in written treaty documents at the Nin.Da.Waab.Jig Heritage Centre, Walpole Island First Nation.

29 McNab, *Circles of Time*, 156.

30 Raymond Williams, *The Country and the City* (New York: Oxford University Press, 1973), 12.

31 MacKenzie, *Baldoon*, 28.

32 Shawn Wilson defines ontological as "belief in reality," epistemological as "how one thinks," and axiological as "a set of morals or a set of ethics." Shawn Wilson, "What Is an Indigenous Research Methodology?" *Canadian Journal of Native Education* 25, no. 2 (2001): 175.

33 Jace Weaver, "Indigenousness and Indigeneity," in *A Companion to Postcolonial Studies: An Historical Introduction*, ed. Henry Schwarz and Sangeeta Ray (Malden, MA: Blackwell Publishing, 2004), 230.

34 Louise Erdrich, *Books and Islands in Ojibwe Country* (Washington, DC: National Geographic, 2003), 34.

35 Erdrich, *Books and Islands*, 34.

36 Sheridan and Longboat, "Haudenosaunee Imagination," 369.

37 Dean Jacobs, "'We have but our hearts and the traditions of our old men': Understanding the Traditions and History of Bkejwanong," in *Gin Das Winan: Documenting Aboriginal History in Ontario*, ed. Dale Standen and David McNab (Toronto: Champlain Society, 1996), 4.

38 Theresa S. Smith, *The Island of the Anishinaabeg: Thunderers and Water Monsters in the Traditional Ojibwe Life-World* (Moscow, ID: University of Idaho Press, 1995), 19.

39 Bkejwanong Natural Heritage Program, *E-Niizaanag Wii-Ngoshkaag Maampii Bkejwanong—Species at Risk on the Walpole Island First Nation* (Nin.Da.Waabe.Jig, 2006), 26.

40 Bkejwanong Natural Heritage Program, *E-Niizaanag Wii-Ngoshkaag*, 13.

41 Vine Deloria, *For This Land: Writings on Religion in America* (New York: Routledge, 1998), 247.

42 Weaver, "Indigeousness and Indigeneity," 230; Bill Ashcroft, Gareth Griffiths, and Helen Tiffin, *The Empire Writes Back: Theory and Practice in Post-Colonial Literatures* (New York: Routledge, 1989), 25.

43 Weaver, "Indigeousness and Indigeneity," 230; Ashcroft, Griffiths, and Tiffin, *The Empire Writes Back*, 25.

44 Turner, *Beyond Geography*, 32.

45 Turner, *Beyond Geography*, 41.

46 Lynn White Jr., "The Historical Roots of Our Ecological Crisis," *Science* 155 (1967), http://www.uvm.edu/~gflomenh/ENV-NGO-PA395/articles/Lynn-White.pdf (accessed 6 November 2007).

47 Joe Sheridan, "The Rains Wept Time in the Badlands," *Space and Culture* 5, no. 2 (2002): 125.

48 Clark, *Baldoon Settlement Lands*.

49 Jacobs, "We have but our hearts," 12.

50 Dominque Temple, "The Policy of the 'Severed Flower,'" *INTERculture* 98 (1988): 11, 14–15.

51 Wendall Berry, *The Unsettling of America: Culture and Agriculture* (San Francisco: Sierra Club, 1977), 4.

52 Donna Haraway, *Simians, Cyborgs and Women: The Reinvention of Nature* (New York: Routledge, 1991), 191.

53 Lawrence Gross, "*Bimaadiziwin*, or the 'Good Life,' as a Unifying Concept of Anishinaabe Religion," *American Indian Culture and Research Journal* 26, no. 1 (2002): 19.

54 Gross, "*Bimaadiziwin*," 16.

55 Robert M. Vanwynsberghe, *AlterNatives: Community, Identity and Environmental Justice on Walpole Island* (Boston: Pearson Education, 2002), 21.

56 Jacobs, "We have but our hearts," 11–12.

57 John Livingstone defines the "other than human" community (animal, plant, biotic, aquatic, and terrestrial) as possessing a level of awareness that has been entirely excluded from Western ontology, see John Livingstone, *Rogue Primate: An Exploration of Human Domestication* (Toronto: Key Porter, 1994), 110–18.

58 Jacobs, "Bkejwanong," 9.

59 White, "The Historical Roots."

60 Willis Jenkins, "Biodiversity and Salvation: Thomistic Roots for Environmental Ethics," *Journal of Religion* 83, no. 3 (2003): 401.

61 Jenkins, "Biodiversity and Salvation," 402.

62 Jenkins, "Biodiversity and Salvation," 403.

63 Jenkins, "Biodiversity and Salvation," 414.

## Chapter 9: "Nativism's Bastard: Neolin, Tenskwatawa, and the Anishinabeg Methodist Movement," by Catherine Murton Stoehr

The author wishes to thank the reviewers for their clear and useful corrections, Karl Hele for creating the opportunity to present and publish this paper, and James Murton for his insightful comments and suggestions.

1 Jeremy Adelman and Stephen Aron, "From Borderlands to Borders: Empires, Nation-States, and the Peoples in Between in North American History," *American Historical Review* 104, no. 3 (1999): 816.

2 Works on Anishinabe Methodism have been written from the time of the movement in the mid-nineteenth century until the present. Contemporary chroniclers of the movement all wrote as Methodist believers and so had an ideological motivation to ignore the similarities between the movement and what they perceived to be the much more radical movement of Nativism. See Peter Jacobs, *Journal of the Reverend Peter Jacobs, Indian Wesleyan Missionary from Rice Lake to the Hudson's Bay Territory and Returning; Commencing May, 1852; With a Brief Account of His Life and a Short History of the Wesleyan Mission in that Country* (New York: Published for the Author, 1857); George Copway, *The Traditional History and Characteristic Sketches of the Ojibway Nation* (London: Charles Gilpin, 1850); Peter Jones, *History of the Ojebway Indians; With Especial Reference to Their Conversion to Christianity* (London: A. W. Bennett, 1861); and John Carroll, *Case and His Contemporaries; or, The Canadian Itinerants' Memorial; Con-*

stituting a Biographical History of Methodism in Canada from Its Introduction into the Province, till the Death of the Rev. Wm. Case in 1855 (Toronto: Samuel Rose, 1867).

A second group of authors wrote about the Anishinabe Methodist movement from the perspective of Methodist church history and did not explore its connection to the Nativist movements. See John Webster Grant, *Moon of Wintertime: Missionaries and the Indians of Canada in Encounter since 1534* (Toronto: University of Toronto Press, 1984); and Neil Semple, *The Lord's Dominion: The History of Canadian Methodism* (Montreal: McGill-Queen's University Press, 1996).

A third group contrasts Anishinabe Methodism with earlier Anishinabe practices but fails to identify how those practices had been affected by nativism. See Elizabeth Graham, *Medicine Man to Missionary: Missionaries as Agents of Change among the Indians of Southern Ontario, 1784–1867* (Toronto: Peter Martin, 1975); Hope MacLean, "The Hidden Agenda: Methodist Attitudes to the Ojibwa and the Development of Indian Schooling in Upper Canada, 1821–1860" (MA thesis, University of Toronto, 1978); Christopher Vecsey, *Traditional Ojibwa Religion and Its Historical Changes* (Philadelphia: American Philosophical Society, 1983); Donald B. Smith, *Sacred Feathers: The Reverend Peter Jones (Kahkewaquonaby) and the Mississauga Indians* (Toronto: University of Toronto Press, 1987); and Michael Ripmeester and Brian Osborne, "It Is Scarcely to Be Believed": The Mississauga Indians and the Grape Island Mission, 1826–1836," *Canadian Geographer* 39, no. 2 (1995): 157–68.

3  In this essay, the term "Nativist" is used in the anthropological sense to indicate a revivalist, anti-colonial cultural movement rather than a general attitude of chauvinism toward an outside group; see Anthony F. C. Wallace, "Nativism and Revivalism," in *International Encyclopedia of the Social Sciences*, ed. David L. Sills (New York: Macmillan Company and Free Press, 1968), 11:75–79.

4  Gregory Evans Dowd, *A Spirited Resistance: The North American Indian Struggle for Unity, 1745–1815* (Baltimore: Johns Hopkins University Press, 1992), xix.

5  James Clifton describes the Pottawattamie, Ottawa, and Ojibwa migrating together in *A Place of Refuge for All Time: Migration of the American Potawatomi into Upper Canada, 1830 to 1850* (Ottawa: National Museums of Canada, 1975), 8.

6  Nineteenth-century historian William Whipple Warren observed that the three groups known as the Ottawa, Pottawattamie, and Ojibwa nations were thought of as a single group until approximately 1585. Warren, *History of the Ojibway People* (1885; reprint, St. Paul: Minnesota Historical Society Press, 1984), 81, 82.

7  Dowd, *A Spirited Resistance*, 106.

8  Cole Harris, "How Did Colonialism Dispossess? Comments from an Edge of Empire," *Annals of the Association of American Geographers* 94, no. 1 (2004): 166.

9  Harris, "How Did Colonialism Dispossess?" 179.

10  Peter S. Schmalz, *The Ojibwa of Southern Ontario* (Toronto: University of Toronto Press, 1991), 111–19.

11  Donald B. Smith, "The Dispossession of the Mississauga Indians: A Missing Chapter in the Early History of Upper Canada," *Ontario History* 73, no. 2 (1981): 76–78; and Peter Schmalz, *Ojibwa*, 90–94.

12  Smith, "The Dispossession of the Mississauga," 68; Schmalz, *Ojibwa*, 89–98, 105–10; and Harris, "How Did Colonialism Dispossess?" 179.

13  See Dowd's comparison of "accomadationist" leaders Joseph Brant and Alexander McGillivray to the Nativist leaders Pontiac and Tecumseh. Dowd also observes that the "two traditions [became] mutually tolerant during the Revolution." Dowd, *A Spirited Resistance*, 91, 90–115.

14  Alfred A. Cave, "The Delaware Prophet Neolin: A Reappraisal," *Ethnohistory* 46, no. 2 (1999): 268.

15  Cave, "The Delaware Prophet Neolin," 268.

16  Cave, "The Delaware Prophet Neolin," 269.

17  Delawares, who left their home east of the Allegheny Mountains to escape settler expansion and moved to the Ohio Valley in 1766, are more correctly known as the Lenape.

18  Historians have often credited the Ottawa war leader Pontiac with organizing the former French allies into the new pan-Native alliance, but some now believe that his position as an Ottawa leader allowed him to take the lead in a spontaneous development between leaders in various communities. The Ottawas were middlemen in the fur trade, and, as an Ottawa chief, Pontiac had deep relationships with many surrounding communities. For a concise analysis of the historiographic debate, see Gregory Evans Dowd, *War under Heaven: Pontiac, the Indian Nations, and the British Empire* (Baltimore: Johns Hopkins University Press, 2002), 5–10.

19  Cave, "The Delaware Prophet Neolin," 272.

20  From *Journals of Charles Beatty*, quoted in Gregory Dowd, *A Spirited Resistance*, 33.

21  Dowd, *A Spirited Resistance*, 33.

22  Donald B. Smith, "Who Are the Mississauga?" *Ontario History* 67, no. 4 (1975); and Schmalz, *Ojibwa*, 65.

23  Schmalz, *Ojibwa*, 72.

24  For Wabbicommicot's relationship with Sir William Johnson, see Jane E. Graham, "Wabbicomicot, 1780–1820," in *Dictionary of Canadian Biography (DCB)*, vol. 3, *1741–1770* (Toronto: University of Toronto Press, 1974), 651–52.

25  Schmalz, *Ojibwa*, 72.

26  Schmalz, *Ojibwa*, 72.

27  Schmalz, *Ojibwa*, 73.

28  Schmalz, *Ojibwa*, 72.

29  Schmalz, *Ojibwa*, 80.

30  Schmalz, *Ojibwa*, 77.

31  In a recent article, Gregory Dowd argues that in the eighteenth century First Nations people were very aware of, and concerned about, their status with respect to the British. Gregory Evans Dowd, "'We Subdue the Globe'—'We Are Not Your Slaves'—Imperial Mastery, Indigenous Resistance, and American Indian Status, 1760–1795," *GSC [Global Security and Cooperation] Quarterly* 14 (2005), <http://programs.ssrc.org/gsc/publications/quarterly14/dowd.pdf> (accessed 7 June 2007).

32  Schmalz, *Ojibwa*, 80–84.

33  Schmalz, *Ojibwa*, 100.

34  Dowd, *A Spirited Resistance*, 95.

35  Smith, *Sacred Feathers*, 26.

36  Dowd, *A Spirited Resistance*, xxii.

37  Dowd, *A Spirited Resistance*, 126.

38 David R. Edmunds, *The Shawnee Prophet* (Lincoln: University of Nebraska Press, 1983), 34–38.

39 Edmunds, *Shawnee Prophet*, 27, 38.

40 John Tanner relayed an account of a visit of one of the prophet's messengers and the effect that it had on his community. Benjamin Drake, *Life of Tecumseh, and of His Brother the Prophet: With a Historical Sketch of the Shawanoe Indians* (Cincinnati: E. Morgan, 1841), 103.

41 Edmunds, *Shawnee Prophet*, 40.

42 Richard White, *The Middle Ground: Indians, Empires, and Republics in the Great Lakes Region, 1650–1815* (New York: Cambridge University Press, 1991), 510.

43 Drake, *Life of Tecumseh*, 105.

44 R. David Edmunds, *Tecumseh and the Quest for Indian Leadership* (Toronto: Little, Brown, 1984), 119.

45 A British man at Amherstburg reported on the tensions aroused by the prophet, noting that he [Elliot] was unsure of his information, "Elliot" observed that the "Ottawas and Chippewas are much displeased with him [Tenskwatawa]" and that some of the Shawnees at Amherstburg had been killed and scalped. "Letter from Elliot" re: Shawnee Prophet, 19 May 1809. Records of the Governor General and Lieutenant Governor, Upper Canada, Civil Control, 1796–1816, 1841–1843, RG 10, A1, Indian Affairs, Library and Archives Canada, Ottawa, ON.

46 Peter Jones, "To the Editor," *Christian Guardian* [Toronto], 1 August 1832.

47 New Revised Standard Version.

48 John Sunday, "An Indian Chief's Conversion," *Christian Guardian*, 22 October 1834.

49 Benjamin Slight, *Indian Researches, or Facts Concerning the North American Indians; Including Notices of their Present State of Improvement, in their Social, Civil, and Religious Condition; with Hints for their Future Advancement* (Montreal: Printed for the Author, by J. E. L. Miller, 1844), 87.

50 Adelman and Aron, "From Borderlands to Borders," 816.

## Chapter 10: "Borders Within: Anthropology and the Six Nations of the Grand River," by Michelle A. Hamilton

1 Postcard, File 1898–June 1900, MU 5422, F 1139, Ontario Historical Society Papers, Archives of Ontario (AO), Toronto, ON; Brant-Sero to Boyle, 26 October 1899, Box 1, David Boyle Correspondence, Royal Ontario Museum, Toronto, ON (ROM); Penny Petrone, ed., *First Peoples, First Voices* (Toronto: University of Toronto Press, 1983), 138; and "Germans Hear Mohawk Yell," *New York Times*, 6 May 1901.

2 For informants and anthropologists seen as "cultural brokers," those bicultural individuals who skilfully negotiated between Native and non-Native worlds, see Frances E. Karttunen, *Between Worlds: Interpreters, Guides, and Survivors* (New Brunswick: Rutgers University Press, 1994), 170–240; Dorothy R. Parker, "D'Arcy McNickle: Living a Broker's Life," in *Between Indian and White Worlds: The Cultural Broker*, ed. Margaret Connell Szasz (Norman: University of Oklahoma Press, 1994), 240–54; Peter Iverson, "Speaking Their Language: Robert W. Young and the Navajos, in *Between Indian and White Worlds*, 255–72; Beatrice Medicine, "Ella C. Deloria: The Emic Voice," in *Learning to Be an*

*Anthropologist and Remaining "Native,"* ed. Beatrice Medicine and Sue-Ellen Jacobs (Urbana: University of Illinois Press, 2001), 269–88. For other individuals who engaged in a variety of ways with anthropology, see, for example, Margot Liberty, ed., *American Indian Intellectuals of the Nineteenth and Early Twentieth Centuries* (Lincoln: University of Nebraska Press, 2002); Jeanne Cannizzo, "George Hunt and the Invention of Kwakiutl Culture," *Canadian Review of Sociology and Anthropology* 20, no. 1 (1983): 44–58; James A. Clifton, ed., *Being and Becoming Indian: Biographical Sketches of North American Frontiers* (Chicago: Dorsey Press, 1989); Douglas Cole, *Captured Heritage: The Scramble for Northwest Coast Artifacts* (Seattle: University of Washington Press, 1985); Ira Jacknis, *The Storage Box of Tradition: Museums, Anthropologists and Kwakiutl Art, 1881–1981* (Washington, DC: Smithsonian Institution Press, 2002); Sally Weaver, "Seth Newhouse and the Grand River Confederacy at Mid-Nineteenth Century," in *Extending the Rafters: Interdisciplinary Approaches to Iroquoian Studies,* ed. Michael K. Foster, Jack Campisi, and Marianne Mithun (Albany: State University of New York Press, 1984), 165–82; Trudy Nicks, "Dr. Oronhyatekha's History Lessons: Reading Museum Collections as Texts," in *Reading Beyond Words: Contexts for Native History,* ed. Jennifer S. H. Brown and Elizabeth Vibert (Peterborough: Broadview Press, 2003), 459–90; Joy Porter, *To Be Indian: The Life of Iroquois-Seneca Arthur Caswell Parker* (Norman: University of Oklahoma Press, 2001); Joan Mark, "Francis La Flesche: The American Indian as Anthropologist," *Isis* 73, no. 4 (1982): 497–510; Charles Briggs and Richard Bauman, "The Foundation of All Future Researches: Franz Boas, George Hunt, Native American Texts, and the Construction of Modernity," *American Quarterly* 51, no. 3 (1999): 479–528; and Wendy Wickwire, "We Shall Drink from the Stream and So Shall You: James A. Teit and Native Resistance in British Columbia, 1908–22," *Canadian Historical Review* 79, no. 2 (1998): 199–236.

3  The study of the involvement of these individuals in anthropology is brief. Gerald Killan, *David Boyle: From Artisan to Archaeologist* (Toronto: University of Toronto Press, 1983), 183, noted some of those who helped Boyle. For the involvement of the Confederacy Council in the Ontario Historical Society (OHS), see Gerald Killan, *Preserving Ontario's Heritage: A History of the Ontario Historical Society* (Ottawa: Love Print Service, 1967), 42–44. For the Johnson sisters, see Veronica Strong-Boag and Carole Gerson, *Paddling Her Own Canoe: The Times and Texts of E. Pauline Johnson Tekahionwake* (Toronto: University of Toronto Press, 2000), 41, 54–57. For Brant-Sero, see Penny Petrone, ed., *First People, First Voices,* 125, 138; Penny S. Petrone, "John Ojijatekah Brant-Sero," in *Dictionary of Canadian Biography (DCB),* vol. 14, *1911–1920* (Toronto: University of Toronto Press, 1998), 137–39; Karl Markus Kreis, "John O. Brant-Sero's Adventures in Europe," *European Review of Native American Studies* 15, no. 2 (2001): 27–30; and Cecilia Morgan, "A Wigwam to Westminster: Performing Mohawk Identity in Imperial Britain, 1890s–1990s," *Gender and History* 15, no. 2 (2003): 319–41.

4  For an extensive discussion of their childhood, see Sheila M. F. Johnston, *Buckskin and Broadcloth: A Celebration of E. Pauline Johnson—Tekahionwake, 1861–1913* (Toronto: Natural Heritage/Natural History, 1997); Betty Kellar, *Pauline: A Biography of Pauline Johnson* (Vancouver: Douglas and McIntyre, 1981), and *Pauline Johnson: First Aboriginal Voice of Canada* (Montreal: XYZ Publishing, 1999); Strong-Boag and Gerson, *Paddling Her Own Canoe;* and Charlotte Gray,

*Flint and Feather: The Life and Times of E. Pauline Johnson*, Tekahionwake (Toronto: HarperFlamingo Canada, 2002).

5  Ontario, Legislative Assembly, *Annual Archaeological Report Being Part of Appendix to the Report of the Minister of Education, Ontario, 1896–97* (Toronto, 1897), 14; and Ontario, Legislative Assembly, *Annual Archaeological Report; Being Part of Appendix to the Report of the Minister of Education, Ontario, 1897–98* (Toronto: 1898), 5.

6  Hale to Johnson, July 1896, File 6, Box 1, E. Pauline Johnson Papers, William Ready Division of Archives and Research Collections, McMaster University, Hamilton, ON.

7  Johnson to Boyle, 13 July 1896, File 19, Box 2, David Boyle Papers, ROM.

8  Johnson to Boyle, 4 August 1897, Box 1, David Boyle Correspondence, ROM.

9  Johnson to Boyle, 13 July 1896, File 19, Box 2, Boyle Papers, ROM.

10  Johnson to Seton, 2 August 1905, vol. 16, MG 29, Ernest Thompson Seton Papers, Library and Archives Canada, Ottawa, ON (LAC).

11  Whale to Currelly, 9 April 1943, Reginald W. Whale Papers, ROM.

12  Horatio Hale, *Chief George H. M. Johnson, Onwanonsyshon: His Life and Work among the Six Nations* (New York: A. S. Barnes, 1885), 134–35; William N. Fenton, *The False Faces of the Iroquois* (Norman: University of Oklahoma Press, 1987), 464; E. H. C. Johnson, Normal School Accession Files, ROM; E. Pauline Johnson, "The Delaware Idol," in *The Shagganappi* (Toronto: Ryerson Press, 1913), 223–35; and E. Pauline Johnson to Boyle, 4 August 1897, Box 1, Boyle Correspondence, ROM.

13  Evelyn Johnson, "Chiefswood," chap. 2, p. 4, MS 4, MU 4642, Miscellaneous Indian Manuscripts, AO.

14  Gray, Flint and Feather, 175; and Johnson to Heye, 23 March 1906, George Gustav Heye Correspondence, National Museum of the American Indian (NMAI), Smithsonian Institution, Washington, DC.

15  Hess to Boyle, 17 October 1904, file 3, box 2, Boyle Papers, ROM; Hess to Boyle, 25 October 1904 and 9 January 1905, box 2, Boyle Correspondence, ROM; Brant-Sero to Carnochan, 7 December 1899, Niagara Historical Society Papers, Niagara Historical Museum, Niagara-on-the-Lake; Ontario, Legislative Assembly, *Annual Archaeological Report Being Part of Appendix to the Report of the Minister of Education, Ontario, 1898* (Toronto: 1898), 157–59, and *Annual Archaeological Report; Being Part of Appendix to the Report of the Minister of Education, Ontario, 1899* (Toronto: 1900), 28–29.

16  For an analysis of the significance, purpose, and treatment of False Face masks, and examples of the consequences of the neglect or ridicule of them, see Fenton, *False Faces*.

17  Kellar, *Pauline: A Biography; Kellar, Pauline Johnson: First Aboriginal Voice of Canada*; Strong-Boag and Gerson, *Paddling Her Own Canoe*; Gray, *Flint and Feather*.

18  Johnson to Boyle, 4 August 1897, box 1, Boyle Correspondence, ROM.

19  Johnson to Seton, 2 August 1905, vol. 16, MG 29, Seton Papers, LAC.

20  Johnson to Heye, 17 March 1906, 20 March 1906, 23 March 1906, 31 March 1906, 4 April 1906, and 10 April 1906, George Heye Correspondence, NMAI; Contract entered into this Twenty-sixth day of March, Nineteen Hundred and Six, between Miss E. Pauline Johnson, of Hamilton, Ontario, and Mr. George G. Heye, of New York City, New York, George Heye Correspondence. I am indebted to Paul Williams, Haudenosaunee Standing Committee on Burial Rules and Regulations, for these references.

21 Johnson to Lighthall, 7 April 1907, file 19, box 1, MS 216, William Douw Lighthall Papers, Rare Book Room, McGill University, Montreal, QC.

22 Strong-Boag and Gerson, *Paddling Her Own Canoe*, 22.

23 Fenton, *False Faces*, 178.

24 Hale, *Chief George H. M. Johnson, Onwanonsyshon*, 134–35; and Johnson, "The Delaware Idol," 228, 231.

25 E. Pauline Johnson, "Hoolool of the Totem Poles," in *E. Pauline Johnson Tekahion-wake: Collected Poems and Selected Prose*, ed. Carole Gerson and Veronica Strong-Boag (Toronto: University of Toronto Press, 2002), 257–60; and Strong-Boag and Gerson, *Paddling Her Own Canoe*, 40, 41.

26 Johnson to Seton, 2 August 1905, vol. 16, MG 29, Seton Papers, LAC.

27 Johnson to Boyle, 20 August 1906, E. H. C. Normal School Accession Files, ROM.

28 "Miss Johnson's Relics for Brantford Museum," *Globe* [Toronto], 12 May 1913; "Relics of Indian Poet Offered to Brantford," *Globe*, 16 May 1924; Whale to Currelly, 9 April 1943, Reginald W. Whale Papers, ROM.

29 Johnson to Currelly, 16 January 1916, 30 January 1916, and 10 October 1922, Charles Trick Currelly Correspondence, ROM. I am indebted to Paul Williams, Haudenosaunee Standing Committee on Burial Rules and Regulations, for these references.

30 For the history of these eleven belts, see William N. Fenton, "Return of Eleven Wampum Belts to the Six Nations Iroquois Confederacy on Grand River, Canada," *Ethnohistory* 36, no. 4 (1989): 392–410; and Elisabeth Tooker, "A Note on the Return of Eleven Wampum Belts to the Six Nations Iroquois Confederacy on Grand River, Canada," *Ethnohistory* 45, no. 2 (1998): 219–36.

31 E. H. C. Johnson, "Chief John Smoke Johnson," *Ontario Historical Society Papers and Records* 12 (1914): 112.

32 Johnson to Harcourt, 6 January 1902, Boyle to Harcourt, 9 January 1902, Department of Education, Ontario, RG 2-42-0-3549, AO.

33 Brant-Sero to Mooney, 3 May 1900, Brant-Sero to Boas, 3 May 1900, file 21, box 2, General Correspondence, 1894–1907, Division of Anthropology Archives, American Museum of Natural History, New York, NY (AMNH). I am indebted to Arni Brownstone, ROM, for these references to Brant-Sero's correspondence with the AMNH.

34 Brant-Sero to Coyne, 2 June 1900, file 20, box 4018, James H. Coyne Papers, Archives and Research Collections Centre, University of Western Ontario, London, ON (ARCC).

35 Boyle to Ross, 5 January 1898, Department of Education, Ontario, RG 2-42-0-3669, AO; and Ontario Historical Society, *Catalogue, Canadian Historical Exhibition Victoria College, Queen's Park, Toronto under the Patronage of the His Excellency the Governor-General and the Countess of Minto* (Toronto: William Briggs, 1899), 94–96.

36 Brant-Sero to Boyle, 29 September 1899, 3 October 1899, and 5 October 1899, box 1, Boyle Correspondence, ROM.

37 Brant-Sero to Boyle, 9 December 1899, 6 January 1900, and 15 February 1900, box 1, Boyle Correspondence, ROM. This manuscript was likely published as J. Ojijatekha Brant-Sero, "Some Descendants of Joseph Brant," *Ontario Historical Society Papers and Records* 1 (1899): 113–17.

38 Brant-Sero to Boyle, 15 February 1900, box 1, Boyle Correspondence, ROM.

39 Ojijatekha to Powell, 13 December 1889, Box 17; and Brant-Sero to Powell, 16

February 1900, box 2, Correspondence, Letters Received 1888–1906, Records of the Bureau of American Ethnology, National Anthropological Archives, Suitland, MD.

40 Brant-Sero to Mooney, 3 May 1900, Thwaites to Boas, 4 May 1900, and Boas to Brant-Sero, 16 May 1900, file 21, box 2, General Correspondence, 1894–1907, Division of Anthropology Archives, AMNH; Mooney to Boyle, 20 May 1900, file 3, box 2, Boyle Papers, ROM; Brant-Sero to Boas, 20 October 1900, file 21, box 2, General Correspondence, 1894–1907, AMNH.

41 Brant-Sero to Carnochan, 19 June 1899 and 7 December 1899, box 6, Niagara Historical Society Correspondence, Niagara Historical Society Museum, Niagara-on-the-Lake, ON.

42 Brant-Sero to Boas, 2 October 1902, file 21, box 2, General Correspondence, 1894–1907, AMNH.

43 Brant-Sero to Boas, 3 May 1900, Brant-Sero to Mooney, 3 May 1900, and Brant-Sero to Boas, 20 October 1900, file 21, box 2, General Correspondence, 1894–1907, AMNH.

44 J. Ojijatekha Brant-Sero, "The Six Nations Indians in the Province of Ontario, Canada," *Transactions of the Wentworth Historical Society* 2 (1899): 62.

45 Brant-Sero to Boas, 2 October 1902, file 21, box 2, General Correspondence, 1894–1907, AMNH. Petrone, "Brant-Sero," 39, argued that Brant-Sero changed his depiction of the Iroquois depending on his audience.

46 "Stands Up for Redskin," *New York Times*, 1 July 1910; "A Mohawk Makes a Mistake," *New York Times*, 2 July 1910.

47 Killan, *David Boyle*, 183.

48 Brant-Sero to Coyne, 7 March 1911, file 20, box 4018, Coyne Papers, ARCC.

49 *Indian Magazine*, "Council Notes," January 1896.

50 Sergei Kan, ed., *Strangers to Relatives: The Adoption and Naming of Anthropologists in Native North America* (Lincoln: University of Nebraska Press, 2001), 4–12.

51 Sally M. Weaver, "The Iroquois: The Grand River Reserve in the Late Nineteenth and Early Twentieth Centuries, 1875–1945," in *Aboriginal Ontario: Historical Perspectives on the First Nations*, ed. Edward S. Rogers and Donald B. Smith (Toronto: Dundurn Press, 1994), 240.

52 See Weaver, "The Iroquois," 233–40, 243.

53 Annemarie Anrod Shimony, *Conservatism among the Iroquois at the Six Nations Reserve* (Syracuse: Syracuse University Press, 1994), xxxii–xxxiii.

54 Weaver, "The Iroquois," 233–40, 243.

55 1 June 1898, Minute Book, 10–11, MS249, reel 1, F 1139, Ontario Historical Society Papers, AO, OHSP, recorded 400 Six Nations people; and Ontario Historical Society, *Annual Report of the Ontario Historical Society 1898* (Toronto: Warwick Brothers and Rutter, 1898), 7, recorded the number of Six Nations people as 200.

56 Ontario Historical Society, *Annual Report 1898*, 41, 42; "Old Niagara," *Globe*, 12 June 1897; and Killan, *Preserving Ontario's Heritage*, 43.

57 Norman Knowles, *Inventing the Loyalists: The Ontario Loyalist Tradition and the Creation of Usable Pasts* (Toronto: University of Toronto Press, 1997), 86–88.

58 E. Yates Farmer, "The Six Nations Celebrate the Jubilee," *Saturday Globe*, 16 October 1897.

59 "U. E. L. Association," *Globe*, 12 May 1898. He is called "Chief C. I. Johnson" in "U. E. Loyalist Association," *Globe*, 13 May 1898.

60 "U. E. Loyalist Association," *Globe*, 13 May 1898, 5; "Women's Historical Society," *Globe*, 6 May 1898.

61 Hill to Cumberland, 19 May 1909, and Cumberland to Hill, 3 June 1909, MU 5424, F 1139, OHSP.

62 Ontario Historical Society, *Annual Report of the Ontario Historical Society 1911* (Toronto: The Society, 1911), 43–47.

63 Killan, *Preserving Ontario's Heritage*, 44.

64 Scott Michaelsen, *The Limits of Multiculturalism: Interrogating the Origins of American Anthropology* (Minneapolis: University of Minnesota Press, 1999), xiii. Joan Mark, "Francis La Flesche: The American Indian as Anthropologist," *Isis* 73, no. 4 (1982): 497–510, suggests that La Flesche was an anthropologist in his own right rather than an "informant." For the terms "auto" and "anti-anthropologist," see Michaelsen, *Limits of Multiculturalism*, xiii, 1–32. Other scholars who define the concept of auto-anthropology include Marilyn Strathern, "The Limits of Auto-Anthropology," in *Anthropology at Home*, ed. Anthony Jackson (London: Tavistock Publications, 1987), 16–37; and Mary Louise Pratt, *Imperial Eyes: Travel Writing and Transculturation* (London: Routledge, 1992). For a brief overview of the historiography of these terms, see Deborah E. Reed-Donahay, ed., *Auto/Ethnography: Rewriting the Self and the Social* (Oxford: Berg, 1987), 4–9.

## Chapter 11: "The Grand General Indian Council of Ontario and Indian Status Legislation," by Norman Shields

1 For the most recent, and sustained, argument in this direction, see Joyce Audry Green, "Exploring Identity and Citizenship: Aboriginal Women, Bill C-31 and the Sawridge Case" (PhD diss., University of Alberta, 1997), 2–3 and passim. For a counterpoint, though not complete refutation, see Patricia Monture-Angus, "Organizing Against Oppression: Aboriginal Women, Law and Feminism," in *Thunder in My Soul: A Mohawk Woman Speaks* (Halifax: Fernwood Publishing, 1995), 169–88.

2 For a general history of the Grand Council, see Norman Shields, "Anishinabek Political Alliance in the Post-Confederation Period: The Grand General Indian Council of Ontario, 1870–1936" (MA thesis, Queen's University, 2001).

3 John L. Tobias, "Protection, Civilization, Assimilation: An Outline History of Canada's Indian Policy," in *Sweet Promises: A Reader on Indian–White Relations in Canada*, ed. J. R. Miller (Toronto: University of Toronto Press, 1991), 129. For an account of early legislation, see Kathleen Jamieson, *Indian Women and the Law in Canada: Citizens Minus* (Supply and Services Canada, 1978), 26.

4 Canada, An Act Providing for the Organization of the Department of the Secretary of State of Canada, and for the Management of Indian and Ordnance Lands, Statutes of Canada 1868, 31 Vict., c. 42: 91–100, 93–94; Canada, An Act for the Gradual Enfranchisement of Indians, the Better Management of Indian Affairs, and to Extend the Provisions of the Act, 31st Victoria, Chapter 42, Statutes of Canada 1869, 32–33 Vict., c. 6: 22–27, 23; Canada, Indian Act, Statutes of Canada 1876, 39 Vict., c. 18: 43–73, 43–44; and Canada, An Act to Amend and Consolidate the Laws Respecting Indians. Statutes of Canada 1880, 43 Vict., c. 28: 202–35, 204.

5 Canada, Indian Act, Statutes of Canada 1876, 39 Vict., c. 18: 43–73, 43–44; Canada, An Act to Amend and Consolidate the Laws Respecting Indians,

Statutes of Canada 1880, 43 Vict., c. 28: 202–35, 204; and Jamieson, *Indian Women and the Law*, 59–60.

6 Jamieson, *Indian Women and the Law*, 67–72.

7 Jamieson, *Indian Women and the Law*, 72.

8 Susanne E. Miskimmin, "'Nobody Took the Indian Blood Out of Me': An Analysis of Algonquian and Iroquoian Discourse Surrounding Bill C-31" (MA thesis: University of Western Ontario, 1997), 98.

9 For discussion, see Jamieson, *Indian Women and the Law*, 79–88.

10 Jamieson, *Indian Women and the Law*, 79–88.

11 Jamieson, *Indian Women and the Law*, 84; Kathleen Jamieson, "Multiple Jeopardy: The Evolution of a Native Women's Movement," *Atlantis* 4, no. 2 (1979): 167–68.

12 Jamieson, "Multiple Jeopardy," 169.

13 Liliane E. Krosenbrink-Gelissen, "The Canadian Constitution, the Charter, and Aboriginal Women's Rights: Conflicts and Dilemmas," *International Journal of Canadian Studies* 7–8 (1993): 207–24, 210.

14 Native Women's Association of Canada, "The Impact of State Policy: Women's Responses to State Action," *Resources for Feminist Research* 17, no. 3 (1988): 125–28, 126.

15 Krosenbrink-Gelissen, "The Canadian Constitution," 215–18; and Jamieson, "Multiple Jeopardy," 162.

16 Jamieson, *Indian Women and the Law*, 13.

17 General Council of the Six Nations, *The General Council of the Six Nations, and Delegates from Different Bands in Western and Eastern Canada; June 10, 1870*, Minutes (Hamilton, ON: Spectator, 1870), 16–19, 25. For discussion on "immoral tendency," see Jamieson, *Indian Women and the Law*, 38.

18 Janet Chute, *The Legacy of Shingwaukonse: A Century of Native Leadership* (Toronto: University of Toronto Press, 1998), 199.

19 General Council, *Minutes of the Eighth Grand General Indian Council, Held upon the Cape Crocker Reserve … Sept. 10th to Sept. 15th, 1884* (Hagersville, ON: Indian Publishing Company, 1885), 18.

20 Carole T. Corcoran and Roger J. Augustine, "Moose Deer Point First Nation Inquiry: Pottawatomi Rights," Indian Claims Commission, March 1999, 69.

21 One exception was the Mohawk Gibson band, which emigrated from Lake of Two Mountains, present-day Oka, in 1881, and which appears to have sent a delegation to the 1886 council, but probably no more.

22 The minutes for 1886, 1888, 1890, 1892, and 1898 have yet to be located. The legislation may very well have been discussed during those years as well.

23 *Grand General Indian Council, 1894*, 14–16, RG 10, vol. 2639, file 129,690–1, Library and Archives Canada, Ottawa, ON (LAC).

24 Grand General Indian Council 1894, 14–16, LAC: Jamieson, *Indian Women and the Law*, 38. The customs and extensiveness of the adoption system in the nineteenth century are worthy of detailed research.

25 General Council, *Minutes, 1884*, 15.

26 General Council, *Minutes, 1884*, 15–16.

27 *Grand General Indian Council, 1894*, 14–16, LAC.

28 Quoted in Anthony J. Hall, "The Red Man's Burden: Land, Law, and the Lord in the Indian Affairs of Upper Canada, 1791–1858" (PhD diss., University of Toronto, 1984), 204.

29 Not only for his bombastic approach to Indian Affairs: Sir Bond Head presided over the Upper Canada Rebellion and gerrymandered the Upper Canada 1836 election by actively, aggressively campaigning for the Tories, all the while decrying the Reformers' democratic impulse. For the latter episode, see Sean T. Cadigan, "Paternalism and Politics: Sir Francis Bond Head, the Orange Order, and the Election of 1836," *Canadian Historical Review* 72, no. 3 (1991): 319–47.

30 As both Karl Hele and Phil Bellfy have remarked, the American government also tried to woo First Nations with Presents and land. The competition between Britain and the United States for Aboriginal allies sometimes produced comic results. "Lines Drawn Upon the Water: The First Nations Experience in the Great Lakes Borderlands," London, ON, February 11–12, 2005.

31 Britain, *British Parliamentary Papers* 34 (1839): 323: 217; Sir F. B. Head, Bart., to Lord Glenelg, Toronto, 22 August 1837; Sir F. B. Head, K. C. H., to Lord Glenelg, Toronto, 20 November 1836; Sir F. B. Head, Bart., K. C. H., to Lord Glenelg, Toronto, 11 July 1837. A greater value of Presents was given during times of war.

32 Hall, "The Red Man's Burden," 197–203.

33 James A. Clifton, *A Place of Refuge for All Time: The Potawatomi Emigration to Upper Canada, 1830–1850* (Ottawa: National Museums of Canada, 1975), 34.

34 Hall, "The Red Man's Burden," 209.

35 Peter S. Schmalz, *The History of the Saugeen Indians* (Toronto: Ontario Historical Society, 1977), 14–15.

36 Clifton, *A Place of Refuge*, 89, 100.

37 Clifton, *A Place of Refuge*, 47.

38 Clifton, *A Place of Refuge*, 57, 85, 95, 97; Schmalz, *History of the Saugeen Indians*, 43–44; and Hall, "The Red Man's Burden," 202.

39 Schmalz, *History of the Saugeen Indians*, 36–43, 54.

40 Quoted in Clifton, *A Place of Refuge*, 92.

41 Clifton, *A Place of Refuge*, 90.

42 Clifton, *A Place of Refuge*, 95–96.

43 Clifton, *A Place of Refuge*, 96.

44 The issue of treaty land and annuity for Canada's Aboriginal allies recently went before the Indian Claims Commission. The commission suggested that the Aboriginal allies should be compensated for the discontinuance of Presents, and recommended further study to "further define Canada's obligations arising from the Crown's promises of 1837 and to verify whether those obligations have been fulfilled ... [and] if Canada's obligations have not been fulfilled, the claim be accepted for negotiation under the Specific Claims Policy." Then-minister of Indian Affairs and Northern Development Robert Nault declined further study, stating "Under the Specific Claims Policy, Canada is mandated to enter into negotiations where it is determined that there is an outstanding lawful obligation ... After a fully researched claim submission, consideration by Canada, a full ISCC [Indian Specific Claims Commission] inquiry and, I understand, very able representation by the First Nation's counsel, the very substance of the treaty rights Canada is alleged to have breached cannot be defined with any certainty. Given these circumstances, I am not prepared to authorize a joint research project with the First Nation." See Carole T. Corcoran and Roger J. Augustine, "Moose Deer Point First Nation Inquiry: Pottawatomi Rights; Report 2," Indian Claims Commission, March 1999; and Minister of Indian Affairs and Northern Development, Recommendations to

Daniel J. Bellegarde and James Prentice, QC, co-chairs, Indian Specific Claims Commission, 29 March 2001.

45 *Grand General Indian Council, 1894,* 14–16.

46 *Grand Indian Council, 1900,* 13, RG 10, vol. 2639, file 129,690-1, LAC; *Minutes of the Twenty-First Grand General Indian Council of Ontario, St. John the Baptist Parish Hall, Walpole Island Reserve, June 14th, 1910,* 3–4, 6–7; and *Abstract of the Proceedings of the Grand General Indian Council of Ontario, October 2nd, 1917,* 2, RG 10, vol. 2640, files 129,690–2, 129,690–3, LAC.

## Chapter 12: "'This is a pipe and I know hash': Louise Erdrich and the Lines Drawn upon the Waters and the Lands," by Ute Lischke

1 King published his short story "Borders" in his collection *One Good Story, That One* (New York: HarperCollins, 1993), 129–45. The Blackfoot tribe has a homeland that does not recognize the "international" border between the United States and Canada; in this story, a mother who stubbornly refuses to acknowledge Canadian citizenship and affirms her status as Blackfoot finally succeeds in crossing the border when the threat of a media circus undermines the authority of the customs officials.

2 See Penny Van Toorn, "Aboriginal Writing," in *The Cambridge Companion to Canadian Literature,*" ed. Eva-Marie Kroeller (Cambridge: Cambridge University Press, 2004), 25.

3 Bonita Lawrence, *"Real" Indians and Others: Mixed-Blood Urban Native Peoples and Indigenous Nationhood* (Lincoln: University of Nebraska Press, 2004), 8.

4 See Randy Bass, ed., *Border Texts: Cultural Readings for Contemporary Writers* (Boston: Houghton Mifflin, 1999).

5 Van Toorn, "Aboriginal Writing," 44.

6 Thomas King, *The Truth About Stories: A Native Narrative* (Toronto: Anansi, 2003), 2.

7 Louise Erdrich, *The Blue Jay's Dance: A Birth Year* (New York: HarperCollins Publishers, 1995), 98–99.

8 David T. McNab, "'Time Is a Fish': The Spirit of Nanapush and the Power of Transformation in the Stories of Louise Erdrich," in *(Ad)dressing Our Words: Aboriginal Perspectives on Aboriginal Literature,* ed. Armand Garnet Ruffo (Penticton, BC: Theytus Press, 2001), 181–204.

9 Erdrich has two clans on her mother's side of her family, both of which are significant. On her Anishinabe side, Erdrich is a "Be-nays." Be-nays is a bird—likely of the Great Blue Heron Clan—as indicated repeatedly in her autobiography *a birth year.* In the Anishinabe clan system, birds are spiritual leaders. Edward Benton Banai has described birds as "noted for their intuition and sense of knowledge of what the future would bring. They were said to have the characteristics of the eagle, the head of their clan, in that they pursued the higher elevations of the mind just as the eagle pursued the higher elevations of the sky." Benton-Banai, *The Mishomis Book* (Minneapolis: Red School House, 1988), 74–78. All of Erdrich's literary works are filled with her storytelling—the higher elevations of the mind, a keen sense of knowledge, and, above all, the gift of *ah-mun'-ni-soo-win* (intuition), which includes the ability of *nee-goni-wa'bun-gi-gay-win* (to see into the future). On her mother's side of

the family, she is also Cree of the Bear Clan. Erdrich, *The Blue Jay's Dance*, 81–82. Spiritual messages through storytelling, warnings, and healing are the dominant themes in all of her works. This is made even more potent because she has the female spirit of the bear within her—the gift of prophecies. The Birds are also the spirit protectors of the Bears. Her two clans are powerfully linked together.

10  Erdrich, *The Blue Jay's Dance*, 70.

11  Erdrich, *The Blue Jay's Dance*, 98.

12  Erdrich, *The Blue Jay's Dance*, 99.

13  Erdrich, *The Blue Jay's Dance*, 186.

14  Erdrich, *The Blue Jay's Dance*, 138.

15  Louise Erdrich, *The Bingo Palace* (New York: HarperCollins Publishers, 1995), 31.

16  Erdrich, *The Bingo Palace*, 31.

17  Erdrich, *The Bingo Palace*, 31–32.

18  Erdrich, *The Bingo Palace*, 39.

19  Erdrich, *The Bingo Palace*, 34.

20  Erdrich, *The Bingo Palace*, 34–35.

21  Erdrich, *The Bingo Palace*, 37–39.

22  Louise Erdrich and Michael Dorris, *Route 2* (Northridge: Lord John Press, 1990), 3.

23  Erdrich and Dorris, *Route 2*, 4.

24  Erdrich and Dorris, *Route 2*, 15.

25  Erdrich and Dorris, *Route 2*, 15.

26  Erdrich and Dorris, *Route 2*, 23.

27  Erdrich and Dorris, *Route 2*, 34.

28  See A. LaVonne Brown Ruoff and Donald B. Smith, introduction to *Life, Letters and Speeches*, by George Copway (Kahgegagahbowh) (Lincoln: University of Nebraska Press, 1997).

29  Louise Erdrich, *Books and Islands in Ojibwe Country* (Washington, DC: National Geographic, 2003), 11.

30  Erdrich, *Books and Islands*, 3.

31  Erdrich, *Books and Islands*, 81.

32  Erdrich, *Books and Islands*, 83.

33  Erdrich, *Books and Islands*, 85.

34  Erdrich, *Books and Islands*, 94.

35  Erdrich, *Books and Islands*, 95.

36  Erdrich, *Books and Islands*, 96. Erdrich is quoting from W. G. Sebald's *Austerlitz*.

37  Erdrich, *Books and Islands*, 96–97.

38  Erdrich, *Books and Islands*, 100–101.

# BIBLIOGRAPHY

## I. Archival Collections

Anglican General Synod Archives, Toronto, ON

Archives and Research Collections Centre, University of Western Ontario, London, ON.

      James H. Coyne Papers

      Alexander Vidal Papers

      Wawanosh Family Papers

Archives of Ontario, Toronto, ON

      Buell Family Papers

      Catholic Archdiocesan Collection (Toronto)

      Commission of Crown Lands, Letters Received

      Crown Land Surveys Account Ledgers, Records, and Files

      Department of Education, Ontario

      Ermatinger Family Papers (photocopies)

      George Gordon Papers

      Amelius Irving Papers

      Ontario Historical Society Papers

      Ontario Marriage Index

      Miscellaneous Indian Manuscripts

      Peter Russell Papers

      Bishop Strachan Papers

      Hiram Walker Papers

Bayliss Public Library, Sault Ste. Marie, MI

Bishophurst, Sault Ste. Marie, ON

      Colloton Papers

Bruce Mines Museum, Bruce Mines, ON

Clarke Historical Library, Michigan Central University, Mt. Pleasant, MI

Abel Bingham Papers, 1796–1909

P.S. Church Diaries (Sault Ste. Marie Collection)

George Johnston Papers, 1792–1851, American Fur Company Papers (Sault Ste. Marie Collection)

Jeremiah Porter's Diaries, Jeremiah Porter Papers

Records of the Michigan Superintendency of Indian Affairs, 1814–1851

Henry Rowe Schoolcraft Papers

Detroit Public Library, Burton Historical Collection

J. B. Barthe Papers

George Johnston Papers

Division of Anthropology Archives, American Museum of Natural History, New York City, NY

Hudson's Bay Company Archives, Winnipeg, MB

HBC Sault Ste. Marie – post number B. 194 1818–1864

B. 194/a/1-9 Post Journals 1824–1836 Reel No. 1M131

B. 194/b/1-15 Correspondence Books 1824–1850 Reel 1M224

B. 194/b/16 1826–1853 Reel 1M225

B. 194/c/1 Correspondence Inward 1824–1861 1M381

B. 194/e/1-8 Reports on Districts 1825–1835 1M782

B. 194/z/1 Miscellaneous Items 1818–1864 1M1670 & 1M1671

Library and Archives Canada, Ottawa, ON

Ernest Thompson Seton Papers

Northern Superintendency—Correspondence (Manitoulin Island)

Indian Affairs, RG 10

Chief Superintendent, Upper Canada, Samuel Peters Jarvis—Correspondence

Map Collection

National Anthropological Archives, Suitland, MD

Records of the Bureau of American Ethnology

Correspondence of the Northern Superintendent of Indian Affairs

National Archives and Records Administration, Washington, DC

Records of the Bureau of Indian Affairs, RG 75.

Green Bay Agency

La Pointe Agency

Letters Received by the Office of Indian Affairs, 1824–1881

National Museum of the American Indian, Smithsonian Institution, Washington, DC

George Gustav Heye Correspondence

New York Historical Society, New York

Stuyvesant-Rutherford Papers

Niagara Historical Museum, Niagara-on-the-Lake, ON

Niagara Historical Society Papers

Nin.Da.Waab.Jig (Walpole Island Heritage Centre), Walpole Island First Nation

Rare Book Room, McGill University, Montreal, QC

William Douw Lighthall Papers

Royal Ontario Museum, Toronto, ON
    David Boyle Correspondence
    David Boyle Papers
    Charles Trick Currelly Correspondence
    E. H. C. Normal School Accession Files
    Reginald W. Whale Papers
Sault Ste. Marie Public Library, Sault Ste. Marie, ON
    John Prince Papers (disbursement microfilm)
Shawanaga First Resource Centre
    Elias Journals
Toronto Metropolitan Library, Toronto, ON
    Anderson Papers
William Ready Division of Archives and Research Collections, McMaster University, Hamilton, ON
    E. Pauline Johnson Papers

## II. Government Documents

Britain. *British Parliamentary Papers*. 34 (1839).

Cadotte, Michael. Affadavit. In Report No. 42, Land Cessions in Michigan, United States Committee on Public Lands, 20th Congress, House of Representatives.

Canada. An Act for the Gradual Enfranchisement of Indians, the Better Management of Indian Affairs, and to Extend the Provisions of the Act, 31st Victoria, Chapter 42. Statutes of Canada 1869, 32–33 Vict., c. 6.

———. An Act Providing for the Organization of the Department of the Secretary of State of Canada, and for the Management of Indian and Ordnance Lands. Statutes of Canada, 31 Vict., c. 42.

———. An Act to Amend and Consolidate the Laws Respecting Indians. Statutes of Canada 1880, 43 Vict., c. 28.

———. *Gathering Strength—Canada's Aboriginal Action Plan*. Ottawa: Indian Affairs and Northern Development, 1997.

———. Indian Act. Statutes of Canada 1876, 39 Vict., c. 18.

———. Indian Advancement Act. Statutes of Canada 1884, 47 Vict., c. 28.

———. *Indian Treaties and Surrenders*. 3 vols. 1891. Reprint, Saskatoon: Fifth House Publishers, 1992.

Canada. Indian Affairs. *Annual Report, 1893. Sessional Papers* (1894): 9. http://www.collectionscanada.gc.ca/indianaffairs/020010-119.01-e.php?page_id_nbr=8794&PHPSESSIS=et4hc0a2c0vvs6o33fpingmpc5.

———. Indian and Northern Affairs. *First Nations in Canada*. Ottawa: Queen's Printer, 1997.

———. Indian Affairs and Northern Development. Minister's Recommendations to Daniel J. Bellegarde and James Prentice, QC, co-chairs, Indian Specific Claims Commission, 29 March 2001.

Canada (Province of). An Act for the Better Protection of the Lands and Property of the Indians in Lower Canada. Statutes of the Province of Canada 1851, 14 Vict., c. 42.

———. An Act for the Protection of the Indians of Upper Canada from the Imposition, and the Property Occupied or Enjoyed by Them from Trespass or Injury. Statutes of the Province of Canada 1850, 13 Vict., c. 74.

———. An Act to Encourage the Gradual Civilization of the Indian Tribes in the Province, and to Amend the Laws Respecting Indians. Statutes of the Province of Canada 1857, 20 Vict., c. 26.

———. An Act to Make Better Provision for the Administration of Justice in the Unorganized Tracts of Country of Upper Canada. Statutes of the Province of Canada 1853, 16 Vict., c. 56.

Corcoran, Carole T., and Roger J. Augustine. "Moose Deer Point First Nation Inquiry: Pottawatomi Rights; Report 2." Indian Claims Commission, March 1999.

Fletcher, Alice C. *Indian Education and Civilization.* Bureau of Education Special Report Prepared in Answer to Senate Resolution of 23 February 1885. 1988. Senate Executive Document no. 95. 48th Congress, 2nd Session (serial 2264).

Gover, Kevin. Remarks at the Ceremony Acknowledging the 175th Anniversary of the Establishment of the Bureau of Indian Affairs. 8 September 2000. <www.tahtonka.com/apaology.html> (accessed 14 June 2005).

Ontario Legislative Assembly. *Annual Archaeological Report; Being Part of Appendix to the Report of the Minister of Education, Ontario, 1896–97.* Toronto: 1897.

———. *Annual Archaeological Report; Being Part of Appendix to the Report of the Minister of Education, Ontario, 1897–98.* Toronto: 1898.

———. *Annual Archaeological Report; Being Part of Appendix to the Report of the Minister of Education, Ontario, 1898.* Toronto: 1898.

———. *Annual Archaeological Report; Being Part of Appendix to the Report of the Minister of Education, Ontario, 1899.* Toronto: 1900.

*Mitchell v. M.N.R.*, [2001] 1 S.C.R. 911, 2001 SCC 33.

*R. v. Powley*, [2003] 2 S.C.R. 207, 2003 SCC 43.

Royal Commission on Aboriginal Peoples. *Volume I: Looking Forward, Looking Back.* Ottawa: Canada Communication Group Publishing, 1996.

United Kingdom. Quebec Act, 1774, 14 George III, c. 83.

United States. An Act to Provide for the Allotment of Lands in Severalty to Indians on the Various Reservations [General Allotment Act or Dawes Act], 1887, United States Statutes at Large 24, 388–91.

## III. Newspapers

*Boston Globe* (Boston)
*British Colonist* (Toronto)
*Chatham Chronicle* (Chatham)
*Christian Guardian* (Toronto)

*Empire* (Toronto)
*Globe* (Toronto)
*Indian News* (Ottawa)
*Montreal Gazette* (Montreal)
*New York Christian Advocate* (New York, NY)
*New York Times* (New York, NY)
*Sault Evening News* (Sault Ste. Marie, MI)
*Sault Express* (Sault Ste. Marie, MI)
*Sault Star* (Sault Ste. Marie, ON)

## IV. Published Works, Theses, and Dissertations

Abbott, John, Graeme S. Mount, and Michael J. Mulloy. *The History of Fort St. Joseph*. Toronto: Dundurn Group, 2000.

Adelman, Jeremy, and Stephen Aron. "From Borderland to Borders: Empires, Nation-States, and the Peoples in Between in North American History." *American Historical Review* 104, no. 3 (1999): 814–41.

———. "Of Lively Exchanges and Larger Perspectives." *American Historical Review* 104, no. 4 (1999): 1235–39.

Allen, Robert S. "Dickson, Robert." In *Dictionary of Canadian Biography*, vol. 6, *1821–1835*, 209–11. Toronto: University of Toronto Press, 1987.

———. *His Majesty's Indian Allies: British Indian Policy in the Defence of Canada, 1774–1815*. Toronto: Dundurn Press, 1991.

———. "McDougall, Robert." In *Dictionary of Canadian Biography*, vol. 7, *1836–1850*, 556–57. Toronto: University of Toronto Press, 1988.

———. "McKay, William." In *Dictionary of Canadian Biography*, vol. 6, *1821–1835*, 464–66. Toronto: University of Toronto Press, 1987.

American Indian Movement (AIM). "Brief to the Committee on Indian Affairs and Northern Development of the House of Commons (Canada)." Ms. University of Regina, SK, 1973.

Anonymous. *The Baldoon Mystery*. Wallaceburg: Wallaceburg Press, 1915.

Anonymous. "General Cass at Sault Ste. Marie in 1820." In *Wisconsin Historical Collections*, ed. Lyman Copeland Draper, 5: 410–16. 1869. Reprint, Madison: State Historical Society of Wisconsin, 1907.

Aquila, Richard. *The Iroquois Restoration: Iroquois Diplomacy on the Colonial Frontier, 1701–1754*. 1983. Reprint, Lincoln: University of Nebraska Press, 1997.

Arbic, Bernie. *City of the Rapids: Sault Ste. Marie's Heritage*. Allegan Forest, MI: Priscilla Press, 2003.

Armour, David A. "Cadot (Cadotte), Jean-Baptiste." In *Dictionary of Canadian Biography*, vol. 5, *1801–1820*, 128–30. Toronto: University of Toronto Press, 1983.

———. "Henry, Alexander." In *Dictionary of Canadian Biography*, vol. 6, *1821–1835*, 316–19. Toronto: University of Toronto Press, 1987.

———. "Johnston, John." In *Dictionary of Canadian Biography*, vol. 6, *1821–1835*, 356–59. Toronto: University of Toronto Press, 1987.

————. "Madjeckewiss." In *Dictionary of Canadian Biography*, vol. 5, *1801–1820*, 567–68. Toronto: University of Toronto Press, 1983.

————. "Mitchell, David." In *Dictionary of Canadian Biography*, vol. 6, *1821–1835*, 508–10. Toronto: University of Toronto Press, 1987.

Arthur, Elizabeth. "Beyond Superior: Ontario's New-Found Land." In *Patterns of the Past: Interpreting Ontario's History*, ed. Roger Hall, William Westfall, and Laurel S. MacDowell, 130–49. Toronto: Oxford Press, 1988.

————. "Dawson, Simon James." In *Dictionary of Canadian Biography*, vol. 13, *1901–1910*, 261–63. Toronto: University of Toronto Press, 1994.

————. "General Dickson and the Indian Liberating Army in the North." *Ontario History* 61, no. 3 (1970): 151–62.

————. *Simon J. Dawson, C. E.* Thunder Bay: Thunder Bay Historical Museum Society, 1987.

————. "Siveright, John." In *Dictionary of Canadian Biography*, vol. 7, *1851–1860*, 820–22. Toronto: University of Toronto Press, 1988.

Ashcroft, Bill, Gareth Griffiths, and Helen Tiffin. *The Empire Writes Back: Theory and Practice in Post-Colonial Literatures*. New York: Routledge, 1989.

Ashworth, William. *The Late, Great Lakes: An Environmental History*. Detroit: Wayne State University Press, 1987.

Bald, F. Clever. *The Seigneury at Sault Ste. Marie*. Sault Ste. Marie, MI: Sault Express, 1937.

Barron, F. L. "Victimizing His Lordship: Lord Selkirk and the Upper Canadian Courts." *Manitoba History* 7 (1984): 14–22.

Barry, James P. *Georgian Bay: The Sixth Great Lake*. Toronto: Clarke, Irwin, 1968.

Bass, Randy, ed. *Border Texts: Cultural Readings for Contemporary Writers*. Boston: Houghton Mifflin, 1999.

Bate, Jonathan. *The Song of the Earth*. London, UK: Pan Macmillan, 2000.

Bauman, Richard. *Verbal Art as Performance*. Prospect Heights, IL: Waveland Press, 1984.

Bauman, Robert F. "The Migration of the Ottawa Indians from the Maumee Valley to Walpole Island." *Northwest Ohio Quarterly* 21, no. 3 (1949): 86–112.

Bayliss, Joseph E., and Estelle Bayliss. *Historic St. Joseph Island*. Cedar Rapids, IA: Torch Press, 1938.

————. *River of Destiny: The Saint Mary's*. Detroit: Wayne State University Press, 1955.

Beaven, James. *Recreations of a Long Vacation; or, A Visit to Indian Missions in Upper Canada*. Toronto: H. and W. Roswell, 1846.

Bechard, Henri. "Joseph Togouiroui." In *Dictionary of Canadian Biography*, vol. 1, *1000–1700*, 650–51. Toronto: University of Toronto Press, 1966.

Beck, David R. M. "Siege and Survival: Menominee Responses to an Encroaching World." PhD diss., University of Illinois at Chicago, 1994.

Bellfy, Philip C. "Division and Unity, Dispersal and Permanence: The Anishinabeg of the Lake Huron Borderlands." PhD diss., Michigan State University, 1995.

Benedict, Ruth. *Zuni Mythology*. New York: AMS Press, 1969.

Benton-Banai, Edward. *The Mishomis Book*. Minneapolis: Red School House, 1988.

Berkhofer, Robert F. "The North American Frontier as Process and Context." In *The Frontier in History: North American and South Africa Compared*, ed. Howard Lamar and Leonard Thompson, 43–75. New Haven, CT: Yale University Press, 1981.

Berry, Wendell. *The Unsettling of America, Culture and Agriculture*. San Francisco: Sierra Club Books, 1977.

Berton, Pierre. *The Invasion of Canada, 1812–1813*. Toronto: McClelland and Stewart, 1980.

Bieder, Robert E. "Sault Ste. Marie and the War of 1812: A World Turned Upside Down in the Old Northwest." *Indiana Magazine of History* 95, no. 1 (1999): 1–13.

———. *Science Encounters the Indian, 1820–1880: The Early Years of American Ethnology*. Norman: University of Oklahoma Press, 1986.

Bigsby, John J. *The Shoe and Canoe; or, Pictures of Travel in the Canadas*. 2 vols. London: Chapman and Hall, 1850.

Birk, Douglas A. "John Sayer and the Fond du Lac Trade: The North West Company in Minnesota and Wisconsin." In *Rendezvous: Selected Papers of the Fourth North American Fur Trade Conference*, ed. Thomas C. Buckley, 51–63. St. Paul: North American Fur Trade Conference, 1981.

———, ed., *John Sayer's Snake River Journal, 1804–1805: A Fur Trade Diary from East Central Minnesota*. Minneapolis: Institute from Minnesota Archaeology, 1989.

———. "Sayer, John." In *Dictionary of Canadian Biography*, vol. 5, *1801–1820*, 741–42. Toronto: University of Toronto Press, 1983.

Bkejwanong Natural Heritage Program. *E-Niizaanag Wii-Ngoshkaag Maampii Bkejwanong–Species at Risk on the Walpole Island First Nation*. Walpole Island First Nation: Nin.Da.Waab.Jig, 2006.

Blackbird, Andrew J. *History of the Ottawa and Chippewa Indians of Michigan*. Ypsilanti, MI: Ypsilanti Job Printing House, 1887.

Blackburn, George M. "George Johnston: Indian Agent and Copper Hunter." *Michigan History* 54, no. 2 (1970): 108–21.

Bolkcom, Christopher. "Homeland Security: Unmanned Aerial Vehicles and Border Surveillance." *Congressional Research Service Reports on Homeland Security*. Federation of American Scientists, <http://www.fas.org/sgp/crs/homesec/RS21698.pdf> (accessed 22 March 2006).

Bolton, Herbert Eugene. *The Spanish Borderlands: A Chronicle of Old Florida and the Southwest*. New Haven, CT: Yale University Press, 1921.

Bolton, Herbert E., and Mary Ross. *The Debatable Land: A Sketch of the Anglo-Spanish Contest for the Georgia Country*. New York: Russell and Russell, 1968.

Bothwell, Robert. *A Short History of Ontario*. Edmonton: Hurtig Publishers, 1986.

Bowsfield, Hartwell, ed. *The Letters of Charles John Brydges, 1879–1882: Hudson's Bay Company Land Commissioner*. Winnipeg: Hudson's Bay Record Society, 1977.

Brandâo, José Antonio. *"Your Fire Shall Burn No More": Iroquois Policy Toward New France and Its Native Allies to 1701*. Lincoln: University of Nebraska Press, 1997.

Brandâo, J.A., and William Starna. "The Treaties of 1701: A Triumph of Iroquois Diplomacy." *Ethnohistory* 43, no. 2 (1996): 209–44.

Brant-Sero, J. Ojijatekha. "The Six Nations Indians in the Province of Ontario, Canada." *Transactions of the Wentworth Historical Society* 2 (1899): 62.

———. "Some Descendants of Joseph Brant." *Ontario Historical Society Papers and Records* 1 (1899): 113–17.

Bray, R. Matthew. "Borron, Edward Barnes." In *Dictionary of Canadian Biography*, vol. 14, *1910–1920*, 101–2. Toronto: University of Toronto Press, 2001.

Brazer, Marjorie Cahn. *Harps Upon the Willows: The Johnston Family of the Old Northwest*. Ann Arbor: Historical Society of Michigan, 1993.

Briggs, Charles, and Richard Bauman. "The Foundation of All Future Researches: Franz Boas, George Hunt, Native American Texts, and the Construction of Modernity." *American Quarterly* 51, no. 3 (1999): 479–528.

Brode, Patrick. "Rankin, Arthur." In *Dictionary of Canadian Biography*, vol. 12, *1891–1900*, 884–85. Toronto: University of Toronto Press, 1990.

Brooks, James. *Captives and Cousins: Slavery, Kinship, and Community in the Southwest Borderlands*. Chapel Hill: University of North Carolina Press, 2002.

Brown, Jennifer S. H. *Strangers in Blood: Fur Trade Families in Indian Country*. Vancouver: University of British Columbia Press, 1980.

Bryant, William Cullen. *The Letters of William Cullen Bryant, 1836–1849*. Ed. William Cullen Bryant II and Thomas G. Voss. New York: Fordham University Press, 1977.

Bumstead, J. M. *Fur Trade Wars: The Founding of Western Canada*. Winnipeg: Great Plains Publications, 1999.

———. *The Red River Rebellion*. Winnipeg: Watson and Dwyer, 1996.

Burke, Thomas E., Jr. *Mohawk Frontier: The Dutch Community of Schenectady, New York, 1661–1710*. Ithaca, NY: Cornell University Press, 1991.

Burrows, Dorothy M. *Central through the Years: Sault Ste. Marie, Ontario; A History of Our Church, 1851–1975*. Sault Ste. Marie: Central United Church, 1975.

Cadigan, Sean T. "Paternalism and Politics: Sir Francis Bond Head, the Orange Order, and the Election of 1836." *Canadian Historical Review* 72, no. 3 (1991): 319–47.

Calloway, Colin G. "The Abenakis and the Anglo-French Borderlands." *Dublin Seminar for New England Folklife* 14 (1989): 18–27.

Campbell, Marjorie Wilkins. "Ogilvy, John." In *Dictionary of Canadian Biography*, vol. 5, *1801–1820*, 635–37. Toronto: University of Toronto Press, 1983.

Campey, Lucille H. *The Silver Chief: Lord Selkirk and the Scottish Pioneers of Belfast, Baldoon and Red River*. Toronto: Natural Heritage Books, 2003.

Cannizzo, Jeanne. "George Hunt and the Invention of Kwakiutl Culture." *Canadian Review of Sociology and Anthropology* 20, no. 1 (1983): 44–58.

Capp, Edward H. *The Story of Bow-a-ting, Being the Annals of Sault Sainte Marie, Ontario*. Sault Ste. Marie: Sault Star Presses, 1904.

Careless, J. M. S. *Frontier and Metropolis: Regions, Cities, and Identities in Canada Before 1914; The Donald Creighton Lectures, 1987*. Toronto: University of Toronto Press, 1987.

Carroll, Francis M. *A Good and Wise Measure: The Search for the Canadian–American Boundary, 1783–1842*. Toronto: University of Toronto Press, 2001.

Carroll, John. *Case and his Cotemporaries; or, The Canadian Itinerants' Memorial: Constituting a Biographical History of Methodism in Canada from Its Introduction into the Province, till the Death of the Rev. Wm. Case in 1855*. Toronto: Samuel Rose, 1867.

Carter-Edwards, Dennis. "Ironside, George." In *Dictionary of Canadian Biography*, vol. 6, *1821–1835*, 340–41. Toronto: University of Toronto Press, 1987.

Cass, Lewis. "Governor Cass to the Secretary of War, Sault St. Marie, June 17, 1820." In *The Territory of Michigan*, vol. 11 of *The Territorial Papers of the United States*, ed. Clarence Edwin Carter, 36–37. Washington: Government Printing Office, 1942.

Catlin, George. *Letters and Notes on Manners, Customs, and Condition of the North American Indians*. 1844. Reprint, New York: Dover Publications, 1973.

Cave, Alfred A. "The Delaware Prophet Neolin: A Reappraisal." *Ethnohistory* 46, no. 2 (1999): 265–90.

Cayton, Andrew R. L., and Fredrika J. Teute. "Introduction: On the Connection of Frontiers." In *Contact Points: American Frontiers from the Mohawk Valley to the Mississippi, 1750–1830*, ed. Andrew R. L. Cayton and Fredrika J. Teute, 1–15. Chapel Hill: University of North Carolina Press, for the Omohundro Institute of Early American History and Culture, 1998.

Chance, James. "Letter, 21 Feb. 1871." In *History of the New England Company, from its incorporation in the seventeenth century to the present time. Including A Detailed Report of the Company's Proceedings for the Civilization and Conversion of Indians, Blacks, and Pagans in the Dominion of Canada, British Columbia, the West Indies and S. Africa, during the two years 1869–1870*. London: Taylor and Co., 1871.

Chapman, Charles H. "The Historic Johnston Family of the Soo." In *Michigan Pioneer and Historical Collections*, 36:305–28. Lansing: Wyncoop Hallenbeck Crawford Company, State Printers, 1908.

Chaput, Donald. "The Missus Nolin of Red River." *Beaver* 306, no. 3 (1975): 14–17.

———. "Nolin, Jean-Baptiste." In *Dictionary of Canadian Biography*, vol. 6, *1821–1835*, 546–48. Toronto: University of Toronto Press, 1987.

Chisholm, Barbara, and Andrea Gutsche. *Lake Superior: Under the Shadow of the Gods*. Toronto: Lynx Images, 1998.

Chittenden, Hiram M. *The American Fur Trade and the Far West*. 1903. Reprint, New York: Press of the Pioneers, 1935.

Christian, Shirley. *Before Lewis and Clark: The Story of the Chouteaus, the French Dynasty That Ruled America's Frontier*. New York: Farrar, Straus and Giroux, 2004.

Chute, Janet E. "A Century of Native Leadership: Shingwaukonse and His Heirs." PhD diss., McMaster University, 1986.

———. *The Legacy of Shingwaukonse: A Century of Native Leadership*. Toronto: University of Toronto Press, 1998.

———. "Ojibwa Leadership During the Fur Trade Era at Sault Ste. Marie." In *New Faces of the Fur Trade: Selected Papers of the Seventh North American Fur Trade Conference, Halifax, Nova Scotia, 1995*, ed. JoAnne Fiske, Susan Sleeper-Smith, and William Wicken, 153–72. East Lansing: Michigan State University Press, 1998.

———. Preservation of Ethnic Diversity at Garden River: A Key to Ojibwa Strength." *Papers of the Twenty-Eighth Algonquian Conference*, ed. David H. Pentland, 44–70. Winnipeg: University of Manitoba Press, 1997.

———. "Shingwauk, George (Menissino, Menissinowini, also known as George Pine)." In *Dictionary of Canadian Biography*, vol. 15, *1921–1930*, 1095–97. Toronto: University of Toronto, 2005.

———. "A Unifying Vision: Shingwaukonse's Plan for the Future of the Great Lakes Ojibwa." *Journal of the Canadian Historical Association* 7 (1996): 55–80.

Chute, Janet E., and Alan Knight. "Taking Up the Torch: Simon J. Dawson and the Upper Great Lake's Native Resourse Campaign of the 1860s, 1870s and 1880s." In *With Good Intentions: Euro-Canadian and Aboriginal Relations in Colonial Canada*, ed. Celia Haig-Brown and David Nock, 106–31. Vancouver: University of British Columbia Press, 2006.

Clark, James Lloyd. "The Baldoon Settlement Lands: The Effects of Changing Drainage Technology, 1804–1967." MA thesis, University of Western Ontario, 1970.

Clarke, John. "McKee, Thomas." In *Dictionary of Canadian Biography*, vol. 5, *1801–1820*, 535–36. Toronto: University of Toronto Press, 1983.

Cleland, Charles E. *The Place of the Pike (Gnoozhekaaning): A History of the Bay Mills Indian Community*. Ann Arbor: University of Michigan Press, 2001.

———. *Rites of Conquest: The History and Culture of Michigan's Native Americans*. Ann Arbor: University of Michigan Press, 1992.

Clifton, James A., ed. *Being and Becoming Indian: Biographical Sketches of North American Frontiers*. Chicago: Dorsey Press, 1989.

———. *A Place of Refuge for All Time: Migration of the American Potawatomi into Upper Canada, 1830 to 1850*. Ottawa: National Museums of Canada, 1975.

———. *The Prairie People*. Lawrence: Regents Press of Kansas, 1977.

———. "Visiting Indians in Canada." Ms. prepared for the Fort Malden National Historical Park, Parks Canada, 1979.

Cole, Douglas. *Captured Heritage: The Scramble for Northwest Coast Artifacts*. Seattle: University of Washington Press, 1985.

Colonial Church and School Society. "Mrs. Chance, 14 Mar. 1861." *Annual Report of the Colonial Church and School Society*. n.pub: n.p., 1862.

Columbo, John. "The Baldoon Mystery." In *Ghost Stories of Ontario*. Toronto: Hounslow Press, 1996.

Comaroff, Jean, and John L. Comaroff. "The Colonization of Consciousness in South Africa." *Economy and Society* 18, no. 3 (1989): 267–96.

Cook, S. *Drummond Island: The Story of the British Occupation, 1815–1828.* 1896. Reprint, Ann Arbor: UMI, 1997.

Copway, George. *The Traditional History and Characteristic Sketches of the Ojibway Nation.* London: Charles Gilpin, 1850.

Cormier, Louis-Phillippe. "Perrault, Jean-Baptiste." In *Dictionary of Canadian Biography*, vol. 7, *1836–1850*, 686–87. Toronto: University of Toronto Press, 1988.

Danziger, Edmund Jefferson. *The Chippewas of Lake Superior.* Norman: University of Oklahoma Press, 1978.

Darroch, Sue. "Poltergeist of Baldoon." 2005. *Ontario Ghosts and Hauntings Research Society.* <http://www.torontoghosts.org/chathamkent/baldoon1.htm> (accessed 8 April 2007).

Davis, Natalie Zemon. "Iroquois Women, European Women." *In Women, "Race," and Writing in the Early Modern Period*, ed. Margo Hendricks and Patricia Parker, 243–58. New York: Routledge, 1994.

Delafield, Major Joseph. *The Unfortified Boundary: A Diary of the First Survey of the Canadian Boundary Line from St. Regis to the Lake of the Woods*, ed. Robert McElroy and Thomas Biggs. Privately printed, 1943.

de l'Incarnation, Marie. *Word from New France: The Selected Letters of Marie de l'Incarnation*, ed. Joyce Marshall. Toronto: Oxford University Press, 1967.

Deloria, Vine. *For This Land: Writings on Religion in America.* New York: Routledge, 1998.

Demers, Paul Andrew. "The Formation and Maintenance of the Canada–United States Border in the St. Mary's River and Lake Huron Borderlands, 1780–1860." PhD diss., Michigan State University, 2001.

Dempsey, Hugh A. "Peguis, Chief." In *Dictionary of Canadian Biography*, vol. 9, *1861–1870*, 626–27. Toronto: University of Toronto Press, 1976.

Dennis, Matthew. *Cultivating a Landscape of Peace: Iroquois–European Encounters in Seventeenth-Century America.* Ithaca, NY: Cornell University Press, 1993.

Derome, Robert. "Rosseau, Dominque." In *Dictionary of Canadian Biography*, vol. 6, *1821–1835*, 663–67. Toronto: University of Toronto Press, 1987.

Descartes, René. *A Discourse on Method.* 1637. Project Gutenberg, <http://www.gutenberg.org/dirs/etext93/dcart10.txt> (accessed 25 August 2006).

Dickason, Olive P. *Canada's First Nations: A History of Founding Peoples from Earliest Times.* Toronto: Oxford University Press, 1992, 1997. Reprint, Don Mills, ON: Oxford University Press, 2002.

Dippie, Brian W. *The Vanishing American: White Attitudes and U.S. Indian Policy.* Kansas: University of Kansas Press, 1982.

Douglas, Alan R., ed. *John Prince: A Collection of Documents.* Toronto: Champlain Society, 1980.

Dowd, Gregory Evans. *A Spirited Resistance: The North American Indian Struggle for Unity, 1745–1815.* Baltimore: Johns Hopkins University Press, 1992.

————. *War under Heaven: Pontiac, the Indian Nations, and the British Empire*. Baltimore: Johns Hopkins University Press, 2002.

————. "'We Subdue the Globe'—'We Are Not Your Slaves'—Imperial Mastery, Indigenous Resistance, and American Indian Status, 1760–1795," *GSC* [*Global Security and Cooperation*] *Quarterly* 14 (2005), <http://programs.ssrc .org/gsc/publications/quarterly14/dowd.pdf> (accessed 7 June 2007).

Drake, Benjamin. *Life of Tecumseh, and of His Brother the Prophet: With a Historical Sketch of the Shawanoe Indians*. Cincinnati: E. Morgan, 1841.

Dufour, Pierre, and Marc Ouellet. "Pierre de Rastel de Rocheblave." In *Dictionary of Canadian Biography*, vol. 7, *1836–1850*, 735–39. Toronto: University of Toronto Press, 1988.

Duncan, Hugh Dalziel. *Symbols and Social Theory*. New York: Oxford University Press, 1969.

Dunn, Shirley W. *The Mohicans and Their Land, 1609–1730*. Fleischmanns, NY: Purple Mountain Press, 1994.

Eccles, W. J. *Canada under Louis XIV, 1663–1701*. Toronto: University of Toronto Press, 1964.

————. "Daniel de Remy de Courcelle." In *Dictionary of Canadian Biography*, vol. 1, *1000–1700*, 569–72. Toronto: University of Toronto Press, 1966.

Edmunds, David R. *The Shawnee Prophet*. Lincoln: University of Nebraska Press, 1983.

————. *Tecumseh and the Quest for Indian Leadership*. Toronto: Little, Brown, 1984.

Erdrich, Louise. *The Antelope Wife*. New York: Harper Flamingo, 1998.

————. *The Beet Queen*. 1986. Reprint, New York: Harper Flamingo, 1998.

————. *The Bingo Palace*. New York: HarperCollins Publishers, 1995.

————. *The Blue Jay's Dance: A Birth Year*. New York: HarperCollins Publishers, 1995.

————. *Books and Islands in Ojibwe Country*. Washington, DC: National Geographic, 2003.

————. *The Last Report on the Miracles at Little No Horse*. New York: HarperCollins Publishers, 2001.

Erdrich, Louise, and Michael Dorris. *Route 2*. Northridge: Lord John Press, 1990.

Evans, Sterling, ed. *The Borderlands of the American and Canadian Wests: Essays on Regional History of the Forty-Ninth Parallel*. Lincoln: University of Nebraska Press, 2006.

Falkner, Frederick J. "Narrative Re: Sault Ste. Marie, Ontario." Paper presented to the Sault Ste. Marie Historical Society on its founding, 20 June 1921. Sault Ste. Marie Historical Society Archives, Sault Public Library, Sault Ste. Marie, ON.

Farmer, E. Yates. "The Six Nations Celebrate the Jubilee." *Saturday Globe* (Toronto), 16 October 1897.

Farrell, David R. "Askin, John." In *Dictionary of Canadian Biography*. Vol. 5, *1801–1820*, 37–39. Toronto: University of Toronto Press, 1983.

Fenton, William N. *The False Faces of the Iroquois*. Norman: University of Oklahoma Press, 1987.

———. *The Great Law and the Longhouse: A Political History of the Iroquois Confederacy*. Norman: University of Oklahoma Press, 1998.

———. "Return of Eleven Wampum Belts to the Six Nations Iroquois Confederacy on Grand River, Canada." *Ethnohistory* 36, no. 4 (1989): 392–410.

Ferri-Pisani, Camille. *Prince Napoleon in America, 1861: Letters from His Aide-de-Camp*. Trans. George J. Joyaux. Bloomington: Indiana University Press, 1959.

Fierst, John. "Return to 'Civilization': John Tanner's Troubled Years at Sault Ste. Marie." *Minnesota History* 50, no. 1 (1986): 23–36.

Fowle, Otto. *Sault Ste. Marie and Its Great Waterway*. New York: G. P. Putnam's Sons, 1925.

Franchère, Gabriel. "Narrative of a Voyage to the Northwest Coast of America, in the Years 1811, 1812, 1813 and 1814, or the First American Settlement on the Pacific." In *Early Western Travel*, ed. Reuben Gold Thwaites, 167–410. 1854. Reprint, New York: AMS Press, 1966.

Fulford, George. "The Pictographic Account Book of an Ojibwa Fur Trader." *Papers of the Twenty-Third Algonquian Conference*, ed. William Cowan, 190–233. Ottawa: Carleton University, 1992.

Gehring, Charles T. *Fort Orange Court Minutes, 1652–1660*. Vol. 16, pt. 2. New Netherland Documents. Syracuse, NY: Syracuse University Press, 1990.

General Council of the Six Nations. *The General Council of the Six Nations, and Delegates from Different Bands in Western and Eastern Canada; June 10, 1870*. Minutes. Hamilton, ON: Spectator, 1870.

General Council. *Minutes of the Eighth Grand General Indian Council, Held upon the Cape Crocker Reserve … Sept. 10th to Sept. 15th, 1884*. Hagersville, ON: Indian Publishing Company, 1885.

Gibson, Arrell M. *The American Indian: Prehistory to the Present*. Lexington, MA: D. C. Heath, 1980.

Gilpin, Alec R. *The War of 1812 in the Old Northwest*. East Lansing: Michigan State University Press, 1958.

Glazebrook, G. P. de T., ed. *The Hargrave Correspondence, 1821–43*. Toronto: Champlain Society, 1938.

Goffman, Erving. *Frame Analysis: An Essay on the Organization of Experience*. New York: Harper and Row, 1974.

Gough, Barry. *Fighting Sail on Lake Huron and Georgian Bay: The War of 1812 and Its Aftermath*. St. Catharines: Vanwell Publishing, 2002.

———. *Through Water, Ice and Fire: Schooner Nancy of the War of 1812*. Toronto: Dundurn Group, 2006.

Graham, Elizabeth. *Medicine Man to Missionary: Missionaries as Agents of Change among the Indians of Southern Ontario, 1784–1867*. Toronto: Peter Martin, 1975.

———. *The Mush Hole, Life at Two Indian Residential Schools*. Waterloo, ON: Heffle Publishing, 1997.

Graham, Jane E. "Wabbicomicot." In *Dictionary of Canadian Biography*, vol. 3, *1741–1770*, 651–52. Toronto: University of Toronto Press, 1974.

Grant, John Webster. *Moon of Wintertime: Missionaries and the Indians of Canada in Encounter since 1534*. Toronto: University of Toronto Press, 1984.

Grant, Peter. "The Saulteaux Indians about 1804." In *Les Bourgeois de la Compagnie du Nord-Quest, 1889–90*, ed. R. L. Masson, 231–366. New York: Antiquarian Press, 1960.

Grant, Valerie. "The Crane and Sucker Indians of Sandy Lake." In *Actes du quatorzième congres des algonquinistes*, ed. William Cowan, 75–90. Ottawa: Carleton University, 1983.

Grassman, Thomas. "Flemish Bastard," In *Dictionary of Canadian Biography*, vol. 1, *1000–1700*, 307–8. Toronto: University of Toronto Press, 1966.

Gray, Charlotte. *Flint and Feather: The Life and Times of E. Pauline Johnson, Tekahionwake*. Toronto: HarperFlamingo Canada, 2002.

Gray, Susan E. "Limits and Possibilities: White–Indian Relations in Western Michigan in the Era of Removal." *Michigan Historic Review* 20, no. 2 (1994): 71–91.

Green, Joyce Audry. "Exploring Identity and Citizenship: Aboriginal Women, Bill C-31 and the Sawridge Case." PhD diss., University of Alberta, 1997.

Greer, Allan L., ed. *The Jesuit Relations: Natives and Missionaries in Seventeenth-Century North America*. Boston: Bedford/St. Martin's, 2000.

Gressley, Gene M. "Lord Selkirk and the Canadian Courts." In *Canadian History Before Confederation: Essays and Interpretations*, ed. J. M. Bumstead, 287–306. Georgetown: Irwin-Dorsey, 1972.

Gross, Lawrence W. "*Bimaadiziwin*, or the 'Good Life,' as a Unifying Concept of Anishinaabe Religion." *American Indian Culture and Research Journal* 26, no. 1 (2002): 15–31.

Gump, James O. *The Dust Rose Like Smoke: The Subjugation of the Zulu and the Sioux*. Lincoln: University of Nebraska Press, 1994.

Gutsche, Andrea, Barbara Chisholm, and Russel Floren. *The North Channel and St. Mary's River*. Toronto: Lynx Images, 1997.

Haefeli, Evan. "A Note on the Use of North American Borderlands." *American Historical Review* 104, no. 4 (1999): 1222–25.

Haefeli, Evan, and Kevin Sweeney. *Captors and Captives: The 1704 French and Indian Raid on Deerfield*. Amherst: University of Massachusetts Press, 2003.

Hagedorn, Nancy L. "Brokers of Understanding: Interpreters as Agents of Cultural Exchange in Colonial New York." *New York History* 76, no. 4 (1995): 379–408.

Hale, Horatio. *Chief George H. M. Johnson, Onwanonsyshon: His Life and Work among the Six Nations*. New York: A. S. Barnes, 1885.

Halkett, John. *Statement Respecting The Earl of Selkirk's Settlement upon the Red River in North America, its Destruction in 1815 and 1816; and the Massacre of Governor Semple and His Party*. London: John Murray, 1817.

Hall, Anthony J. "The Red Man's Burden: Land, Law, and the Lord in the Indian Affairs of Upper Canada, 1791–1858." PhD diss., University of Toronto, 1984.

Hallowell, A. Irving. *Role of Conjuring in Saulteaux Society*. Philadelphia: University of Pennsylvania Press, 1942.

Hambleton, Elizabeth, and Elizabeth Warren Stoutamire, eds. *The John Johnston Family of Sault Ste. Marie.* Sault Ste. Marie, MI: Johnston Family Association, 1993.

Haraway, Donna. *Simians, Cyborgs and Women: The Reinvention of Nature.* New York: Routledge, 1991.

Harmon, Daniel William. *A Journal of Voyages and Travels in the Interior of North America.* Toronto: Courier Press, 1911.

Harrington, Carolyn Jane. "The Influence of Location on the Development of an Indian Community at the Rapids of the St. Mary's River." MA thesis, University of Western Ontario, 1979.

Harris, Cole. "How Did Colonialism Dispossess? Comments from an Edge of Empire." *Annals of the Association of American Geographers* 94, no. 1 (2004): 165–82.

Hart, William B. "For the Good of Our Souls: Mohawk Authority, Accommodation, and Resistance to Protestant Evangelism, 1700–1780." PhD diss., Brown University, 1998.

Hatfield, April Lee. *Atlantic Virginia: Intercolonial Relations in the Seventeenth Century.* Philadelphia: University of Pennsylvania Press, 2004.

Heath, Francis M. *Sault Ste. Marie: City by the Rapids; An Illustrated History.* Burlington: Windsor Publications, 1988.

Hele, Karl. "'By the Rapids': The Anishinabeg–Missionary Encounter at Bawating (Sault Ste. Marie), c. 1821 to 1871." PhD diss., McGill University, 2002.

———. "Conflict and Cooperation at Garden River First Nation: Missionaries, Ojibwa, and Government Interactions, 1854–1871." *Journal of the Canadian Church Historical Society* 47, no. 1 (2005): 75–117.

———. "'How to Win Friends and Influence People': Missions to Bawating, 1830–1840." In *Historical Papers, 1996: Canadian Society of Church History,* ed. Bruce L. Guenther, 155–76. Canada: Canadian Society of Church History, 1997.

———. "James D. Cameron: Baptist and Mixed-Blood Minister at Bawating: 1831–1859." In *Papers of the 35th Algonquian Conference,* ed. H. C. Wolfart, 137–61. Manitoba: University of Manitoba Press, 2004.

Hellmuth, Isaac. *The Annual Address of the Rt. Reverend I. Hellmuth, PDDCL, Bishop of Huron.* London: Evening Herald Steam Printing, 1873.

Henry, Alexander. *Travels and Adventures in Canada and the Indian Territories Between the Years 1760 and 1776.* Pt. 1. New York: I. Riley, 1809.

Heriot, George. *Travels Through the Canadas.* 1806. Reprint, Edmonton: Hurtig, 1971.

Higham, C. L. *Noble, Wretched, and Redeemable: Protestant Missionaries to the Indians in Canada and the United States, 1820-1900.* Albuquerque: University of New Mexico Press, 2000.

Hooker, LeRoy. *Baldoon.* Toronto: Poole Publishing, 1900.

Hornsby, Stephen J., Victor A. Konrad, and James J. Herlan, eds. *The Northeastern Borderlands: Four Centuries of Interaction.* Fredericton: Acadiensis Press, 1989.

Horsman, Reginald. "Scientific Racism and the American Indian in Mid-Nineteenth Century." *American Quarterly* 27, no. 2 (1975): 152–68.

———. "United States Indian Policies, 1776–1815." In *Handbook of North American Indians. Volume 4: History of Indian–White Relations,* ed. Wilcomb E. Washburn, 29–39. Washington: Smithsonian Institution, 1988.

Hoxie, Frederick E. *A Final Promise: The Campaign to Assimilate the Indians, 1880–1920.* Lincoln: University of Nebraska Press, 1984.

———, ed. *Talking Back to Civilization: Indian Voices from the Progressive Era.* Boston: Bedford/St. Martin's, 2001.

Huckins, Philip Cate. "Broken Vows, Broken Arrows: An Analysis of the U.S. Government's Off-Reservation Boarding School Program, 1879–1900." PhD diss., Boston College, 1995.

Hymes, Dell. *Ethnography, Linguistics, Narrative Inequality.* London: Taylor and Francis, 1996.

*Indian Magazine.* "Council Notes." January 1896.

Iverson, Peter. "Speaking Their Language: Robert W. Young and the Navajos." In *Between Indian and White Worlds: The Cultural Broker,* ed. Margaret Connell Szasz, 255–72. Norman: University of Oklahoma Press, 1994.

Jacknis, Ira. *The Storage Box of Tradition: Museums, Anthropologists and Kwakiutl Art, 1881–1981.* Washington, DC: Smithsonian Institution Press, 2002.

Jacobs. *Legend and Memory: Ontario's First Nations.* TV Ontario, 29 March 2002.

Jacobs, Dean. "'We have but our hearts and the traditions of our old men': Understanding the Traditions and History of Bkejwanong." In *Gin Das Winan: Documenting Aboriginal History in Ontario,* ed. Dale Standen and David McNab, 1–13. Toronto: Champlain Society, 1996.

Jacobs, Peter. *Journal of the Reverend Peter Jacobs, Indian Wesleyan Missionary from Rice Lake to the Hudson's Bay Territory and Returning; Commencing May, 1952; With a Brief Account of His Life and a Short History of the Wesleyan Mission in that Country.* New York: Author, 1857.

Jahoda, Gloria. *The Trail of Tears.* New York: Holt, Rinehart and Winston, 1975.

Jameson, Anna Brownell. *Winter Studies and Summer Rambles in Canada.* 1838. Reprint, Toronto: McClelland and Stewart, 1990.

Jamieson, Kathleen. *Indian Women and the Law in Canada: Citizens Minus.* Supply and Services Canada, 1978.

———. "Multiple Jeopardy: The Evolution of a Native Women's Movement." *Atlantis* 4, no. 2 (1979): 157–78.

Jasen, Patricia. *Wild Things: Nature, Culture, and Tourism in Ontario, 1790–1914.* Toronto: University of Toronto Press, 1995.

Jenkins, Willis. "Biodiversity and Salvation: Thomistic Roots for Environmental Ethics." *Journal of Religion* 83, no. 3 (2003): 401–20.

Jennings, Francis. *The Ambiguous Iroquois Empire: The Covenant Chain Confederation of Indian Tribes with English Colonies from Its Beginnings to the Lancaster Treaty of 1744.* New York: Norton, 1984.

Johnson, E. H. C. "Chief John Smoke Johnson." *Ontario Historical Society Papers and Records* 12 (1914): 112.

Johnson, E. Pauline. "The Delaware Idol." In *The Shagganappi*. Toronto: Ryerson Press, 1913.

———. "Hoolool of the Totem Poles." In *E. Pauline Johnson Tekahionwake: Collected Poems and Selected Prose*, ed. Carole Gerson and Veronica Strong-Boag, 257–60. Toronto: University of Toronto Press, 2002.

Johnson, J. K. *Becoming Prominent: Regional Leadership in Upper Canada, 1791–1841*. Montreal: McGill-Queen's University Press, 1989.

Johnston, George. "Reminiscences by Geo. Johnston of Sault Ste Mary's, 1815 (1), 1816 (2) and 1820 (3)." In *Michigan Pioneer and Historical Collections*, ed. Henry S. Bartholomew, 12:605–11. Lansing: Wyncoop Hallenbeck Crawford Company State Printers, 1887.

Johnston, John. "An Account of Lake Superior (1809)." In *Les Bourgeois de la Compagnie du Nord-Ouest: Récits de Voyages, Lettres et Rapports Inédits Relatifs au Nord-Ouest Canadien, 1889–1890*, ed. L. R. Masson, 144–74. New York: Antiquarian Press, 1960.

Johnston, Sheila M. F. *Buckskin and Broadcloth: A Celebration of E. Pauline Johnson—Tekahionwake, 1861–1913*. Toronto: Natural Heritage/Natural History, 1997.

Jones, Peter (Kahkewaquonaby). *History of the Ojebway Indians*. London: Houlston and Wright; A. W. Bennett, 1861.

Kan, Sergei, ed. *Strangers to Relatives: The Adoption and Naming of Anthropologists in Native North America*. Lincoln: University of Nebraska Press, 2001.

Kappler, Charles J., ed. *Treaties, 1778–1883*. Vol. 2 in *Indian Affairs: Laws and Treaties*, ed. Kappler. New York: Interland Publisher, 1972.

———. *Indian Affairs: Laws and Treaties*. Washington, DC: Government Printing Office, 1904.

Karttunen, Frances E. *Between Worlds: Interpreters, Guides, and Survivors*. New Brunswick: Rutgers University Press, 1994.

———. *Pauline Johnson: First Aboriginal Voice of Canada*. Montreal: XYZ Publishing, 1999.

Kellar, Betty. *Pauline: A Biography of Pauline Johnson*. Vancouver: Douglas and McIntyre, 1981.

Kellogg, Louise Phelps. *The French Regime in Wisconsin and the Northwest*. Madison: State Historical Society of Wisconsin, 1925.

Killan, Gerald. *David Boyle: From Artisan to Archaeologist*. Toronto: University of Toronto Press, 1983.

———. *Preserving Ontario's Heritage: a History of the Ontario Historical Society*. Ottawa: Love Print Service, 1967.

King, Thomas. "Borders." In *One Good Story, That One*, 129–45. HarperCollins, 1993.

———. *The Truth about Stories: A Native Narrative*. Toronto: Anansi, 2003.

Kingsford, William. "John Johnston of Sault Ste. Marie: A Passage in Canadian History." *Rose Bedford's Canadian Monthly and National Review*, July 1881.

Klein, Kerwin Lee. *Frontiers of the Historical Imagination: Narrating the European Conquest of Native America, 1890–1990*. Berkeley: University of California Press, 1999.

Knight, Alan. "'A Study in Failure': The Anglican Mission at Sault Ste. Marie, 1832–1841." *Journal of the Canadian Church Historical Society* 45, no. 2 (2003): 133–224.

Knight, Alan, and Janet E. Chute. "A Visionary on the Edge: Allan Macdonell and the Championing of Native Resource Rights." In *With Good Intentions: Euro-Canadian and Aboriginal Relations in Colonial Canada*, ed. David Nock and Celia Haig-Brown, 87–105. Vancouver: University of British Columbia Press, 2006.

Knowles, Norman. *Inventing the Loyalists: The Ontario Loyalist Tradition and the Creation of Usable Pasts*. Toronto: University of Toronto Press, 1997.

Kohl, J. G. *Kitchi-Gami: Life among the Lake Superior Ojibway*. 1860. Reprint, St. Paul, MN: Minnesota Historical Society Press, 1985.

Kreis, Karl Markus. "John O. Brant-Sero's Adventures in Europe." *European Review of Native American Studies* 15, no. 2 (2001): 27–30.

Kristof, Ladis K. D. "The Nature of Frontiers and Boundaries." *Annals of the Association of American Geographers* 49, no. 1 (March 1959): 269–82.

Krosenbrink-Gelissen, Liliane E. "The Canadian Constitution, the Charter, and Aboriginal Women's Rights: Conflicts and Dilemmas." *International Journal of Canadian Studies* 7–8 (1993): 207–24.

Kupperman, Karen Ordahl. "International at the Creation: Early Modern American History." In *Rethinking American History in a Global Age*, ed. Thomas Bender, 103–22. Berkeley: University of California Press, 2002.

Labov, William. "Transformation of Experience in Narrative Syntax." In *Language in the Inner City*, ed. William Labov, 354–96. Philadelphia: University of Pennsylvania Press, 1972.

Labov, William, and J. Waletzky. "Narrative Analysis." In *Essays on the Verbal and Visual Arts*, ed. J. Helm, 12–44. Seattle: University of Washington Press, 1967.

Lamontagne, Leopold. "Alexandre de Prouville de Tracy." In *Dictionary of Canadian Biography*, vol. 1, *1000–1700*, 554–57. Toronto: Toronto University Press, 1966.

Lauriston, Victor. *Romantic Kent: More Than Three Centuries of History, 1626–1952*. Chatham: Shepherd Printing, 1952.

Lavender, D. S. *The Fist in the Wilderness*. New York: Doubleday, 1964.

Lawrence, Bonita. *"Real" Indians and Others: Mixed-Blood Urban Native Peoples and Indigenous Nationhood*. Lincoln: University of Nebraska Press, 2004.

LeBlanc, Jean-Marie. "Bonne de Missegle (Misele), Louis de." In *Dictionary of Canadian Biography*, vol. 3, *1741–1770*, 69–70. Toronto: University of Toronto Press, 1974.

Lefebvre, Andrew. "Prohibition and the Smuggling of Intoxicating Liquors Between the Two Saults." *Northern Mariner* 11, no. 3 (2001): 33–40.

Leighton, Douglas. *The Historical Development of the Walpole Island Community*. Occasional Paper no. 22. Wallaceburg, ON: Walpole Island Research Centre, 1986.

––––––. "Ironside, George [Jr.]." In *Dictionary of Canadian Biography*, vol. 9, *1861–1870*, 407–8. Toronto: University of Toronto Press, 1976.

Lewis, Janet. *The Invasion: A Narrative of the Events Concerning the Johnston Family of the St. Mary's*. New York: Harcourt and Brace, 1932. Reprint, *The Invasion*, East Lansing: Michigan State University Press, 2000.

Liberty, Margot, ed. *American Indian Intellectuals of the Nineteenth and Early Twentieth Centuries*. Lincoln: University of Nebraska Press, 2002.

Livingston, John A. *Rogue Primate: An Exploration of Human Domestication*. Toronto: Key Porter, 1994.

Long, John. *Voyages and Travels of an Indian Interpreter and Trader*. 1971. Reprint, Toronto: Coles Publishing, 1971.

Long, Stephen H. *The Northern Expeditions of Stephen H. Long: The Journals of 1817 and 1823 and Related Documents*. Ed. Lucile M. Kane, June D. Holmquist, and Carolyn Gilman. St. Paul: Minnesota Historical Society, 1978.

Lovisek, Joan. "The Ojibway vs. the Gerrymander: The Evolution of the Robinson Huron and William Treaties Boundaries." In *Actes du trente-deuxième congrès des Algonquinistes*, ed. John D. Nichols, 278–303. Winnipeg: University of Manitoba, 2001.

Lowensteyn, Peter. "The Role of Chief Canaqueese in the Iroquois Wars." 5 November 2006. *Lowensteyn Family Online: Humanities*, http://lowensteyn.com/iroquois/canaqueese.html (accessed 26 December 2006).

MacDonald, Graham Alexander. "Commerce, Civility and Old Sault Ste. Marie." *Beaver* 312, no. 3 (1981): 52–59.

———. "The Saulteur–Ojibway Fishery at Sault Ste Marie, 1640–1920." MA thesis, University of Waterloo, 1977.

MacGregor, J. G. *Peter Fidler: Canada's Forgotten Explorer 1769–1822*. Toronto: McClelland & Stewart, 1966.

MacKenzie, A. E. D. *Baldoon: Lord Selkirk's Settlement in Upper Canada*. London: Phelps Publishing, 1978.

Mackenzie, Alexander. *Alexander Mackenzie's Voyages*. London: n.p., 1802.

Mackenzie, John M. *The Empire of Nature: Hunting, Conservation and British Imperialism*. Manchester: Manchester University Press, 1988.

———. *Empires of Nature and the Nature of Empires: Imperialism, Scotland and the Environment*. East Linton: Tuckwell Press, 1997.

MacLean, Hope. "The Hidden Agenda: Methodist Attitudes to the Ojibwa and the Development of Indian Schooling in Upper Canada, 1821–1860." MA thesis, University of Toronto, 1978.

Madsen, Axel. *John Jacob Astor: America's First Multimillionaire*. New York: John Wiley and Sons, 2001.

Magnaghi, Russell. *A Guide to the Indians of Michigan's Upper Peninsula, 1621–1900*. Marquette: Belle Fontaine Press, 1984.

Mahon, John K. *History of the Second Seminole War, 1835–1842*. Gainesville: University of Florida Press, 1967.

Malinowski, Bronislaw. *Malinowski and the Work of Myth*. Princeton, NJ: Princeton University Press, 1992.

Mark, Joan. "Francis La Flesche: The American Indian as Anthropologist." *Isis* 73, no. 4 (1982): 497–510.

Marshall, Joyce, trans. and ed. *Word from New France: The Selected Letters of Marie de l'Incarnation*. Toronto: University of Oxford Press, 1967.

Martin, Joel W. *The Land Looks After Us: A History of Native American Religion*. New York: Oxford University Press, 2001.

Mason, Philip P. *Schoolcraft's Expedition to Lake Itasca: The Discovery of the Source of the Mississippi*. East Lansing: Michigan State University Press, 1958.

———, ed., *Schoolcraft's Ojibwa Lodge Stories: Life on the Lake Superior Frontier*. East Lansing: Michigan State University Press, 1997.

Mason, Roger Burford, ed. *Travels in the Shining Island: The Story of James Evans and the Invention of the Cree Syllabary Alphabet*. Toronto: Natural Heritage Books, 1996.

McCrady, David G. *Living with Strangers: The Nineteenth-Century Sioux and the Canadian–American Borderlands*. Lincoln: University of Nebraska Press, 2006.

McDonald, Lois Halliday, ed. *Fur Trade Letters of Francis Ermatinger, Written to His Brother Edward During His Service with the Hudson's Bay Company, 1818–1833*. Glendale, CA: Arthur H. Clarke, 1980.

McDonald, Neil T. *The Belledoon Mysteries: An O'er True Story*. 1871, 1895. Reprint, Wallaceburg, ON: Wallaceburg News Book and Job Print, 1905.

McKenney, Thomas L. *Sketches of a Tour to the Lakes*. Minneapolis: Ross and Haines, 1827.

McLaughlin, Andrew Cunningham. *Lewis Cass*. 1899. Reprint, New York: Chelsea House, 1980.

McLeod, Neal. "Plains Cree Identity: Borderlands, Ambiguous Genealogies and Narrative Irony." *Canadian Journal of Native Studies* 20, no. 2 (2000): 437–54.

McManus, Sheila. *The Line Which Separates: Race, Gender, and the Making of the Alberta–Montana Borderlands*. Edmonton: University of Alberta Press, 2005.

———. "Mapping the Alberta–Montana Borderlands: Race, Ethnicity and Gender in the Late Nineteenth Century." *Journal of American Ethnic History* 20, no. 3 (2001): 71–87.

———. "'Their Own Country': Race, Gender, Landscape, and Colonization Around the 49th Parallel, 1862–1900." *Agricultural History* 73, no. 2 (1999): 168–82.

McNab, David. "Borders of Water and Fire: Islands as Sacred Places and as Meeting Grounds." In *Aboriginal Cultural Landscapes*, ed. Jill Oakes, Rick Riewe, et al., 35–45. Winnipeg: Aboriginal Issues Press, 2004.

———. *Circles of Time: Aboriginal Land Rights and Resistance in Ontario*. Waterloo: Wilfrid Laurier University Press, 1999.

———. "Conjoining Mindscape and Landscape: The Borders of Knowledge in Indigenous Thought and the Written Word of Ezhaaswe (William A. Elias [1856–1929])." Paper presented at the Austrian Association for American Studies Conference, University of Vienna, Vienna, Austria, 16 November 2006.

———, ed. *Earth, Water, Air and Fire: Studies in Canadian Ethnohistory*. Waterloo: Wilfrid Laurier University Press, 1998.

———, ed. *Gin Das Winan: Documenting Aboriginal History in Ontario*. Toronto: Champlain Society, 1996.

————. "Herman Merivale and Colonial Office Indian Policy in the Mid-Nineteenth Century." In *As Long as the Sun Shines and Water Flows: A Reader in Canadian Native Studies*, ed. Ian A. L. Getty and Antoine S. Lussier, 85–103. Vancouver: University of British Columbia Press, 1990.

————. "'The land was to remain ours'": The St. Anne Island Treaty of 1796 and Aboriginal Title and Rights in the Twenty-first Century." In *Native American Speakers of the Eastern Woodlands: Selected Speeches and Critical Analyses*, ed. Barbara Alice Mann, 229–50. New York: Greenwood Press, 2001.

————. "Landscape and Mindscape Conjoined: The Empire of Nature and the Nature of Empire in William A. Elias' (1856–1929) Journals." In *The Empire of Nature and the Nature of Empire*, ed. Karl S. Hele. Waterloo: Wilfrid Laurier University Press (forthcoming).

————. "Sovereignty and Trade and Bkejwanong Territory: A Retrospective on Meeting Grounds." Draft report. 2000.

————. "'Time is a Fish': The Spirit of Nanapush and the Power of Transformation in the Stories of Louise Erdrich." In *(Ad)dressing Our Words: Aboriginal Perspectives on Aboriginal Literature*, ed. Armand Garnet Ruffo, 181–204. Penticton, BC: Theytus Press, 2001.

McNab, David T., Bruce W. Hodgins, and Ute Lischke. *Blockades and Resistance: Studies in Actions of Peace and the Temagami Blockades of 1988–89*. Waterloo: Wilfrid Laurier University Press, 2003.

McNab, David, Bruce Hodgins, and Dale Standen. "'Black with Canoes': Aboriginal Resistance and the Canoe: Diplomacy, Trade and Warfare in the Meeting Grounds of Northeastern North America, 1600–1821." In *Technology, Disease and Colonial Conquests, Sixteenth to Eighteenth Centuries: Essays Reappraising the Guns and Germs Theories*, ed. George Raudzens, 237–92. Leiden, The Netherlands: Brill International, 2001.

McNeice, Gladys. *The Ermatinger Family of Sault Ste. Marie*. Sault Ste. Marie, ON: Creative Printing House, 1984.

Medicine, Beatrice. "Ella C. Deloria: The Emic Voice." In *Learning to Be an Anthropologist and Remaining "Native,"* ed. Beatrice Medicine and Sue-Ellen Jacobs, 269–88. Urbana: University of Illinois Press, 2001.

Merideth, Alden G., ed. *Mary's Rosedale and Gossip of "Little York."* Ottawa: Graphic Publishers, 1928.

Merrell, James H. "'The Cast of His Countenance': Reading Andrew Montour." In *Through a Glass Darkly: Reflections on Personal Identity in Early America*, ed. Ronald Hoffman, Mechal Sobel, and Fredrika J. Teute, 13–39. Chapel Hill: University of North Carolina Press for the Institute of Early American History and Culture, 1997.

————. *Into the American Woods: Negotiators on the Pennsylvania Frontier*. New York: Norton, 1999.

Merwick, Donna. *Possessing Albany, 1630–1710: The Dutch and English Experiences*. New York: Cambridge University Press, 1990.

Métis National Council. Statement to the United Nations Working Group on Indigenous Populations. August 1984. Geneva, Switzerland.

Meuwese, Marcus P. "'For the Peace and Well-Being of the Country': Intercultural Mediators and Dutch–Indian Relations in New Netherland and Dutch Brazil, 1600–1664." PhD diss., University of Notre Dame, 2003.

Michaelsen, Scott. *The Limits of Multiculturalism: Interrogating the Origins of American Anthropology*. Minneapolis: University of Minnesota Press, 1999.

Miller, J. R. "Introduction." In *Aboriginal Peoples of Canada: A Short Introduction*, ed. Paul Robert Magocsi, 3–38. Toronto: University of Toronto Press, 2002.

———. *Shingwauk's Vision: A History of Native Residential Schools*. Toronto: University of Toronto Press, 1996.

———. *Skyscrapers Hide the Heavens: A History of Indian–White Relations in Canada*. Toronto: University of Toronto Press, 1991.

Milliken, Barry, in collaboration with Rachel Shawkence. *Annie Rachel: Mshkiki-ikwe; Stories from an Elder of the Kettle and Stony Point First Nation*. London: Centre for Research and Teaching of Canadian Native Languages, 1996.

Millman, Thomas. "Anderson, Thomas." In *Dictionary of Canadian Biography*, vol. 10, *1871–1880*, 11–13. Toronto: University of Toronto Press, 1972.

Milloy, John S. "The Early Indian Acts: Developmental Strategy and Constitutional Change." In *As Long as the Sun Shines and Water Flows: A Reader in Canadian Native Studies*, ed. Ian A. L. Getty and Antoine S. Lussier, 39–55. Vancouver: University of British Columbia Press, 1990.

———. *"A National Crime": The Canadian Government and the Residential School System, 1879–1986*. Winnipeg: University of Manitoba Press, 1999.

Miskimmin, Susanne E. "'Nobody Took the Indian Blood Out of Me': An Analysis of Algonquian and Iroquoian Discourse Surrounding Bill C-31." MA thesis, University of Western Ontario, 1997.

*Mitchell v. M.N.R.*, [2001] 1 S. C. R. 911, 2001 SCC 33.

Momryk, Myron. "Ermatinger (Ermintinger, Armitinger), Charles Oakes." In *Dictionary of Canadian Biography*, vol. 6, *1821–1835*, 236–37. Toronto: University of Toronto Press, 1987.

———. "Ermatinger, Lawrence." In *Dictionary of Canadian Biography*, vol. 4, *1771–1800*, 262–63. Toronto: University of Toronto Press, 1974.

Montgomerie, Deborah Anne. "Coming to Terms: Ngai Tahu, Robeson County Indians and the Garden River Band of Ojibwa, 1840–1940: Three Studies of Colonialism in Action." PhD diss., Duke University, 1993.

Montgomery, M. R. *Jefferson and the Gunmen: How the West Was Almost Lost*. New York: Crown Publishers, 2000.

Monture-Angus, Patricia. *Thunder in My Soul: A Mohawk Woman Speaks*. Halifax, NS: Fernwood Publishing, 1995.

Morgan, Cecilia. "A Wigwam to Westminster: Performing Mohawk Identity in Imperial Britain, 1890s–1990s." *Gender and History* 15, no. 2 (2003): 319–41.

Morrison, Jean. "Grant, Peter." In *Dictionary of Canadian Biography*, vol. 7, *1836–1850*, 356–57. Toronto: University of Toronto Press, 1988.

———. "Mackenzie, Kenneth." In *Dictionary of Canadian Biography*, vol. 5, *1801–1820*, 543–44. Toronto: University of Toronto Press, 1983.

————. "McKay, Alexander." In *Dictionary of Canadian Biography*, vol. 5, *1801–1820*, 532–34. Toronto: University of Toronto Press, 1983.

————, ed. *The North West Company in Rebellion: Simon McGillivray's Fort William Notebook, 1815*. Thunder Bay: Thunder Bay Historical Museum, 1988.

Morton, W. L. *Manitoba: A History*. Toronto: University of Toronto Press, 1957.

Mount, Graeme S. "Drums along the St. Mary's: Tensions on the International Border at Sault Ste. Marie." *Michigan History* 73, no. 4 (1989): 32–36.

Mount, Graeme S., John Abbott, and Michael J. Mulloy. *The Border at Sault Ste. Marie*. Toronto: Dundurn Press, 1995.

Mount, Graeme S., and Michael J. Mulloy, "Rivals and Friends at the Sault." *Beaver* 70, no. 3 (1990): 48–51.

Mumford, Jeremy. "Mixed-Race Identity in a Nineteenth-Century Family: The Schoolcrafts of Sault Ste. Marie, 1824–27." *Michigan Historical Review* 25, no. 1 (1999): 1–23.

Murphy, Lucy Eldersveld. *A Gathering of Rivers: Indians, Métis, and Mining in the Western Great Lakes, 1737–1832*. Lincoln: University of Nebraska Press, 2000.

Native Women's Association of Canada. "The Impact of State Policy: Women's Responses to State Action." *Resources for Feminist Research* 17, no. 3 (1988): 125–28.

Necheff, Julia. "U.S. to Use Air Patrols along Canadian Border." *CNEWS* <http://www.canoe.ca/CNEWS/home.html> (accessed 3 February 2006).

Neumeyer, Elizabeth A. "Indian Removal in Michigan, 1833–1855." MA thesis, Central Michigan University, 1968.

New England Company. *History of the New England Company, from its incorporation in the seventeenth century to the present time. Including A Detailed Report of the Company's Proceedings for the Civilization and Conversion of Indians, Blacks, and Pagans in the Dominion of Canada, British Columbia, the West Indies and S. Africa during the two years 1869–1870*. London: Taylor and Co., 1871.

————. *Report of the Proceedings of the New England Company, for the Civilization and Conversion of Indians, Blacks, and Pagans in the Dominion of Canada, South Africa, and the West Indies, During the Two Years 1871–1872*. London: Taylor and Co., 1874.

Nichols, Roger L. *Indians in the United States and Canada: A Comparative History*. Lincoln: University of Nebraska Press, 1998.

Nicks, Trudy. "Dr. Oronhyatekha's History Lessons: Reading Museum Collections as Texts." In *Reading Beyond Words: Contexts for Native History*, ed. Jennifer S. H. Brown and Elizabeth Vibert, 459–90. Peterborough: Broadview Press, 2003.

Norrie, Kenneth, and Douglas Owram. *A History of the Canadian Economy*. Toronto: Harcourt Brace Jovanovich, 1991.

Nute, Grace Lee. "The American Fur Company's Fishing Enterprises on Lake Superior." *Mississippi Valley Historical Review* 12, no. 4 (1926): 483–503.

————. "James Dickson: A Filibuster in Minnesota in 1836." *Mississippi Valley Historical Review* 10, no. 2 (1923): 127–39.

O'Callaghan, E. B., and Berthold Fernow, eds. *Documents Relative to the Colonial History of the State of New York.* 15 vols. Albany: Weed, Parsons and Company, 1856–1887.

O'Meara, F. A. *Appeal on Behalf of Indian Missions in the Diocese of Toronto.* Toronto: Diocesan Church Society, 1856.

Ontario Historical Society. *Annual Report of the Ontario Historical Society, 1898.* Toronto: Warwick Brothers and Rutter, 1898.

———. *Annual Report of the Ontario Historical Society, 1911.* Toronto: The Society, 1911.

———. *Catalogue, Canadian Historical Exhibition Victoria College, Queen's Park, Toronto under the Patronage of the His Excellency the Governor-General and the Countess of Minto.* Toronto: William Briggs, 1899.

Osborne, A. C. "The Migration of Voyageurs from Drummond Island to Penetanguishene in 1828." *Ontario Historical Society Papers and Records* 3 (1901): 123–66.

Owram, Doug. *Promise of Eden: The Canadian Expansionist Movement and the Idea of the West, 1856–1900.* Toronto: University of Toronto Press, 1980.

Pannekoek, Fritz. *A Snug Little Flock: The Social Origins of the Riel Resistance of 1869–70.* Winnipeg: Watson and Dwyer, 1991.

———. "Some Comments on the Social Origins of the Riel Protest of 1869." *Historical and Scientific Society of Manitoba, Transactions* 3, nos. 34–35 (1977–1979): 39–48.

Parker, Dorothy R. "D'Arcy McNickle: Living a Broker's Life." In *Between Indian and White Worlds: The Cultural Broker,* ed. Margaret Connell Szasz, 240–54. Norman: University of Oklahoma Press, 1994.

Parkman, Francis. *The Conspiracy of Pontiac and the Indian War after the Conquest of Canada.* Vol. 1. Boston: Little, Brown, 1883.

Perrault, Jean Baptiste. "Narrative of the Travels and Adventures of a Merchant Voyageur in the Savage Territories of Northern America, Leaving Montreal the 28th of May, 1783 (to 1820)." In *Michigan Pioneer and Historical Collections,* 37:508–619. Lansing: Wynkoop, Hallenbeck Crawford, 1909–1910.

Perrot, Nicholas. "Memoirs on the Manners, Customs, and Religion of the Savages of North America." In *The Indian Tribes of the Upper Mississippi Valley and Region of the Great Lakes.* 2 vols. Trans. and ed. Emma Helen Blair. Cleveland: Burrows Brothers, 1911.

Peterson, Jacqueline. "Many Roads to Red River: Métis Genesis in the Great Lakes Region, 1680–1815." In *The New Peoples: Being and Becoming Métis in North America,* ed. Jacqueline Peterson and Jennifer S. H. Brown, 37–52. Winnipeg: University of Manitoba Press, 1985.

Petrone, Penny, ed. *First Peoples, First Voices.* Toronto: University of Toronto Press, 1983.

———. "John Ojijatekah Brant-Sero." In *Dictionary of Canadian Biography,* vol. 14, *1911–1920,* 137–39. Toronto: University of Toronto Press, 1998.

Pitezel, John H. *Lights and Shades of Missionary Life.* Cincinnati: Printed at the Western Book Concern for the author, 1857.

Porter, Joy. *To Be Indian: The Life of Iroquois-Seneca Arthur Caswell Parker*. Norman: University of Oklahoma Press, 2001.

Pratt, Mary Louise. *Imperial Eyes: Travel Writing and Transculturation*. London: Routledge, 1992.

Preston, David Lee. "The Texture of Contact: European and Indian Settler Communities in the Iroquoian Borderlands, 1720–1780." PhD diss., College of William and Mary, 2002.

Price, John. *Native Studies: American and Canadian Indians*. Toronto: McGraw-Hill, 1978.

Prucha, Francis Paul, ed. *Americanizing the American Indians: Writings by the "Friends of the Indian," 1880–1900*. Cambridge, MA: Harvard University Press, 1973.

———. *The Great Father: The United States Government and the American Indians*. Vol. 1. Lincoln: University of Nebraska Press, 1984.

———. *The Great Father: The United States Government and the American Indians*. Abridged ed. Lincoln: University of Nebraska Press, 1996.

Quaife, Milo, ed. *The Akin Papers*. 2 vols. Detroit: Detroit Public Library, Burton Historical Collection, 1928.

Quinn, David B., ed. *Early Maryland in a Wider World*. Detroit: Wayne State University Press, 1982.

Ray, Arthur J. *Indians in the Fur Trade: Their Role as Hunters, Trappers, and Middlemen in the Lands Southwest of Hudson Bay, 1660–1870*. Toronto: University of Toronto Press, 1974.

Rea, J. E. "Logan, Robert." In *Dictionary of Canadian Biography*, vol. 9, *1861–1870*, 472–73. Toronto: University of Toronto Press, 1976.

Reed-Donahay, Deborah E., ed. *Auto/Ethnography: Rewriting the Self and the Social*. Oxford: Berg, 1987.

Reid, C. S. "Paddy." In *Mansion in the Wilderness: The Archaeology of the Ermatinger House*. Toronto: Ontario Ministry of Culture and Recreation, Historical Planning and Research Branch, 1977.

Rezek, Antoine Ivan. *History of the Diocese of Sault Ste. Marie and Marquette*. 2 vols. Houghton, MI: M. A. Donohue, 1907.

Richardson, Boyce. "Kind Hearts of Forked Tongues?" *Beaver* 67, no. 1 (1987): 16–41.

Richardson, John. *A Journal of a Boat Voyage Through Rupert's Land to the Arctic Sea*. New York: Harper Brothers, 1854.

Richardson, Major John. *Tecumseh and Richardson: The Story of a Trip to Walpole Island and Port Sarnia*. Toronto: Ontario Book Company, 1924.

Richter, Daniel K. "Cultural Brokers and Intercultural Politics: New York–Iroquois Relations, 1664–1701." *Journal of American History* 75, no. 1 (1988–1989): 40–67.

———. "Iroquois Confederacy." In *The Encyclopedia of New York State*, ed. Peter Eisenstadt, 791–94. Syracuse, NY: Syracuse University Press, 2005.

———. "Iroquois versus Iroquois: Jesuit Missions and Christianity in Village Politics, 1642–1686." *Ethnohistory* 32, no. 1 (1985): 1–16.

————. *The Ordeal of the Longhouse: The Peoples of the Iroquois League in the Era of European Colonization*. Chapel Hill: University of North Carolina Press for the Institute of Early American History and Culture, 1992.

————. "Ordeals of the Longhouse: The Five Nations in Early American History." In *Beyond the Covenant Chain: The Iroquois and Their Neighbors in Indian North America, 1600–1800*, ed. Daniel K. Richter and James H. Merrell, 11–27. Syracuse, NY: Syracuse University Press, 1987.

————. "War and Culture: The Iroquois Experience." *William and Mary Quarterly* 40, no 4 (1983): 528–59.

Ripmeester, Michael, and Brian Osborne. "It Is Scarcely to Be Believed": The Mississauga Indians and the Grape Island Mission, 1826–1836." *Canadian Geographer* 39, no. 2 (1995): 157–68.

Rogers, Edward S. "Northern Algonquians and the Hudson's Bay Company, 1821–1890." In *Aboriginal Ontario: Historical Perspectives on the First Nations*, eds. Edward S. Rogers and Donald Smith, 307–43. Toronto: Dundurn Press, 1994.

Rogers, Edward S., and Mary Black Rogers. "Who Were the Cranes? Groups and Group Identity in Northern Ontario." In *Approaches in Algonquin Archaeology: Proceedings of the Thirteenth Annual Conference of the University of Calgary Archaeological Association*, ed. Margaret Hanna, 247–88. Calgary: University of Calgary Press, 1982.

Ross, Catherine Sheldrick, ed. *Recovering Canada's First Novelist: Proceedings from the John Richardson Conference*. Erin, ON: Porcupine's Quill, 1984.

Ruggles, Richard E. "McMurray, William." In *Dictionary of Canadian Biography*, vol. 12, *1891–1900*, 680–82. Toronto: University of Toronto Press, 1990.

Ruoff, A. LaVonne Brown, and Donald B. Smith. Introduction to *Life, Letters and Speeches*, by George Copway (Kahgegagahbowh). Lincoln: University of Nebraska Press, 1997.

Russell, Hilary. "Bethune, Angus." In *Dictionary of Canadian Biography*, vol. 8, *1851–1860*, 85–86. Toronto: University of Toronto Press, 1985.

Salisbury, Neal. "Toward the Covenant Chain: Iroquois and Southern New England Algonquians, 1637–1684." In *Beyond the Covenant Chain: The Iroquois and Their Neighbors in Indian North America, 1600–1800*, ed. Daniel K. Richter and James H. Merrell, 61–73. Syracuse, NY: Syracuse University Press, 1987.

Salway, Peter. *The Frontier People of Roman Britain*. London: Cambridge University Press, 1965.

Schama, Simon. *Landscape and Memory*. New York: Random House, 1996.

Schenck, Theresa. "Lewis Saurin Johnston, 1793–1825." In *The John Johnston Family of Sault Ste. Marie*, ed. Elizabeth Hambleton and Elizabeth Warren Stoutamire, 27–28. Sault Ste. Marie, MI: Johnston Family Association, 1993.

———— *The Voice of the Crane Echoes Afar: The Sociopolitical Organization of the Lake Superior Ojibway, 1640–1855*. New York: Garland, 1997.

Schmalz, Peter S. *The History of the Saugeen Indians*. Toronto: Ontario Historical Society, 1977.

——— *The Ojibwa of Southern Ontario*. Toronto: University of Toronto Press, 1991.

Schoolcraft, Henry Rowe. "Memoir of John Johnston." In *Michigan Pioneer and Historical Collections*, vol. 36, ed. Clarence Burton, 53–90. Lansing, Wyncoop, Hallenbeck, Crawford, 1908.

———. *Personal Memoirs of a Residence of Thirty Years with the Indian Tribes on the American Frontiers: With Brief Notices of Passing Events, Facts, and Opinions, A.D. 1812 to A.D. 1842*. Philadelphia: Lippincott, Grambo, 1851.

Schwarz, Henry, and Sangeeta Ray. *A Companion to Postcolonial Studies: A Historical Introduction*. Malden, MA: Blackwell Publishing, 2004.

Semple, Neil. *The Lord's Dominion: The History of Canadian Methodism*. Montreal: McGill-Queen's University Press, 1996.

Sheridan, Joe. "The Rains Wept Time in the Badlands." *Space and Culture* 5, no. 2 (2002): 122–39.

Sheridan, Joe, and Dan Roronhiake:wen Longboat. "The Haudenosaunee Imagination and Ecology of the Sacred." *Space and Culture* 9, no. 4 (2006): 365–81.

Shields, Norman. "Anishinabek Political Alliance in the Post-Confederation Period: The Grand General Indian Council of Ontario, 1870–1936." MA thesis, Queen's University, 2001.

Shillinger, Sarah. "'They Never Told Us They Wanted to Help Us': An Oral History of Saint Joseph's Indian Industrial School." PhD diss., University of Pennsylvania, 1995.

Shimony, Annemarie Anrod. *Conservatism among the Iroquois at the Six Nations Reserve*. Syracuse: Syracuse University Press, 1994.

Sleeper-Smith, Susan. "Furs and Female Kin Networks: The World of Marie Madeleine Réaume L'Archevêque Chevalier." In *New Faces of the Fur Trade: Selected Papers of the Seventh North American Fur Trade Conference*, ed. JoAnne Fiske, Susan Sleeper-Smith, and William Wicken, 53–72. East Lansing: Michigan State University Press, 1998.

———. *Indian Women and French Men: Rethinking Cultural Encounter in the Western Great Lakes*. Amherst: University of Massachusetts Press, 2001.

Slight, Benjamin. *Indian Researches, or Facts Concerning the North American Indians; Including Notices of their Present State of Improvement, in their Social, Civil, and Religious Condition; with Hints for their Future Advancement*. Montreal: Printed for the Author, by J. E. L. Miller, 1844.

Smith, Dan. *The Seventh Fire: The Struggle for Aboriginal Government*. Toronto: Key Porter, 1993.

Smith, Derek G., ed. *Canadian Indians and the Law: Selected Documents, 1663–1972*. Toronto: McClelland and Stewart, 1975.

Smith, Donald B. "The Dispossession of the Mississauga Indians: A Missing Chapter in the Early History of Upper Canada." *Ontario History* 73, no. 2 (1981): 67–87.

————. *Sacred Feathers: The Reverend Peter Jones (Kahkewaquonaby) and the Missis-sauga Indians*. Lincoln: University of Nebraska Press, 1987.

————. "Who Are the Mississauga?" *Ontario History* 67, no. 4 (1975): 211–22.

Smith, Linda Tuhiwai. *Decolonizing Methodologies: Research and Indigenous Peoples*. London: Zed Books, 1999.

Smith, Theresa S. *The Island of the Anishnaabeg: Thunderers and Water Monsters in the Traditional Ojibwe Life-World*. Moscow, ID: University of Idaho Press, 1995.

Soetebier, Virginia M. *Woman of the Green Glade: The Story of an Ojibway Woman on the Great Lakes Frontier*. Saline, MI: McNaughton and Gunn, 2000.

Sprague, D. N., and R. P. Frye. *The Genealogy of the First Métis Nation*. Winnipeg: Pemmican Publications, 1983.

Spry, Irene M. "The Metis and Mixed-Bloods of Rupert's Land before 1870." In *The New Peoples: Being and Becoming Metis in North America*, ed. Jacqueline Peterson and Jennifer S. H. Brown, 96–118. Winnipeg: University of Manitoba Press, 1985.

Stagg, Ronald J. "Elmes Yelverton Steele." In *Dictionary of Canadian Biography*, vol. 9, *1861–1870*, 743–44. Toronto: University of Toronto Press, 1976.

Steele, Sam. *Forty Years in Canada*. 1915. Reprint, Toronto: Prospero, 2000.

Stone-Gordon, Tammy. "The Other Schoolcraft." *Michigan History* 78, no. 2 (1994): 24–27.

Strathern, Marilyn. "The Limits of Auto-Anthropology." In *Anthropology at Home*, ed. Anthony Jackson, 16–37. London: Tavistock Publications, 1987.

Strong-Boag, Veronica, and Carole Gerson. *Paddling Her Own Canoe: The Times and Texts of E. Pauline Johnson Tekahionwake*. Toronto: University of Toronto Press, 2000.

Sturm, John. "Farewell to the Swan Creek Chippewa." *Chronicle: The Quarterly Magazine of the Historical Society of Michigan* 21, no. 2 (1985): 20–25.

Surtees, Robert J. "Canadian Indian Policies." In *Handbook of North American Indians*. Vol. 4, *History of Indian–White Relations*, ed. Wilcomb E. Washburn, 81–95. Washington: Smithsonian Institution, 1988.

Szasz, Margaret Connell, ed. *Between Indian and White Worlds: The Cultural Broker*. Norman: University of Oklahoma Press, 1994.

Tallemite, Etienne. "Legardeur De Repentigny, Louis." In *Dictionary of Canadian Biography*, vol. 4, *1771–1800*, 447–48. Toronto: University of Toronto Press, 1974.

Tanner, Helen Hornbeck, ed. *Atlas of Great Lakes Indian History*. Norman: University of Oklahoma Press, 1987.

————. "The Glaize in 1792: A Composite Indian Community." *Ethnohistory* 25, no. 1 (1978): 15–39.

Tanner, John. *A Narrative of the Captivity and Adventures of John Tanner (U.S. Interpreter at the Saut de Ste. Marie) During Thirty Years Residence among the Indians in the Interior of North America*. Ed. Edwin James. 1830. Reprint, Minneapolis: Ross and Haines, 1956.

Taylor, Alan. *The Divided Ground: Indians, Settlers, and the Northern Borderland of the American Revolution*. New York: Alfred A. Knopf, 2006.

Telford, Rhonda. "The Sound of the Rustling of the Gold Is under My Feet Where I Stand: We Have a Rich Country; A History of Aboriginal Mineral Resources in Ontario." PhD diss., University of Toronto, 1996.

Temple, Dominique. "Policy of the 'Severed Flower.'" *INTERculture* 98 (1988): 10–35.

Terrell, John U. *Furs by Astor: The Full Story of the Founding of a Great American Fortune*. New York: William Morrow, 1963.

Thompson, Albert Edward. *Chief Peguis and His Descendents*. Winnipeg: Pequis Press, 1973.

Thompson, Arthur N. "John West: A Study of the Conflict Between Civilization and the Fur Trade." *Journal of the Canadian Church Historical Society* 12, no. 3 (1970): 44–57.

Thorman, George E. "Oakes, Forrest." In *Dictionary of Canadian Biography*, vol. 4, *1771–1800*, 585–86. Toronto: University of Toronto Press, 1974.

Thorne, Tanis C. "Crooks, Ramsay." In *Dictionary of Canadian Biography*, vol. 8, *1851–1860*, 190–91. Toronto: University of Toronto Press, 1985.

Thwaites, Reuben G., ed. *The Jesuit Relations and Allied Documents*. 73 vols. Cleveland: Burrows Brothers, 1896–1900.

Titley, E. Brian. *A Narrow Vision: Duncan Campbell Scott and the Administration of Indian Affairs in Canada*. Vancouver: University of British Columbia Press, 1986.

Tobias, John L. "Protection, Civilization, Assimilation: An Outline History of Canada's Indian Policy." In *As Long as the Sun Shines and Water Flows: A Reader in Canadian Native Studies*, eds. Ian L. Getty and Antoine S. Lussier, 39–64. Vancouver: University of British Columbia Press, 1990.

———. "Protection, Civilization, Assimilation: An Outline History of Canada's Indian Policy." Reprint, in *Sweet Promises: A Reader on Indian–White Relations in Canada*, ed. J. R. Miller, 127–45. Toronto: University of Toronto Press, 1991.

Tooker, Elisabeth. "A Note on the Return of Eleven Wampum Belts to the Six Nations Iroquois Confederacy on Grand River, Canada." *Ethnohistory* 45, no. 2 (1998): 219–36.

Trap, Paul. "Mouet de Langlade, Charles-Michel." In *Dictionary of Canadian Biography*, vol. 4, *1771–1800*, 563–64. Toronto: University of Toronto Press, 1974.

Travers, Karen J. "The Drummond Island Voyageurs and the Search for Great Lakes Métis Identity." In *The Long Journey of a Forgotten People: Métis Identities and Family Histories*, ed. Ute Lischke and David T. McNab, 219–44. Waterloo: Wilfrid Laurier University Press, 2007.

Trelease, Allen W. *Indian Affairs in Colonial New York: The Seventeenth Century*. Ithaca, NY: Cornell University Press, 1960.

Tulchinsky, Gerald. *Taking Root: The Origins of the Canadian Jewish Community*. Toronto: Stoddart Publishing, 1992.

Turner, Frederick Jackson. *The Frontier in American History*. 1920. Reprint, New York: Dover Publications, 1996.

Turner, Frederick W. *Beyond Geography: The Western Spirit Against the Wilderness*. New York: Viking Press, 1980.

Valentine, Lisa Philips. *Making It Their Own: Severn Ojibwe Communicative Practices*. Toronto: University of Toronto Press, 1995.

Valentine, Lisa Philips, and Allan K. McDougall. "Imposing the Border: The Detroit River from 1786 to 1807." *Journal of Borderland Studies* 19, no. 1 (2004): 13–22.

van den Bogaert, Harmen Meyndertsz. *A Journey into Mohawk and Oneida Country, 1634–1635: The Journal of Harmen Meyndertsz van den Bogaert*. Trans. and ed. Charles T. Gehring and William A. Starna. Wordlist and linguistic notes by Gunther Michelson. Syracuse, NY: Syracuse University Press, 1988.

Van Kirk, Sylvia. "Ballenden, Sarah McLeod." In *Dictionary of Canadian Biography*, vol. 8, *1851–1860*, 573–75. Toronto: University of Toronto Press, 1985.

———. "Cameron, John Dugald." In *Dictionary of Canadian Biography*, vol. 8, *1851–1860*, 121–22. Toronto: University of Toronto Press, 1985.

———. *Many Tender Ties: Women in Fur Trade Society, 1670–1879*. Winnipeg: Watson and Dwyer, 1980.

———. "What If Mama Is an Indian?: The Cultural Ambivalence of the Alexander Ross Family." In *The New Peoples: Being and Becoming Metis in North America*, ed. Jacqueline Peterson and Jennifer S. H. Brown, 207–17. Winnipeg: University of Manitoba Press, 1985.

van Laer, A. J. F., trans. and ed. *Fort Orange and Beverwijck Records: Court Minutes, 1652–1660*. 2 vols. Albany: University of the State of New York, 1920–1923.

Van Toorn, Penny. "Aboriginal Writing." In *The Cambridge Companion to Canadian Literature*, ed. Eva-Marie Kroeller, 22–48. Cambridge: Cambridge University Press, 2004.

Van Zandt, Cynthia J. "Negotiating Settlement: Colonialism, Cultural Exchange, and Conflict in Early Colonial Atlantic North America, 1580–1660." PhD diss., University of Connecticut, 1998.

VanWynsberghe, Robert M. *AlterNatives: Community, Identity, and Environmental Justice on Walpole Island*. Boston: Pearson Education, 2002.

Vecsey, Christopher. *Traditional Ojibwa Religion and Its Historical Changes*. Philadelphia: American Philosophical Society, 1983.

Wallace, Anthony F. C. "Nativism and Revivalism." In *International Encyclopedia of the Social Sciences*, ed. David L. Sills, 11: 75–80. New York: Macmillan Company and the Free Press, 1968.

Wallace, W. S., ed. *Documents Relating to the North West Company*. Toronto: Champlain Society, 1934.

Warren, William W. *History of the Ojibway Nation*. 1885. Reprint, Minneapolis: Ross and Haines, 1970. Also reprinted as *History of the Ojibway People*. St. Paul: Minnesota Historical Society Press, 1984.

Washburn, Wilcomb E., ed. *The American Indian and the United States: A Documentary History*. New York: Random House, 1973.

Weaver, Jace. "Indigenousness and Indigeneity." In *A Companion to Postcolonial Studies: An Historical Introduction*, ed. Henry Schwarz and Sangeeta Ray, 221–35. Malden, MA: Blackwell Publishing, 2004.

Weaver, Sally M. "The Iroquois: The Grand River Reserve in the Late Nineteenth and Early Twentieth Centuries, 1875–1945." In *Aboriginal Ontario:*

*Historical Perspectives on the First Nations*, ed. Edward S. Rogers and Donald B. Smith, 213–57. Toronto: Dundurn Press, 1994.

———. "Seth Newhouse and the Grand River Confederacy at Mid-Nineteenth Century." In *Extending the Rafters: Interdisciplinary Approaches to Iroquoian Studies*, eds. Michael K. Foster, Jack Campisi, and Marianne Mithun, 165–82. Albany: State University of New York Press, 1984.

Weber, David J. "Turner, the Boltonians, and the Borderlands." *American Historical Review* 91 (February 1986): 66–81.

Weeks, Philip. *Farewell, My Nation: The American Indian and the United States, 1820–1890*. Arlington Heights, IL: Harlan Davidson, 1990.

Westfall, William. *Two Worlds: The Protestant Culture of Nineteenth-Century Ontario*. Montreal: McGill-Queen's University Press, 1989.

White, H. *Metahistory: The Historical Imagination in Nineteenth-Century Europe*. Baltimore: Johns Hopkins Press, 1973.

White, Lynn, Jr. "The Historical Roots of Our Ecological Crisis." *Science* 155 (1967): 1203–7.

White, Randall. *Ontario, 1610–1985: A Political and Economic History*. Toronto: Dundurn Press, 1985.

White, Richard. *The Middle Ground: Indians, Empires and Republics in the Great Lakes Region, 1650–1815*. Cambridge: Cambridge University Press, 1991.

White, Bruce M. "Cadotte, Joseph." In *Dictionary of Canadian Biography*, vol. 6, *1821–1835*, 99–101. Toronto: University of Toronto Press, 1987.

Wickwire, Wendy. "We Shall Drink from the Stream and So Shall You: James A. Teit and Native Resistance in British Columbia, 1908–22." *Canadian Historical Review* 79, no. 2 (1998): 199–236.

Widdis, Randy William. "Borderland Interaction in the International Region of the Great Plains: An Historic-Geographical Perspective." *Great Plains Research* 7, no. 1 (1997): 103–37.

Williams, Glyndwr. "McLeod, Roderick." In *Dictionary of Canadian Biography*, vol. 7, *1836–1850*, 569–70. Toronto: University of Toronto Press, 1988.

Williams, J. Fletcher. "Memoir of William W. Warren," in Warren, *History of the Ojibway Nation*, 11–12.

Williams, Raymond. *The Country and the City*. New York: Oxford University Press, 1973.

Wilson, Edward Francis. *Missionary Work among the Ojebway Indians*. New York: E. and J. B. Young, 1886.

Wilson, James. *The Earth Shall Weep: A History of Native America*. New York: Grove Press, 1998.

Wilson, Shawn. "What Is an Indigenous Research Methodology?" *Canadian Journal of Native Education* 25, no. 2 (2001): 175–79.

Woodcock, George. *Gabriel Dumont*. Edmonton: Hurtig Publishers, 1975.

Wunder, John E., and Pekka Hamalainen. "Of Lethal Places and Lethal Essays." *American Historical Review* 104, no. 4 (1999): 1229–34.

# LIST OF CONTRIBUTORS

**Phil Bellfy** is an associate professor in the American Indian Studies program at Michigan State University. He is also an enrolled member of the White Earth Band of Minnesota Chippewa and is active in the Native community.

**Janet E. Chute** teaches anthropology and ethnohistory at Mount Saint Vincent University, and is an adjunct professor with the School for Resource and Environmental Studies at Dalhousie University. She acts as a consultant in land claims and identity cases with many Aboriginal nations across Canada.

**Edmund J. Danziger Jr.**, Distinguished Teaching Professor at Bowling Green University in Ohio, has written extensively on Great Lakes Aboriginal history topics—north and south of the international border.

**Rick Fehr** is a doctoral student in the Faculty of Environmental Studies at York University, where he is researching the historic and contemporary relationships between Anishinaabe and settler communities in southwestern Ontario. His research is aimed at exploring how these relationships can enact positive land ethics.

**Michelle A. Hamilton** is a postdoctoral fellow at the University of Guelph researching the history of amateur archaeological collecting and has worked in museums across Canada.

**Karl S. Hele** is an Anishinabeg historian, the Director of the First Nations Studies program and assistant professor of anthropology and history at the University of Western Ontario.

**Alan Knight** is an Anglican clergy and archivist for the Diocese of Algoma and a sessional lecturer in Canadian history at Algoma University College in Sault Ste. Marie.

**Ute Lischke** teaches German literature, film studies, and cultural perspectives at Wilfrid Laurier University, where she is associate professor in the Department of English and Film Studies.

**Allan K. McDougall**, professor emeritus from the University of Western Ontario, is a political scientist whose expertise is in political communication, public policy, and law.

**David T. McNab** is a Métis historian who has worked for three decades on Aboriginal land and treaty rights issues in Canada. David teaches in the School of Arts and Letters in the Atkinson Faculty of Liberal and Professional Studies at York University in Toronto, where he is associate professor of Indigenous Studies. Since 1992 he has also been a claims advisor for Nin.Da.Waab.Jig., Walpole Island Heritage Centre, Bkejwanong First Nations.

**Mark Meuwese** is assistant professor in the history department of the University of Winnipeg. His research interests include Indigenous peoples in the early modern world.

**Catherine Murton Stoehr** is a doctoral student at Queen's University. Her dissertation discusses the Anishinabe encounter with Methodism in early-nineteenth-century Upper Canada.

**Lisa Philips**, professor and chair of anthropology at the University of Alberta, is a linguistic anthropologist who has worked extensively on First Nations–state relations.

**Norman Shields** is a historian for Parks Canada. His principal research interest is inter-village Anishinabek alliances in the nineteenth and twentieth centuries.

# INDEX

## Books in the Aboriginal Studies Series
### Published by Wilfrid Laurier University Press

*Blockades and Resistance: Studies in Actions of Peace and the Temagami Blockades of 1988–89* / Bruce W. Hodgins, Ute Lischke, and David T. McNab, editors / 2003 / xi + 276 pp. / map, illustrations / ISBN 978-0-88920-381-5

*Indian Country: Essays on Contemporary Native Culture* / Gail Guthrie Valaskakis / 2005 / x + 293 pp. / photos / ISBN 978-0-88920-479-9

*Walking a Tightrope: Aboriginal People and Their Representations* / Ute Lischke and David T. McNab, editors / 2005 / xix + 377 pp. / photos / ISBN 978-0-88920-484-3

*The Long Journey of a Forgotten People: Métis Identities and Family Histories* / Ute Lischke and David T. McNab, editors / 2007 / viii + 386 pp. / maps, photos / ISBN 978-0-88920-523-9

*Words of the Huron* / John L. Steckley / 2007 / xvii + 259 pp. / ISBN 978-0-88920-516-1

*Essential Song: Three Decades of Northern Cree Music* / Lynn Whidden / 2007 / xvi + 176 pp. / photos, musical examples, audio CD / ISBN 978-0-88920-459-1

*From the Iron House: Imprisonment in First Nations Writing* / Deena Rymhs / 2008 / ix + 152 pp. / ISBN 978-1-55458-021-7

*Lines Drawn upon the Water: First Nations and the Great Lakes Borders and Borderlands* / Karl S. Hele, editor / 2008 /xxiv + 354 pp. / maps, illustrations/ ISBN 978-1-55458-004-0